ADDISON-WESLEY MATHEMATICS

Robert E. Eicholz

Phares G. O'Daffer

Charles R. Fleenor

Randall I. Charles

Sharon Young

Carne S. Barnett

Addison-Wesley Publishing Company

Menlo Park, California Reading, Massachusetts London Amsterdam Don Mills, Ontario Sydney

Illustration Acknowledgments

Sherry Balestra 81
Dave Blanchette 8–9, 37, 84–85, 192–193, 232, 370–371, 398–399
Ellen Blonder 354–355, 388
David Broad 51, 110, 111
Cindy Brodie 52, 73, 82, 86, 88–89, 94–95, 129, 206 (top), 207, 208, 215, 282, 294–295, 394–395
Kirk Caldwell 236–237
Liz Callen 120–121, 140–141, 159, 164, 165 (top), 188, 198–199, 238–239, 312–313, 344–345, 365, 400–401, 403
Randy Chewing 116–117, 260–261
Dick Cole 80, 167
Sam Daijogo 2–3, 200–201
Helen K. Davie 39, 105, 146–147, 148–149
Bert Dodson 83, 92–93, 142–143
Hal Frenck 138–139
Tom Garcia 16–17, 34–35, 66–67
Barry Geller 101, 256–257, 280, 290, 374–375
John Goodell 226–227, 328–329
Pat Hoggan 62–63
Susan Jaekel 20, 25, 44, 57, 70, 76–77, 96, 123, 126–127, 132–133, 150–151, 156, 172–173, 174, 178–179, 182–183, 190–191, 210–211, 212, 244, 262–263, 266, 296, 310–311, 350, 376–377
Tony Kenyon 30–31, 145, 162–163, 165 (bottom), 171, 175, 196–197, 202–203, 346, 358, 359
Heather King 220–221, 230–231, 274–275, 302–303
Susan Lexa 56, 68–69, 87, 118, 119, 176, 254–255, 265, 286, 332–333, 356–357, 372–373, 396–397
Carlos Marchiori 22, 46, 72, 98, 128, 158, 184, 213–214, 246, 268, 298, 316, 340–341, 364, 384–385, 404–405
Jane McCreary 21, 58–59, 71, 97, 108–109, 134–135, 136–137, 157, 194–195, 204–205, 334, 348
Jim McGuinness 32–33 (top)
Masami Miyamoto 291, 306, 410–411
Debby Morse 24, 33 (bottom), 115, 124–125
Susan Nelson 90
Dennis Nolan 4–5, 15, 54–55, 114, 122, 224–225, 326–327
Bill Ogden 106–107, 222–223
Sharron O'Neil 234–235, 337, 368–369
Sandra Popovich 29, 47, 144, 177, 185
Sue Rother 28
Doug Roy 168–169, 180
Judy Sakaguchi 60–61, 253
Doug Smith 1, 27, 40–41, 49, 75, 103, 131, 152–153, 161, 187, 219, 249, 271, 276–277, 301, 308–309, 321, 343, 367, 387
Sandra Spiedel 378–379
Linda Storm 181
Dalia Sudavicius 99
Susan Swan 6–7, 10, 12–13, 18–19, 79, 206 (bottom), 228–229, 250–251, 284–285, 304–305, 330–331, 352–353, 360–361, 380–381, 390–391

Photograph Acknowledgments

Gene Ahrens/Bruce Coleman Inc.: 174–175
© **Jim Anderson/Woodfin Camp & Associates:** 196
© **Craig Aurness/West Light:** 113
© **David Austen/After-Image:** 318
© **1982 Dennis Brack/Black Star:** 155
© **1982 John deNisser/Black Star:** 242 bottom left
© **1981 Doris DeWitt/Atoz Images:** 343
© **1982 Donald Dietz/Stock, Boston:** 278
© **Francisco Erize/Bruce Coleman Inc.:** 243 top left

Focus On Sports: 75
Jeff Foott/Bruce Coleman Inc.: 131 top
Owen Franken/Stock, Boston: 301 bottom
George B. Fry III*: 43 (both), 103, 194, 231, 325
John Gerlach/Tom Stack & Associates: 187 bottom
Raoul Hackel/Stock, Boston: 307 bottom left
© **1978 Jim Harrison/Stock, Boston:** 282 center
© **Carol Hughes/Bruce Coleman Inc.:** 243 bottom right
© **1982 Ken King/After-Image:** 307 top left
Glen A. Knudsen/Tom Stack & Associates: 242 bottom right
© **1980 Larry Lee/West Light:** 1
Wayland Lee*/Addison-Wesley Publishing Company: 11, 14, 36 top left, 36 top right, 36 center left, 36 bottom right, 209 (all), 240 (both), 252, 272 (all), 282 left, 282 right, 294, 314, 315, 321, 322 (both), 338, 339 (both), 362, 382 (poster © 1981 Ron Kimball), 383, 402
© **1981 Andy Levin/Black Star:** 249
© **1980 David Madison/Focus On Sports:** 219
© **1980 James Mason/Black Star:** 170
© **Coco McCoy/Rainbow:** 409
© **1982 Steven Monti/Bruce Coleman Inc.:** 154
© **Charles Moore/Black Star:** 112
Hank Morgan/Rainbow: 36 center right
Chuck Muhlstock/Focus On Sports: 258
© **Norman Myers/Bruce Coleman Inc.:** 367
NASA: 64, 65, 242 top left
M. Timothy O'Keefe/Bruce Coleman Inc.: 307 right
© **Chuck O'Rear/Woodfin Camp & Associates:** 49
© **Chuck O'Rear/West Light:** 271 top
Brian Parker/Tom Stack & Associates: 131 bottom
© **1980 Mark Perlstein/Black Star:** 217
© **W. E. Ruth/Bruce Coleman Inc.:** 187 top, 243 bottom left
Frank Siteman/Stock, Boston: 230
Tom Stack/Tom Stack & Associates: 104
© **Harald Sund:** 301 top
© **Tom Tracy:** 406, 407
© **Tom Tracy/Black Star:** 216
Mark Tuschman*: 324, 387
© **1982 Jim Tuten/Black Star:** 27
© **Jerry Wachter/Focus On Sports:** 259
Wells Fargo Bank History Department: 161
J. Westley: 271 bottom
Baron Wolman*: 166
© **1979 Arnold Zann/Black Star:** 306

*Photographs provided expressly for the publisher.

Cover Photograph
©**Marvin Ickow/Folio Inc.**

ISBN 0-201-24500-0

EFGHIJKL-KR-8765

Contents

CHAPTER 5   Multiplication, 103

CHAPTER 6   Division: 1-Digit Divisors, 131

CHAPTER 7   Division: 2-Digit Divisors, 161

CHAPTER 8   Measurement, 187

CHAPTER 9 Fractions: Addition and Subtraction, 219

CHAPTER 10 Larger Fractions, 249

CHAPTER 11 Geometry, 271

CHAPTER 12 Fractions: Multiplication and Division, 301

Basic Facts

Sharon and her brother enjoyed telling their friends about their vacation trip to the Indian cliff dwellings of the southwest. These mud and stone houses were built high on the edges of rocky cliffs. Four park guides led groups of 8 visitors along winding paths up to the apartment-like houses. Many of the houses were 2, 3, or 4 stories high. On some floors there were only 2 or 3 rooms. Other floors had as many as 6 or 7 rooms. The only way to reach the rooms on the first, second, or third floor was by climbing steep ladders to the roof. When the Indians were attacked, they just pulled up the ladders. Sharon and her brother wondered what caused the Indians to leave these strange homes 700 years ago. No one knows for sure.

Addition Facts

We learn math to help us solve problems.

We use **addition** when a problem involves finding the total when two amounts are *put together*.

Problem

The United States flag has one stripe for each of the original American colonies. The flag has 7 red stripes and 6 white stripes. How many colonies were there?

We can show addition in two ways.

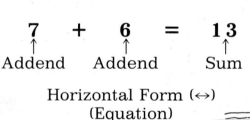

$$7 \leftarrow \text{Addend}$$
$$\underline{+\ 6} \leftarrow \text{Addend}$$
$$13 \leftarrow \text{Sum}$$

Vertical Form (↕)

$$7 \quad + \quad 6 \quad = \quad 13$$
Addend   Addend   Sum

Horizontal Form (↔)
(Equation)

The flag has 13 stripes, so there were 13 colonies.

Warm Up   Give the sums.

1.   7
  + 3

2.   4
  + 5

3.   8
  + 3

4.   9
  + 4

5.   9
  + 7

6.   7
  + 8

7.   6
  + 0

8.   3
  + 9

9.   5
  + 5

10.   7
  + 5

11.   4
  + 7

12.   9
  + 8

13. $7 + 7$

14. $8 + 0$

15. $6 + 7$

16. $3 + 6$

17. $6 + 6 = n$

18. $9 + 5 = n$

19. $8 + 8 = n$

20. $6 + 9 = n$

Add.

1. 5
   + 0

2. 2
   + 2

3. 6
   + 6

4. 3
   + 1

5. 3
   + 3

6. 0
   + 1

7. 9
   + 1

8. 1
   + 1

9. 2
   + 6

10. 3
   + 0

11. 4
   + 3

12. 5
   + 1

13. 4
   + 4

14. 0
   + 8

15. 2
   + 9

16. 3
   + 5

17. 1
   + 6

18. 8
   + 5

19. 3
   + 2

20. 9
   + 0

21. 0
   + 0

22. 4
   + 9

23. 0
   + 2

24. 3
   + 8

25. 6
   + 6

26. 8
   + 1

27. 6
   + 5

28. 5
   + 7

29. 1
   + 2

30. 7
   + 9

31. 5
   + 4

32. 4
   + 2

33. 7
   + 6

34. 7
   + 4

35. 4
   + 6

36. $3 + 7$

37. $8 + 8$

38. $4 + 8$

39. $7 + 2$

40. $5 + 9 = n$

41. $1 + 7 = n$

42. $2 + 8 = n$

43. $9 + 3 = n$

44. What is the sum of 9 and 6?

45. Add 8 and 7.

46. What number is 4 more than 9?

★ Give the missing addends.

47. $5 + n = 7$

48. $n + 8 = 13$

49. $6 + n = 6$

50. $n + 9 = 16$

Think

Logical Reasoning

At the end of the third inning the baseball scoreboard looked like this.

Reds	0	0	2
Cubs	0	0	4

The final score was 7 to 3.
Who won the game?
How do you know?

Math

Subtraction Facts

We use **subtraction** when a problem involves *taking away, comparing,* or *finding how many more are needed.*

Problem 1

Brenda had 10 tickets for the football game. Her uncle bought 3 of them. How many tickets did she have left?

Problem 2

In the first half the Tigers threw 10 passes. The Bulldogs threw 3. How many more passes did the Tigers throw than the Bulldogs?

Problem 3

The Bulldogs football team leads the Tigers 10 to 3. How many points do the Tigers need to tie the score?

We can show subtraction in two ways. The labels show how addition and subtraction are related.

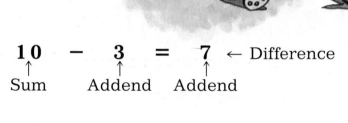

$$\begin{array}{r} 10 \leftarrow \text{Sum} \\ -\ 3 \leftarrow \text{Addend} \\ \hline \text{Difference} \rightarrow 7 \leftarrow \text{Addend} \end{array}$$

$$? + 3 = 10$$

$$\underset{\text{Sum}}{10} - \underset{\text{Addend}}{3} = \underset{\text{Addend}}{7} \leftarrow \text{Difference}$$

The answer to each problem is 7.

Warm Up Find the differences.

1. $\begin{array}{r}11\\-\ 5\\\hline\end{array}$	**2.** $\begin{array}{r}9\\-\ 4\\\hline\end{array}$	**3.** $\begin{array}{r}13\\-\ 8\\\hline\end{array}$	**4.** $\begin{array}{r}10\\-\ 6\\\hline\end{array}$	**5.** $\begin{array}{r}16\\-\ 7\\\hline\end{array}$	**6.** $\begin{array}{r}17\\-\ 9\\\hline\end{array}$

7. $14 - 6$ **8.** $13 - 7$ **9.** $18 - 9$ **10.** $11 - 3$ **11.** $15 - 9$

12. $12 - 4 = n$ **13.** $9 - 9 = n$ **14.** $14 - 7 = n$ **15.** $8 - 0 = n$

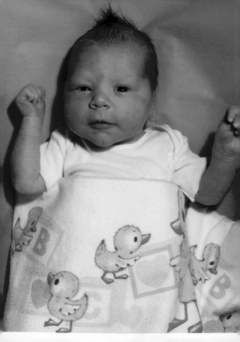

Elizabeth Ann

2-24-'89

Subtract.

1. $\begin{array}{r} 9 \\ -3 \\ \hline \end{array}$	**2.** $\begin{array}{r} 11 \\ -2 \\ \hline \end{array}$	**3.** $\begin{array}{r} 8 \\ -6 \\ \hline \end{array}$	**4.** $\begin{array}{r} 5 \\ -5 \\ \hline \end{array}$	**5.** $\begin{array}{r} 9 \\ -1 \\ \hline \end{array}$	**6.** $\begin{array}{r} 7 \\ -6 \\ \hline \end{array}$	**7.** $\begin{array}{r} 4 \\ -0 \\ \hline \end{array}$
8. $\begin{array}{r} 10 \\ -2 \\ \hline \end{array}$	**9.** $\begin{array}{r} 12 \\ -8 \\ \hline \end{array}$	**10.** $\begin{array}{r} 10 \\ -6 \\ \hline \end{array}$	**11.** $\begin{array}{r} 11 \\ -8 \\ \hline \end{array}$	**12.** $\begin{array}{r} 7 \\ -4 \\ \hline \end{array}$	**13.** $\begin{array}{r} 11 \\ -7 \\ \hline \end{array}$	**14.** $\begin{array}{r} 12 \\ -4 \\ \hline \end{array}$
15. $\begin{array}{r} 16 \\ -9 \\ \hline \end{array}$	**16.** $\begin{array}{r} 14 \\ -6 \\ \hline \end{array}$	**17.** $\begin{array}{r} 8 \\ -5 \\ \hline \end{array}$	**18.** $\begin{array}{r} 14 \\ -7 \\ \hline \end{array}$	**19.** $\begin{array}{r} 18 \\ -9 \\ \hline \end{array}$	**20.** $\begin{array}{r} 12 \\ -9 \\ \hline \end{array}$	**21.** $\begin{array}{r} 12 \\ -3 \\ \hline \end{array}$
22. $\begin{array}{r} 9 \\ -4 \\ \hline \end{array}$	**23.** $\begin{array}{r} 6 \\ -6 \\ \hline \end{array}$	**24.** $\begin{array}{r} 17 \\ -8 \\ \hline \end{array}$	**25.** $\begin{array}{r} 11 \\ -9 \\ \hline \end{array}$	**26.** $\begin{array}{r} 12 \\ -5 \\ \hline \end{array}$	**27.** $\begin{array}{r} 8 \\ -0 \\ \hline \end{array}$	**28.** $\begin{array}{r} 13 \\ -8 \\ \hline \end{array}$
29. $\begin{array}{r} 14 \\ -5 \\ \hline \end{array}$	**30.** $\begin{array}{r} 14 \\ -9 \\ \hline \end{array}$	**31.** $\begin{array}{r} 13 \\ -7 \\ \hline \end{array}$	**32.** $\begin{array}{r} 15 \\ -7 \\ \hline \end{array}$	**33.** $\begin{array}{r} 11 \\ -4 \\ \hline \end{array}$	**34.** $\begin{array}{r} 13 \\ -6 \\ \hline \end{array}$	**35.** $\begin{array}{r} 14 \\ -8 \\ \hline \end{array}$

36. $13 - 9$ **37.** $16 - 7$ **38.** $17 - 9$ **39.** $11 - 6$ **40.** $15 - 9$

41. $10 - 9$ **42.** $15 - 8$ **43.** $13 - 5$ **44.** $12 - 7$ **45.** $13 - 4$

46. $15 - 6 = n$ **47.** $7 - 0 = n$ **48.** $10 - 4 = n$ **49.** $13 - 5 = n$

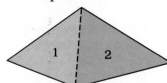

50. What is 7 subtracted from 15?

51. What is 5 less than 14?

52. How much greater is 13 than 7?

Think

Discovering a Pattern

Study the figures below. Then copy and complete the table.

How many triangles would there be for a 100-sided figure?

Number of **sides**	Number of **triangles**
4	2
5	3
6	?
7	?
8	?

Math

Addition and Subtraction Properties

Addition properties help us find sums.
Subtraction properties help us find differences.

Addition Properties

Order Property, +
When the order of the addends is changed, the sum is the same.

> $7 + 3 = 10$,
> so $3 + 7 = 10$
> This means I have fewer facts to remember.

0 Property, +
When one addend is 0, the sum is the other addend.

> This helps me know facts like $9 + 0 = 9$.

Grouping Property, +
When the grouping of the addends is changed, the sum is the same.

> I can add either pair of numbers first and the sum is the same.
> $$\left.\begin{array}{r}7\\2\\+\ 8\end{array}\right\}$$
> $$17$$

Subtraction Properties

Subtracting 0
When 0 is subtracted from a number, the difference is that number.

> This helps me know facts like $8 - 0 = 8$.

Doubles Facts
Since $8 + 8 = 16$, I know that
> 1 more than $8 + 8$

$8 + 9 = 17$
and
$8 + 7 = 15$
> 1 less than $8 + 8$

Subtracting a Number from Itself
When a number is subtracted from itself, the difference is 0.

> I see! $8 - 8 = 0$

Addition and Subtraction Are Related
Adding "undoes" subtracting. Subtracting "undoes" adding.

> I can use addition to check subtraction!
> $$\begin{array}{r}15\ \text{S}\\-\ 7\ \text{A}\\\hline 8\ \text{A}\end{array} \qquad \begin{array}{r}8\ \text{A}\\+7\ \text{A}\\\hline 15\ \text{S}\end{array}$$

Remember! There is *no* order property for subtraction. $7 - 2$ equals 5, but $2 - 7$ does *not* equal 5.

Practice the Facts

1. 9
   + 4

2. 4
   + 9

3. 8
   + 6

4. 6
   + 8

5. 9
   + 8

6. 8
   + 9

7. 7
   + 0

8. 0
   + 7

9. 9
   − 0

10. 6
    − 6

11. 5
    + 0

12. 8
    − 8

13. 7
    + 7

14. 7
    + 8

15. 7
    + 6

16. 13
    − 7

17. 16
    − 9

18. 7
    + 9

19. 9
    + 9

20. 9
    + 7

21. 17
    − 8

22. 6
    − 0

23. 18
    − 9

24. 7
    − 7

Find the sums by adding **down**. Add **up** to check.

25. 5
    3
   + 4

26. 3
    6
   + 2

27. 8
    1
   + 8

28. 6
    2
   + 4

29. 2
    3
   + 5

30. 5
    4
   + 2

Add. **31.** 6 + 3 + 4   **32.** 7 + 2 + 7   **33.** 5 + 3 + 6

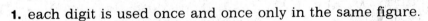

Think

Number Puzzle

Copy and solve this puzzle!
Write numbers in the empty circles so that

1. each digit is used once and once only in the same figure.

2. the **target sum** is the sum of the numbers in each line.

Digits: 1–9
Target Sum: 16

Digits: 1–5
Target Sum: 8

Digits: 1–5
Target Sum: 10

Digits: 1–7
Target Sum: 13

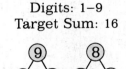

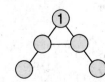

Math

Problem Solving: The 5-Point Checklist

QUESTION
DATA
PLAN
ANSWER
CHECK

To Solve a Problem
1. **Understand the Question**
2. **Find the needed Data**
3. **Plan what to do**
4. **Find the Answer**
5. **Check back**

These five steps can help you solve problems.
Follow them to solve this problem.

Mary bought 2 records and some cleaner
for $15. Jane bought 1 record for $6.
How much more did Mary spend than Jane?

1. **Understand the Question**
   How many more dollars did Mary
   spend than Jane?

2. **Find the needed Data**
   Mary: $15   Jane: $6

3. **Plan what to do**
   Since we want to compare the
   amounts, we subtract.

4. **Find the Answer**
   $15 - 6 = 9$
   Mary spent $9 more than Jane.

5. **Check back**
   Since $9 + 6 = 15$, $15 - 6 = 9$.
   Read the problem again.
   The answer seems reasonable.

Solve. Use the 5-Point Checklist.

1. At 7:00, 5 of Tina's friends came
   to her record party. At 8:00, 7
   more friends arrived. How many
   people were at the party then?
   (Don't forget Tina!)

2. Jeff had $14 to buy presents for
   3 friends. He spent $5 for a
   record for 1 friend. How much
   money did he have left to buy
   presents for his other 2 friends?

Solve.

1. Marcie had 9 records. She bought 6 records on sale for $20. How many records did she have then?

2. Jim has 17 records in his collection. Elena has 12 in hers, and Todd has only 9 in his. How many more records does Jim have than Todd?

3. Sam has 7 records. How many records can he buy before his storage rack is full? The rack holds 15 records.

6. Lola has 15 minutes to listen to records. Two of her favorite songs together take 8 minutes to play. How much time does she have left to listen?

7. Jack had 9 records. He gave 2 away. Then he bought 8 more. How many records did he have then?

4. One clerk in the record store sold 9 records before 12 o'clock. She sold 7 records in the afternoon. How many did she sell that day?

5. A record store owner sold 7 out of a collection of 16 records that were on sale. How many did she have left?

8. Erin bought 3 records. One cost $4, one cost $5, and the other cost $6. She then sold one of the records to a friend for $7. What was her final cost for the two records she kept?

9. Adrian had 9 records. She traded 4 of her records to Julio for 2 nearly new records. How many records did Adrian have after the trade?

Multiplication Facts

We use **multiplication** when a problem involves combining a number of equal sets to find the total number.

Problem

Marcella uses 6 ropes of clay like these to make the sides of a vase. How many ropes would she need to make 8 vases?

We can show multiplication in two ways.

$$
\begin{array}{r}
6 \leftarrow \text{Factor} \\
\times\, 8 \leftarrow \text{Factor} \\
\hline
48 \leftarrow \text{Product}
\end{array}
$$

$$\underset{\text{Factor}}{8} \times \underset{\text{Factor}}{6} = \underset{\text{Product}}{48}$$

Marcella would need 48 ropes of clay.

Because 48 is the product of 6 and another whole number, we say 48 is a **multiple** of 6.
Here are some other multiples of 6: 0, 6, 12, 18, 24, 30, 36, 42, . . .
We also say 48 is a multiple of 8.
Here are some other multiples of 8: 0, 8, 16, 24, 32, 40, . . .

Warm Up   Write the next 6 facts for exercises 1–8.

1.

$1 \times 2 = 2 \quad 2 \times 2 = 4 \quad 3 \times 2 = 6$

2.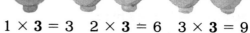

$1 \times 3 = 3 \quad 2 \times 3 = 6 \quad 3 \times 3 = 9$

3. $1 \times 4 = 4 \quad 2 \times 4 = 8 \quad 3 \times 4 = 12$

4. $1 \times 5 = 5 \quad 2 \times 5 = 10 \quad 3 \times 5 = 15$

5. $1 \times 6 = 6 \quad 2 \times 6 = 12 \quad 3 \times 6 = 18$

6. $1 \times 7 = 7 \quad 2 \times 7 = 14 \quad 3 \times 7 = 21$

7. $1 \times 8 = 8 \quad 2 \times 8 = 16 \quad 3 \times 8 = 24$

8. $1 \times 9 = 9 \quad 2 \times 9 = 18 \quad 3 \times 9 = 27$

9. Write nine multiples of 5. Use 5 as the first multiple.

10. Write nine multiples of 7. Use 7 as the first multiple.

Multiply.

1. 8×3	**2.** 7×1	**3.** 2×1	**4.** 6×6	**5.** 6×1	**6.** 2×3	**7.** 3×4
8. 5×8	**9.** 0×0	**10.** 4×2	**11.** 1×0	**12.** 7×6	**13.** 9×2	**14.** 7×4
15. 7×7	**16.** 6×2	**17.** 0×4	**18.** 7×3	**19.** 8×6	**20.** 2×0	**21.** 5×3
22. 1×4	**23.** 0×6	**24.** 5×5	**25.** 5×0	**26.** 2×2	**27.** 5×4	**28.** 7×0
29. 0×8	**30.** 3×3	**31.** 9×0	**32.** 6×9	**33.** 5×1	**34.** 1×8	**35.** 4×8

36. 3×1 **37.** 2×7 **38.** 1×9 **39.** 6×4

40. $7 \times 5 = n$ **41.** $9 \times 8 = n$ **42.** $6 \times 5 = n$ **43.** $5 \times 9 = n$

44. What is 7 multiplied by 9?   **45.** What is the product of 9 and 4?

46. Start with 8 and write the next eight multiples of 8.

★ Find the missing factors.

47. $5 \times n = 30$ **48.** $7 \times n = 0$

49. $n \times 6 = 42$ **50.** $n \times 9 = 81$

Think

Number Relationships

Start with 0. Skip count by twos to get the **EVEN** (E) numbers.

0, 2, 4, 6, 8, 10, 12 . . .

Start with 1. Skip count by twos to get the **ODD** (O) numbers.

1, 3, 5, 7, 9, 11, 13 . . .

Copy and complete these tables.

+	E	O
E		O
O		

×	E	O
E	E	E
O	O	

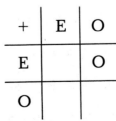

Math

Multiplication Properties

We can use these properties to help us find products.

Order Property
When the order of the factors is changed, the product is the same.

$3 \times 9 = 27$, so $9 \times 3 = 27$ This means I have fewer facts to remember.

0 Property
When either factor is 0, the product is 0.

This makes facts like $9 \times 0 = 0$ easy.

1 Property
When either factor is 1, the product is the other factor.

This helps me know facts like $8 \times 1 = 8$.

Grouping Property
When the grouping of three factors is changed, the product is the same.

Since $(3 \times 4) \times 10$ or 12×10 is 120, I know $3 \times (4 \times 10)$ or 3×40 is 120.

Multiplication-Addition Property
When two products have a common factor, you can "add" them to find a new product having that same factor.

$3 \times 4 = 12$ and $5 \times 4 = 20$ so $8 \times 4 = 32$ This helps me use products I know to find products I may not know.

Use the multiplication properties to help you find the missing products.

1. Since $4 \times 7 = 28$, then $7 \times 4 = n$.

2. Since one factor is 0, then $0 \times 6 = n$.

3. Since one factor is 1, then $9 \times 1 = n$.

4. Since $(8 \times 7) \times 10 = 560$, then $8 \times (7 \times 10) = n$.

5. Since $4 \times 8 = 32$ and $3 \times 8 = 24$, then $7 \times 8 = n$.

Practice the Facts

Try some zeros and ones.

| **1.** $\begin{array}{r} 0 \\ \times\, 0 \\ \hline \end{array}$ | **2.** $\begin{array}{r} 0 \\ \times\, 6 \\ \hline \end{array}$ | **3.** $\begin{array}{r} 0 \\ \times\, 9 \\ \hline \end{array}$ | **4.** $\begin{array}{r} 1 \\ \times\, 3 \\ \hline \end{array}$ | **5.** $\begin{array}{r} 1 \\ \times\, 5 \\ \hline \end{array}$ | **6.** $\begin{array}{r} 1 \\ \times\, 8 \\ \hline \end{array}$ |

> Check the 0 and the 1 properties!

Try some twos.

| **7.** $\begin{array}{r} 2 \\ \times\, 3 \\ \hline \end{array}$ | **8.** $\begin{array}{r} 2 \\ \times\, 4 \\ \hline \end{array}$ | **9.** $\begin{array}{r} 2 \\ \times\, 5 \\ \hline \end{array}$ | **10.** $\begin{array}{r} 2 \\ \times\, 6 \\ \hline \end{array}$ | **11.** $\begin{array}{r} 2 \\ \times\, 7 \\ \hline \end{array}$ | **12.** $\begin{array}{r} 2 \\ \times\, 8 \\ \hline \end{array}$ |

> Remember:
> The twos are just doubles!

Try some fives.

| **13.** $\begin{array}{r} 5 \\ \times\, 3 \\ \hline \end{array}$ | **14.** $\begin{array}{r} 5 \\ \times\, 4 \\ \hline \end{array}$ | **15.** $\begin{array}{r} 5 \\ \times\, 6 \\ \hline \end{array}$ | **16.** $\begin{array}{r} 5 \\ \times\, 7 \\ \hline \end{array}$ | **17.** $\begin{array}{r} 5 \\ \times\, 8 \\ \hline \end{array}$ | **18.** $\begin{array}{r} 5 \\ \times\, 9 \\ \hline \end{array}$ |

> Have you tried counting by fives?
>
> 5, 10, 15, 20, 25, 30, 35, 40, 45, . . .

Try some "squares."

| **19.** $\begin{array}{r} 2 \\ \times\, 2 \\ \hline \end{array}$ | **20.** $\begin{array}{r} 3 \\ \times\, 3 \\ \hline \end{array}$ | **21.** $\begin{array}{r} 4 \\ \times\, 4 \\ \hline \end{array}$ | **22.** $\begin{array}{r} 5 \\ \times\, 5 \\ \hline \end{array}$ |

| **23.** $\begin{array}{r} 6 \\ \times\, 6 \\ \hline \end{array}$ | **24.** $\begin{array}{r} 7 \\ \times\, 7 \\ \hline \end{array}$ | **25.** $\begin{array}{r} 8 \\ \times\, 8 \\ \hline \end{array}$ | **26.** $\begin{array}{r} 9 \\ \times\, 9 \\ \hline \end{array}$ |

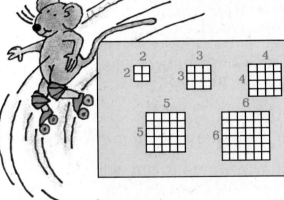

Try some others.

| **27.** $\begin{array}{r} 1 \\ \times\, 2 \\ \hline \end{array}$ | **28.** $\begin{array}{r} 3 \\ \times\, 4 \\ \hline \end{array}$ | **29.** $\begin{array}{r} 3 \\ \times\, 6 \\ \hline \end{array}$ | **30.** $\begin{array}{r} 3 \\ \times\, 7 \\ \hline \end{array}$ | **31.** $\begin{array}{r} 3 \\ \times\, 8 \\ \hline \end{array}$ |

| **32.** $\begin{array}{r} 3 \\ \times\, 9 \\ \hline \end{array}$ | **33.** $\begin{array}{r} 4 \\ \times\, 6 \\ \hline \end{array}$ | **34.** $\begin{array}{r} 4 \\ \times\, 7 \\ \hline \end{array}$ | **35.** $\begin{array}{r} 4 \\ \times\, 8 \\ \hline \end{array}$ | **36.** $\begin{array}{r} 4 \\ \times\, 9 \\ \hline \end{array}$ |

| **37.** $\begin{array}{r} 6 \\ \times\, 7 \\ \hline \end{array}$ | **38.** $\begin{array}{r} 6 \\ \times\, 8 \\ \hline \end{array}$ | **39.** $\begin{array}{r} 6 \\ \times\, 9 \\ \hline \end{array}$ | **40.** $\begin{array}{r} 7 \\ \times\, 8 \\ \hline \end{array}$ | **41.** $\begin{array}{r} 7 \\ \times\, 9 \\ \hline \end{array}$ |

> Remember the Multiplication-Addition Property.
>
> $\begin{array}{r} 8 \\ \times\, 5 \\ \hline 40 \end{array}$ $\qquad$ $\begin{array}{r} 8 \\ \times\, 2 \\ \hline 16 \end{array} \rightarrow$ $\begin{array}{r} 8 \\ \times\, 7 \\ \hline 56 \end{array}$

QUESTION
DATA
PLAN
ANSWER
CHECK

Problem Solving:
Understanding the Question

In problem solving,
it is very important to
understand the question.

Answer the question given for the problem.

Now decide which of the questions below can be answered using the data in the problem. Give the answers when you can.

1. How much more does a hardback book cost than a paperback book?

2. How much does it cost to buy a paperback and a hardback?

3. How much change do you get back if you buy 1 hardback?

4. Which cost more, 8 paperbacks or 4 hardbacks?

Problem
At the bookstore paperback books cost $5 and hardback books cost $9.

Question
What is the cost of 6 paperback books?

Write a question for each problem. Then solve the problem.

5. Roberto wants to buy 9 books. Each book costs $5.

6. Carol has $15 to spend on books. She wants to buy one that is on sale for $9.

7. Mr. Timms makes $3 profit on the sale of each $15 travel book. He sold 8 of these books.

8. Jenny worked 8 days putting books on shelves. Then she worked 9 days as a sales clerk.

9. Mr. Timms had 17 copies of an exciting travel book in stock. He sold 9 copies in one day.

10. Linda must mark the prices on all the books in 9 boxes. Each box holds 8 books.

11. Jan sold 8 books before lunch, 7 books in the afternoon, and 2 books in the evening.

12. Carl works 6 hours during the day and 2 hours in the evening. He earns $4 per hour.

QUESTION
DATA
PLAN
ANSWER
CHECK

Problem Solving: Using Data from a Story

Sometimes you must search for data needed to solve a problem.

Use data from this story to solve the problems.

1. The spaceship passed a giant star 5 hours after it took off. What time was this?

2. The spaceships traveled in flight groups of 6. They always had the same number of crew members. How many crew members were in a flight group?

3. How many kilograms did the crew of one spaceship weigh?

4. It took the crew 8 seconds to swallow their daily food pills. How far did the spaceship travel during this time?

5. How many days will it take the spaceship to reach the unknown planet?

★ 6. Give the next 3 numbers in the laser beep pattern.

The Adventure

The spaceship blasted off from the small planet Juno at 6:00 a.m. Each of the 7 crew members weighed exactly the same—8 kg—so the ship had no trouble reaching its cruising speed of 9 km/s (kilometers per second). It would take the ship 5 weeks to reach its target. The target was an unknown planet. Strange radio signals had been coming from the planet. The signals were a series of beeps in the pattern 1, 1, 2, 3, 5, 8, 13, ... The crew had quickly recognized the pattern, but who was sending the signals?

15

Division Facts

We use **division** to solve problems that involve finding *how many equal sets* there are or *how many are in each equal set.*

Problem 1

There are 42 students in the marching band. If 7 students march in each row, how many rows are there?

Problem 2

There are 42 students in the marching band. If the students march in 7 rows, how many students are in each row?

We can show division in two ways.

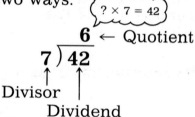

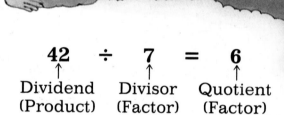

The answer to each problem is 6.

Warm Up Divide. Think about missing factors.

1. $5\overline{)20}$ 2. $3\overline{)12}$ 3. $6\overline{)24}$ 4. $5\overline{)40}$ 5. $9\overline{)72}$

6. $4\overline{)32}$ 7. $2\overline{)10}$ 8. $9\overline{)27}$ 9. $3\overline{)15}$ 10. $2\overline{)18}$

11. $1\overline{)4}$ 12. $6\overline{)54}$ 13. $7\overline{)49}$ 14. $4\overline{)36}$ 15. $5\overline{)5}$

16. $14 \div 7$ 17. $36 \div 6$ 18. $18 \div 3$ 19. $9 \div 1$

20. $8 \div 8 = n$ 21. $28 \div 4 = n$ 22. $54 \div 6 = n$ 23. $45 \div 9 = n$

16

Divide.

1. $4\overline{)12}$ 2. $1\overline{)5}$ 3. $6\overline{)30}$ 4. $9\overline{)18}$ 5. $7\overline{)28}$

6. $8\overline{)56}$ 7. $8\overline{)64}$ 8. $9\overline{)72}$ 9. $4\overline{)36}$ 10. $9\overline{)45}$

11. $7\overline{)63}$ 12. $6\overline{)48}$ 13. $5\overline{)45}$ 14. $7\overline{)56}$ 15. $9\overline{)81}$

16. $6\overline{)42}$ 17. $9\overline{)63}$ 18. $7\overline{)49}$ 19. $8\overline{)72}$ 20. $7\overline{)35}$

21. $24 \div 4$ 22. $18 \div 6$ 23. $15 \div 5$ 24. $14 \div 2$ 25. $25 \div 5$

26. $20 \div 5$ 27. $18 \div 3$ 28. $28 \div 4$ 29. $10 \div 2$ 30. $8 \div 8$

31. $12 \div 4$ 32. $10 \div 5$ 33. $30 \div 5$ 34. $24 \div 6$ 35. $21 \div 3$

36. $32 \div 4$ 37. $36 \div 6$ 38. $28 \div 7$ 39. $21 \div 3$ 40. $35 \div 5$

41. $40 \div 8 = n$ 42. $54 \div 6 = n$ 43. $48 \div 8 = n$ 44. $63 \div 7 = n$

45. What is 32 divided by 8?

46. What is the quotient of 49 and 7?

47. What is the quotient when the dividend is 36 and the divisor is 9?

Think

Discovering Patterns

Try these input-output tables!

Study the example. Then give the missing numbers and the rule for tables A and B.

Example:

Rule
Divide by 6

Input	Output
18	3
24	4
48	8
54	9
36	6
30	5

A Rule

Input	Output
27	3
45	5
1. 18	
2. 54	
3. 72	
4. 63	

B Rule

Input	Output
28	4
14	2
5. 21	
6. 56	
7.	9
8.	5

Rule
Divide by 6

Input
18

Output
3

→ **Math** ←

Division Properties

We can use these properties to help us find quotients.

Dividing by 1

Any number divided by 1 is that number.

This helps me know facts like 9 ÷ 1 = 9.

Dividing a Number by Itself

Any number divided by itself is 1.

I see! 8 ÷ 8 = 1

Multiplication and Division Are Related

Dividing "undoes" multiplying. Multiplying "undoes" dividing.

I can use multiplication to check division!

$$\begin{array}{r} F \quad 6 \; F \\ 7\overline{)42} \; P \end{array} \qquad \begin{array}{r} 6 \; F \\ \times \; 7 \; F \\ \hline 42 \; P \end{array}$$

Remember!

We can divide 0 by a number, but **we never divide by 0!**

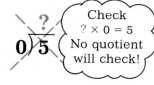
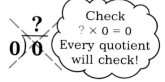

$$1\overline{)0} \overset{0}{} \qquad 2\overline{)0} \overset{0}{} \qquad 0\overline{)5} \overset{?}{} \qquad 0\overline{)0} \overset{?}{}$$

Check 0 × 1 = 0   *Check 0 × 2 = 0*   *Check ? × 0 = 5 No quotient will check!*   *Check ? × 0 = 0 Every quotient will check!*

Divide.

1. $6 \div 1$ **2.** $4 \div 1$ **3.** $7 \div 7$ **4.** $6 \div 6$ **5.** $0 \div 4$

6. $24 \div 3$ **7.** $56 \div 8$ **8.** $24 \div 8$ **9.** $7 \div 1$ **10.** $42 \div 6$

11. $9 \div 9$ **12.** $0 \div 7$ **13.** $8 \div 1$ **14.** $0 \div 3$ **15.** $54 \div 9$

16. $2\overline{)2}$ **17.** $8\overline{)72}$ **18.** $1\overline{)4}$ **19.** $8\overline{)8}$ **20.** $6\overline{)0}$

Which problems cannot be solved? Give the quotients for the others.

21. $1\overline{)3}$ **22.** $0\overline{)4}$ **23.** $6\overline{)0}$ **24.** $0\overline{)7}$ **25.** $7\overline{)0}$
   ?   ?   ?   ?   ?

Using More Than One Operation

Parentheses tell which operation to do first.

Some problems have more than one operation.

$$(12 \div 3) + 9$$
$$4 \qquad + 9$$
$$13$$

Do these operations in the order shown by the parentheses. Give the answer.

1. $(36 \div 4) + 5$

2. $(3 + 4) \times 6$

3. $(13 - 7) \times 8$

4. $(15 - 7) + 9$

5. $(6 + 8) - 9$

6. $(24 \div 3) \times 4$

7. $13 - (45 \div 9)$

8. $9 + (4 \times 2)$

9. $16 - (3 \times 3)$

10. $49 \div (3 + 4)$

11. $72 \div (16 - 7)$

12. $(15 - 9) \times 9$

13. $(63 \div 9) \times 8$

14. $17 - (40 \div 5)$

15. $(81 \div 9) + 5$

16. $(6 \times 4) \div 8$

17. $7 + (11 - 4)$

18. $8 \times (5 + 3)$

19. $(13 - 8) \times 9$

20. $(3 \times 2) \times 7$

21. $6 + (56 \div 7)$

Copy and put in the parentheses to show which operation has been done first.

22. $4 \times 2 + 5 = 13$

23. $8 \times 4 + 5 = 72$

24. $3 \times 4 - 3 = 9$

25. $4 + 2 \times 3 = 10$

26. $3 \times 5 + 4 = 27$

27. $18 \div 6 + 3 = 2$

Skillkeeper

Add, subtract, or multiply.

1. $7 + 4$

2. $3 + 9$

3. $8 + 0$

4. $6 + 9$

5. $9 + 8$

6. $8 + 7$

7. $13 - 5$

8. $12 - 6$

9. $14 - 8$

10. $18 - 9$

11. $14 - 9$

12. $16 - 7$

13. 7×5

14. 6×3

15. 8×5

16. 9×6

17. 7×0

18. 8×7

Problem Solving: Choose the Operations

Some problems can be solved by using a single operation (+, −, ×, ÷). Other problems are solved by using two or more operations. A problem-solving **strategy** that can be used to solve such problems is called

CHOOSE THE OPERATIONS

Try This Nancy plans to mow lawns for regular customers once a week for 9 weeks. She has 3 lawns to mow in Westside and 5 to mow in Lakeview. How many lawns will she mow during the 9 weeks?

+
- Finding the total after putting together?

−
- Taking away?
- Comparing?
- Finding how many more are needed?

×
- Finding the total for a number of equal sets?

÷
- Finding the number of equal sets?
- Finding the number in each equal set?

Can I use +, −, ×, ÷?

Since I want to find the total number of lawns, I ADD

Westside: 3 lawns
Lakeview: 5 lawns
3 + 5 = 8
8 lawns in all

I see! Since I want to find the total for 9 eights, I MULTIPLY!

8 lawns
Mow each lawn
9 times.
9 × 8 = 72

Nancy will mow 72 lawns.

Solve.

1. There are 17 students in Fred's class. 6 of them are 10 years old. 3 are 12 years old. The others are 11 years old. How many are 11 years old?

2. Jerry has collected 32 team flags. He began to collect them when he was 8 years old. He collected the same number of flags each year. If he is now 12, how many flags did he collect each year?

Chapter Review-Test

Add.

1. 5   +4

2. 7   +3

3. 8   +4

4. 4   +8

5. 9   +0

6. 8   +8

7. $8 + 9$

8. $5 + 3 + 6$

9. $0 + 5 + 7$

10. $4 + 5 + 4$

Subtract.

11. 11   − 5

12. 14   − 6

13. 10   − 7

14. 8   − 0

15. 18   − 9

16. 7   − 7

17. $17 − 8$

18. $9 − 9$

19. $13 − 5$

20. $14 − 9$

Multiply.

21. 5   × 4

22. 4   × 5

23. 8   × 6

24. 9   × 0

25. 7   × 5

26. 8   × 1

27. $7 × 7$

28. $9 × 6$

29. $1 × 7$

30. $0 × 8$

Divide.

31. $6 \overline{)24}$

32. $7 \overline{)0}$

33. $3 \overline{)27}$

34. $6 \overline{)48}$

35. $7 \overline{)56}$

36. $24 ÷ 8$

37. $0 ÷ 6$

38. $56 ÷ 8$

39. $32 ÷ 4$

Do the operations in the order shown by the parentheses.

40. $(5 + 3) × 7$

41. $45 ÷ (13 − 4)$

42. $(16 − 7) × 6$

Solve.

43. Sandy works at the skating rink 6 days a week. If she works a total of 48 days, how many weeks does she work?

44. Derek has $9. He wants to buy 3 records that cost $5 each. How much more money does he need?

Another Look

6 ← Addend → 9   2)6
+ 9 ← Addend → + 6   + 3
15 ← Sum → 15   11

(2 + 6)

17 Use addition
− 8 to check.
 9   (? + 8 = 17)

4 ← Factor → 3
× 3 ← Factor → × 4
12 ← Product → 12

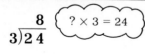

    8   (? × 3 = 24)
3)2 4

Use multiplication
to check.

Add.

1. 7 + 8	**2.** 8 + 7	**3.** 9 + 8	**4.** 7 + 6
5. 5 3 + 4	**6.** 6 2 + 5	**7.** 8 1 + 7	**8.** 7 2 + 6

Subtract. Check by adding.

9. 13 − 4	**10.** 16 − 7	**11.** 12 − 8	**12.** 11 − 6
13. 11 − 3	**14.** 12 − 5	**15.** 14 − 8	**16.** 15 − 9
17. 17 − 9	**18.** 15 − 7	**19.** 13 − 6	**20.** 18 − 9

Multiply.

21. 5 × 4	**22.** 8 × 4	**23.** 7 × 6	**24.** 8 × 5
25. 9 × 4	**26.** 3 × 9	**27.** 6 × 3	**28.** 6 × 4
29. 9 × 6	**30.** 8 × 7	**31.** 6 × 8	**32.** 7 × 9

Divide. Check by multiplying.

33. 2)10	**34.** 3)21	**35.** 4)24	**36.** 5)30
37. 6)18	**38.** 7)28	**39.** 8)56	**40.** 9)63
41. 3)27	**42.** 5)40	**43.** 7)42	**44.** 8)64

Shape Perception

Jim labeled a circle with 5 evenly spaced dots. He started at dot 1 and connected dots in this order: [1, 3, 5, 2, 4, 1]. The finished drawing was a **star polygon.**

Copy the circles below and connect the dots in the orders given to make star polygons. Color each star polygon in an interesting way.

1.

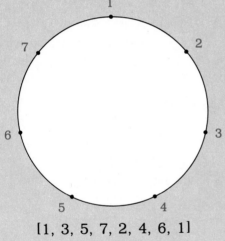

[1, 3, 5, 7, 2, 4, 6, 1]

2.

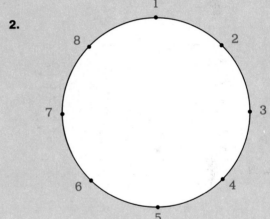

[1, 4, 7, 2, 5, 8, 3, 6, 1]

3.

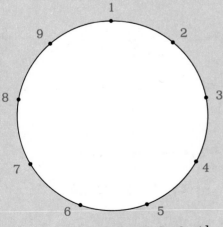

[1, 5, 9, 4, 8, 3, 7, 2, 6, 1]

4.

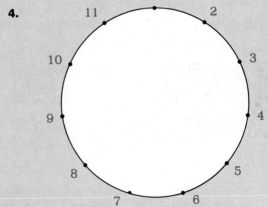

How many different 11-dot star polygons can you draw? List the order for connecting the dots.

23

Technology

Using a Calculator

You can solve many problems most easily and quickly in your head:

$$7 + 5 = n$$

You can use a calculator to help you solve problems that involve larger numbers:

$$2{,}895 + 486 - (26 \times 28) = n$$

When you use a calculator, follow these steps:
1. Write the problem.
2. Estimate the answer mentally.
3. Use a calculator to find the answer.
4. Compare the calculator answer to your estimate.

Example

Diana and David want to build a Rocket I and use 3 high-power engines to test it. They also need to buy glue and a launching pad. What will their total cost be?

Rocket I kit	$3.95
Rocket II kit	2.59
Launching pad	3.25
Low-power engine	0.79
High-power engine	0.98
Rocket glue	1.15

	Rocket	Engines	Glue	Pad	
1. Write the problem	3.95	+ (3 × 0.98)	+ 1.15	+ 3.25	= n
2. Estimate the answer.	4	+ 3	+ 1	+ 3	= 11

3. Use a calculator to find the answer.

   A Press the ⬚ON button or switch.

   B Do the operation inside the parentheses first. (3 × 0.98)
   Press ⬚3 → Press ⬚× → Press ⬚· → Press ⬚9 → Press ⬚8 → Press ⬚=
   The calculator should show 2.94.

   C Add the rest of the costs to 2.94.
   2.94 → ⬚+ → ⬚3 → ⬚· → ⬚9 → ⬚5 → ⬚+ → ⬚1 → ⬚· → ⬚1 → ⬚5 →
   ⬚+ → ⬚3 → ⬚· → ⬚2 → ⬚5 → ⬚=
   The calculator should show 11.29.

4. Compare the calculator answer to your estimate.

   The calculator answer of 11.29 and the estimate of 11 are reasonably close. The calculator answer makes sense.

The total cost of the items is $11.29.

24

Another Example

How much change would Diana and David get back from a $10 bill if they buy 6 low-power engines?

1. Write the problem. $10 - (6 \times 0.79) = n$

2. Estimate the answer. $10 - 6 = 4$

3. Use a calculator to find the answer.

   Remember: Do the operation inside the parentheses first. Record the answer.

   A $\boxed{\text{CLEAR}} \rightarrow \boxed{6} \rightarrow \boxed{\times} \rightarrow \boxed{\cdot} \rightarrow \boxed{7} \rightarrow \boxed{9} \rightarrow \boxed{=}$

   The calculator should show 4.74 (the cost of 6 engines). Record the answer.

   B Subtract 4.74 from 10.

   $\boxed{\text{CLEAR}} \rightarrow \boxed{1} \rightarrow \boxed{0} \rightarrow \boxed{-} \rightarrow \boxed{4} \rightarrow \boxed{\cdot} \rightarrow \boxed{7} \rightarrow \boxed{4} \rightarrow \boxed{=}$

   The calculator should show 5.26.

4. Compare the calculator answer to your estimate. The calculator answer of 5.26 and the estimate of 4 are reasonably close.

Diana and David should get $5.26 in change.

Use a calculator to solve these problems. Follow the 4-step method.

1. $3{,}985 + (4 \times 1{,}027) - 2{,}117 = n$

2. $(79{,}387 - 7{,}337) - 9 = n$

3. Ella wants to buy these items for the Model Rockets Club: 3 Rocket I kits, 2 Rocket II kits, 5 Low-power engines. Use the list on page 24 to find the prices. What is the total cost?

4. The Model Rockets Club has $28 to spend. How much will they have left if they buy 1 tube of rocket glue, 2 launching pads, and 5 Rocket I kits?

5. Is $65 enough money to pay for 25 High-power engines, 10 Rocket I kits, and 2 tubes of glue?

25

Cumulative Review

Add.

1. 4
    + 0

    A 0
    B 8
    C 4
    D not given

2. 8 + 7

    A 16
    B 13
    C 15
    D not given

3. 6
    2
    + 7

    A 18
    B 16
    C 15
    D not given

Subtract.

4. 18
    − 9

    A 9
    B 27
    C 10
    D not given

5. 11
    − 4

    A 7
    B 6
    C 15
    D not given

6. 12 − 7

    A 4
    B 6
    C 19
    D not given

Multiply.

7. 9
    × 3

    A 27
    B 25
    C 12
    D not given

8. 8
    × 5

    A 35
    B 45
    C 40
    D not given

9. 7 × 0

    A 7
    B 0
    C 70
    D not given

Divide.

10. 54 ÷ 6

    A 7
    B 9
    C 8
    D not given

11. 9)‾72

    A 8
    B 7
    C 6
    D not given

12. Fifth grade students won 5 prizes for paintings and 6 prizes for craft works at the arts and crafts show. How many prizes did they win in all?

    A 13   B 11
    C 12   D not given

13. A shipping clerk has 72 books to pack in boxes. Each box will hold 8 books. How many boxes does he need?

    A 9   B 7
    C 8   D not given

2

Numbers and Place Value

Damion and his classmates looked eagerly upward. They were among 450,000 people who had gathered at Edwards Air Force Base to view the historic landing of the space shuttle *Columbia*. From 270 km above the earth's surface, the pilots would guide the spaceship to the landing strip. Temperatures on the ship's surface would reach 363°C as it sped back to earth. Damion and the others wondered how the 31,000 tiles that formed the outer shell could stand such great heat. Everyone cheered loudly when at last the *Columbia* flew into view and then glided smoothly to the runway. Damion and his classmates were thankful that they had been able to see this great event. Many of them dreamed of the day when they might make a space flight.

Place Value—Hundreds

We use numbers every day to describe our world and help us solve problems.

The **digits**

0 1 2 3 4 5 6 7 8 9

are the only symbols we need for writing all whole numbers.

We **see** this number in **standard form**:   **354**

We **can think** about these blocks and **place value**:

3 hundreds   5 tens   4 ones

We **read:** "three hundred fifty-four"

Warm Up   Think about the blocks and read each number.

1. 463	**2.** 837	**3.** 79	**4.** 876	**5.** 987	**6.** 999
7. 600	**8.** 608	**9.** 458	**10.** 45	**11.** 749	**12.** 711
13. 504	**14.** 90	**15.** 101	**16.** 683	**17.** 875	**18.** 750

Give the missing numbers.

1. 3 hundreds, 5 tens, 6 ones → __?__ ▦ __?__ | __?__ ▫

2. 4 tens, 2 hundreds, 7 ones → __?__ ▦ __?__ | __?__ ▫

3. → __?__ hundreds, __?__ tens, __?__ ones

4. → __?__ hundreds, __?__ tens, __?__ ones

5. → number in standard form __?__

6. 135 → __?__ ▦ __?__ | __?__ ▫

7. 378 → __?__ hundreds, __?__ tens, __?__ ones

8. 249 → __?__ tens, __?__ ones, __?__ hundreds

9. 4 hundreds, 0 tens, 5 ones → number in standard form __?__

10. 6 tens, 2 ones, 3 hundreds → number in standard form __?__

Think

Money and Place Value

Suppose you have these bills.

How would you write a number in standard form to show the total value of your money?

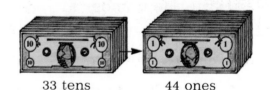

33 tens   44 ones

Hint: Think about making as many of these trades as you can:

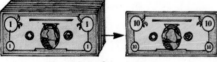
10 ones for 1 ten

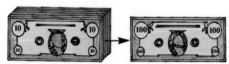
10 tens for 1 hundred

Math

Thousands

Only three states are smaller in area than Hawaii, but the islands of Hawaii stretch across a distance of 2,451 km. This distance is almost as great as the distance between Dallas and Philadelphia!

We see this number in **standard form:** **2,451**

We can think about these blocks:

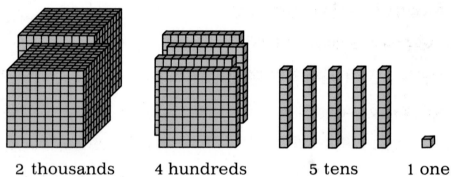

| 2 thousands | 4 hundreds | 5 tens | 1 one |

We read: "two thousand, four hundred fifty-one"

We can write the number in **expanded form:** **2,000 + 400 + 50 + 1**

Warm Up Read each number. Give the place value of each red digit.

1. 4,657	**2.** 2,635	**3.** 6,719	**4.** 4,582	**5.** 3,045
6. 7,436	**7.** 1,988	**8.** 2,073	**9.** 6,508	**10.** 1,524
11. 1,370	**12.** 2,700	**13.** 3,695	**14.** 8,475	**15.** 3,976
16. 5,309	**17.** 4,264	**18.** 8,999	**19.** 6,103	**20.** 6,798

Which number in the list has

1. 8 tens?　　　　**2.** 9 ones?　　　　**3.** 7 hundreds?

4. 6 thousands?　　**5.** 8 hundreds?　　**6.** 7 thousands?

7. 7 tens?　　　　**8.** 8 ones?　　　　**9.** 9 hundreds?

10. 9 thousands?　　**11.** 6 tens?　　　**12.** 6 hundreds?

9,876
8,769
7,698
6,987

Give each number in standard form.

13. 3 hundreds
8 tens
6 thousands
0 ones

14. 8 thousands
9 tens
4 hundreds
6 ones

15. 6 tens
8 ones
0 hundreds
7 thousands

16. 9 ones
6 thousands
3 tens
8 hundreds

17. five hundred, seventy-one

18. six thousand, four hundred thirty-seven

19. four thousand, fifty-three

20. eight thousand, nine hundred two

21. seven thousand, six hundred twenty

22. 8,000 + 500 + 30 + 8

23. 9,000 + 600 + 20 + 7

24. 70 + 6,000 + 2 + 800

25. 3,000 + 400 + 80 + 3

26. 8,000 + 70 + 5

27. 8 + 200 + 4,000

28. 7,000 + 5

29. 800 + 30 + 9

Write the numbers in expanded form.

30. 748　　　　**31.** 3,602　　　　**32.** 4,500　　　　**33.** 7,468

Think

Place Value

Find the secret number!

Thousands　Hundreds　Tens　Ones

Clues:
1. The number of hundreds plus the number of thousands is 1.
2. The number of tens is 7 times the number of thousands.
3. The number of ones is 5 times the number of hundreds.

Math

More About Thousands

All of the numbers below show a certain number of thousands. Each group of 3 digits in a number is called a **period**. The periods help us read larger numbers.

On an Average Day in America . . .

9,077 babies are born.

10,205 people give blood.

147,671 people ride a trolley.

191,952 clothespins are manufactured.

833,000 packages are delivered.

We see: **191,952**

We can think:

Thousands Period			Ones Period		
hundred thousands	ten thousands	one thousands	hundreds	tens	ones
1	9	1 ,	9	5	2

We read: "one hundred ninety-one thousand, nine hundred fifty-two"

We can write the number in expanded form:

100,000 + 90,000 + 1,000 + 900 + 50 + 2

Read each number in the "Average Day" list.

Warm Up Read each number. Give the place value of each red digit.

1. 143,047
2. 449,616
3. 5,872
4. 406,741
5. 635,251

6. 187,976
7. 257
8. 642,297
9. 508,264
10. 90,768

11. 8,627
12. 13,928
13. 17,886
14. 359,273
15. 206,375

16. 468,046
17. 84,915
18. 610,682
19. 84,864
20. 973,156

Which numbers in the number list have

1. 6 in the tens place?
2. 3 in the thousands place?
3. 5 in the ten thousands place?
4. 2 in the hundreds place?
5. 0 in the ones place?
6. 3 in the hundred thousands place?

Number List

632
4,320
6,253
5,146
13,564
62,015
50,461
326,274
563,421
652,153

Write in standard form.

7. 5,000 + 300 + 40 + 3

8. 80,000 + 4,000 + 300 + 5

9. 600,000 + 70,000 + 400 + 9

10. 90,000 + 6,000 + 800 + 20 + 7

Write in expanded form.

11. 857

12. 3,254

13. 5,897

14. 15,386

15. 29,307

16. 45,086

17. 379,604

18. 820,945

Write in standard form.

19. fifty-four thousand, two hundred seventy-one

20. eighty-six thousand, three hundred four

21. three hundred sixty-seven thousand, nine hundred thirty-two

22. 27 thousand

23. 568 thousand

Think

Place Value/Calculator

Enter this number into a calculator. Can you change the 3 to 0 by using just one operation? (All other digits must stay the same!)

234567

Now try to do these in one operation:

1. Change the 6 in 87653 to 0.
2. Change the 3 in 121314 to 0.
3. Change the 4 in 956145 to 0.

Math

Millions and Billions

What is the population of the world?

World Population Data

Africa	471,769,000
Asia	2,696,082,000
Australia	14,588,000
Europe	684,824,000
North America	366,628,000
Pacific Islands	8,162,000
South America	240,818,000
World Total	**4,482,871,000**

The chart below will help you read and understand numbers like the one that gives the world's population.

Periods	Billions			Millions			Thousands			Ones		
Place Values	hundred billions	ten billions	billions	hundred millions	ten millions	millions	hundred thousands	ten thousands	thousands	hundreds	tens	ones
	4,	4	8	2,	8	7	1,	0	0		0	

We read: "four billion, four hundred eighty-two million, eight hundred seventy-one thousand"

Read each number in the population table.

Warm Up Read the number. Give the digits in the period named.

Example: 8,900,006,000
(millions period)

Answer: eight billion, nine hundred million, six thousand; 900

1. 967,384,647
(thousands period)

2. 8,736,900,863
(millions period)

3. 763,800,794,368
(ones period)

4. 96,834,700,287
(billions period)

5. 937,842,386,248
(millions period)

6. 8,764,387
(thousands period)

Read each number. Give the place value of each red digit.

7. 376,000,000

8. 5,937,862

9. 3,476,850,400

10. 9,367,000,800

11. 935,467,854

12. 836,975,123,468

13. 94,367,800,672

14. 9,436,874

15. 436,843,700,965

A recent census gave the population of the United States as **226,504,825**.

Give the digit that is in each of the following places.

1. thousands
2. ten millions
3. ones
4. hundreds
5. hundred thousands
6. tens
7. ten thousands
8. hundred millions

Write the number in standard form.

9. billions period: 396
   millions period: 154
   thousands period: 872
   ones period: 600

10. millions period: 563
    thousands period: 200
    billions period: 387
    ones period: 418

11. 400,000,000 + 30,000,000 + 5,000,000 + 700,000 + 50,000

12. 3,000,000,000 + 800,000,000 + 40,000,000 + 6,000,000

13. six hundred forty-nine million, three hundred fifty-four thousand

14. three billion, five hundred ninety-six million

15. one billion, five hundred ninety-two million, six hundred eighty-eight thousand

Skillkeeper

Multiply or divide.

1. 6
   × 2

2. 9
   × 4

3. 8
   × 3

4. 7
   × 0

5. 1
   × 8

6. 9
   × 9

7. 48 ÷ 6

8. 42 ÷ 6

9. 63 ÷ 9

10. 45 ÷ 5

11. 7 × 8

12. 6)‾54

13. 5)‾40

14. 9 × 8

15. 7 × 7

16. 9 × 7

Problem Solving: Using Estimation

Choose the best estimate.

1.

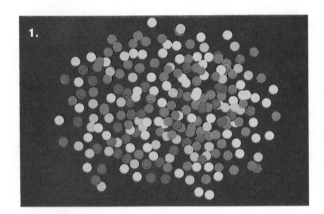

About how many dots are in the picture?

A 50   **B** 150   **C** 1,500

2.

About how many pennies are in this pile?

A 40   **B** 4,000   **C** 400

3.

About how many oranges are in the box?

A 100   **B** 40   **C** 1,000

4.

About how many people are in the picture?

A 7,000   **B** 70,000   **C** 700

5. DATA HUNT About how many more whole peanuts are in a 1-quart jar than are in 1 cup? Estimate first. Then check.

Roman Numerals

For hundreds of years many people used Roman numerals to write numbers. Study these ideas to help you read the Roman numerals in the picture.

Basic Roman numerals:

I	V	X	L	C	D	M
1	5	10	50	100	500	1,000

Some numerals where letter values are added:

II	VI	XI	XV	XX	LX	CL	CC	DC	MM
2	6	11	15	20	60	150	200	600	2,000

Some numerals where the first letter value is subtracted from the second letter value:

IV	IX	XL	XC	CD	CM
(5 − 1)	(10 − 1)	(50 − 10)	(100 − 10)	(500 − 100)	(1,000 − 100)
4	9	40	90	400	900

Study these other examples.

L XXX IV   CD XL IX   M   CM   XC   I   M   M   I
↓   ↓   ↓   ↓   ↓   ↓   ↓   ↓   ↓   ↓   ↓   ↓   ↓
50 + 30 + 4   400 + 40 + 9   1,000 + 900 + 90 + 1   1,000 + 1,000 + 1

       84   449   1,991   2,001

Write the Roman numeral.

1. 11   2. 14   3. 18   4. 19

5. 22   6. 25   7. 29   8. 30

9. 34   10. 37   11. 41   12. 95

13. 149   14. 275   15. 842   16. 1,998

Write the standard numeral.

17. CDIX   18. XCVIII

19. CDXXIX   20. MCMLXXXVIII

Comparing and Ordering Numbers

The list shows the lengths of some important rivers of North America.

Compare the lengths of the St. Lawrence and the Rio Grande by finding which length is greater.

River	Length (km)
St. Lawrence, Canada	3,058
Yukon, U.S. and Canada	2,849
Mackenzie, Canada	4,241
Rio Grande, U.S.	3,034
Missouri, U.S.	3,726
Mississippi, U.S.	3,779

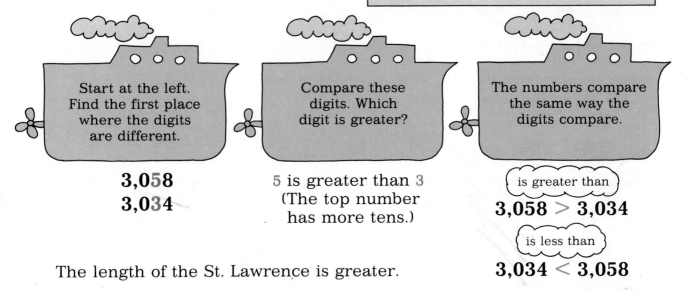

Start at the left. Find the first place where the digits are different.

3,0**5**8
3,0**3**4

Compare these digits. Which digit is greater?

5 is greater than 3 (The top number has more tens.)

The numbers compare the same way the digits compare.

is greater than
3,058 > 3,034

is less than
3,034 < 3,058

The length of the St. Lawrence is greater.

Order the lengths of the rivers by listing them from greatest to least. Do this by comparing them two at a time.

4,241 ← greatest
3,779
3,726
3,058
3,034
2,849 ← least

Warm Up Write > (greater than) or < (less than) for each ▦.

1. 415 ▦ 398
2. 567 ▦ 576
3. 5,196 ▦ 5,164
4. 6,038 ▦ 6,039
5. 8,701 ▦ 7,802
6. 7,905 ▦ 7,991
7. 46,873 ▦ 4,698
8. 1,999 ▦ 8,101
9. 358,960 ▦ 36,897
10. 7,638 ▦ 7,549
11. 367,934 ▦ 369,734
12. 10,000 ▦ 8,990

13. Order these areas of lakes from least to greatest.

Michigan, North America	57,800 km^2	Tanganyika, Africa	32,900 km^2
Baykal, Asia	31,500 km^2	Great Bear, North America	31,300 km^2

Write >, <, or = for each ⦀.

1. 743 ⦀ 758
2. 3,976 ⦀ 3,980
3. 9,999 ⦀ 1,001
4. 16,378 ⦀ 16,783
5. 54,079 ⦀ 54,079
6. 786,300 ⦀ 786,099
7. 365 thousand ⦀ 356,000
8. 979,000,000 ⦀ 236 billion
9. 34 thousand ⦀ 34,000
10. 49 billion ⦀ 490,000

Order from greatest to least.

11. 936; 1,010; 945; 989
12. 5,976; 5,967; 5,971; 5,987
13. 56,234; 56,324; 56,432
14. 374,900; 385,800; 379,900

Order from least to greatest.

15. 1,536; 1,540; 1,551; 1,531
16. 29,035; 28,799; 29,110; 28,990
17. 324,386; 386,324; 328,834
18. 9,475; 8,990; 9,587; 9,209

Give the number that is 1,000 more.

19. 376
20. 2,457
21. 56,394

Think

History of Math

The Egyptians of long ago used pictures called **hieroglyphics** to represent numbers. They did not use place value, but simply added the value of each symbol to get the number.

Egyptian Hieroglyphic Numerals

Stroke	Arch	Coiled Rope	Lotus Flower	Pointed Finger	Tadpole	Surprised Person
|	∩	?	⚱	ℳ	⌒	⚲
1	10	100	1,000	10,000	100,000	1,000,000

The Nile River is 6,671 km long. The hieroglyphic numeral for this is

⚱⚱⚱⚱⚱⚱ ????? ∩∩∩∩∩∩∩ \|

Can you write the year you were born using Egyptian numerals? The present year?

Math

Rounding Numbers

Odometers use a place-value system to show distances traveled.

When we want to show only the approximate distance traveled, we **round numbers.**

A The trip shown on the auto odometer is 483 km. What is 483 rounded to the **nearest ten?**

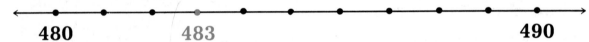

483 is closer to 480 than to 490.
483 **rounded to the nearest ten** is 480.

B What is 483 rounded to the **nearest hundred?**

483 is closer to 500 than to 400.
483 **rounded to the nearest hundred** is 500.

C What is 1,500 rounded to the **nearest thousand?**

When a number is halfway between, it is rounded **up.**
1,500 **rounded to the nearest thousand** is 2,000.

Round to the nearest ten.

1. 374 **2.** 568 **3.** 295 **4.** 8,643 **5.** 7,685

6. 3,528 **7.** 7,401 **8.** 694 **9.** 3,655 **10.** 7,237

Round to the nearest hundred.

11. 874 **12.** 3,426 **13.** 7,550 **14.** 3,051 **15.** 2,899

16. 16,543 **17.** 27,986 **18.** 3,748 **19.** 5,655 **20.** 3,095

Round to the nearest thousand.

21. 8,352 **22.** 7,605 **23.** 12,397 **24.** 4,500 **25.** 26,987

26. 42,349 **27.** 16,999 **28.** 52,498 **29.** 9,499 **30.** 8,537

Remember!

To round to **any** place
- Look at the digit to the right of the place you want to round to.
- Round **up** if the digit is 5 or more. Round **down** if the digit is less than 5.

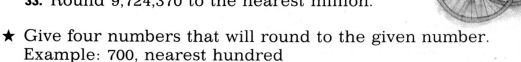

31. Round 326,975 to the nearest ten thousand.

32. Round 754,386 to the nearest hundred thousand.

33. Round 9,724,370 to the nearest million.

★ Give four numbers that will round to the given number.
Example: 700, nearest hundred
Answer: 650, 662, 708, 749 (any number from 650 through 749)

34. 60, nearest ten   **35.** 14,000, nearest thousand

Skillkeeper

Add or subtract.

1. 78
+ 21

2. 43
+ 26

3. 203
+ 154

4. 6,314
+ 1,482

5. 25,738
+ 63,251

6. 36
− 10

7. 85
− 25

8. 947
− 321

9. 4,785
− 2,352

10. 76,497
− 53,187

Problem Solving: Organizing Data

Nan gathered data about some classroom activities. She showed the data in three different ways.

A Tally

1. How many more votes did Liz get than Jimmy?

2. How many students altogether voted for the two students who got the most votes?

3. Make a tally like the one above. Show this count of votes for vice president.

Votes for Class President

Steve	ЦЖТ I
Liz	ЦЖТ III
Jimmy	IIII
Phil	ЦЖТ ЦЖТ IIII

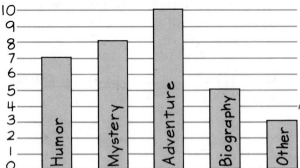

| Bill | Mary | Luisa | Brian |
| 9 votes | 4 votes | 12 votes | 7 votes |

A Table

4. How many students are taller than 137 cm but shorter than 149 cm?

5. How many more girls than boys are 138 cm or taller?

Heights of Students

	Less than 138 cm	138 cm– 148 cm	More than 148 cm
Boys	5	7	2
Girls	4	8	6

A Graph

6. How many more students like mystery and adventure than like humor and biography?

7. **DATA HUNT** How many students in your class like each kind of book best? How many more chose the most-liked favorite than the least-liked favorite?

Favorite Books

Graph showing values — Humor: 7, Mystery: 8, Adventure: 10, Biography: 5, Other: 2 (vertical scale 0 to 10)

8. **Try This** Suppose 5 of the 32 students in the class are absent. What is the largest number of groups of equal size that can be formed? Hint: Choose the operations.

Problem Solving:
Using Data from a Data Bank

A data bank is something we can use to store information until we need it. Microcomputers store large amounts of data on floppy discs. When we want to use the data, a printer types the needed data on paper. Libraries of data, stored in a **data bank,** can be passed from one computer to another over telephone lines for use by people all over the world.

Floppy Discs   Microcomputer

Use the **DATA BANK** on page 409 to solve these problems.

1. In which two Great Lakes States is the population density the same?

2. Which five of the states have the greatest population? List these five populations in order from greatest to least.

Printer

3. Use > or < to compare the areas of
   A Pennsylvania and Minnesota.   **B** Illinois and Wisconsin.

4. Use > or < to compare the yearly incomes in
   A Indiana and Michigan.   **B** Wisconsin and Pennsylvania.

5. Order the list of highest points in the states from greatest to least.

6. **Try This**   For every 5 people who live in cities or towns in New York, 1 lives in the country. About 15 million people live in cities or towns. About how many people live in the country?

Problem Solving: Guess and Check

To solve a problem like this, we must do more than choose and use an operation (+, −, ×, ÷). We use the following **strategy** to help us solve such problems:

Try This Ted has $3 more than Jane. The sum of their amounts is $15. How much money does Jane have?

GUESS and CHECK...

I'll start by guessing Jane's amount.

GUESS

Jane	Ted
$5	$8

$3 more than Jane

Then I'll check my amount. Hmm, too small!

CHECK

5 + 8 = 13
13 is less than 15.

I'll guess again and use a larger number.

GUESS

Jane	Ted
$6	$9

This checks! Jane has $6. Ted has $9.

CHECK

6 + 9 = 15
Correct!

Solve.

1. Les sold 3 less tickets to the school play than Nico. Together the boys sold 17 tickets. How many tickets to the play did each boy sell?

2. Marla told Sandy, "If you give me a nickel, each of us will have the same amount of money." Together they have 36¢. How much money did Marla have at the beginning?

Chapter Review-Test

Give the place value of each red digit.

1. 4,278   2. 6,795   3. 54,936   4. 678,321

5. 3,675   6. 78,965   7. 8,736,243   8. 7,683,436,924

Write the standard number.

9. 8 hundreds, 4 thousands, 3 ones, 7 tens, 6 ten thousands

10. thirty-seven thousand, nine hundred fifty-eight

11. 40,000 + 7,000 + 800 + 40 + 6

12. 300,000 + 50,000 + 2,000 + 700 + 8

13. 346 million   14. 415 thousand   15. 43 billion

Write in expanded form.

16. 5,321   17. 47,830   18. 380,900   19. 70,904,800

Write the standard number.

20. XLIV   21. XCVIII   22. MDCLXXVI

Write > or < for each ▦.   Order from greatest to least.

23. 450 ▦ 449   24. 5,019 ▦ 5,100   25. 2,114; 2,410; 3,000; 2,069

Round to the place named.

26. 5,674 (nearest ten)   27. 9,486 (nearest hundred)

28. 75,546 (nearest thousand)   29. 359,406 (nearest ten thousand)

Use the table for problems 30 and 31.

30. How many more girls than boys weigh more than 32 kg?

31. How many students are in the class?

Weights of Students in Our Class			
	26-32 kg	33-40 kg	41-55 kg
Number of boys	4	7	1
Number of girls	2	6	9

Another Look

Periods

Millions	Thousands	Ones
3 6,	5 7 6,	3 8 4

ten millions
hundred thousands
millions
ten thousands
thousands
hundreds
tens
ones

To compare two numbers:

Find the first place where the digits are different.

5,7**3**6   5,7**4**2

(is less than)

3 < 4

so 5,736 < 5,742

(is greater than)

also 5,742 > 5,736

To round a number to the nearest *hundred:*

Step 1 Find the *hundreds* place.
↓
5,376
↑
Step 2 If the digit to the right of the *hundreds* place is 5 or more, round **up.** If it is less than 5, round **down.** 5,375 rounded to the nearest *hundred* is 5,400.

Give the place value of each red digit.

1. 6,421

2. 37,689

3. 42,406

4. 48,762,195

Write the standard number.

5. 600 + 50 + 3

6. 2,000 + 400 + 8

7. 800,000 + 60,000 + 900 + 70

Write > or < for each 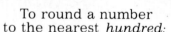.

8. 6,785 ▓ 6,892

9. 15,049 ▓ 15,094

10. 47,200 ▓ 47,005

11. 360,499 ▓ 361,000

12. 5,000,000 ▓ 500,000

13. 649,000 ▓ 65,000

Round to the place named.

14. 427 (nearest ten)

15. 5,938 (nearest thousand)

16. 6,452 (nearest hundred)

17. 56,834 (nearest thousand)

18. 372,945 (nearest ten)

19. 8,699 (nearest hundred)

20. 765,832 (nearest ten thousand)

Enrichment

Logical Reasoning

The words **and, or, not** and **if-then** are used in everyday life and in mathematics to state ideas clearly. The **figure card** exercises on this page will help you practice using these words correctly.

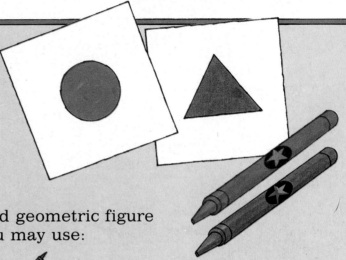

A figure card must have one colored geometric figure on it. To make each figure card, you may use:

▶ one of 2 **colors**, red or blue

▶ one of 3 **figures**, a square, a circle, or a triangle ☐ ○ △

▶ one of 2 **sizes**, large or small △ △

1. How many different figure cards can be made?

2. How many cards have figures that are both blue **and** circular?

3. How many cards have figures that are red **and** small?

4. How many cards have figures that are blue **or** square?

5. How many cards have figures that are triangular **or** large?

6. How many cards have figures that are **not** circles?

7. How many cards have figures that are **not** red?

8. **If** a figure is not blue, **then** it must be what color?

Clues may be written on the backs of the figure cards.
Which figure would be on the front of each clue card below?

9. **Clue Card**
It is small.
It is a square.
It is **not** red.
What is it?

10. **Clue Card**
It is **not** small.
It is **not** blue.
It is a circle.
What is it?

11. **Clue Card**
It is **not** large.
It is **not** red.
It is **not** a circle.
It is **not** a square.
What is it?

12. **Clue Card**
It is **not** blue
or small.
It has four sides.
What is it?

13. Make a clue card and give it to a classmate to solve.

Cumulative Review

Add.

1.
$$\begin{array}{r} 6 \\ + 9 \\ \hline \end{array}$$
A 14
B 16
C 15
D not given

2.
$$\begin{array}{r} 2 \\ 4 \\ + 8 \\ \hline \end{array}$$
A 114
B 14
C 13
D not given

3.
$$\begin{array}{r} 9 \\ + 8 \\ \hline \end{array}$$
A 18
B 17
C 19
D not given

Subtract.

4.
$$\begin{array}{r} 13 \\ - 8 \\ \hline \end{array}$$
A 21
B 5
C 4
D not given

5.
$$\begin{array}{r} 15 \\ - 6 \\ \hline \end{array}$$
A 9
B 11
C 10
D not given

6.
$$\begin{array}{r} 16 \\ - 8 \\ \hline \end{array}$$
A 8
B 7
C 12
D not given

Multiply.

7.
$$\begin{array}{r} 5 \\ \times 6 \\ \hline \end{array}$$
A 32
B 30
C 35
D not given

8.
$$\begin{array}{r} 7 \\ \times 9 \\ \hline \end{array}$$
A 60
B 63
C 62
D not given

9.
$$\begin{array}{r} 3 \\ \times 8 \\ \hline \end{array}$$
A 18
B 21
C 24
D not given

Divide.

10. $4\overline{)20}$
A 24
B 5
C 6
D not given

11. $7\overline{)0}$
A 0
B 7
C 1
D not given

12. $54 \div 6$
A 60
B 9
C 8
D not given

13. Conrad bought 13 post cards, but he had stamps for only 6 of the cards. How many more stamps did he need?

A 5   B 6
C 2   D not given

14. Leona worked 4 hours a day at the senior citizens center. One week she worked 6 days. How many hours did she work that week?

A 25   B 20
C 24   D not given

3

Addition and Subtraction

Arlene James has been a travel agent for almost 15 years. Three years ago she proudly opened her own business, Dreamlands Travel. Ms. James enjoys helping others with their travel plans almost as much as she enjoys traveling herself. She was particularly pleased when her good friends, the Javits, asked her to help them plan a trip to New Orleans. Ms. James found that the regular air fare for the family would total $495 each way. She also found, though, that they could save $120 each way if they flew on a weekday night. The Javits were very grateful for the help Ms. James gave them and promised to send her a post card when they reached New Orleans.

Estimating Sums: Mental Math

In the problems below, an answer close to the exact answer is all that is needed. To **estimate** the answer, we can **round** the addends and find a simpler sum.

A radio costs $29.
A tape recorder costs $53.
About how much do they cost together?

Round to the nearest ten.

$$\begin{array}{rcr} \$29 & \rightarrow & \$30 \\ +53 & \rightarrow & +50 \\ \hline & & \$80 \end{array}$$

The radio and tape recorder cost about $80.

The store had 379 customers on Tuesday.
It had 521 customers on Wednesday.
About how many customers were there during these two days?

Round to the nearest hundred.

$$\begin{array}{rcr} 379 & \rightarrow & 400 \\ +521 & \rightarrow & +500 \\ \hline & & 900 \end{array}$$

The store had about 900 customers during these two days.

Other Examples

Round to the nearest thousand.

$$\begin{array}{rcr} 4,523 & \rightarrow & 5,000 \\ +7,198 & \rightarrow & +7,000 \\ \hline & & 12,000 \end{array}$$

Round to the nearest dollar.

$$\begin{array}{rcr} \$1.95 & \rightarrow & \$2.00 \\ +7.29 & \rightarrow & +7.00 \\ \hline & & \$9.00 \end{array}$$

Warm Up   Estimate by rounding to the place named.

Nearest ten

1.	52	2.	78	3.	32
	+ 39		+ 69		+ 49

Nearest hundred

4.	523	5.	499	6.	875
	+ 388		+ 819		+ 629

Nearest thousand

7.	5,273	8.	4,109	9.	2,999
	+ 8,769		+ 7,784		+ 5,532

Nearest dollar

10.	$ 5.98	11.	$ 9.69	12.	$ 3.75
	+ 4.15		+ 7.39		+ 8.29

Find these sums.

1.	80 + 70	**2.** 300 + 700	**3.** 900 + 800	**4.** 8,000 + 6,000	**5.** $ 8.00 + 5.00

Estimate by rounding to the nearest ten.

6.	93 + 27	**7.** 37 + 55	**8.** 79 + 25	**9.** 18 + 47	**10.** 72 + 69

Estimate by rounding to the nearest hundred.

11.	487 + 241	**12.** 731 + 498	**13.** 617 + 376	**14.** 805 + 396	**15.** 898 + 682

Estimate by rounding to the nearest thousand or the nearest dollar.

16.	1,843 + 2,107	**17.** 3,862 + 7,516	**18.** 4,371 + 8,643	**19.** 2,417 + 5,864	**20.** 6,089 + 3,752

21.	$ 2.98 + 6.15	**22.** $ 7.98 + 3.37	**23.** $ 4.08 + 9.27	**24.** $ 6.59 + 8.43	**25.** $ 9.19 + 7.50

26. In November 189 TV sets were sold. In December 314 sets were sold. Estimate the total number of sets sold.

27. The main parts of a stereo set cost $219, $398, and $329. Estimate the total cost of these parts.

Think

Number Patterns

Look for a pattern. Give the next three numbers in each sequence.

1. 2, 4, 8, 16, 32, ▯, ▯, ▯

2. 1, 4, 9, 16, 25, ▯, ▯, ▯

3. 1, 3, 6, 10, 15, 21, ▯, ▯, ▯

4. 1, 5, 3, 10, 5, 15, 7, 20, ▯, ▯, ▯

Math

Adding: One Trade

Students who paid for their class picture before Wednesday were given a lower price. How many students were given the lower price?

Since we want to find the total of the two amounts, we add.

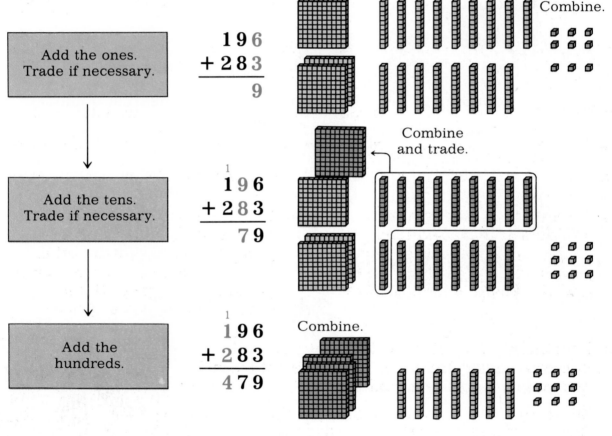

| Add the ones. Trade if necessary. | $\begin{array}{r} 196 \\ +283 \\ \hline 9 \end{array}$ |

Combine.

| Add the tens. Trade if necessary. | $\begin{array}{r} {}^{1} \\ 196 \\ +283 \\ \hline 79 \end{array}$ |

Combine and trade.

| Add the hundreds. | $\begin{array}{r} {}^{1} \\ 196 \\ +283 \\ \hline 479 \end{array}$ |

Combine.

479 students were given the lower price.

Other Examples

$\begin{array}{r} {}^{1} \\ 58 \\ +29 \\ \hline 87 \end{array}$
$\qquad$
$\begin{array}{r} 506 \\ +853 \\ \hline 1,359 \end{array}$
$\qquad$
$\begin{array}{r} {}^{1} \\ 360 \\ +59 \\ \hline 419 \end{array}$
$\qquad$
$\begin{array}{r} {}^{1} \\ 437 \\ +8 \\ \hline 445 \end{array}$
$\qquad$
$\begin{array}{r} {}^{1} \\ 5,265 \\ +3,473 \\ \hline 8,738 \end{array}$

Warm Up   Decide if you have to make a trade. Find the answer.

1. $\begin{array}{r} 46 \\ +28 \\ \hline \end{array}$

2. $\begin{array}{r} 565 \\ +74 \\ \hline \end{array}$

3. $\begin{array}{r} 409 \\ +348 \\ \hline \end{array}$

4. $\begin{array}{r} 3,436 \\ +2,158 \\ \hline \end{array}$

5. $\begin{array}{r} 2,436 \\ +5,912 \\ \hline \end{array}$

Find the sums.

1. 69 + 46	**2.** 247 + 136	**3.** 523 + 175	**4.** 368 + 29	**5.** 306 + 468
6. 324 + 8	**7.** 636 + 291	**8.** 570 + 139	**9.** 826 + 643	**10.** 495 + 230
11. 854 + 138	**12.** 474 + 319	**13.** 1,328 + 458	**14.** 1,578 + 391	**15.** 3,571 + 4,257
16. 4,372 + 1,519	**17.** 6,582 + 1,253	**18.** 7,943 + 526	**19.** 4,374 + 8,123	**20.** 5,038 + 2,847

21. 74 + 85

22. 357 + 820

23. 4,685 + 92

24. 684 + 295

25. 8,643 + 755

26. 5,763 + 4,193

27. Add 246 and 329.

28. What number is 308 more than 971?

29. A total of 197 fifth grade students and 242 sixth grade students bought a class picture. How many students in these grades bought a class picture?

30. Use the problem and payment record on page 52 for this problem. On Friday the other 113 students paid for their class picture. How many students did not get the lower price?

 31. Find the total number of class pictures sold in these 4 cities. Round to the nearest thousand and estimate to check your answer.

Milltown: 1,976   Newton: 5,128
Bay City: 3,285   Plainville: 2,597

Think

Logical Reasoning

Finding the missing digits. Copy and complete each problem.

3▒▒▒ + ▒▒▒5 6 3	4▒▒▒3 + ▒▒9▒▒ 7 6 8	▒▒▒, 7▒▒2 + 5,▒▒5▒▒ 9, 5 9 9	▒▒▒, 6 0 7 + 1,▒▒▒▒5 10, 8 4 2

Math

Adding: Two or More Trades

In Los Angeles 488 passengers board the *U.S.S. Goodspeed*. At the next port of call, Seattle, another 244 passengers board the ship. What is the total number of passengers who board the ship in these two ports?

Since we want to find the total number for the two ports, we add.

Add the ones. Trade if necessary.	Add the tens. Trade if necessary.	Add the hundreds.

$$\begin{array}{r} \overset{1}{4}88 \\ +244 \\ \hline 2 \end{array}$$
12 ones is 1 ten and 2 ones.

$$\begin{array}{r} \overset{1}{4}\overset{1}{8}8 \\ +244 \\ \hline 32 \end{array}$$
13 tens is 1 hundred and 3 tens.

$$\begin{array}{r} \overset{1}{4}\overset{1}{8}8 \\ +244 \\ \hline 732 \end{array}$$

The total number of passengers who board in the two ports is 732.

Other Examples

$$\begin{array}{r} \overset{1}{5},\overset{1}{3}48 \\ +8,079 \\ \hline 13,427 \end{array}$$

$$\begin{array}{r} \overset{1}{4}\overset{1}{8},\overset{1}{7}94 \\ +24,630 \\ \hline 73,424 \end{array}$$

$$\begin{array}{r} \overset{1}{\$}\overset{1}{5}.98 \\ +2.45 \\ \hline \$8.43 \end{array}$$ ←

To add money, think of pennies and add as with whole numbers. Write the answer as dollars and cents.

Warm Up Add.

1. $$\begin{array}{r} 576 \\ +49 \\ \hline \end{array}$$

2. $$\begin{array}{r} 926 \\ +897 \\ \hline \end{array}$$

3. $$\begin{array}{r} 9,156 \\ +8,375 \\ \hline \end{array}$$

4. $$\begin{array}{r} 57,364 \\ +18,906 \\ \hline \end{array}$$

5. $$\begin{array}{r} \$24.98 \\ +17.34 \\ \hline \end{array}$$

Add.

1. 467
    + 548

2. 379
    + 45

3. 840
    + 796

4. 389
    + 157

5. 4,374
    + 867

6. 5,289
    + 76

7. 6,034
    + 2,993

8. 5,738
    + 499

9. 5,638
    + 2,947

10. 51,764
    + 27,896

11. 68,347
    + 24,862

12. 87,036
    + 94,628

13. $ 5.69
    + 3.46

14. $ 8.34
    + 7.90

15. $ 12.75
    + 8.43

16. $ 24.98
    + 16.37

17. 365 + 278

18. 5,476 + 384

19. 567 + 89

20. 4,078 + 2,653

21. 2,480 + 4,679

22. 58,632 + 974

23. What is the sum of 8,167 and 3,798? Estimate to check your answer.

24. A cargo ship unloads 479 vans of produce in Tampa, Florida. It unloads 464 vans in Galveston, Texas. How many vans in all does the ship unload in the two ports?

25. Write a question that can be answered using the data below. Then solve the problem.

On one Atlantic Ocean crossing the liner *QE II* carried 1,795 passengers and 860 crew members.

Think

Discovering a Pattern

A **palindrome** is a number that is the same whether read from left to right or right to left. You can make a palindrome by adding. Sometimes this takes many steps.

What are the palindromes for these numbers?

```
   76 start
 + 67 reverse
  143 sum
+ 341 reverse
  484 palindrome
```

1. 87   2. 678   3. 3,279   4. 125,698

Math

Column Addition

Maria formed these three words while playing a word game. Her score for each word is shown next to it. What is her total score for the three words?

Since we want to find the total score for the three words, we add.

Triple Word

| P₃ | L₁ | A₁ | Y₄ | $\dfrac{27}{\text{Score}}$ |

| W₄ | H₄ | I₁ | C₃ | H₄ | $\dfrac{16}{\text{Score}}$ |

Double Word

| B₃ | L₁ | A₁ | C₃ | K₅ | $\dfrac{36}{\text{Score}}$ |

Double Letter

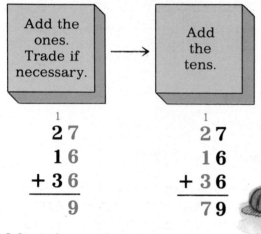

```
  1              1
  2 7            2 7
  1 6            1 6
+ 3 6          + 3 6
───────        ───────
    9            7 9
```

Maria's total score is 79.

Other Examples

```
    2           1 2           1 2         1 2  2 1
   7 9          3 8 5         3 6 8       5 4 , 6 2 8
   3 6              9         4 7 9           9 , 7 5 3
 + 5 7          + 7 8       + 6 0 6               8 5 6
 ─────          ─────       ───────       +   4 , 3 7 0
 1 7 2          4 7 2       1 , 4 5 3      ─────────────
                                           6 9 , 6 0 7
```

Warm Up Add.

1.	58	2.	279	3.	509	4.	743	5.	3,255
	46		186		64		7		1,318
	+ 87		+ 427		+ 283		+ 69		+ 1,699

6.	5,078	7.	4,178	8.	87,563	9.	7,086	10.	3,574
	365		6,039		9,875		3,975		398
	+ 29		+ 2,654		74		2,840		6,407
				+	386	+	8,694	+	58,612

56

Add.

1.	45 58 + 75	2.	594 385 + 257	3.	893 74 + 783	4.	624 9 + 48	5.	745 863 + 900

6.	22 73 + 98	7.	65 93 + 451	8.	249 37 + 786	9.	894 521 + 4,367	10.	6,576 937 + 8,142

11.	3,586 489 + 7,692	12.	6,837 4,079 + 3,605	13.	$ 57,836 4,927 + 398	14.	$ 4,367 295 8 + 46	15.	$ 57.63 29.48 67.00 + 89.76

16. 5,693 + 843 + 78 + 7,854

17. 5,429 + 8,239 + 568

18. 4,738 + 4,607 + 386

19. 14,349 + 38 + 274

20. Ben formed words with scores 19, 28, and 37. What is his total score for these three plays?

21. Make up the missing data and solve: Jill played three word games. Her scores for the first two games were 236 and 419. What is the total score for all three games?

Round each number to the nearest thousand and estimate the sum. Then find the actual sum. Do your results have a difference of more than 1,000?

22. 9,367 + 8,542 + 6,099 + 7,642 + 8,519 + 2,468

23. 6,988 + 4,023 + 5,555 + 3,746 + 8,499 + 7,023

Skillkeeper

Write > (greater than) or < (less than) for each ▓.

1. 451 ▓ 541   **2.** 8,195 ▓ 8,159   **3.** 36,726 ▓ 3,676

Do the operations in the order shown by the parentheses.

4. (6 + 2) × 3   **5.** (9 + 1) ÷ 2   **6.** 3 + (2 × 4)

7. 63 ÷ (3 + 4)   **8.** (18 ÷ 3) − 5   **9.** 15 − (3 × 2)

Problem Solving: Using Mental Math

No pens or pencils please!

The Grouping Property tells us that we can regroup numbers in addition to find the answer. It helps us solve problems **mentally** ("in our head").

HOBBY SHOW TODAY!

Sal collects hats. He brought 8 of them to the hobby show. He has 34 more at home. How many hats does he have in all?

$34 + 8$ is **30 + 12** or 42.

Van and Wendy both grow rare plants. Van has 35 plants. Wendy has 43. How many plants do Van and Wendy have altogether?

$35 + 43$ is 78.

Solve mentally. Write only the answer.

1. Kim has 46 stamps in a book. She also has 7 loose stamps. How many stamps does she have?

2. One showcase has 32 rocks in it. Another case has 27 rocks. What is the total number of rocks in the two cases?

3. Fiona has 52 Indian head pennies. She also has 9 Buffalo head nickels. How much money is this in all?

4. Kyle is putting 9 photos on each page of his album. He has already filled 37 pages. He has 45 more photos to put in the album. How many pages of photos will he have in all?

5. Tina's hobby is making pottery. She has made 26 bowls, 32 plates, and 7 vases. How many pieces of pottery has she made?

6. **Try This** Kerry has a total of 40 model planes and cars. She has 4 more planes than cars. How many cars does she have? Hint: Guess and check.

Problem Solving:
Using Data from a Distance Table

QUESTION
DATA
PLAN
ANSWER
CHECK

We can use this table to find the distance from one city to another. We read across the **row** for one city until we reach the **column** for the other city. The red arrows show the number in the Denver row and the Miami column. The distance from Denver to Miami is 3,293 km.

Driving Distances (kilometers)	Chicago	Dallas	Denver	Miami	New York	Seattle
Chicago		1,506	1,614	2,189	1,352	3,261
Dallas	1,506		1,265	2,107	2,586	3,399
Denver	1,614	1,265	→	3,293	2,979	2,117
Miami	2,189	2,107	3,293	↑	2,140	5,506
New York	1,352	2,586	2,979	2,140		4,674
Seattle	3,261	3,399	2,117	5,506	4,674	

Solve.

1. How far is a trip from Chicago to Seattle?

2. How far is a trip from New York to Miami to Dallas?

3. How far is a trip from Chicago to Denver to Seattle and directly back to Chicago?

4. How far is a trip from Seattle to Denver to Dallas and a return to Seattle the same way?

5. What are the 5 longest distances in the table? List them in order from greatest to least. Do not list the same distance more than once.

6. Choose a trip that starts at Miami and goes through each of the other cities in the table only once and ends in Seattle. Find how long this trip is.

7. **Try This** Mr. Blake drove 25 km farther on Tuesday than on Monday. He drove a total of 109 km on the two days. How far did he drive on Monday? Hint: Guess and check.

59

Estimating Differences: Mental Math

In the problems below, an answer close to the exact answer is all that is needed. To **estimate** the answer, we can round and solve a simpler problem.

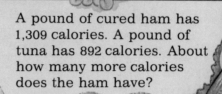

The energy we get from the food we eat is measured using a unit called a **calorie**. We get 38 calories when we eat a peach. We get 76 calories from an apple. About how many more calories do we get from an apple?

A pound of cured ham has 1,309 calories. A pound of tuna has 892 calories. About how many more calories does the ham have?

Round to the nearest ten.

$$
\begin{array}{rcr}
76 & \rightarrow & 80 \\
-38 & \rightarrow & -40 \\
\hline
& & 40
\end{array}
$$

We get about 40 more calories from an apple.

Round to the nearest hundred.

$$
\begin{array}{rcr}
1,309 & \rightarrow & 1,300 \\
-\quad 892 & \rightarrow & -\quad 900 \\
\hline
& & 400
\end{array}
$$

The ham has about 400 more calories.

Other Examples

Round to the nearest thousand.

$$
\begin{array}{rcr}
2,975 & \rightarrow & 3,000 \\
-1,198 & \rightarrow & -1,000 \\
\hline
& & 2,000
\end{array}
$$

Round to the nearest dollar.

$$
\begin{array}{rcr}
\$9.29 & \rightarrow & \$9.00 \\
-4.98 & \rightarrow & -5.00 \\
\hline
& & \$4.00
\end{array}
$$

Warm Up Estimate by rounding to the place named.

Nearest ten

1.	2.	3.
53	72	153
− 27	− 38	− 67

Nearest hundred

4.	5.	6.
812	1,392	1,507
− 386	− 785	− 689

Nearest thousand

7.	8.	9.
7,865	8,946	16,078
− 1,976	− 2,198	− 8,799

Nearest dollar

10.	11.	12.
$8.69	$14.39	$16.54
− 1.98	− 5.78	− 7.69

Find these differences.

1.	120 − 70	**2.**	1,100 − 500	**3.**	9,000 − 4,000	**4.**	12,000 − 9,000	**5.**	$ 17.00 − 8.00

Estimate by rounding to the nearest ten.

6.	93 − 38	**7.**	76 − 29	**8.**	123 − 57	**9.**	152 − 79	**10.**	168 − 75

Estimate by rounding to the nearest hundred.

11.	832 − 367	**12.**	908 − 176	**13.**	1,271 − 736	**14.**	1,384 − 899	**15.**	1,576 − 898

Estimate by rounding to the nearest thousand or the nearest dollar.

16.	9,176 − 2,847	**17.**	7,777 − 2,675	**18.**	6,473 − 4,516	**19.**	14,362 − 9,143	**20.**	15,866 − 8,678
21.	$ 8.25 − 1.89	**22.**	$ 6.79 − 2.87	**23.**	$ 9.75 − 3.88	**24.**	$ 16.44 − 7.56	**25.**	$ 12.83 − 2.89

26. Scrambled egg: 116 calories
Boiled egg: 79 calories
Estimate how many more
calories from the scrambled
egg by rounding to the
nearest ten.

27. If Tom has already taken in
1,067 calories but he needs
2,950 calories, how many more
calories does he need? Round
to the nearest thousand.

Think

Estimation

1. Use estimation to try to pick the two numbers
from the list that have a difference closest to 500.

2. Use a calculator to find the actual difference.

The winner is the person whose numbers have
a difference closest to 500!

Number List

257	1,275	749
798	698	1,203
136	1,657	612
1,098	1,409	1,894
897	937	384
419	1,386	1,562
1,805		1,184

Math

Subtracting: One Trade

A king cobra is 356 cm long. A bull snake is 162 cm long. How much longer is the king cobra?

Since we want to compare the lengths, we subtract.

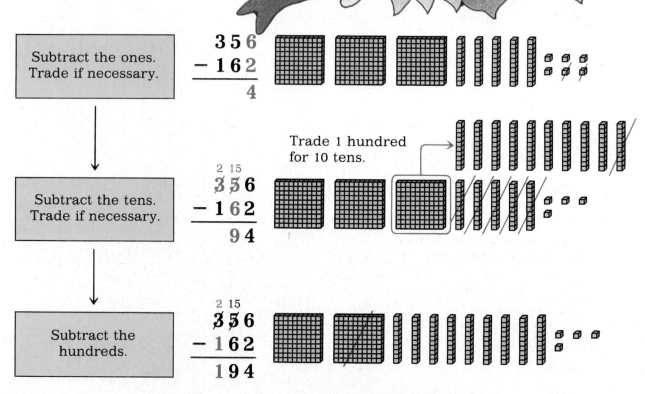

| Subtract the ones. Trade if necessary. | $\begin{array}{r} 3\,5\,6 \\ -\,1\,6\,2 \\ \hline 4 \end{array}$ |

Trade 1 hundred for 10 tens.

| Subtract the tens. Trade if necessary. | $\begin{array}{r} {\scriptstyle 2\;15} \\ 3\,\cancel{5}\,6 \\ -\,1\,6\,2 \\ \hline 9\,4 \end{array}$ |

| Subtract the hundreds. | $\begin{array}{r} {\scriptstyle 2\;15} \\ \cancel{3}\,\cancel{5}\,6 \\ -\,1\,6\,2 \\ \hline 1\,9\,4 \end{array}$ |

The king cobra is 194 cm longer. Check: 194 + 162 = 356

Other Examples

$\begin{array}{r} {\scriptstyle 7\;14} \\ \cancel{8}\,\cancel{4} \\ -\,2\,8 \\ \hline 5\,6 \end{array}$
$\qquad$
$\begin{array}{r} {\scriptstyle 4\;12} \\ \cancel{5}\,\cancel{2}\,7 \\ -\,4\,5\,4 \\ \hline 7\,3 \end{array}$
$\qquad$
$\begin{array}{r} {\scriptstyle 3\;12} \\ \cancel{4},\cancel{2}\,8\,5 \\ -\,1,5\,7\,2 \\ \hline 2,7\,1\,3 \end{array}$
$\qquad$
$\begin{array}{r} {\scriptstyle 3\;15} \\ \$9.\cancel{4}\,\cancel{5} \\ -\,3.1\,7 \\ \hline \$6.2\,8 \end{array}$

> To subtract money, think of pennies and subtract as with whole numbers. Write the answer as dollars and cents.

Warm Up   Subtract. Check by adding.

1.	2.	3.	4.	5.
$\begin{array}{r} 92 \\ -\,37 \\ \hline \end{array}$	$\begin{array}{r} 638 \\ -\,372 \\ \hline \end{array}$	$\begin{array}{r} 643 \\ -\,81 \\ \hline \end{array}$	$\begin{array}{r} 5,365 \\ -\,2,841 \\ \hline \end{array}$	$\begin{array}{r} \$7.48 \\ -\,2.63 \\ \hline \end{array}$

Find the differences.

1. 74
  − 29

2. 91
  − 47

3. 563
  − 247

4. 827
  − 454

5. 796
  − 623

6. 956
  − 348

7. 735
  − 92

8. 258
  − 29

9. 562
  − 129

10. 836
  − 781

11. 571
  − 262

12. $4.56
  − 1.82

13. $8.43
  − 3.27

14. 7,486
  − 2,916

15. 9,735
  − 4,441

16. $7.78
  − 5.83

17. $16.52
  − 2.33

18. $24.79
  − 18.57

19. 4,741
  − 3,114

20. 8,759
  − 7,164

21. 8,436 − 217

22. 186 − 27

23. 437 − 52

24. How much less than 566 is 249?

25. Estimate the difference of 892 and 324.

26. An indigo snake is 234 cm long. A water snake is 127 cm shorter. How long is the water snake?

27. Some information is missing from this problem. Make up the information and find the answer.

   Pat has a pet python. One of the longest pythons ever caught was 998 cm long. How many centimeters shorter than that is Pat's python?

28. **DATA BANK** How much longer is an anaconda of average length than is each of the next four longest snakes? (See page 409.)

Think

Logical Reasoning

Copy each problem and find the missing digits.

```
  8 ▓▓            ▓▓ 3 ▓▓
− ▓▓ 7          − 2 ▓▓ 7
─────          ─────────
  2 9             4 1 5


  ▓▓ 2 ▓▓          8 7 ▓▓
− 1 ▓▓ 4        − 3 ▓▓ 8
─────────       ─────────
  3 4 3           ▓▓ 5 3
```

Math

Subtracting: Two or More Trades

The rockets used to launch spacecraft travel fast enough to make a round trip between Earth and Venus in 288 days. A round trip between Earth and Mars would take 514 days. How many more days would the Mars trip take than the Venus trip?

Since we want to compare the number of days, we subtract.

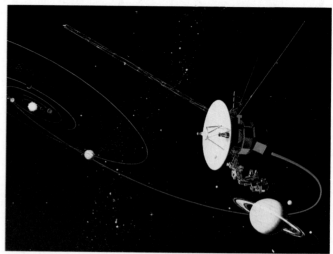

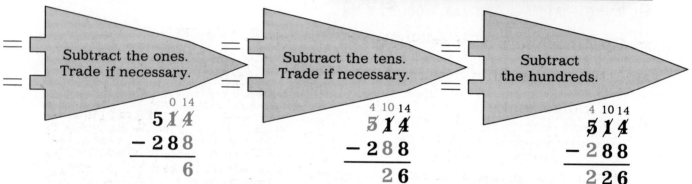

Subtract the ones. Trade if necessary.

$$\begin{array}{r} {\scriptstyle 0\ 14} \\ 5\cancel{1}\cancel{4} \\ -\,2\,8\,8 \\ \hline 6 \end{array}$$

Subtract the tens. Trade if necessary.

$$\begin{array}{r} {\scriptstyle 4\ 10\ 14} \\ \cancel{5}\cancel{1}\cancel{4} \\ -\,2\,8\,8 \\ \hline 2\,6 \end{array}$$

Subtract the hundreds.

$$\begin{array}{r} {\scriptstyle 4\ 10\ 14} \\ \cancel{5}\cancel{1}\cancel{4} \\ -\,2\,8\,8 \\ \hline 2\,2\,6 \end{array}$$

The Mars trip would take 226 more days than the Venus trip.

Other Examples

$$\begin{array}{r} {\scriptstyle 15\ 13} \\ 1\cancel{6}\cancel{3} \\ -\ \ 7\,8 \\ \hline 8\,5 \end{array}$$

$$\begin{array}{r} {\scriptstyle 7\ 12\ 12} \\ \cancel{8}\cancel{3}\cancel{2} \\ -\,7\,5\,9 \\ \hline 7\,3 \end{array}$$

$$\begin{array}{r} {\scriptstyle 8\ 17\ 14} \\ \cancel{9}\cancel{8}\cancel{4} \\ -\ \ 9\,5 \\ \hline 8\,8\,9 \end{array}$$

$$\begin{array}{r} {\scriptstyle 5\ \ \ 12\ 6\ 18} \\ \cancel{6},\cancel{2}\cancel{7}\cancel{8} \\ -\,3,8\,4\,9 \\ \hline 2,4\,2\,9 \end{array}$$

$$\begin{array}{r} {\scriptstyle 4\ 13\ \ \ 12\ 17} \\ \cancel{5}\cancel{4},\cancel{3}\cancel{7}\cancel{5} \\ -\,1\,7,6\,8\,2 \\ \hline 3\,6,6\,9\,3 \end{array}$$

Warm Up   Subtract. Check by adding.

1. $\begin{array}{r} 175 \\ -\ \ 98 \\ \hline \end{array}$

2. $\begin{array}{r} 946 \\ -\,868 \\ \hline \end{array}$

3. $\begin{array}{r} 747 \\ -\ \ 68 \\ \hline \end{array}$

4. $\begin{array}{r} 8,375 \\ -\,2,649 \\ \hline \end{array}$

5. $\begin{array}{r} 83,562 \\ -\,47,195 \\ \hline \end{array}$

6. $\begin{array}{r} 816 \\ -\,237 \\ \hline \end{array}$

7. $\begin{array}{r} 637 \\ -\ \ 89 \\ \hline \end{array}$

8. $\begin{array}{r} 6,247 \\ -\,1,579 \\ \hline \end{array}$

9. $\begin{array}{r} 71,436 \\ -\ \ 8,752 \\ \hline \end{array}$

10. $\begin{array}{r} 732 \\ -\,657 \\ \hline \end{array}$

Subtract.

1.	647 − 278	**2.**	812 − 434	**3.**	174 − 96	**4.**	425 − 377	**5.**	763 − 97

6.	626 − 515	**7.**	133 − 76	**8.**	915 − 847	**9.**	4,328 − 2,875	**10.**	741 − 65

11.	6,437 − 2,818	**12.**	3,572 − 853	**13.**	7,953 − 5,877	**14.**	15,045 − 8,468	**15.**	57,802 − 38,991

16.	9,365 − 4,878	**17.**	25,463 − 9,756	**18.**	647 − 179	**19.**	42,563 − 17,874	**20.**	67,324 − 26,875

21. $5.43 − $2.88

22. 356 − 79

23. 9,634 − 5,798

24. How much less is 629 than 817?

25. What number is 4,865 less than 5,742?

26. Today's spacecraft travel fast enough to fly to Saturn and back to Earth in 4,453 days. How much longer is this than the 514 days it would take to fly to Mars and back to Earth?

27. A round trip to Neptune takes 10,950 days less than a round trip to Pluto and 17,812 more days than a round trip to Mars. A round trip to Pluto takes 33,215 days. How many days does a round trip to Neptune take?

28. DATA BANK How much longer would a round trip space flight to Pluto take than a round trip flight to each of these planets? (See page 410.)

  A Venus   **B** Jupiter

  C Saturn   **D** Uranus

Think

An Addition-Subtraction Pattern

Start with a 3-digit number.

$$\begin{array}{r} 471 \\ -174 \\ \hline 297 \end{array}$$

Reverse the digits and subtract the smaller number from the larger.

$$\begin{array}{r} +792 \\ \hline 1,089 \end{array}$$

Reverse and add.

Try this with at least five other 3-digit numbers. What do you discover?

→ Math ←

More Practice, page 417, Set B

Subtracting: With Zeros

The graph shows how many cars there are for every 1,000 people in the given countries.

United Kingdom	260
West Germany	308
Canada	389
United States	507

Passenger Cars per 1,000 People

How many more cars per 1,000 people are there in the United States than in Canada?

Since we want to compare the two numbers, we subtract.

| Subtract the ones. Trade if necessary. | → | Subtract the tens. Trade if necessary. | → | Subtract the hundreds. |

$$\begin{array}{r} {\scriptstyle 4\ 9\ 17} \\ 5\,0\,7 \\ -\,3\,8\,9 \\ \hline 8 \end{array}$$

$$\begin{array}{r} {\scriptstyle 4\ 9\ 17} \\ 5\,0\,7 \\ -\,3\,8\,9 \\ \hline 1\,8 \end{array}$$

$$\begin{array}{r} {\scriptstyle 4\ 9\ 17} \\ 5\,0\,7 \\ -\,3\,8\,9 \\ \hline 1\,1\,8 \end{array}$$

There are 118 more cars per 1,000 people in the United States than in Canada.

Other Examples

$$\begin{array}{r} {\scriptstyle 3\ 9\ 10} \\ 4\,0\,0 \\ -\,2\,3\,7 \\ \hline 1\,6\,3 \end{array}$$
$$\begin{array}{r} {\scriptstyle 5\ 10} \\ 6\,0\,4 \\ -\,3\,6\,1 \\ \hline 2\,4\,3 \end{array}$$
$$\begin{array}{r} {\scriptstyle 5\ \ 9\ 15\,14} \\ 6{,}0\,6\,4 \\ -\,2{,}7\,9\,6 \\ \hline 3{,}2\,6\,8 \end{array}$$
$$\begin{array}{r} {\scriptstyle 6\ \ 9\ 9\,13} \\ 7{,}0\,0\,3 \\ -\,4{,}3\,2\,7 \\ \hline 2{,}6\,7\,6 \end{array}$$
$$\begin{array}{r} {\scriptstyle 8\ 9\ \ 9\ 9\,10} \\ 9\,0{,}0\,0\,0 \\ -\,5\,3{,}2\,4\,7 \\ \hline 3\,6{,}7\,5\,3 \end{array}$$

Warm Up Subtract. Check by adding.

1.
$$\begin{array}{r} 700 \\ -\ 463 \\ \hline \end{array}$$

2.
$$\begin{array}{r} 802 \\ -\ 531 \\ \hline \end{array}$$

3.
$$\begin{array}{r} 9{,}075 \\ -\ 3{,}687 \\ \hline \end{array}$$

4.
$$\begin{array}{r} 8{,}006 \\ -\ 5{,}458 \\ \hline \end{array}$$

5.
$$\begin{array}{r} 80{,}000 \\ -\ 27{,}438 \\ \hline \end{array}$$

6.
$$\begin{array}{r} 705 \\ -\ 648 \\ \hline \end{array}$$

7.
$$\begin{array}{r} 803 \\ -\ 76 \\ \hline \end{array}$$

8.
$$\begin{array}{r} 107 \\ -\ 49 \\ \hline \end{array}$$

9.
$$\begin{array}{r} 8{,}307 \\ -\ 4{,}539 \\ \hline \end{array}$$

10.
$$\begin{array}{r} 56{,}000 \\ -\ 28{,}325 \\ \hline \end{array}$$

Subtract.

1.	804 − 579	**2.**	600 − 436	**3.**	703 − 361	**4.**	560 − 387	**5.** 506 − 47

6.	5,304 − 3,267	**7.**	8,042 − 4,561	**8.**	4,050 − 1,309	**9.**	9,206 − 6,178	**10.** 7,008 − 2,456

11.	7,003 − 3,736	**12.**	6,206 − 1,893	**13.**	7,037 − 2,440	**14.**	6,000 − 3,665	**15.** 6,300 − 2,616

16.	95,070 − 34,368	**17.**	82,004 − 57,328	**18.**	52,057 − 26,483	**19.**	$9.04 − 3.69	**20.** $30.07 − 8.59

21. 803 − 739

22. 705 − 66

23. 5,008 − 1,269

24. How much more is 6,800 than 2,975?

25. What is 4,876 subtracted from 9,004?

26. Estimate the difference of 7,907 and 2,098.

27. Use the graph on page 66. How many more cars per 1,000 people are there in West Germany than in the United Kingdom?

28. In a recent year there were 7,065 thousand licensed drivers in Illinois and 3,588 thousand licensed drivers in Indiana. How many more licensed drivers were there in Illinois?

Skillkeeper

Estimate by rounding to the nearest ten.

1. 48 + 51

2. 57 + 92

3. 175 − 88

4. 92 − 53

5. $71 + $68

6. 153 − 76

Estimate by rounding to the nearest hundred.

7. 339 + 688

8. 985 − 448

9. $451 + $738

10. 1090 − 348

11. 759 + 609

12. $1567 − $879

Problem Solving: Using Estimation

For each problem,

A. **estimate** the answer by rounding to the nearest dollar.

B. find the **exact** answer.

C. find the **difference** between the exact answer and the estimate.

1. A chain costs $5.95. Pedals cost $3.69 a pair. What is the cost of a pair of pedals and a chain?

2. A new bike tire costs $7.49 in one store. It costs $9.65 in another store. How much do you save if you buy the tire at the lower price?

3. A handle bar costs $9.69. New handle grips cost $1.35 a pair, and a new headlight costs $4.98. How much would these new parts cost?

4. Bike reflectors cost $1.00 each if bought separately. A set of 5 reflectors costs $3.89. How much do you save on 5 reflectors if you buy the set?

5. If Tim has his old bike repaired, parts will cost $39.57 and the labor cost will be $29.75. A new bike costs $120.49. How much will he save if he decides to have his bike repaired?

6. **DATA HUNT** What is the actual total cost if you buy these extras for your bike: an odometer, a horn, and a headlight? Get the prices from a catalog or a store.

7. **Try This** Dawn made 2 round trips on her bike to a state park 29 km away. After these trips her bike odometer read 402 km. What did it read before she made the trips?

Problem Solving: Practice

Solve.

1. A food stand at a zoo sold 123,678 bags of peanuts one year and 137,458 the next year. How many more bags were sold the second year?

2. What would be the total cost of 7 pairs of socks for $4.00 a pair and a shirt for $9.89?

3. Wade worked 9 hours for $4.00 an hour. He used part of the money he earned to buy a shirt for $8.98. How much money did he have left?

4. The attendance at 3 baseball games was 32,794; 35,669; and 49,708. Of the total, 5,276 fans were admitted free. How many fans paid to see the three games?

5. The Rose Bowl in Pasadena, California, has 101,025 seats. Memorial Coliseum in Los Angeles has 93,791 seats. How many more seats does the Rose Bowl have?

6. Annette Low paid $369.00 for a 35-mm camera. She also bought a special lens for $297.00, a tripod for $47.29, and 2 rolls of film for $3.29 a roll. What was the total cost?

7. A patrol of 9 scouts is chosen from a group of 63 scouts. The rest of the scouts are divided into work groups of 6. How many work groups are there?

8. Write a question that can be answered using this data. Then solve the problem. A gray whale weighed 1,882 kg when it was brought to Sea World in March. In November the whale weighed 3,447 kg.

9. **Try This** Mrs. Carl has twice as many children in her class as Mr. Perez has. There are 48 children in the two classes. How many children are in Mr. Perez's class?

Problem Solving: Draw a Picture

Sometimes it is easier to solve a problem if you use a strategy called

DRAW A PICTURE

Try This Rockton is 572 km from Millville. Roy's family started at Millville and drove 258 km toward Rockton. Cassie's family started at Rockton and drove 219 km toward Millville during the same time. How far apart were the two families then?

First I show all the information in a picture and label it carefully.

Then I see that I first must add, then subtract to find the answer.

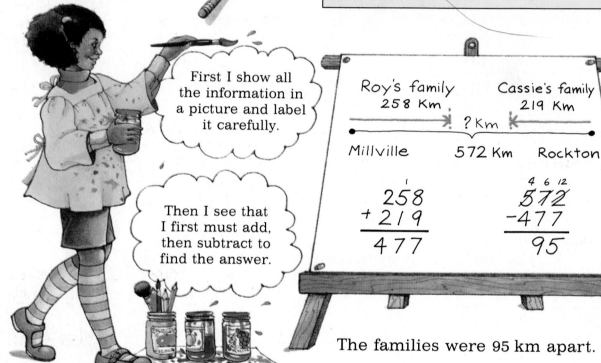

Roy's family
258 Km

Cassie's family
219 Km

? Km

Millville   572 Km   Rockton

$$\begin{array}{r} 258 \\ +219 \\ \hline 477 \end{array}$$

$$\begin{array}{r} 572 \\ -477 \\ \hline 95 \end{array}$$

The families were 95 km apart.

Solve.

1. Alton, Benton, Clinton, and Dunlap are towns on the same highway. Dunlap is between Alton and Clinton. Dunlap is 189 km from Alton. Clinton is between Dunlap and Benton. Clinton is 237 km from Benton. Alton and Benton are 671 km apart. How far apart are Dunlap and Clinton?

2. Sara's family are taking a 1,024-km trip from Bayview to Forest City. On the way they will go through only two other towns, first Oakville and then Durham. It is 587 km from Bayview to Durham and 96 km from Durham to Oakville. How many kilometers farther is it between Bayview and Oakville than between Durham and Forest City?

70

Chapter Review-Test

Estimate the sums by rounding to the place named.

1. Nearest ten
82
+ 29

2. Nearest hundred
367
+ 782

3. Nearest thousand
4,798
+ 8,127

4. Nearest dollar
$ 5.46
+ 8.55

Add.

5. 257
+ 549

6. 6,483
+ 8,329

7. 59,380
+ 47,825

8. $ 29.39
+ 5.68

9. 6,738
489
+ 72,803

10. 179 + 86

11. $3.75 + $8.89

12. 25,947 + 865

Estimate the differences by rounding to the place named.

13. Nearest ten
94
− 39

14. Nearest hundred
1,365
− 645

15. Nearest thousand
7,429
− 2,058

16. Nearest dollar
$ 16.75
+ 8.53

Subtract.

17. 73
− 25

18. 638
− 572

19. 503
− 178

20. 6,002
− 4,765

21. $ 80.83
− 37.65

22. 196 − 38

23. 704 − 257

24. 12,008 − 199

Solve.

25. Can a trip from Chicago to St. Louis to Denver and back to Chicago be completed without driving more than 3,000 km? How much more or less than 3,000 km is the trip?

Distances	
Chicago to St. Louis	468 km
St. Louis to Denver	1,388 km
Denver to Chicago	1,614 km

26. A set of front and rear bike lights costs $11.31. A front light alone costs $7.49, and a rear light costs $5.38. How much less does it cost to buy the set than to buy the lights separately?

71

Another Look

```
  1  1 1              1 ten
  9,569        ╭─────────────────╮
+ 4,875        │ 14 ones = 1 ten and │
─────────      │        4 ones      │
 14,444        ╰─────────────────╯
                      4 ones
```

14 tens = 1 hundred and 4 tens

14 hundreds = 1 thousand and
4 hundreds

14 thousands = 1 ten thousand and
4 thousands

Add.

1.	465 + 329	**2.**	567 + 745	**3.**	879 + 94
4.	6,048 + 9,576	**5.**	9,846 + 2,784	**6.**	83,570 + 9,657
7.	579 836 + 408	**8.**	3,654 237 + 29	**9.**	498 7 + 3,865

```
  ╭────────────────────────╮
  │ 6 thousands = 600 tens = │
  │  599 tens and 10 ones    │
  ╰────────────────────────╯
              ╭──────────╮
              │ Need more │
  5  9 9 12   │  ones!    │
  6,002       ╰──────────╯
- 3,765              1  1 1
─────────   Check:   3,765
  2,237            + 2,237
                   ─────────
                     6,002
```

Subtract. Check by adding.

10.	5,003 – 68	**11.**	701 – 74	**12.**	368 – 199
13.	500 – 276	**14.**	8,004 – 2,975	**15.**	7,000 – 2,431
16.	802 – 54	**17.**	4,083 – 2,657	**18.**	8,706 – 4,978

```
  ╭──────────────────────╮
  │ Think about pennies and │
  │ add as with whole numbers. │
  ╰──────────────────────╯
            723¢
          + 459¢

  ╭──────────╮     1
  │ Write the │   $ 7.23
  │  answer   │  + 4.59
  │ as dollars │  ─────────
  │ and cents. │  $ 11.82
  ╰──────────╯
```

Find the sum or difference.

19.	$ 8.45 + 3.76	**20.**	$ 9.24 – 5.73	**21.**	$ 12.57 + 8.46
		22.	$ 7.36 – 1.98	**23.**	$ 24.20 – 16.59
				24.	$ 24.75 + 36.89

Enrichment

The Microcomputer—Inputs, Rules, and Outputs

A microcomputer can be programmed so that when you type in an INPUT NUMBER (for example, 5) it will use a RULE (for example, N + N − 1) and print an OUTPUT NUMBER (in this case, 9).

```
INPUT: 5
RULE: N + N - 1
OUTPUT: 9
```

The computer can be instructed to print tables like those below. Give any missing **inputs**, **outputs**, or **rules**.

Rule: $(8 \times N) + 3$

	Input	Output
	5	43
1.	8	—
2.	7	—
3.	4	—
4.	9	—

Rule: $(N \div 9) - 2$

	Input	Output
	81	7
5.	36	—
6.	45	—
7.	63	—
8.	54	—

Rule: $(N \times N) - 1$

	Input	Output
	3	8
9.	4	—
10.	7	—
11.	9	—
12.	5	—

Rule: $(3 \times N) + 1$

	Input	Output
	2	7
	3	10
	4	13
13.	—	22
14.	—	28

15. **Rule:** ?

	Input	Output
	3	0
	4	1
	10	7
16.	13	—
17.	—	15

18. **Rule:** ?

	Input	Output
	2	3
	5	9
	10	19
	50	99
	100	199

19. Make up some tables with input and output numbers and ask a classmate to guess your rule.

Cumulative Review

Add, subtract, multiply, or divide.
Watch the signs.

1.
```
   9
 + 7
```
A 17
B 16
C 15
D not given

2.
```
  14
 - 9
```
A 23
B 5
C 6
D not given

3. 8 × 7
A 58
B 54
C 15
D not given

4. 54 ÷ 6
A 9
B 48
C 8
D not given

5. 7)42
A 4
B 6
C 14
D not given

6. What is the place value of the 7 in 607,342?

A hundreds   B thousands
C tens   D not given

7. Which three digits are in the millions period of 674,368,942,681?

A 942   B 674
C 368   D not given

8. Give the standard number for 1,000 + 900 + 70 + 6.

A 1,976   B 10,976
C 19,706 D not given

Which sign should go in the ▓?

9. 1,234 ▓ 1,243

A <   B >   C =

10. 46,090 ▓ 46,900

A <   B >   C =

11. What is 383 rounded to the nearest ten?

A 400   B 370
C 390   D not given

12. What is 7,398 rounded to the nearest hundred?

A 7,400   B 8,000
C 7,300   D not given

13. Alan ordered a model car kit for $27.98, a model boat kit for $22.79, and a model airplane kit for $30. What was the total amount of his order?

A $79.67   B $51.07
C $80.77   D not given

14. Inez was given a $150 bonus for outstanding work on her job. She spent $28 of the bonus for a new tennis racket and $13 for a pair of shorts. How much bonus money did she have left?

A $122   B $109
C $135   D not given

Decimals: Addition and Subtraction

Niels got his first pair of ice skates when he was only two years old. During his early years, he spent many happy hours racing with his cousin Elise on the frozen lakes near their home in Minnesota. As the two grew older, though, what once had been just a pleasant pastime became a very important part of their lives. Summer and winter they trained—bicycling, running, and practicing their turns around the ice rink. By the time they were 16, Niels was able to skate 500 meters in only 40.65 seconds, and Elise took only 2.5 seconds longer than that to cover the same distance. Very soon they would be good enough to try to win a place on their country's Olympic speed skating team.

Decimal Place Value: Tenths

Mario painted one whole section of a fence and 3 of the 10 boards in the next section. How can he use numbers to tell someone about the amount of the fence he has painted?

Using a fraction

One whole section
↓
$1\dfrac{3}{10}$

3 ← Number of boards painted in the next section

10 ← Total number of boards in a section

We read: "one and three tenths"

Using a decimal

One whole section
↓
1.3 ← Number of boards painted in the next section out of a total of ten

We read: "one and three tenths"

Mario can say that he has painted 1.3 sections of fence.

In this chapter we will use decimals. Study these other examples.

A.

ones	tenths
2	8

We write: 2.8

We read: "two and eight tenths"

B.

ones	tenths
0	2

We write: 0.2

We read: "two tenths"

Warm Up Write and read a decimal for the amount painted in each exercise.

1.

2.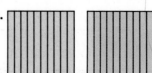

3.

76

Match the words for the amount painted with each picture.

A. two and one tenth
B. one tenth
C. one and two tenths
D. two tenths

1.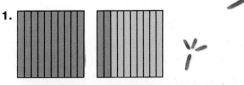

2.

3.

4.

Write a decimal for the amount painted in each exercise.

5.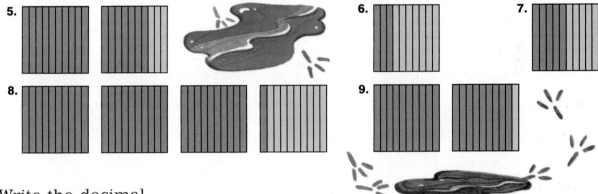

6.

7.

8.

9.

Write the decimal.

10. seven tenths

11. one and three tenths

12. four and eight tenths

13. twenty-five and six tenths

Write the word name for each decimal.

14. 0.4   15. 3.7   16. 32.6   17. 40.1

Think

Estimation

Estimate the location of each of these numbers by giving the correct letter from the number line below.

1. 1.7   2. 1.3   3. 2.5   4. 2.8   5. 0.8   6. 0.3

```
   A   B   C   D       E   F   G   H   I   J   K   L
←──•───•───•───•───┼───•───•───•───•───•───•───•───•──→
  0                 1               2               3
```

Math

77

Hundredths

Cathy began covering a tiled
floor with squares of green carpet.
How can she use numbers to tell
someone about the amount of the
floor she has covered with carpet?

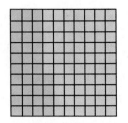

Using a fraction

$\dfrac{34}{100}$ ← Number of carpeted squares
← Total number of squares

We read: "thirty-four hundredths"

Using a decimal

0.34 ← Number of squares
carpeted out of a
total of 100

We read: "thirty-four hundredths"

Cathy can say that she has carpeted 0.34 of the floor.

Study these other examples.

A.

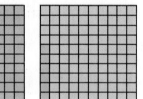

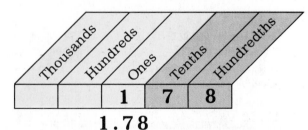

1.06
"one and six hundredths"

B.

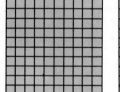 

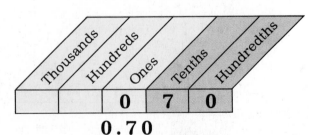

1.78
"one and seventy-eight hundredths"

C.

7 tenths is the same as
70 hundredths. 0.7 = 0.70

0.70
"seventy hundredths"

Write the decimal for each picture.

1.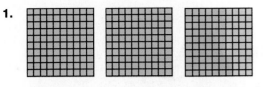

two and sixty-three hundredths

2.

one and seven hundredths

3.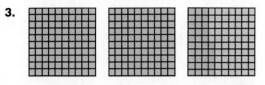

4.

5.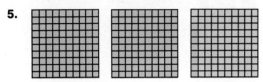

6. Give the missing numbers.

▥ tenths are shaded.

▥ hundredths are shaded.

Write the decimal.

7. one and forty-three hundredths

8. five and seven hundredths

9. seventeen and eight tenths

10. four and ninety-nine hundredths

11. two and thirty hundredths

12. two and three hundredths

Write the word name for each decimal.

13. 1.56

14. 3.60

15. 7.08

16. 30.41

17. 10.62

18. 6.09

Think

Money and Decimals

Can you write a decimal for each blank?

A ⬤ is ___?___ of a [bill]

A ⬤ is ___?___ of a [bill]

A ⬤ is ___?___ of a [bill]

A ⬤ is ___?___ of a [bill]

Math

Thousandths

Engineers measured the heads of more than 2,000 women and men to find the best shape for a new telephone. They used decimals like the one shown in the picture to describe the measurements of the new telephone.

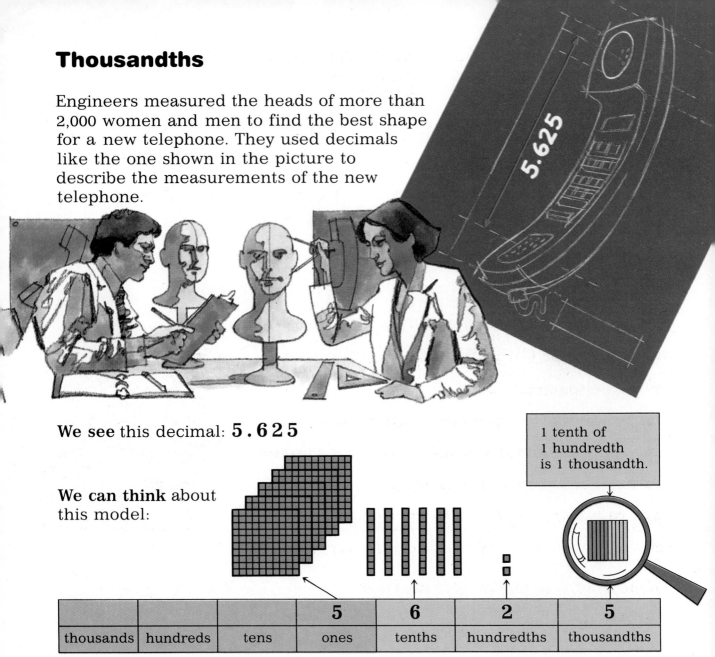

5.625

We see this decimal: **5.625**

1 tenth of
1 hundredth
is 1 thousandth.

We can think about this model:

thousands	hundreds	tens	ones	tenths	hundredths	thousandths
			5	6	2	5

We read: "five and six hundred twenty-five thousandths"

Warm Up

Write and read a decimal for each exercise.

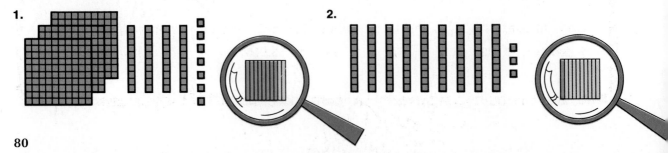

1.

2.

Read each decimal. Give the place value of each red digit. Example: 2.076 Answer: "two and seventy-six thousandths"; 7 hundredths

1. 3.451
2. 0.254
3. 12.643
4. 57.635
5. 18.036
6. 2.854
7. 865.5
8. 0.561
9. 4.002
10. 8.705
11. 50.04
12. 67.057
13. 0.379
14. 86.437
15. 0.001
16. 608.302
17. 3.142
18. 101.01
19. 9,427.683
20. 5,963.418

Write the decimal.

21. four and two hundred eighty-six thousandths
22. one hundred fifty-seven thousandths
23. seventy-four thousandths
24. ninety-six and forty-two hundredths
25. sixty-two and three hundred two thousandths
26. nine and thirty-four hundredths
27. five hundred eighty-nine thousandths
28. one hundred fifty-three and nine tenths

Write a word name for each decimal.

29. 3.678
30. 0.525
31. 0.402
32. 8.005

Think

Decimal Place Value

 Enter the decimal 56.478 into a calculator.

Can you make the calculator show the decimal with the 7 changed to a 0 by using just one operation on the calculator?

Change these digits to a 0. (Remember: Use only one operation!)

1. the 5 in 8.532
2. the 3 in 13.965
3. the 2 in 9.427

Math

Comparing and Ordering Decimals

Sandra asked this trivia question about baseball history: "Who had the higher batting average, Ty Cobb in 1917 or Rogers Hornsby in 1923?"

Compare the two averages to see which is greater.

Batting Averages of Some Great Hitters of the Past		
1917	Ty Cobb	0.383
1923	Rogers Hornsby	0.384
1924	Babe Ruth	0.378
1934	Lou Gehrig	0.363

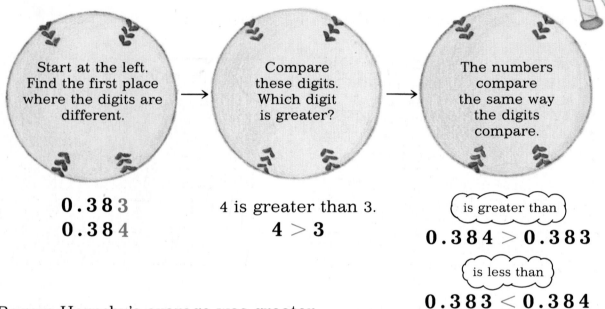

Start at the left. Find the first place where the digits are different. → Compare these digits. Which digit is greater? → The numbers compare the same way the digits compare.

0.383
0.384

4 is greater than 3.
4 > 3

is greater than
0.384 > 0.383

is less than
0.383 < 0.384

Rogers Hornsby's average was greater.

Order the averages shown in the table by listing them from greatest to least. Do this by comparing them two at a time.

0.384 ← greatest
0.383
0.378
0.363 ← least

Warm Up   Write >, <, or = for each ▥.

1. 4.6 ▥ 4.8   **2.** 1.336 ▥ 1.431   **3.** 9.05 ▥ 9.01   **4.** 0.039 ▥ 0.390

5. 1.7 ▥ 1.70   **6.** 0.90 ▥ 0.89   **7.** 37.73 ▥ 36.73   **8.** 0.008 ▥ 0.100

9. 4.96 ▥ 5.02   **10.** 0.002 ▥ 0.020   **11.** 9.3 ▥ 9.30   **12.** 1.686 ▥ 1.868

13. Order from greatest to least: 3.549; 3.594; 3.459; 3.954; 4.345

14. Order from least to greatest: 7.089; 7.421; 6.984; 7.500; 6.099

Write >, <, or = for each .

1. 3.7 ⬤ 3.09
2. 0.314 ⬤ 0.317
3. 0.8 ⬤ 0.58
4. 2.9 ⬤ 2.90

5. 9 ⬤ 8.79
6. 1.00 ⬤ 0.99
7. 6.20 ⬤ 6.02
8. 0.51 ⬤ 0.49

9. 6.8 ⬤ 8.6
10. 0.457 ⬤ 0.475
11. 16.0 ⬤ 16.00
12. 6.41 ⬤ 64.1

13. 0.99 ⬤ 1.01
14. 8.3 ⬤ 8.29
15. 0.47 ⬤ 0.470
16. 12.6 ⬤ 9.8

17. 0.7 ⬤ 0.699
18. 3.1 ⬤ 13
19. 0.54 ⬤ 45
20. 160 ⬤ 16.0

List the decimals in each table from greatest to least.

21.

Some Other Great Hitters' Batting Averages		
1939	Joe DiMaggio	0.381
1941	Ted Williams	0.406
1948	Stan Musial	0.376
1954	Willie Mays	0.345
1959	Hank Aaron	0.355

22.

Champions of Long Ago Winning Records		
1901	Pirates	0.647
1902	Pirates	0.741
1903	Pirates	0.650
1904	Giants	0.693
1905	Giants	0.686

23. One year the leading pitcher in the National League had an earned run average of 1.98. In the American League the leading average was 1.91. Which average was greater?

24. In a recent year the pitchers on one team had an earned run average of 3.93. The pitchers on another team had an average of 4.02. Which average was greater?

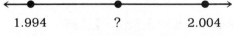
Think

Number Line—Decimals

What is the number for the point halfway between 1.994 and 2.004?

1.994   ?   2.004

Math

Rounding Decimals

The largest pearl on record was found in the shell of a giant clam in the Philippine Islands in 1934. It is valued at over four million dollars and weighs 6.378 kg. What is this weight rounded to the nearest whole number?

To round to the nearest **whole number,** look at the digit in the tenths place.

If the digit is less than 5, drop the decimal part. If the digit is 5 or more, drop the decimal part and round up.

6.378

6.378 rounded to the nearest whole number is **6.**

The pearl weighs about 6 kg.

Other Examples

Look at the digit to the right of the place you want to round to!

6.569 rounded to the nearest **whole number** is **7.**

4.265 rounded to the nearest **tenth** is **4.3.**

7.349 rounded to the nearest **tenth** is **7.3.**

Warm Up   Round to the nearest whole number.

1. 5.3	**2.** 8.7	**3.** 6.5	**4.** 12.38	**5.** 6.427
6. 9.501	**7.** 7.499	**8.** 7.65	**9.** 9.387	**10.** 23.501

Round to the nearest tenth.

11. 0.72	**12.** 0.45	**13.** 0.76	**14.** 3.523	**15.** 0.379
16. 0.46	**17.** 0.852	**18.** 0.507	**19.** 0.079	**20.** 0.637

Round to the nearest whole number.

1. 7.8	**2.** 3.4	**3.** 0.62	**4.** 1.45	**5.** 9.56
6. 0.980	**7.** 5.05	**8.** 1.632	**9.** 5.49	**10.** 1.55
11. 13.4	**12.** 7.49	**13.** 29.5	**14.** 0.89	**15.** 6.48

Round to the nearest tenth.

16. 0.94	**17.** 6.45	**18.** 0.736	**19.** 8.802	**20.** 5.095
21. 1.956	**22.** 7.49	**23.** 3.150	**24.** 2.094	**25.** 9.982
26. 0.963	**27.** 2.05	**28.** 0.848	**29.** 5.163	**30.** 0.609

31. What is 3.461 rounded to the nearest whole number?

32. Round 8.753 to the nearest tenth.

33. One of the largest emeralds ever found has a diameter of 24.75 cm. What is its diameter rounded to the nearest whole number?

34. A very large diamond was sold in 1969 for $1.05 million. How much is this to the nearest tenth of a million?

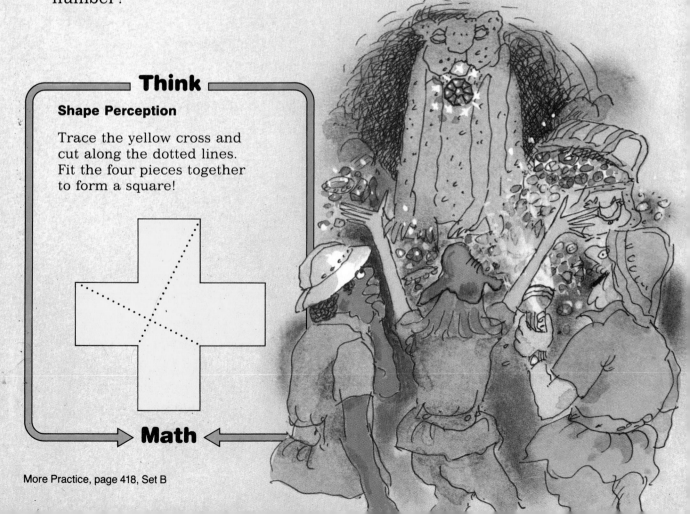

Think

Shape Perception

Trace the yellow cross and cut along the dotted lines. Fit the four pieces together to form a square!

Math

More Practice, page 418, Set B

Estimating Sums and Differences: Mental Math

Sometimes an answer close to the exact answer is all that is needed. To estimate the sum or difference of two decimals, you can **round to the nearest whole number** and find the whole-number sum or difference.

A

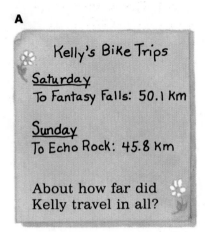

Kelly's Bike Trips

Saturday
To Fantasy Falls: 50.1 km

Sunday
To Echo Rock: 45.8 km

About how far did Kelly travel in all?

B

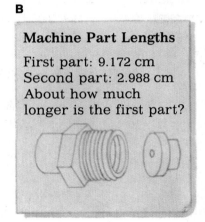

Machine Part Lengths

First part: 9.172 cm
Second part: 2.988 cm
About how much longer is the first part?

C

Sales Slip

QTY.	DESCRIPTION	TOTAL
1	Book	$8.95
1	Record	$7.19

About how much do the two items cost together?

Solutions to the problems:

A.
$$50.1 \rightarrow 50$$
$$+45.8 \rightarrow +46$$
$$96$$

Kelly traveled about 96 km in all.

B.
$$9.172 \rightarrow 9$$
$$-2.988 \rightarrow -3$$
$$6$$

The first part is about 6 cm longer.

C.
$$\$8.95 \rightarrow \$9$$
$$+7.19 \rightarrow +7$$
$$\$16$$

The two items cost about $16.

Estimate by rounding to the nearest whole number.

1. 8.6 + 7.9	**2.** 6.2 + 8.6	**3.** 4.52 + 9.74	**4.** 20.35 + 8.76	**5.** 9.768 + 6.547
6. 16.3 − 8.9	**7.** 14.7 − 6.8	**8.** 17.89 − 9.42	**9.** 25.137 − 19.864	**10.** 12.207 − 7.541
11. 8.36 + 9.75	**12.** 15.762 − 8.457	**13.** 35.178 − 29.436	**14.** 49.764 + 50.147	**15.** 16.783 − 9.199
16. $19.57 + 29.99	**17.** 40.489 − 29.683	**18.** 8.799 + 9.346	**19.** $299.87 − 99.76	**20.** 14.368 − 4.976

Problem Solving: Using Estimation

Estimate the answers by rounding to the nearest whole number.

1. Tanya saw some silver earrings that cost $16.78. She saw some cheaper ones for $9.42. About how much was the difference in the costs?

2. Elton bought two music boxes as gifts. One music box cost $19.69 and the other cost $30.49. About how much did the two boxes cost together?

3. Jessica bought 6 charms for her bracelet. They cost $7.95 each. About how much was the total cost of the charms?

4. Tico bought 5 cups for $5.98 each. He also bought a large pitcher for $10.38. About how much did these items cost?

5. Martina has $25. Does she have enough money to pay for a $9.97 desk set, a $7.86 desk pen, and a $6.18 pencil sharpener? (No sales tax)

6. If you have 3 ten-dollar bills, can you buy 8 rolls of film for $3.19 a roll and a slide tray for $6.75?

7. A set of 6 carving knives is on sale for $53.79. About how much does each of the knives cost?

8. Lyle has only $20. He wants to buy a $14.79 sweater and a $9.24 shirt. About how much more money does he need?

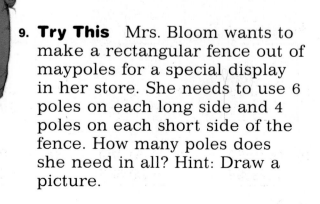

9. **Try This** Mrs. Bloom wants to make a rectangular fence out of maypoles for a special display in her store. She needs to use 6 poles on each long side and 4 poles on each short side of the fence. How many poles does she need in all? Hint: Draw a picture.

Adding with Decimals

The microcomputer screen shows how many milligrams (mg) of vitamin C are in the food Mr. Parr had for lunch. He needs at least 60 mg of vitamin C each day. Do the baked potato and the tomato give him that much vitamin C?

```
VITAMIN C
IN MILLIGRAMS
BAKED POTATO      31.86
FISH               1.24
SLICED TOMATO     28.39
MILK   1 GLASS     1.87
```

Since we want the total amount of vitamin C in 2 items, we add.

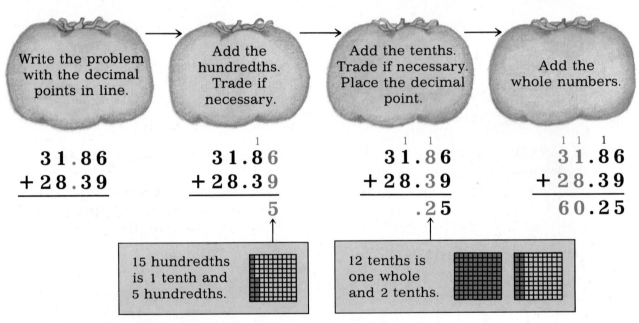

Write the problem with the decimal points in line.

$$31.86$$
$$+28.39$$

Add the hundredths. Trade if necessary.

$$31.8\overset{1}{6}$$
$$+28.39$$
$$5$$

15 hundredths is 1 tenth and 5 hundredths.

Add the tenths. Trade if necessary. Place the decimal point.

$$3\overset{1}{1}.\overset{1}{8}6$$
$$+28.39$$
$$.25$$

12 tenths is one whole and 2 tenths.

Add the whole numbers.

$$\overset{1}{3}\overset{1}{1}.\overset{1}{8}6$$
$$+28.39$$
$$60.25$$

The baked potato and the tomato give him 60.25 mg of vitamin C. This is more than the amount he needs.

Other Examples

$$\begin{array}{r} \overset{1}{1}3.7 \\ +34.8 \\ \hline 48.5 \end{array} \qquad \begin{array}{r} \overset{1}{\$7}.80 \\ +9.65 \\ \hline \$17.45 \end{array} \qquad \begin{array}{r} \overset{1}{9}.\overset{1}{5}\overset{1}{7}6 \\ +0.489 \\ \hline 10.065 \end{array} \qquad \begin{array}{r} \overset{2}{0}.\overset{1}{7}63 \\ 4.69 \\ +1.8 \\ \hline 7.253 \end{array}$$

Warm Up Find the sums.

1. $\begin{array}{r} 26.6 \\ +42.9 \\ \hline \end{array}$
2. $\begin{array}{r} 16.37 \\ +17.96 \\ \hline \end{array}$
3. $\begin{array}{r} \$6.70 \\ +8.54 \\ \hline \end{array}$
4. $\begin{array}{r} 7.864 \\ +0.189 \\ \hline \end{array}$
5. $\begin{array}{r} 6.478 \\ 0.7 \\ +2.85 \\ \hline \end{array}$

88

Add.

1.   46.8
  + 59.7

2.   37.8
  + 9.6

3.   6.27
  + 2.88

4.   0.85
  + 4.36

5.   3.7
  + 2.46

6.   7.386
  + 0.049

7.   36.35
  + 19.2

8.   4.18
  + 3.675

9. $ 5.63
  + 2.48

10. $ 8.98
  + 4.69

11.   36.8
    19.3
  + 26.4

12. 128.7
   36.48
 +   9.867

13.   1.869
  2.088
 + 3.548

14.   0.687
  0.975
  0.836
 + 0.548

15. $ 124.73
  642.80
  376.57
 + 290.17

16. $9.132 + 8.355 + 9.026$

17. $1.663 + 27.65 + 3.78$

18. $12.38 + 9.5 + 8.36$

19. $57.6 + 99.2 + 113.5$

20. What is the sum when the addends are 3.79, 13.872, and 9.6?

21. Here are the vitamin C values of 4 different foods: Orange juice (1 glass) 59.47 mg; 1 apple 5.29 mg; spinach (serving) 49.86 mg; slice of pizza 6.07 mg. How much vitamin C is this in all?

22. Use the information shown in the picture on page 88 to solve this problem. What is the total amount of vitamin C Mr. Parr gets from the foods listed on the screen?

23. **DATA BANK** Use the Data Bank list on page 410 to choose the items you would like to have for breakfast. How much vitamin C would that breakfast give you?

Think

Estimation

Write the equations with decimal points in the addends where needed to make the sums correct.

 Use a calculator to check your answers.

Addends	Sum	Addends	Sum
1. $258 + 16 = 4.18$		**5.** $258 + 16 = 258.16$	
2. $258 + 16 = 41.8$		**6.** $258 + 16 = 16.258$	
3. $258 + 16 = 27.4$		**7.** $258 + 16 = 0.418$	
4. $258 + 16 = 2.74$		**8.** $258 + 16 = 259.6$	

Math

Subtracting with Decimals

A test car traveling at the legal speed limit went 8.31 km on a liter of gas. At a higher speed the car went only 5.94 km. How much farther did the car go at the slower speed?

Since we want to compare the two distances, we subtract.

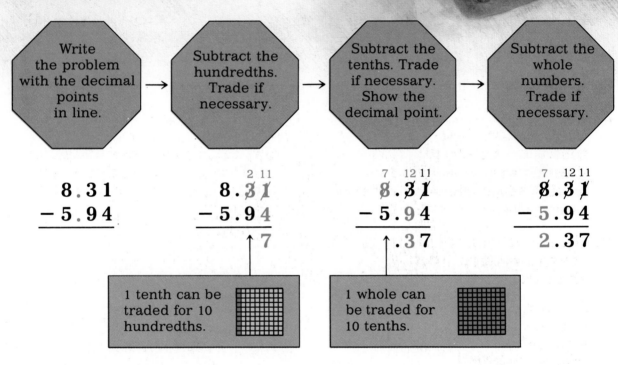

| Write the problem with the decimal points in line. | → | Subtract the hundredths. Trade if necessary. | → | Subtract the tenths. Trade if necessary. Show the decimal point. | → | Subtract the whole numbers. Trade if necessary. |

$$8.31$$
$$-5.94$$

$$\overset{\;2\;11}{8.3\!\!\!/1}$$
$$-5.94$$
$$7$$

$$\overset{7\quad12\,11}{8.3\!\!\!/1}$$
$$-5.94$$
$$.37$$

$$\overset{7\quad12\,11}{8.3\!\!\!/1}$$
$$-5.94$$
$$2.37$$

1 tenth can be traded for 10 hundredths.

1 whole can be traded for 10 tenths.

The car went 2.37 km farther at the slower speed.

Other Examples

$$\overset{3\quad16}{\$4.\!\!\!/6\!\!\!/0}$$
$$-1.80$$
$$\$2.80$$

$$\overset{8\;9\;14}{0.90\!\!\!/4}$$
$$-0.478$$
$$0.426$$

$$856.7$$
$$-534.16$$

→ Write 856.7 as 856.70. →

$$\overset{6\;10}{856.7\!\!\!/0}$$
$$-534.16$$
$$322.54$$

Warm Up Subtract.

1.   6.2
   − 3.8

2.   0.803
   − 0.369

3. $ 47.60
   − 24.15

4.   958.3
   − 423.76

5.   7.523
   − 0.409

Subtract.

1.	8.4 − 3.6	**2.**	8.34 − 4.65	**3.**	57.82 − 18.97	**4.**	304.26 − 96.56	**5.**	7.064 − 1.255
6.	129.7 − 64.43	**7.**	0.832 − 0.076	**8.**	8.054 − 0.655	**9.**	5,638.4 − 2,976.8	**10.**	365.24 − 78.9
11.	596.742 − 258.685	**12.**	9,743.6 − 862.64	**13.**	$89.42 − 64.86	**14.**	$102.51 − 84.38	**15.**	$547.23 − 268.59

16. 4.3 − 0.9   **17.** 3.85 − 1.596   **18.** 547.34 − 98.67

19. 81.05 − 4.3   **20.** 6,734.6 − 87.8   **21.** 972.58 − 846.7

22. What number is 3.592 less than 38.671?

23. A car driven at a slow speed went 8.85 km on a liter of gasoline. At a much higher speed it went 5.94 km. How much farther did it go at the slower speed?

24. One liter of gasoline was put into an empty gas tank on a test car. From these odometer readings, tell how far the car traveled on 1 L.

25. Write a question that can be answered using the data below. Then solve the problem.

A test car went 9.67 km on a liter of ordinary gasoline. It went 12.43 km on a liter of special gasoline.

Odometer Readings

$$5\;3\;5\;8\;.\;8$$

at the beginning of the test

$$5\;3\;6\;7\;.\;3$$

at the end of the test

Skillkeeper

Write >, <, or = for each ▥.

1. 7.30 ▥ 7.03   **2.** 12.6 ▥ 12.60   **3.** 0.95 ▥ 0.89

4. 14.8 ▥ 14.48   **5.** 0.069 ▥ 0.690   **6.** 39.6 ▥ 36.9

Round to the nearest tenth.

7. 0.35   **8.** 4.268   **9.** 0.83   **10.** 0.429

11. 0.97   **12.** 0.09   **13.** 3.57   **14.** 12.34

Money: Making Change

Kara works at a flower stand in a shopping center. A customer bought a small plant for $2.09 and gave Kara a $5 bill. What change should Kara give the customer?

Kara starts with the cost of the plant and counts out enough coins or bills to bring the total to the amount the customer gave her.

Count these coins and bills to see that the total amount of change given back was $2.91. Then check by subtracting $2.09 from $5.00.

$$\begin{array}{r} \overset{4\quad 9\ 10}{\$5.00} \\ -\ 2.09 \\ \hline \$2.91 \end{array}$$

As Kara says:	She gives the customer these coins or bills:
"two oh nine"	
"two ten"	penny
"two fifteen"	nickel
"two twenty-five"	dime
"two fifty"	quarter
"three dollars"	half dollar
"four dollars"	
"five dollars"	

List in order each coin or bill you would count out as change for the costs and payments named. Use the fewest possible coins and bills.

Example: Cost $2.60. Customer paid with $5.00.
Answer: 5¢, 10¢, 25¢, $1, $1

1. Cost $0.78. Customer paid with $1.00.

2. Cost $0.59. Customer paid with $1.00.

3. Cost $3.54. Customer paid with $5.00.

4. Cost $3.45. Customer paid with $10.00.

Problem Solving: Money and Change

For problems 1 through 4

A. write down each coin or bill you would give in change.

B. count the coins and bills and tell the total amount of change.

C. check by subtracting.

1. A customer bought a vase for $3.69. How much change should he receive from a $10 bill?

2. A bag of plant soil cost $3.64. How much change would you give a customer who paid with a $5 bill?

3. Tami bought a bottle of plant food for $2.19. She gave the clerk $3.00. How much change should she be given?

4. Jay bought two copper buckets for $6.38 each. He gave the clerk a $10 bill and a $5 bill. How much change should he get?

Solve.

5. Kara earned $30 for her work one day at the flower stand. She bought a large potted plant for $12.49. How much of the amount she earned did she have left?

6. Mr. Han bought a plant for $11.49, a rose cutting for $2.75, and a gardening book for $3.89. What was the total cost? How much change should he get back from $20?

7. Ernesto bought 2 bunches of spring flowers for $3.56 a bunch. He gave the clerk a $20 bill and 12 cents. How much change should the clerk give him?

8. **DATA HUNT** Find the prices of 3 items that cost less than $30 each in a catalog or newspaper ad. If you pay for them with $100, how much change should you receive?

9. **Try This** Suppose you had 20 coins worth $1.45. If each coin is either a nickel or a dime, how many nickels and dimes do you have? Hint: Guess and check.

Problem Solving:
Using Data from Several Sources

Some of these problems have data that you do not need. For other problems, you must get needed data from the **data source** shown beside the problem.

1. How much greater is the part of body weight that is muscle than the part that is skin?

2. Which makes up a greater part of body weight, the skin and bones together or the muscle? How much greater?

3. An adult's body has 206 bones, and is covered by 1.84 m² of skin. How much less than 0.50 of the body weight is made up of skin and bones?

4. A baby's heart may weigh 28 g. How much less is this than the weight of an adult's heart?

5. The heart pumps blood to the brain and back in 8 seconds. How many times does this happen in 72 seconds?

6. During heavy exercise, a person's heart may beat 140 times per minute. It may pump 9.46 L of blood per minute. How much more blood per minute is this than the average amount per minute?

Data Source:
A **graph** from a magazine

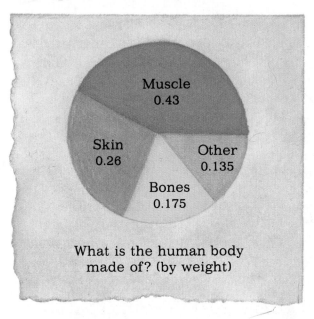

What is the human body made of? (by weight)

Data Source:
Computer printout

The Heart of an Adult

1. Its average weight is 252 g.

2. It is about the size of a fist.

3. It pumps an average of 4.73 L of blood per minute.

4. It beats an average of 70 times per minute.

7. How much less is the average amount of air taken in each breath for a man than the deepest possible intake?

8. What is the difference between the average amount of air taken in each breath by a man and by a woman?

9. A woman may take 21 breaths per minute. Estimate the number of liters of air she takes in with 6 deep breaths.

10. About how long does a human hair grow in a month (4 weeks)? Estimate by rounding the decimal to the nearest whole number.

11. If one hair had the growing power of all your hairs, it could grow 3 cm in a minute. How much could it grow in 9 minutes?

12. How much taller is the average 10-year-old girl than a boy of the same age?

13. Does the average boy or the average girl grow more from age 10 through 14? How much more?

14. **Try This** Bob's goal is to run 25 km each week. He runs 15 km on the weekend. How many kilometers must he run each day during the rest of the week if he runs the same distance each day? Hint: Choose the operations.

Data Source:
Notes from an **interview** with a doctor

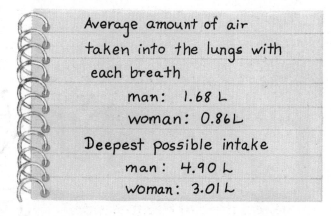

Average amount of air taken into the lungs with each breath
man: 1.68 L
woman: 0.86 L
Deepest possible intake
man: 4.90 L
woman: 3.01 L

Data Source:
A **paragraph** in a reference book

Hair The average human hair grows 3.25 mm a week. It lasts 6 years before falling out.

Data Source:
A **table** from an almanac

Age	Average Height (cm)	
	Boy	Girl
10	137.5	138.3
11	143.3	144.8
12	149.7	151.5
13	156.5	157.1
14	163.1	160.4

Problem Solving: Make a Table

To solve a problem like this, it sometimes helps to show the data in a table. This problem solving strategy is called

MAKE A TABLE

Try This Heidi made 3 free throws out of every 5 shots she tried during the basketball season. How many free throws would you expect her to make in 30 shots?

I'll make a table using the data in the problem.

This data was given in the problem.

Shots tried	5	10	15	20	25	30
Shots made	3	6	9			

I'll use the completed table to find the answer.

This number was given in the problem.

Shots tried	5	10	15	20	25	30
Shots made	3	6	9	12	15	18

This number is the answer to the problem.

You would expect Heidi to make 18 free throws.

Solve. Copy and complete each table. Then give the answer.

1. Darrel needs 4 cups of pancake mix for every 3 cups of milk. How many cups of mix does he need for 15 cups of milk?

Cups of mix	4	8	▦	▦	▦
Cups of milk	3	6	9	12	15

2. Marsha can buy 2 theater tickets for $7. She needs 10 tickets. How much will they cost? $35

Tickets	▦	▦	▦	▦	▦
Cost	▦	▦	▦	▦	▦

Chapter Review-Test

Write the decimal.

1. five and thirty-six hundredths   **2.** six and five tenths

3. nine and seven hundred five thousandths

Write the word name.

4. 6.2   **5.** 0.456

Write the place value of each red digit.

6. 9.4   **7.** 0.32   **8.** 6.759   **9.** 24.008   **10.** 43.527

Write >, <, or = for each .

11. 5.38 5.42   **12.** 0.006 0.060   **13.** 5.7 5.70   **14.** 0.473 0.437

15. Order these decimals from least to greatest:
    4.538   3.485   4.567   4.859   3.962

Round to the place named.

Nearest whole number: **16.** 4.27   **17.** $26.50   **18.** 8.648   **19.** $3.29

Nearest tenth: **20.** 7.348   **21.** 4.55   **22.** 12.239

Add or subtract.

23.   14.8
    + 26.9

24. $3.80
    + 7.64

25.   8.748
    + 0.294

26.   0.684
    5.78
    + 2.5

27.   3.670
    0.086
    + 9.94

28.   6.42
    − 3.85

29.   0.803
    − 0.275

30.   26.8
    − 9.46

31. $5.08
    − 1.97

32.   7,238.2
    − 3,986.7

33. Round to the nearest dollar to estimate how
    much more the highest-priced item
    costs than the lowest-priced item.
    Book: $9.24   Record: $7.96
    Game: $4.95   Calculator: $13.27

Another Look

Each digit in a decimal has a place value.

thousands hundreds tens ones tenths hundredths thousandths

2, 3 4 5 . 7 6 9

two thousand, three hundred forty-five and seven hundred sixty-nine thousandths

Compare **5.724** **5.731**

The decimal on the left has the same number of ones and tenths but has fewer hundredths than the decimal on the right.

5.724 < 5.731

and **5.731 > 5.724**

Round to the nearest whole number:

6.32 → 6

> Less than 5, round down.

to the nearest tenth:

3.752 → 3.8

> 5 or more, round up.

```
  1 1              5 9 1 3
  3.465            9.603
+ 2.75           - 2.418
─────            ───────
  6.215            7.185
```

Add or subtract as you would whole numbers. Trade thousandths, hundredths, and tenths if necessary. Write a decimal point to separate ones from tenths.

Write the decimal.

1. four and thirty-six hundredths

2. six hundred twenty-nine thousandths

3. Write the word name: 2.6

Write the place value of each red digit.

4. 4.3   5. 2.086   6. 6.74

Write >, <, or = for each ▦.

7. 5.7 ▦ 0.57   8. 9.83 ▦ 9.085

9. 3.76 ▦ 3.67   10. 0.80 ▦ 0.8

11. 3.247 ▦ 3.472   12. 5.99 ▦ 6.003

13. 1.01 ▦ 1.010   14. 6.142 ▦ 6.124

Round to the place named.

15. 6.5, nearest whole number

16. 4.76, nearest tenth

17. 8.352, nearest tenth

18. 7.39, nearest whole number

Add or subtract.

19.   4.76   20.   6.538   21.   5.26
     + 3.8   + 7.097   - 2.38

22. 32.075   23.   4.937   24.   8.050
     - 9.368   + 12.34   - 3.642

Space Perception

Suppose you stack 27 cubes as shown below.

Then you draw a funny face on every cube face that shows on the four sides and the top of the stack.

1. How many cubes have no funny face?

2. How many cubes have only 1 funny face?

3. How many cubes have only 2 funny faces?

4. How many cubes have only 3 funny faces?

5. How many cubes have 4 or more funny faces?

6. Is the sum of your answers above equal to 27?

7. Try to answer questions 1 through 5 above for a stack of 64 cubes.

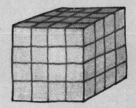

Technology

Flowcharts

A computer can do many important jobs, but it must be given instructions that tell it exactly what to do. Persons who write these instructions often use flowcharts to help them plan the instructions and put them in the most useful order.

Here are some special shapes that are used for flowcharts.

Alert Box	Instruction Box	Decision Box
Used to signal **start** or **stop**	Contains specific instructions on what is to be done	Contains a question that can be answered **yes** or **no**

Here are two sample flowcharts. They give instructions for doing common tasks.

A Playing a Record

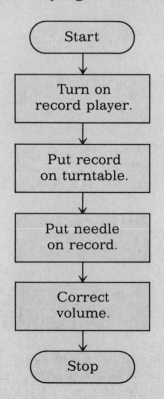

B Diving into a Crowded Pool

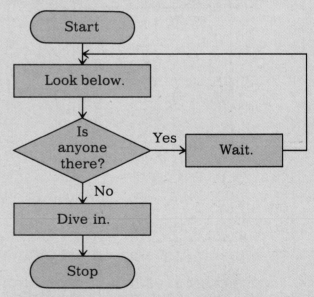

Could the order of steps in flowchart A be changed? How?

Which flowchart has a decision box? What is the question?

100

Study these flowcharts and answer the questions.

1. Finding the "Value" of Your Name

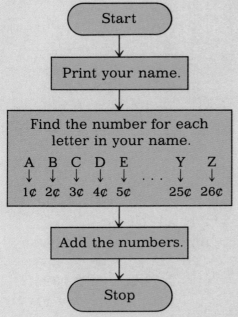

Start

Print your name.

Find the number for each letter in your name.

A B C D E ... Y Z

1¢ 2¢ 3¢ 4¢ 5¢ 25¢ 26¢

Add the numbers.

Stop

2. Finding the Missing Number

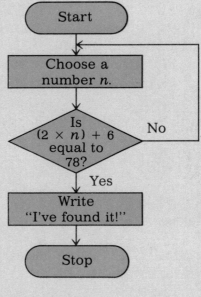

Start

Choose a number n.

Is $(2 \times n) + 6$ equal to 78?   No

Yes

Write "I've found it!"

Stop

A What do you do first? Next?
B What is your name's value?
C Find some other names' values. Can you find a 50¢ name?

A What do you do if twice your number plus 6 is not 78?
B What do you do if it is 78?
C What is the missing number?

3. Use the following instructions to make your own flowchart for calling a friend on the phone.

4. Make a flowchart for
A sharpening a pencil.
B a procedure of your choice.

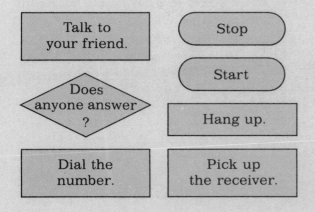

Talk to your friend.

Stop

Does anyone answer?

Start

Hang up.

Dial the number.

Pick up the receiver.

1. What is the place value of the 9 in 9,033?
   A 9 hundreds   B 90 thousands
   C 9 thousands   D not given

2. Give the standard number for 10,000 + 700 + 30 + 8.
   A 17,380   B 1,738
   C 10,738   D not given

Which sign should go in the ?

3. 587 578
   A >   B <   C =

4. 870,598 871,000
   A >   B <   C =

5. What is 53,294 rounded to the nearest thousand?
   A 53,500   B 53,000
   C 54,000   D not given

6. What is 32,415 rounded to the nearest ten thousand?
   A 32,000   B 33,000
   C 30,000   D not given

Add.

7. 762
   + 219
   A 1,081
   B 981
   C 543
   D not given

8. 6,387
   + 2,339
   A 8,726
   B 8,716
   C 8,626
   D not given

9. $1,508
   36
   + 475
   A $2,029
   B $2,009
   C $2,019
   D not given

Subtract.

10. 8,645
    − 2,436
    A 5,219
    B 6,209
    C 6,219
    D not given

11. 607
    − 89
    A 518
    B 596
    C 517
    D not given

12. $3,063
    − 178
    A $2,886
    B $2,858
    C $2,895
    D not given

13. A large theater has enough seats for 1,050 people. If 875 people attend a show, how many empty seats are there?
    A 285   B 175
    C 185   D not given

14. Dominic saved $3.49 from his allowance the first week, $2.86 the second week, and $1.98 the third week. How much did he save altogether in those three weeks?
    A $8.33   B $8.32
    C $8.23   D not given

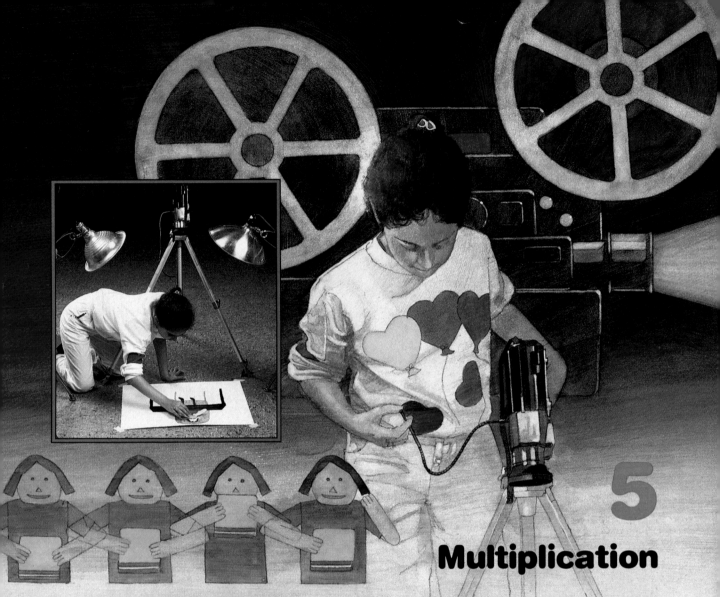

Multiplication

5

At ten years old, Marena is already making her own movies! She always did love to write stories, and now she is learning how to make her stories into animated films. Full-length animated films like *Snow White* and *Charlie Brown* are made from thousands of drawings. Marena, too, must use many drawings to make her films. For each part of her story, Marena draws a background picture. Then she cuts out pictures of her characters. She places the cutouts in different positions on the background and takes a photograph of each one. When these photographs flash by on the movie screen at a speed of 24 per second, the characters appear to be moving. Marena has almost finished making her first 48-second film and looks forward to showing it to her family and friends.

Using Multiplication Facts: Mental Math

A large dolphin eats about 20 kg of fish in a day. About how many kilograms of fish does it eat in a week?

Since the same amount is eaten each day, we multiply.

$$7 \times 2 = 14$$
$$\text{so} \quad 7 \times 20 = 140$$

We can use multiplication facts to help find larger products.

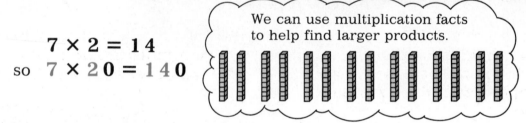

The dolphin eats about 140 kg of fish in a week.

Other Examples

$$9 \times 8 = 72$$
$$\text{so} \quad 9 \times 800 = 7,200$$

$$5 \times 8 = 40$$
$$\text{so} \quad 5 \times 80 = 400$$

$$7 \times 1 = 7$$
$$\text{so} \quad 7 \times 100 = 700$$

$$6 \times 7 = 42$$
$$\text{so} \quad 6 \times 700 = 4,200$$

$$9 \times 1 = 9$$
$$\text{so} \quad 9 \times 1,000 = 9,000$$

$$2 \times 4 = 8$$
$$\text{so} \quad 2,000 \times 4 = 8,000$$

Warm Up Use the multiplication fact to help you find the larger product.

1. 6×3
6×30

2. 3×2
3×200

3. 9×6
$9 \times 6,000$

4. 6×1
6×10

5. 4×7
4×70

6. 5×6
5×600

7. 8×1
$8 \times 1,000$

8. 9×5
$9 \times 5,000$

Multiply.

1. 3 × 90
2. 8 × 60
3. 70 × 5
4. 4 × 600
5. 8 × 500

6. 9 × 10
7. 300 × 4
8. 6 × 2,000
9. 7 × 100
10. 4,000 × 9

11. 8 × 1,000
12. 6 × 80
13. 9 × 800
14. 100 × 4
15. 7 × 6,000

16. 6 × 40
17. 7 × 80
18. 5 × 60
19. 3 × 900
20. 5 × 100

21. 7 × 3,000
22. 3 × 1,000
23. 9 × 40
24. 5 × 600
25. 6 × 900

26. 4 × 7,000
27. 8 × 100
28. 5 × 90
29. 7 × 10
30. 9 × 700

Give each product.

31. 6 × 8
6 × 80
6 × 800
6 × 8,000

32. 7 × 5
7 × 50
7 × 500
7 × 5,000

33. 9 × 1
9 × 10
9 × 100
9 × 1,000

34. 6 × 5
6 × 50
6 × 500
6 × 5,000

35. There are 6 dolphin shows a day. About 2,000 people watch each show. About how many people watch the show each day?

36. A dolphin takes about 4 breaths each minute. About how many breaths does it take in 1 hour?

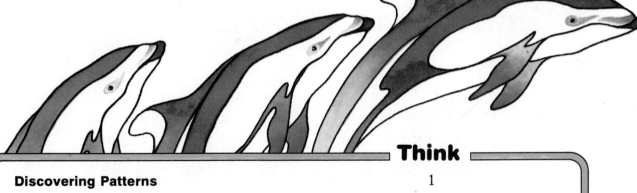

Think

Discovering Patterns

Copy this **multiples triangle** and complete 5 more rows.

Without listing any more rows, can you tell what the last number in row 100 would be?

What other patterns can you find in the multiples triangle?

```
              1
           2     4
        3     6     9
     4     8    12    16
  5    10    15    20    25
```

Math

105

Special Products: Mental Math

A certain TV ad lasts 30 seconds. If this ad is shown 20 times in a week, how many seconds is it shown during a week?

Since the ad lasts 30 seconds each time, we multiply.

$$2 \times 3 = 6$$
so $$20 \times 30 = 600$$

> We can use multiplication facts and basic properties to help us find larger products.
>
> $20 \times 30 = 2 \times 10 \times 3 \times 10$
> $= 6 \times 100$
> $= 600$

The ad is shown 600 seconds during a week.

Other Examples

$40 \times 60 = 2,400$ $30 \times 4,000 = 120,000$

$80 \times 500 = 40,000$ $900 \times 600 = 540,000$

$10 \times 700 = 7,000$ $50 \times 5,000 = 250,000$

Warm Up Find the products.

1. 40×30
2. 50×20
3. 40×80
4. 40×40

5. 30×500
6. 60×300
7. 200×70
8. 400×80

9. $20 \times 6,000$
10. $7,000 \times 40$
11. 300×900
12. 800×700

13. 40×90
14. 70×60
15. 50×700
16. 100×500

17. 10×800
18. 80×80
19. 100×400
20. $6,000 \times 10$

106

Multiply.

1. 30×50
2. 70×40
3. 40×10
4. 70×70

5. 20×900
6. 30×800
7. 100×60
8. 500×40

9. $30 \times 5,000$
10. $6,000 \times 80$
11. $90 \times 1,000$
12. $70 \times 9,000$

13. 400×200
14. 600×500
15. 800×900
16. 300×100

17. 40×60
18. 70×30
19. 40×50
20. 60×90

21. 80×200
22. 90×400
23. 30×600

24. 90×100
25. 400×700
26. 500×900

27. 100×700
28. 600×600
29. $20 \times 3,000$

30. $50 \times 7,000$
31. $20 \times 9,000$
32. $40 \times 1,000$

33. A TV ad lasts 60 seconds. If it is shown 30 times in a week, how many seconds is this?

34. Write a question and solve the problem: A TV station earns $9,000 from the ads on a half-hour program. The program is shown 4 times a month.

35. **DATA HUNT** Suppose it costs $5,000 to run a TV ad for 1 minute. How much would it cost for ad time during your favorite half-hour program? (Round the ad time to the nearest minute.)

Think

Logical Reasoning

A special number pair are we.
100 is our sum you see.
Our product lets you
know some more.
It's our sum
times 24!

Who are we?

Math

Estimating Products

We often estimate products to find **approximate** answers for everyday problems.

There are 38 plants in each row. There are 23 rows. About how many plants are there altogether?

If we get an average of 63 tomatoes from each tomato plant, about how many will we get from 212 plants?

Try these exercises to sharpen your estimation skills. Estimate the products by rounding 2-digit numbers to the nearest ten and 3-digit numbers to the nearest hundred. If the sum of your estimates in a row is the **key number,** your estimates are probably correct.

Key number:

1. 4 × 89
  4 × 90

2. 3 × 38

3. 9 × 74

4. 7 × 92

O 1,740

5. 3 × 298
  3 × 300

6. 2 × 689

7. 6 × 723

8. 8 × 684

O 12,100

9. 63 × 91
  60 × 90

10. 68 × 23

11. 51 × 65

12. 42 × 79

O 13,500

13. 99
  × 45
  (100
  × 50)

14. 83
  × 63

15. 72
  × 49

16. 36
  × 76

O 16,500

17. 287
  × 29
  (300
  × 30)

18. 541
  × 24

19. 798
  × 36

20. 987
  × 25

O 81,000

21. 427
  × 589
  (400
  × 600)

22. 416
  × 235

23. 888
  × 619

24. 324
  × 549

O 1,010,000

More Practice, page 419, Set B

Problem Solving: Using Estimation

Estimate the answers to these travel problems.

1. A car travels at an average speed of 88 km per hour. About how far will it travel in 8 hours?

2. A jet plane flies at an average speed of 896 km per hour. About how far will it travel in 6 hours?

3. A ship averaged 52 km per hour. About how far did it travel during the 7 hours most of the passengers were asleep?

4. If a person can walk 79 m in 1 minute, how far can the person walk in 1 hour (60 minutes)?

5. A traveler flies a small plane at 407 km per hour for 3 hours. The traveler then takes a jet plane that averages 836 km per hour for 7 hours. About how far does the traveler fly?

6. A train averages 109 km per hour. A car averages 88 km per hour. About how many more kilometers does a person go traveling 6 hours by train than traveling 6 hours by car?

7. **DATA BANK** If the world's fastest rocket-engine auto and the world's fastest wheel-driven auto each travel for 3 hours, about how much farther does the rocket auto go? (See the Data Bank on page 411.)

8. **Try This** Tony travels 3 km on his bike for every 11 km Jean travels on her motorcycle. When Tony has traveled 21 km, how far has Jean traveled? Hint: Make a table.

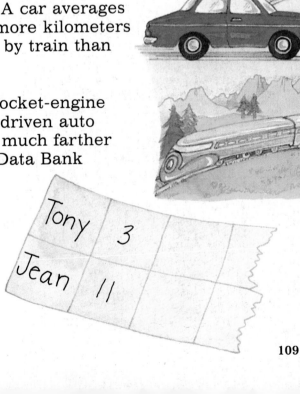

Multiplying by a 1-Digit Factor

A popular film for 35-mm cameras allows you to take 24 pictures on each roll. How many pictures can you take on 3 rolls of this film?

Since we want to find the total for 3 equal amounts, we multiply.

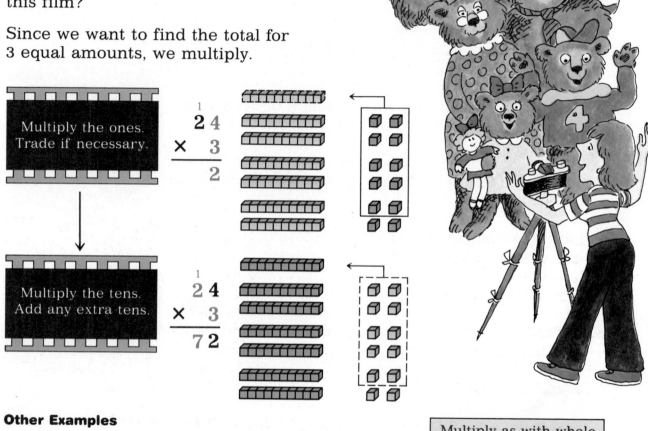

Multiply the ones. Trade if necessary.

$$\begin{array}{r} \overset{1}{}2\,4 \\ \times3 \\ \hline 2 \end{array}$$

Multiply the tens. Add any extra tens.

$$\begin{array}{r} \overset{1}{}2\,4 \\ \times3 \\ \hline 7\,2 \end{array}$$

Other Examples

$$\begin{array}{r} \overset{2}{7}4 \\ \times5 \\ \hline 370 \end{array} \qquad \begin{array}{r} \overset{2\,3}{1}68 \\ \times4 \\ \hline 672 \end{array} \qquad \begin{array}{r} \overset{4}{9}07 \\ \times6 \\ \hline 5{,}442 \end{array} \qquad \begin{array}{r} \overset{2\,2}{\$6}.89 \\ \times3 \\ \hline \$20.67 \end{array}$$

Multiply as with whole numbers. Estimate to help you write the answer in dollars and cents.

About 3 × $7, or $21

Warm Up   Multiply.

1.   38
      × 3

2.   147
       × 4

3.   309
       × 6

4. $4.37
       × 4

5.   75
      × 6

6.   736
       × 4

7.   86
      × 2

8.   652
       × 5

9.   46
      × 9

10. $7.52
       × 6

Multiply.

1.	32 × 3	**2.**	54 × 2	**3.**	19 × 5	**4.**	67 × 6	**5.**	83 × 7
6.	96 × 8	**7.**	79 × 6	**8.**	38 × 5	**9.**	76 × 5	**10.**	98 × 9

11.	143 × 7	**12.**	490 × 6	**13.**	697 × 8	**14.**	504 × 9

15.	975 × 6	**16.**	417 × 8	**17.**	807 × 6

18.	$3.78 × 4	**19.**	$6.23 × 8	**20.**	$9.49 × 3

21. Estimate the product of 578 and 6. How much more or less is your estimate than the actual product?

22. Estimate the product when you multiply 413 by 9. How much more or less is your estimate than the actual product?

23. You can take 36 pictures with a certain roll of film. How many pictures can you take with 3 rolls of film?

24. Write and solve a problem about this slide film.

25. DATA HUNT What is the total cost of buying and developing 3 rolls of 24-picture, 35-mm film at a local photography store?

SLIDE FILM
$3⁴⁹ each
or 4 for $13

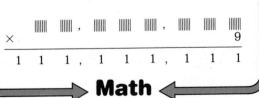

Think

Logical Reasoning

Find the missing digits. They are all different!

$$\begin{array}{r} \blacksquare\blacksquare\blacksquare,\blacksquare\blacksquare\blacksquare,\blacksquare\blacksquare\blacksquare \\ \times \qquad\qquad\qquad 9 \\ \hline 1\ 1\ 1,\ 1\ 1\ 1,\ 1\ 1\ 1 \end{array}$$

Math

More Practice, page 419, Set C

Multiplying Larger Numbers by a 1-Digit Factor

One week the average number of people who went to the San Diego Zoo each weekday was 8,239. What was the total number of people who visited the zoo those 5 days?

Since we want the total of a number of equal amounts, we multiply.

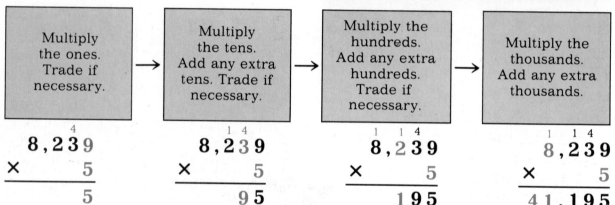

Multiply the ones. Trade if necessary.	Multiply the tens. Add any extra tens. Trade if necessary.	Multiply the hundreds. Add any extra hundreds. Trade if necessary.	Multiply the thousands. Add any extra thousands.
$\overset{4}{8},239$ $\times\ \ \ \ 5$ —— 5	$\overset{1\ 4}{8},239$ $\times\ \ \ \ 5$ —— $9\,5$	$\overset{1}{8},\overset{1\ 4}{2}39$ $\times\ \ \ \ 5$ —— $1\,9\,5$	$\overset{1}{8},\overset{1\ 4}{2}39$ $\times\ \ \ \ 5$ —— $41,195$

During those 5 days 41,195 people went to the zoo.

Other Examples

$$\overset{1}{6},032 \quad \times\ 4 = 24,128$$

$$\overset{2\ \ 2}{2},970 \quad \times\ 3 = 8,910$$

$$\overset{6\,5\ \ 2\,4}{47},625 \quad \times\ 8 = 381,000$$

$$\overset{5\,2\ \ 3}{\$29}.36 \quad \times\ 6 = \$176.16$$

Warm Up Multiply.

1. 4,673
× 8

2. 5,042
× 3

3. 2,360
× 4

4. $19.23
× 4

5. $31.45
× 6

6. 43,628
× 7

7. 37,315
× 6

8. 50,784
× 9

9. 68,000
× 8

10. 64,783
× 5

Multiply.

1. $\begin{array}{r} 56 \\ \times\ 9 \\ \hline \end{array}$
2. $\begin{array}{r} 74 \\ \times\ 7 \\ \hline \end{array}$
3. $\begin{array}{r} 163 \\ \times\ 6 \\ \hline \end{array}$
4. $\begin{array}{r} 274 \\ \times\ 4 \\ \hline \end{array}$
5. $\begin{array}{r} 804 \\ \times\ 5 \\ \hline \end{array}$

6. $\begin{array}{r} 5,637 \\ \times\ 8 \\ \hline \end{array}$
7. $\begin{array}{r} 2,079 \\ \times\ 3 \\ \hline \end{array}$
8. $\begin{array}{r} 4,130 \\ \times\ 2 \\ \hline \end{array}$
9. $\begin{array}{r} 596 \\ \times\ 4 \\ \hline \end{array}$
10. $\begin{array}{r} 3,874 \\ \times\ 7 \\ \hline \end{array}$

11. $\begin{array}{r} 89 \\ \times\ 9 \\ \hline \end{array}$
12. $\begin{array}{r} 695 \\ \times\ 5 \\ \hline \end{array}$
13. $\begin{array}{r} 38,764 \\ \times\ 4 \\ \hline \end{array}$
14. $\begin{array}{r} \$20.49 \\ \times\ 6 \\ \hline \end{array}$
15. $\begin{array}{r} \$86.24 \\ \times\ 3 \\ \hline \end{array}$

16. $\begin{array}{r} 978 \\ \times\ 2 \\ \hline \end{array}$
17. $\begin{array}{r} 8,437 \\ \times\ 8 \\ \hline \end{array}$
18. $\begin{array}{r} 78,324 \\ \times\ 5 \\ \hline \end{array}$
19. $\begin{array}{r} \$75.69 \\ \times\ 7 \\ \hline \end{array}$
20. $\begin{array}{r} \$36.85 \\ \times\ 9 \\ \hline \end{array}$

21. 5×378
22. $7 \times 4,096$

23. $9 \times 2,806$
24. $4 \times 63,946$

25. During August of a recent year an average of 13,080 people went to the zoo each weekday. What was the total number of people who went to the zoo those 5 days?

26. In February the average zoo attendance for each weekend day was 10,658. If there were 4 weekends in February, what was the total weekend attendance? (Be careful!)

27. The average monthly attendance at the San Diego Zoo during a recent year was 250,605 people. Find the total attendance for the year.

Skillkeeper

Add or subtract.

1. $\begin{array}{r} 43.8 \\ +\ 8.5 \\ \hline \end{array}$
2. $\begin{array}{r} 2.9 \\ -\ 2.43 \\ \hline \end{array}$
3. $\begin{array}{r} 0.76 \\ +\ 1.35 \\ \hline \end{array}$
4. $\begin{array}{r} \$86.27 \\ -\ 14.78 \\ \hline \end{array}$

5. $7.3 - 0.9$
6. $\$10.25 + \$2.85$
7. $547.34 - 29.29$

8. $9.375 + 3.602 + 12.789 + 0.144$

Multiplying by Multiples of 10 and 100

Gold bars weigh very close to 400 troy ounces each. A shipment from a mint contained 276 bars. What was the total weight of the shipment?

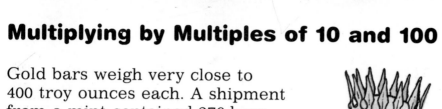

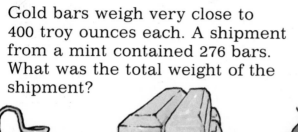

Since we want to find the total for a number of equal amounts, we multiply.

Multiply by the ones.	→	Multiply by the tens.	→	Multiply by the hundreds.

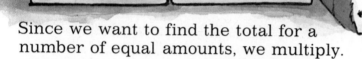

$$\begin{array}{r} 276 \\ \times 400 \\ \hline 0 \end{array}$$

$$\begin{array}{r} 276 \\ \times 400 \\ \hline 00 \end{array}$$

$$\begin{array}{r} \overset{3\ 2}{276} \\ \times 400 \\ \hline 110{,}400 \end{array}$$

The shipment weighed a total of 110,400 troy ounces.

Other Examples

$$\begin{array}{r} \overset{2}{67} \\ \times 40 \\ \hline 2{,}680 \end{array} \qquad \begin{array}{r} \overset{2\ 4}{137} \\ \times 60 \\ \hline 8{,}220 \end{array} \qquad \begin{array}{r} \overset{2}{508} \\ \times 300 \\ \hline 152{,}400 \end{array} \qquad \begin{array}{r} \overset{3}{760} \\ \times 500 \\ \hline 380{,}000 \end{array} \qquad \begin{array}{r} \overset{4}{78} \\ \times 600 \\ \hline 46{,}800 \end{array}$$

Warm Up Multiply.

1. $\begin{array}{r} 47 \\ \times 30 \end{array}$
2. $\begin{array}{r} 38 \\ \times 50 \end{array}$
3. $\begin{array}{r} 26 \\ \times 40 \end{array}$
4. $\begin{array}{r} 143 \\ \times 60 \end{array}$
5. $\begin{array}{r} 459 \\ \times 80 \end{array}$

6. $\begin{array}{r} 321 \\ \times 300 \end{array}$
7. $\begin{array}{r} 496 \\ \times 600 \end{array}$
8. $\begin{array}{r} 380 \\ \times 500 \end{array}$
9. $\begin{array}{r} 66 \\ \times 500 \end{array}$
10. $\begin{array}{r} 970 \\ \times 400 \end{array}$

Multiply.

1. 57×40	**2.** 84×30	**3.** 56×50	**4.** 38×50	**5.** 24×70
6. 342×40	**7.** 351×30	**8.** 704×60	**9.** 643×200	**10.** 576×400
11. 670×300	**12.** 429×80	**13.** 947×20	**14.** 609×700	**15.** 860×500

16. 38×60

17. 159×40

18. 396×30

19. 741×50

20. 921×300

21. 507×80

22. 186×70

23. 420×600

24. 651×700

25. 370×90

26. 53×80

27. 493×800

28. A thin wire 56 km long can be made from 1 troy ounce of gold. How many kilometers of wire can be made from a gold bar that weighs 400 troy ounces?

29. Find the data that is not needed. Then solve this problem: A jeweler buys gold leaf in thin square sheets 9 cm on each side. There are 25 sheets in a book, and books are sold in packs of 20. How many sheets are in a pack?

30. In 1860 the U.S. Mint in San Francisco made 554,950 double eagle gold coins. Each coin was worth $20. Find how much these coins were worth altogether.

Think

Estimation

Estimate which number below is the greatest and which is the smallest.

1. number of seconds in a day

2. number of minutes in a year

3. number of hours in a century

Use a calculator to check your estimates.

1 minute = 60 seconds

1 hour = 60 minutes

1 day = 24 hours

365 days = 1 year

100 years = 1 century

Math

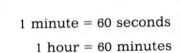

Multiplying by a 2-Digit Factor

About 32 L of water flow from a
slowly running faucet in 1 hour.
About how much water is wasted
when the faucet is left running
for 24 hours?

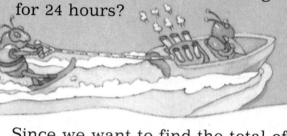

Since we want to find the total of a
number of equal amounts, we multiply.

Multiply by the ones.	→	Multiply by the tens.	→	Add the products.

$$\begin{array}{r} 32 \\ \times\,24 \\ \hline 128 \end{array}$$ (4 × 32)

$$\begin{array}{r} 32 \\ \times\,24 \\ \hline 128 \\ 640 \end{array}$$ (20 × 32)

$$\begin{array}{r} 32 \\ \times\,24 \\ \hline 128 \\ 640 \\ \hline 768 \end{array}$$ (24 × 32)

About 768 L of water are wasted in 24 hours.

Other Examples

$$\begin{array}{r} 67 \\ \times\,43 \\ \hline 201 \\ 2680 \\ \hline 2,881 \end{array} \qquad \begin{array}{r} 308 \\ \times\,65 \\ \hline 1540 \\ 18480 \\ \hline 20,020 \end{array} \qquad \begin{array}{r} 456 \\ \times\,37 \\ \hline 3192 \\ 13680 \\ \hline 16,872 \end{array}$$

Warm Up Multiply.

1. $\begin{array}{r} 59 \\ \times\,28 \\ \hline \end{array}$
2. $\begin{array}{r} 82 \\ \times\,36 \\ \hline \end{array}$
3. $\begin{array}{r} 57 \\ \times\,78 \\ \hline \end{array}$
4. $\begin{array}{r} 36 \\ \times\,84 \\ \hline \end{array}$
5. $\begin{array}{r} 65 \\ \times\,44 \\ \hline \end{array}$

6. $\begin{array}{r} 537 \\ \times\,28 \\ \hline \end{array}$
7. $\begin{array}{r} 315 \\ \times\,16 \\ \hline \end{array}$
8. $\begin{array}{r} 402 \\ \times\,67 \\ \hline \end{array}$
9. $\begin{array}{r} 278 \\ \times\,45 \\ \hline \end{array}$
10. $\begin{array}{r} 609 \\ \times\,85 \\ \hline \end{array}$

Multiply.

1. 63 ✕ 19	**2.** 86 ✕ 27	**3.** 64 ✕ 32	**4.** 35 ✕ 53	**5.** 47 ✕ 36
6. 58 ✕ 35	**7.** 76 ✕ 45	**8.** 99 ✕ 44	**9.** 75 ✕ 75	**10.** 94 ✕ 13
11. 256 ✕ 24	**12.** 138 ✕ 25	**13.** 781 ✕ 47	**14.** 304 ✕ 58	**15.** 514 ✕ 17
16. 640 ✕ 39	**17.** 794 ✕ 36	**18.** 867 ✕ 73	**19.** 908 ✕ 26	**20.** 190 ✕ 66

21. 78 ✕ 53   **22.** 47 ✕ 566   **23.** 36 ✕ 408   **24.** 65 ✕ 45

25. If it takes 56 L of water to wash dishes each day, how much water is used in a month that has 31 days?

26. Supply the missing data and solve the problem: If it takes 136 L of water to fill a bathtub, how much water does a person use for bathing in 1 month?

27. A scientist found that 1,136 L of water are used to grow and prepare the grain that is needed to make 1 loaf of bread. Estimate how much water would be used in making 1 loaf for everyone in your class. Find the actual amount to check your estimate.

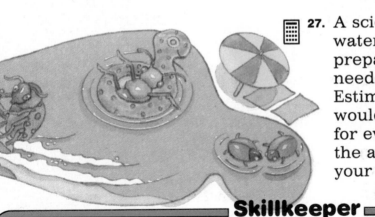

Skillkeeper

Multiply or divide.

1. 7 ✕ 8   **2.** 70 ✕ 8   **3.** 70 ✕ 80   **4.** 70 ✕ 800

5. 6 ✕ 9   **6.** 6 ✕ 90   **7.** 6 ✕ 900   **8.** 600 ✕ 900

9. 40 ÷ 5   **10.** 72 ÷ 8   **11.** 45 ÷ 9   **12.** 49 ÷ 7

13. 35 ÷ 7   **14.** 48 ÷ 6   **15.** 63 ÷ 7   **16.** 81 ÷ 9

Problem Solving: Using the 5-Point Checklist

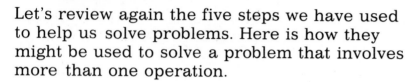

To Solve a Problem
1. **Understand the Question**
2. **Find the needed Data**
3. **Plan what to do**
4. **Find the Answer**
5. **Check back**

Let's review again the five steps we have used to help us solve problems. Here is how they might be used to solve a problem that involves more than one operation.

Felicia's paper route has 79 customers. Every two weeks each customer pays her $3. One time she was also given $14 in tips. What was the total amount she received?

1. Understand the Question
   What was the total amount Felicia was given by her customers, including tips?

2. Find the needed Data
   79 customers, pay $3 each; tips $14

3. Plan what to do
   Two operations are needed. To find how much she was paid for papers, we multiply. Then we add the tips.

4. Find the Answer
   $3 \times 79 = 237$, $237 + 14 = 251$
   The total amount she received was $251.

5. Check back
   The total amount she received for papers is about $3 × 80, or $240. $240 plus tips is $240 + $14, or $254, so $251 seems reasonable.

Solve. Use the 5-Point Checklist.

1. Richie spends 24 hours each month delivering papers. At this rate how many hours does he spend on his job in a year?

2. Leona earns $118 a month from her paper route. At this rate, how much money does she earn from her paper route in a year?

118

Solve.

1. On Monday through Saturday it takes about 45 minutes each day to deliver papers. On Sunday it takes about 125 minutes. How many minutes a week does it take to deliver papers?

2. A certain paper route pays $29 a week. The yearly expenses are $5 for plastic bags and $4 for rubber bands. What is the profit for the year? (Use 52 weeks in a year.)

3. An average paper route has 65 customers. Only 47 of these customers take the Sunday paper. How many papers are delivered each week?

4. An average profit for delivering papers is $26 per week for about 8 hours work. How much more or less is this than the earnings of someone who works the same number of hours at $4 per hour?

5. A paper carrier paid someone else $3 each day for delivering papers. The total income for 2 weeks was $51. After paying the other person for 6 days, what was the carrier's profit for the 2 weeks?

6. **Try This** Steve can deliver 4 papers on his route while his younger brother Jim delivers 3. How many of the total of 63 papers does Steve deliver? Hint: Make a table.

Steve	4	8	12
Jim	3	6	9
Total	7	14	21

Multiplying by a 3-Digit Factor

On an average day at a bowling alley, 476 games are bowled. At this rate, how many games are bowled in a year? (Use 365 days in a year.)

To find the total for a number of equal amounts, we multiply.

Multiply by the ones.	Multiply by the tens.	Multiply by the hundreds.	Add the products.
476	476	476	476
× 365	× 365	× 365	× 365
2380	2380	2380	2380
(5 × 476)	28560	28560	28560
	(60 × 476)	142800	142800
		(300 × 476)	173,740
			(365 × 476)

173,740 games are bowled in a year.

Other Examples

```
      629            237            638            579
    × 274          × 560          × 406          × 800
    2 5 1 6        14220          3 8 2 8        463,200
    4 4 0 3 0      118500         255200
    125800         132,720        259,028
    172,346
```

Warm Up Multiply.

1.	314	2.	137	3.	518	4.	608	5.	455
	× 236		× 346		× 357		× 139		× 268

6.	733	7.	826	8.	385	9.	976	10.	920
	× 506		× 362		× 400		× 670		× 408

Multiply.

1.	542 × 183	**2.**	445 × 622	**3.**	864 × 355	**4.**	759 × 340	**5.**	189 × 538
6.	438 × 367	**7.**	825 × 190	**8.**	396 × 666	**9.**	305 × 183	**10.**	187 × 608
11.	347 × 406	**12.**	518 × 830	**13.**	637 × 586	**14.**	837 × 249	**15.**	950 × 478

16. 536×179 **17.** 704×296 **18.** 380×243 **19.** 555×888

20. If an average of 538 games are bowled each day, how many lines is this in a year (365 days)?

21. A bowling alley owner might take in $435 a day for use of the alleys. How much would this be for a year?

 22. In a recent year there were 8,698 places to bowl in the United States. The average number of lanes in each place was 18. Suppose all these lanes were in use at one time and there were 4 bowlers using each lane. Estimate how many people were bowling. Then find the exact answer.

Think

Space Perception

Cutting across a cube like this gives this **cross section**.

Draw and name the cross sections formed by cutting these space figures as shown.

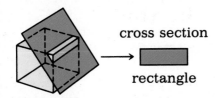

cross section

→ rectangle

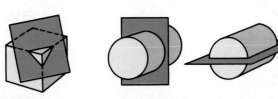

Math

Multiplying: Practice

Find the products.

1. 79 × 5	**2.** 436 × 8	**3.** 207 × 9	**4.** 3,509 × 7	**5.** 6,327 × 6
6. 96 × 54	**7.** 38 × 77	**8.** 83 × 69	**9.** 90 × 80	**10.** 75 × 75
11. 176 × 24	**12.** 263 × 57	**13.** 926 × 43	**14.** 869 × 78	**15.** 375 × 66
16. 807 × 29	**17.** 360 × 47	**18.** 296 × 30	**19.** 703 × 86	**20.** 900 × 70
21. 364 × 172	**22.** 438 × 203	**23.** 569 × 360	**24.** 409 × 670	**25.** 570 × 289

26. 9 × 8 × 7

27. 6 × 7 × 8

28. 9 × 4 × 3

29. 43 × 8 × 4

30. 9 × 56 × 7

31. 6 × 7 × 29

32. 86 × 4 × 23

33. 76 × 34 × 56

34. 29 × 42 × 48

The number in each box is the product of just **three** of the four factors given. Use estimation and computation to find the three factors for each product.

35. 38, 57, 19, 83 │ 89,889 │

36. 23, 79, 54, 97 │ 120,474 │

37. 397, 8, 3, 32 │ 9,528 │

38. 2, 49, 213, 9 │ 20,874 │

Think

Discovering a Pattern

Find this product:

your age × 37 × 91 × 3

Find the product for other ages. What pattern do you find?

Math

122

Problem Solving: Practice

Solve.

1. Boyd must put 16 cans on each section of a shelf. How many cans does he need for 35 sections?

2. A delivery truck travels a 96-km route each day for 19 days during the month. It also makes one longer trip of 238 km. How many kilometers of travel is that in one month?

3. Maxine delivers canned goods to a grocery store. On Friday she delivered 36 cases. Each case held 24 cans. On Saturday she delivered 57 cases. How many cans did she deliver altogether?

4. A special grocery store is open 24 hours a day for 6 days each week. How many hours is the store open in a year (52 weeks)?

5. On Friday a store sold 386 rolls of paper towels. On Saturday it sold 3 times as many. How many rolls in all were sold on those two days?

6. A clerk in a grocery store receives $5 per hour. If she works 35 hours a week, how much does she receive for 6 weeks?

7. A grocery store is located in a city with a population of 87,500. An average of 279 people enter the store each day. How much greater than the population is the number of people who enter the store in a year?

8. **Try This** Carlo is paid $4 an hour for the first 40 hours he works and $6 overtime pay for each additional hour. How much does Carlo earn in a week if he works 57 hours? Hint: Choose the operations.

Problem Solving:
Using Data from a Menu

Soup & Sandwich Shop

Homemade Soups & Homebaked Breads

Soups		Sandwiches		Drinks	
Fresh vegetable	$0.75	Egg salad	$1.24	Juices- small	$0.29
Chicken & noodle	0.87	Tuna salad	1.45	medium	0.49
Split pea w/ham	0.98	Roast beef	1.84	large	0.69
Chili	1.29	Ham	1.78	Milk— medium	0.39
				large	0.59

Lunch Special $2.39
(Soup, Salad, Sandwich, Milk)

Solve. Use data from the menu as needed.

1. Eunice and four friends are having the lunch special. How much will the 5 meals cost?

2. Joy, Amelia, and Robin are each having a large glass of juice and a tuna salad sandwich for lunch. How much will their lunches cost in all?

3. Each person in a party of 6 orders an egg salad sandwich, vegetable soup, and a medium milk. How much will their orders cost in all?

4. The Soup & Sandwich Shop serves an average of 476 customers a day. At this rate, how many customers are served in a year (365 days)?

5. Harry, Keith, Gil, and Jess each are having a large milk and a roast beef sandwich. What will the total cost be?

6. Suppose the shop sells 438 ham sandwiches in one week. At this rate how many will it sell in a year (52 weeks)?

7. Ruth has $3.00. How much will she have left if she buys an egg salad sandwich, a bowl of pea soup, and a medium milk?

8. How much less is the cost of a lunch special than a vegetable soup, a ham sandwich, and a medium milk?

9. How much more does it cost to have chicken soup, an egg salad sandwich, and a large milk than to have chili and a large milk?

10. The shop is open 48 hours a week. It is open the same number of hours on each of 6 days. How many hours is it open each day?

11. One day the shop served 96 groups of people. The average bill for each group was $8. How much money did the shop take in that day?

12. **DATA BANK** How much change would you get back from $20.00 after you pay this bill? Use the Data Bank on page 411 to find the amount of tax.

Soup & Sandwich Shop		
		Amounts
3 egg salad sandwiches	$3	72
2 chilis	2	58
2 medium juices		98
3 large milks	1	77
Food total		
Tax		
Total		

13. **Try This** What two drinks on the menu could you pay for with $1 and receive $0.32 in change? Hint: Guess and check.

Problem Solving:
Make an Organized List

To solve this problem, it helps to write down all the possible numbers. This helpful strategy is called

MAKE AN ORGANIZED LIST

Try This A T-shirt shop can use only these digits to print numbers on their shirts:

1 5 8 9

How many different 2-digit numbers can Dan choose from for his shirt?

First I'll write all the possible numbers starting with 1.

| 11 |
| 15 |
| 18 |
| 19 |

Then I'll write the possible numbers starting with 5, with 8, and with 9.

11	51	81	91
15	55	85	95
18	58	88	98
19	59	89	99

Dan can choose from 16 different 2-digit numbers for his shirt.

Solve.

1. Jan works in a small sandwich shop. A customer can have rye bread or whole wheat bread and one kind of meat—chicken, beef, ham, or turkey. How many different kinds of one-meat sandwiches can be ordered?

2. In a certain part of a state only the letters  J, K, L, M, and N can be used to form a 2-letter beginning for a license plate. How many different 2-letter beginnings are possible?

126

Chapter Review-Test

Multiply.

1. 6 × 70

2. 8 × 900

3. 7 × 100

4. 4 × 3,000

5. 80 × 60

6. 6 × 1,000

7. 70 × 500

8. 400 × 600

Estimate these products. Round 2-digit numbers to the nearest ten and round 3-digit numbers to the nearest hundred.

9.
$$\begin{array}{r} 57 \\ \times\ 6 \\ \hline \end{array}$$

10.
$$\begin{array}{r} 485 \\ \times\ 3 \\ \hline \end{array}$$

11.
$$\begin{array}{r} 92 \\ \times 37 \\ \hline \end{array}$$

12.
$$\begin{array}{r} 547 \\ \times\ 65 \\ \hline \end{array}$$

13.
$$\begin{array}{r} 898 \\ \times 419 \\ \hline \end{array}$$

Find these products.

14.
$$\begin{array}{r} 74 \\ \times\ 3 \\ \hline \end{array}$$

15.
$$\begin{array}{r} 168 \\ \times\ 5 \\ \hline \end{array}$$

16.
$$\begin{array}{r} 307 \\ \times\ 4 \\ \hline \end{array}$$

17.
$$\begin{array}{r} 3,642 \\ \times\ 8 \\ \hline \end{array}$$

18.
$$\begin{array}{r} 57,903 \\ \times\ 6 \\ \hline \end{array}$$

19.
$$\begin{array}{r} 47 \\ \times 30 \\ \hline \end{array}$$

20.
$$\begin{array}{r} 68 \\ \times 42 \\ \hline \end{array}$$

21.
$$\begin{array}{r} 427 \\ \times\ 80 \\ \hline \end{array}$$

22.
$$\begin{array}{r} 708 \\ \times\ 34 \\ \hline \end{array}$$

23.
$$\begin{array}{r} 376 \\ \times\ 58 \\ \hline \end{array}$$

24.
$$\begin{array}{r} 473 \\ \times 200 \\ \hline \end{array}$$

25.
$$\begin{array}{r} 507 \\ \times 369 \\ \hline \end{array}$$

26.
$$\begin{array}{r} 174 \\ \times 340 \\ \hline \end{array}$$

27.
$$\begin{array}{r} 950 \\ \times 348 \\ \hline \end{array}$$

28.
$$\begin{array}{r} 784 \\ \times 369 \\ \hline \end{array}$$

Solve.

29. Corinne's paper route has 86 customers. At the end of two weeks she collects $4 from every customer. If she is also given $18 in tips, what is the total amount she receives?

30. A clerk in a grocery store earns $178 a week. How much is this for 1 year (52 weeks)?

31. At $4.37 an hour, how much does a clerk earn in an 8-hour work day?

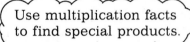

Multiply.

1. 9 × 60

2. 7 × 300

3. 4 × 8,000

4. 8 × 10

5. 30 × 70

6. 800 × 600

7. 8 × 70

8. 7 × 1,000

9. 50 × 40

10. 30 × 60

11. 9 × 500

12. 800 × 700

Use multiplication facts
to find special products.

7   × 4   = 2 8
7   × 4 0   = 2 8 0
7   × 4 0 0 = 2,8 0 0
7   × 4,0 0 0 = 2 8,0 0 0
7 0   × 4 0   = 2,8 0 0
7 0   × 4 0 0 = 2 8,0 0 0
7 0 0 × 4 0 0 = 2 8 0,0 0 0

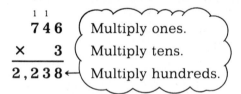

```
  1 1
  7 4 6
×     3
2,2 3 8
```
Multiply ones.
Multiply tens.
Multiply hundreds.

```
    5 7 4
×    2 8
  4 5 9 2  ←—— 8 × 5 7 4
1 1 4 8 0  ←—— 2 0 × 5 7 4
1 6,0 7 2  ←—— 2 8 × 5 7 4
```

Find the products.

13.   56
        × 8

14.   137
         × 4

15.   5,432
         ×   7

16.   609
         × 8

17. 87,523
         ×   6

18. 90,057
         ×   5

19.   96
         × 24

20.   78
         × 35

21.   196
         × 27

22.   804
         × 32

23.   950
         × 79

24.   767
         × 19

25.   187
         × 200

26.   396
         × 50

27.   473
         × 40

28.   507
         × 94

29.   697
         × 84

30.   777
         × 63

Enrichment

History of Mathematics

An arithmetic book printed in Italy in 1478 showed a method of finding products called **lattice multiplication**. Angela used it to check her answer. Here is how it works.

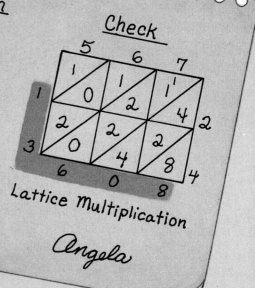

Problem

567
× 24
2268
11340
13,608

Check

Lattice Multiplication

Angela

Set up the lattice.	Fill in the spaces using multiplication facts.	Add the numbers in each diagonal.	Read the product.

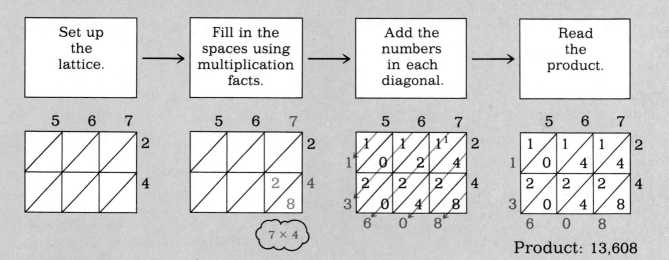

7 × 4

Product: 13,608

Make a lattice for each problem below. Use lattice multiplication to check these products.

1.	2.	3.	4.
225	625	597	746
× 35	× 43	× 86	× 34
7,875	26,875	51,342	25,364

Use lattice multiplication to find these products.

5.	6.	7.	8.
232	785	428	657
× 365	× 694	× 36	× 48

Cumulative Review

1. What is the place value of the 8 in 8,763,419?
   - A 8 million
   - B 8 hundred
   - C 8 thousand
   - D not given

2. Give the standard number for 30,000 + 6,000 + 500 + 40 + 8.
   - A 30,658
   - B 36,548
   - C 36,458
   - D not given

Which sign should go in the ●?

3. 18,060 ● 18,600
   - A >
   - B <
   - C =

4. 105,749 ● 150,749
   - A >
   - B <
   - C =

5. What is 3,550 rounded to the nearest hundred?
   - A 3,500
   - B 4,000
   - C 3,000
   - D not given

6. What is 14,739 rounded to the nearest thousand?
   - A 14,700
   - B 14,800
   - C 15,000
   - D not given

Give the decimals.

7. three tenths
   - A 0.03
   - B 0.3
   - C 0.003
   - D not given

8. one and eight hundredths
   - A 1.80
   - B 0.8
   - C 1.08
   - D not given

Which sign should go in the ●?

9. 8.45 ● 8.045
   - A >
   - B <
   - C =

10. 0.70 ● 0.7
    - A >
    - B <
    - C =

Add.

11. 6.3 + 7.28
    - A 13.58
    - B 13.058
    - C 13.508
    - D not given

Subtract.

12. $36.12 - 14.4$
    - A 21.62
    - B 21.72
    - C 21.08
    - D not given

13. $5.24 - $3.37
    - A $2.97
    - B $1.97
    - C $1.87
    - D not given

14. Carrie rode her bicycle 2.7 km on Monday, 3.5 km on Wednesday, and 12.9 km on Saturday. How far did she ride altogether?
    - A 18.1 km
    - B 18.2 km
    - C 19.1 km
    - D not given

15. Royce earned $15.85 babysitting. He spent $7.48 at the fair. How much did he have left?
    - A $8.47
    - B $8.38
    - C $8.37
    - D not given

130

6

Division: 1-Digit Divisors

It is fall, and the days are growing shorter. Cold breezes are beginning to blow. A monarch butterfly flutters its bright, lacy wings and begins a long journey southward. It stops only once in a while, pausing to sip the sweet juices of flowers along the way. In just 8 days it travels 319 km. No one knows exactly how, but thousands of these monarch butterflies find their way each year to the same small grove of pines on the Pacific Coast. By November the grove is so thick with monarchs that the trees seem to be wrapped in orange and black blankets. Each year the children of nearby towns welcome back the butterflies by dressing in butterfly costumes and marching in a colorful parade.

Using Division Facts: Mental Math

Paul Bunyan and his blue ox, Babe, are the heroes of many stories told by lumberjacks. In these stories, Paul and Babe are giants with strength to match their size.

Try this problem about Babe: When Babe was fitted with ox shoes, he was 3,600 lb heavier. Each of the four shoes weighed the same. How much did one of Babe's shoes weigh?

Since each of Babe's 4 shoes weighed the same, we divide.

$$36 \div 4 = 9$$

so $\quad 3{,}600 \div 4 = 900$

We can use division facts to help us find larger quotients.

Check: $4 \times 900 = 3{,}600$, so the answer is correct.
One of Babe's shoes weighed 900 lb.

Other Examples

$$18 \div 3 = 6$$
so $\quad 180 \div 3 = 60$

$$24 \div 6 = 4$$
so $\quad 24{,}000 \div 6 = 4{,}000$

$$\begin{array}{r} 7 \\ 8{\overline{)5\,6}} \end{array}$$

$$\begin{array}{r} 7\,0\,0 \\ 8{\overline{)5{,}6\,0\,0}} \end{array}$$

Warm Up Divide and check. Use the division fact to help find the larger quotient.

1. $36 \div 9$

   $360 \div 9$

2. $72 \div 8$

   $7{,}200 \div 8$

3. $30 \div 6$

   $300 \div 6$

4. $54 \div 9$

   $54{,}000 \div 9$

5. $7{\overline{)42}}$

   $7{\overline{)420}}$

6. $5{\overline{)40}}$

   $5{\overline{)4{,}000}}$

7. $4{\overline{)28}}$

   $4{\overline{)2{,}800}}$

8. $6{\overline{)48}}$

   $6{\overline{)48{,}000}}$

132

Divide and check.

1. 210 ÷ 3
2. 150 ÷ 5
3. 160 ÷ 8
4. 350 ÷ 7

5. 630 ÷ 9
6. 450 ÷ 5
7. 360 ÷ 4
8. 540 ÷ 6

9. 1,200 ÷ 3
10. 2,400 ÷ 8
11. 4,200 ÷ 6
12. 3,000 ÷ 5

13. 5,400 ÷ 9
14. 7,200 ÷ 8
15. 6,300 ÷ 7
16. 4,200 ÷ 6

17. 16,000 ÷ 4
18. 32,000 ÷ 8
19. 27,000 ÷ 9
20. 48,000 ÷ 8

21. $3\overline{)180}$
22. $8\overline{)240}$
23. $7\overline{)280}$
24. $3\overline{)2,400}$

25. $7\overline{)4,900}$
26. $6\overline{)54,000}$
27. $4\overline{)32,000}$
28. $7\overline{)56,000}$

29. Paul loved pancakes. For breakfast one day he ate 180 pancakes. He ate 6 pancakes in each bite. How many bites was this?

30. Tell what data is not needed, then solve: Paul's skillet was 270 m across. He had people tie strips of bacon on their feet and skate around on it to grease it. One time he hired 360 people to skate in groups of 9. How many groups was this?

★ 31. Make up a Paul Bunyan story problem that can be solved by using this equation:
4,500 ÷ 9 = n.

Think

Using a Calculator

Start with 494
Subtract 38.

```
  494
−  38
  456
```

Subtract 38.

```
−  38
  418
```

Guess how many 38s you must subtract to reach 0. Try it. How many 38s are in 494? What is 494 ÷ 38?

Math

Estimating Quotients

We often estimate quotients to find approximate answers to everyday problems.

The Sky Train carries 234 people in all. The same number of people ride in each of its 6 cars. About how many people ride in each car?

In 4 hours, 2,378 people went on the Giant Slide. About how many people went on the Giant Slide each hour?

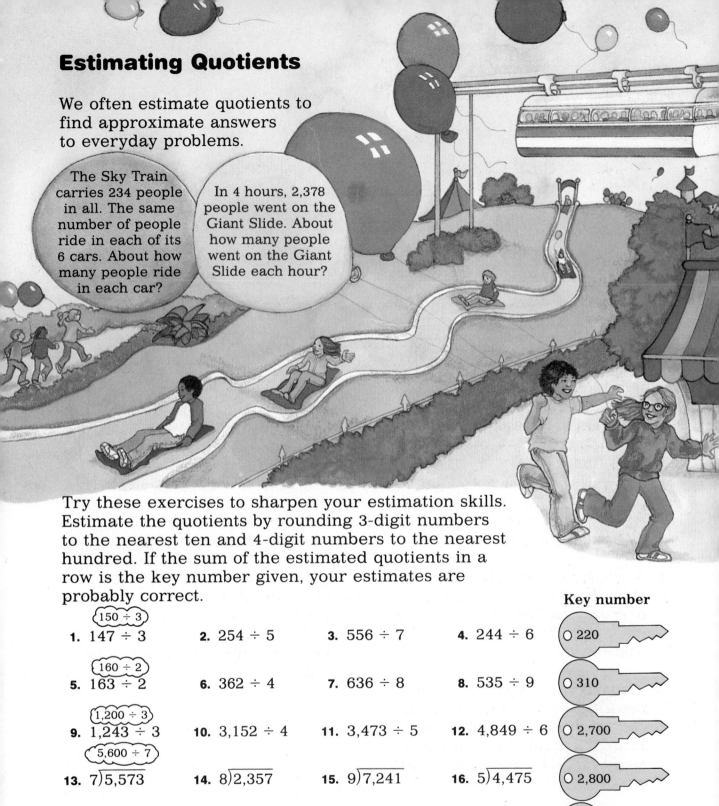

Try these exercises to sharpen your estimation skills. Estimate the quotients by rounding 3-digit numbers to the nearest ten and 4-digit numbers to the nearest hundred. If the sum of the estimated quotients in a row is the key number given, your estimates are probably correct.

Key number

1. $150 \div 3$
   $147 \div 3$
2. $254 \div 5$
3. $556 \div 7$
4. $244 \div 6$ ○ 220

5. $160 \div 2$
   $163 \div 2$
6. $362 \div 4$
7. $636 \div 8$
8. $535 \div 9$ ○ 310

9. $1,200 \div 3$
   $1,243 \div 3$
10. $3,152 \div 4$
11. $3,473 \div 5$
12. $4,849 \div 6$ ○ 2,700

13. $5,600 \div 7$
    $7\overline{)5,573}$
14. $8\overline{)2,357}$
15. $9\overline{)7,241}$
16. $5\overline{)4,475}$ ○ 2,800

17. $4\overline{)355}$
18. $3\overline{)266}$
19. $7\overline{)4,189}$
20. $8\overline{)5,598}$ ○ 1,480

21. $9\overline{)6,279}$
22. $6\overline{)543}$
23. $5\overline{)402}$
24. $7\overline{)4,854}$ ○ 1,570

More Practice, page 421, Set B

Problem Solving:
Using Estimation

Estimate the answers for the problems by rounding each 3-digit number to the nearest ten and each 4-digit number to the nearest hundred. Then write **reasonable** or **not reasonable** for each of the printed answers.

1. Joe's family drove 535 km in 6 hours. About how many kilometers per hour did they drive? Answer: 89

2. There are 195 school days in a school year. How many 5-day weeks is this? Answer: 200

3. Teri put 5 tomatoes into each plastic bag. She filled 197 bags. How many tomatoes did she put into bags? Answer: 40

4. A machine runs 475 minutes each day. It makes one metal part every 8 minutes. How many parts does it make in a day? Answer: 59

5. At an amusement park, 2,686 people took rides on the roller coaster one day. If an average of 30 people rode on each trip, how many trips did the roller coaster make that day? Answer: 900

6. A small airplane flew 304 km per hour for 5 hours. How far did it fly? Answer: 1,520 km

7. A group of 179 people are to be served in the party room of a large restaurant. In another room 124 people are to be served. If 6 people can sit at each table, how many tables are needed? Answer: 51

8. How many more tickets are in 5 bundles of 404 tickets per bundle than are in 6 bundles of 309 tickets per bundle? Answer: 166

9. **Try This** At a restaurant party, the following choices are possible: meat—steak or chicken; potatoes—mashed, baked, or fried; vegetables—green beans or carrots. How many different meal choices are possible if you have one meat dish, one potato dish, and one vegetable dish? Hint: Make an organized list.

Dividing: 1-Digit Quotients

Luann has 52 special flower seeds. She wants to plant 6 seeds in each flower pot. How many flower pots can she prepare? How many seeds will be left over?

Since she wants the same number of seeds in each pot, we divide.

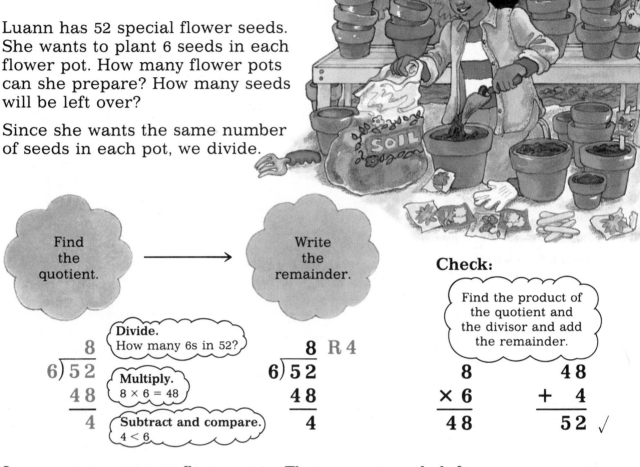

Find the quotient.

Write the remainder.

Check:

Find the product of the quotient and the divisor and add the remainder.

$$\begin{array}{r} 8 \\ 6\overline{)52} \\ 48 \\ \hline 4 \end{array}$$

Divide. How many 6s in 52?

Multiply. $8 \times 6 = 48$

Subtract and compare. $4 < 6$

$$\begin{array}{r} 8 \text{ R } 4 \\ 6\overline{)52} \\ 48 \\ \hline 4 \end{array}$$

$$\begin{array}{r} 8 \\ \times\, 6 \\ \hline 48 \end{array} \qquad \begin{array}{r} 48 \\ +\, 4 \\ \hline 52 \;\checkmark \end{array}$$

Luann can prepare 8 flower pots. There are 4 seeds left over.

Other Examples

$$\begin{array}{r} 2 \text{ R1} \\ 4\overline{)9} \\ 8 \\ \hline 1 \end{array} \qquad \begin{array}{r} 0 \text{ R3} \\ 5\overline{)3} \\ 0 \\ \hline 3 \end{array} \qquad \begin{array}{r} 7 \\ 8\overline{)56} \\ 56 \\ \hline 0 \end{array}$$

Find the quotients and remainders. Check each answer.

1. $9\overline{)56}$ 2. $3\overline{)8}$ 3. $7\overline{)4}$ 4. $4\overline{)36}$ 5. $6\overline{)40}$

6. $5\overline{)19}$ 7. $6\overline{)9}$ 8. $9\overline{)43}$ 9. $7\overline{)46}$ 10. $9\overline{)73}$

11. $4\overline{)3}$ 12. $3\overline{)27}$ 13. $8\overline{)79}$ 14. $8\overline{)5}$ 15. $9\overline{)64}$

16. $3\overline{)20}$ 17. $7\overline{)42}$ 18. $9\overline{)4}$ 19. $4\overline{)31}$ 20. $6\overline{)49}$

More Practice, page 421, Set C

Getting Ready to Divide Larger Numbers

While Ann, Roger, and Miriam were making a garden, they dug up an old metal box. Inside, they found $435! The police could not find the owner, so the children divided the money equally. How much did each child get?

First decide how you would divide the money. Then study the pictures to see how Ann, Roger, and Miriam did it.

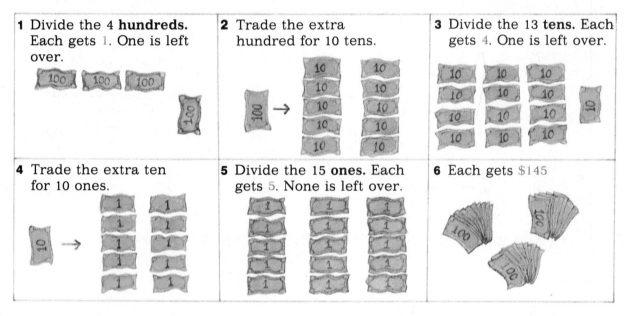

1 Divide the 4 **hundreds.** Each gets 1. One is left over.

2 Trade the extra hundred for 10 tens.

3 Divide the 13 **tens.** Each gets 4. One is left over.

4 Trade the extra ten for 10 ones.

5 Divide the 15 **ones.** Each gets 5. None is left over.

6 Each gets $145

Solve.

1. The fifth grade made $484 by putting on a talent show. They want to divide the money equally among their 4 favorite charities. How much money can they give to each?

2. Vicky won a prize of $855 in a contest. She divided the money equally among her 2 brothers, her 2 sisters, and herself. How much did each get?

3. Warren, Brad, and Julia earned a total of $478 washing cars. They divided the amount equally among themselves. How many dollars did each of them get? How much was left over?

4. The 4 members of a band will earn $276 for playing at a school dance. They will divide the money equally. How much will each get?

Dividing: 2-Digit Quotients

Matt, Julio, and Marty earned $78 by washing cars. They share the money equally. How much does each one get?

Since they share the money equally, we divide.

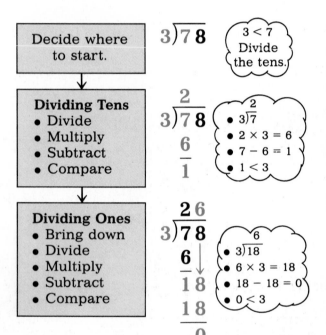

| Decide where to start. | $3\overline{)78}$ | 3 < 7 Divide the tens. |

Dividing Tens
- Divide
- Multiply
- Subtract
- Compare

$$\begin{array}{r} 2 \\ 3\overline{)78} \\ 6 \\ \hline 1 \end{array}$$

- $3\overline{)7}$
- $2 \times 3 = 6$
- $7 - 6 = 1$
- $1 < 3$

Dividing Ones
- Bring down
- Divide
- Multiply
- Subtract
- Compare

$$\begin{array}{r} 26 \\ 3\overline{)78} \\ 6\downarrow \\ \hline 18 \\ 18 \\ \hline 0 \end{array}$$

- $3\overline{)18}$
- $6 \times 3 = 18$
- $18 - 18 = 0$
- $0 < 3$

Each person gets **$26.**

Share $78 among 3 people.

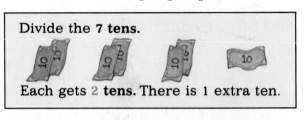

Divide the **7 tens.**

Each gets 2 **tens.** There is 1 extra ten.

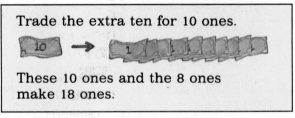

Trade the extra ten for 10 ones.

These 10 ones and the 8 ones make 18 ones.

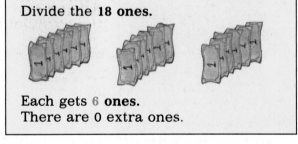

Divide the **18 ones.**

Each gets 6 **ones.**
There are 0 extra ones.

Other Examples

$$\begin{array}{r} 34 \\ 2\overline{)68} \\ 6 \\ \hline 08 \\ 8 \\ \hline 0 \end{array} \qquad \begin{array}{r} 21 \text{ R1} \\ 4\overline{)85} \\ 8 \\ \hline 05 \\ 4 \\ \hline 1 \end{array} \qquad \begin{array}{r} 16 \text{ R2} \\ 6\overline{)98} \\ 6 \\ \hline 38 \\ 36 \\ \hline 2 \end{array}$$

Warm Up Divide.

1. $2\overline{)46}$ 2. $3\overline{)97}$ 3. $5\overline{)83}$ 4. $7\overline{)94}$ 5. $4\overline{)99}$

Divide and check.

1. $3\overline{)69}$ 2. $5\overline{)55}$ 3. $2\overline{)48}$ 4. $4\overline{)84}$ 5. $3\overline{)93}$

6. $7\overline{)87}$ 7. $6\overline{)72}$ 8. $8\overline{)94}$ 9. $9\overline{)99}$ 10. $5\overline{)85}$

11. $4\overline{)64}$ 12. $2\overline{)93}$ 13. $6\overline{)87}$ 14. $7\overline{)91}$ 15. $3\overline{)96}$

16. $5\overline{)78}$ 17. $8\overline{)96}$ 18. $2\overline{)86}$ 19. $6\overline{)75}$ 20. $4\overline{)87}$

21. $4\overline{)57}$ 22. $3\overline{)53}$ 23. $8\overline{)90}$ 24. $5\overline{)95}$ 25. $7\overline{)98}$

26. $60 \div 4$ 27. $98 \div 6$ 28. $87 \div 7$

29. $44 \div 3$ 30. $98 \div 8$ 31. $46 \div 5$

32. What is 97 divided by 3?

33. Estimate the quotient when 87 is divided by 3.

34. Find the quotient when the dividend is 58 and the divisor is 2.

35. Susan, Bill, Hans, and Jeri earned $92 waxing cars. They shared the money equally. How much did each receive?

36. Nina and Oren washed 13 cars for $4 per car. If they divided the money equally, how much did each receive?

37. In six months a car wash business made $33,376 from washing cars at $4 per car. How many cars were washed? First estimate. Then find the exact answer.

Think

Logical Reasoning

Find the missing digits.

1.
```
      ▓▓ ▓▓
   ▓▓)7 ▓▓
     ▓▓
    ─────
      3 ▓▓
     ▓▓ 6
    ─────
        2
```

2.
```
       1 ▓▓
   ▓▓)▓▓7
      ▓▓
    ─────
      3 ▓▓
     ▓▓ 5
    ─────
       ▓▓
```

Math

Dividing: 3-Digit Quotients

The 4 fifth-grade classes at Mott School are blowing up balloons to decorate the gym for Fun Night. There are 580 balloons. If each class has the same number, how many balloons does each class have?

Since the number of balloons is shared equally, we divide.

Decide where to start.

Dividing Hundreds
- Divide
- Multiply
- Subtract
- Compare

Dividing Tens
- Bring down
- Divide
- Multiply
- Subtract
- Compare

Dividing Ones
- Bring down
- Divide
- Multiply
- Subtract
- Compare

$$4\overline{)580}$$

4 < 5 Divide the hundreds

$$\begin{array}{r} 1 \\ 4\overline{)580} \\ 4 \\ \hline 1 \end{array}$$

$$\begin{array}{r} 14 \\ 4\overline{)580} \\ 4\downarrow \\ \hline 18 \\ 16 \\ \hline 2 \end{array}$$

$$\begin{array}{r} 145 \\ 4\overline{)580} \\ 4 \\ \hline 18\downarrow \\ 16 \\ \hline 20 \\ 20 \\ \hline 0 \end{array}$$

Each class has 145 balloons.

Other Examples

$$\begin{array}{r} 171\ R2 \\ 3\overline{)515} \\ 3 \\ \hline 21 \\ 21 \\ \hline 05 \\ 3 \\ \hline 2 \end{array}$$

$$\begin{array}{r} 165 \\ 5\overline{)825} \\ 5 \\ \hline 32 \\ 30 \\ \hline 25 \\ 25 \\ \hline 0 \end{array}$$

$$\begin{array}{r} 212 \\ 4\overline{)848} \\ 8 \\ \hline 04 \\ 4 \\ \hline 08 \\ 8 \\ \hline 0 \end{array}$$

$$\begin{array}{r} 478\ R1 \\ 2\overline{)957} \\ 8 \\ \hline 15 \\ 14 \\ \hline 17 \\ 16 \\ \hline 1 \end{array}$$

Warm Up   Divide and check.

1. $6\overline{)714}$ **2.** $3\overline{)827}$ **3.** $7\overline{)935}$ **4.** $2\overline{)768}$ **5.** $4\overline{)937}$

Divide and check.

1. 4)648   **2.** 3)630   **3.** 2)656   **4.** 6)744   **5.** 3)709

6. 5)713   **7.** 4)985   **8.** 3)933   **9.** 7)900   **10.** 5)734

11. 4)925   **12.** 6)739   **13.** 3)763   **14.** 8)976   **15.** 7)907

16. 3)648   **17.** 8)968   **18.** 2)495   **19.** 4)732   **20.** 8)900

21. 627 ÷ 4   **22.** 379 ÷ 3

23. 804 ÷ 3   **24.** 984 ÷ 8

25. 623 ÷ 4   **26.** 648 ÷ 2

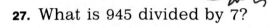

27. What is 945 divided by 7?

28. What is the quotient when 760 is the dividend and 5 is the divisor?

29. Each of 3 school clubs has the same number of tickets to sell for Fun Night. There are 825 tickets to sell in all. How many does each club have?

30. Ask a question and solve: There are 4 special booths at the Fun Night. 496 prizes are to be shared equally by the booths.

31. The school band made $1,848 from a special show they gave. They will use an equal amount of the money for each of 3 road trips. How much money will they use for each trip? Estimate the answer by rounding the amount they have to the nearest hundred. Then find the exact answer.

Skillkeeper

Multiply or divide.

1. 7 × 60   **2.** 90 × 60

3. 3 × 800   **4.** 30 × 100

5. 450 ÷ 9   **6.** 630 ÷ 7

7. 7,200 ÷ 8   **8.** 560 ÷ 8

9. 40 × 50   **10.** 210 ÷ 3

11. 5 × 700   **12.** 2,400 ÷ 40

More Dividing

Shari and 6 of her friends picked up aluminum cans for recycling. They earned $189 and want to divide it equally. How much will each receive?

Since each of the 7 is to get the same amount, we divide.

| Decide where to start. | → | Dividing Tens
• Divide
• Multiply
• Subtract
• Compare | → | Dividing Ones
• Bring down
• Divide
• Multiply
• Subtract
• Compare |

$$7\overline{)189}$$

7 > 1 Not enough hundreds

7 < 18 Divide the tens.

```
   2
7)189
  14
   4
```

```
  27
7)189
  14
   49
   49
    0
```

Each of the 7 will receive $27.

Other Examples

```
   21
6)126
  12
   06
    6
    0
```

```
   53 R1
9)478
  45
   28
   27
    1
```

```
   69 R2
3)209
  18
   29
   27
    2
```

Warm Up Divide and check.

1. $8\overline{)168}$ 2. $6\overline{)144}$ 3. $9\overline{)563}$ 4. $7\overline{)400}$ 5. $5\overline{)345}$

6. $4\overline{)256}$ 7. $7\overline{)\$581}$ 8. $6\overline{)458}$ 9. $9\overline{)705}$ 10. $8\overline{)\$536}$

Divide and check.

1. $3\overline{)174}$ 2. $5\overline{)184}$

3. $4\overline{)228}$ 4. $3\overline{)179}$

5. $6\overline{)170}$ 6. $7\overline{)476}$

7. $3\overline{)200}$ 8. $8\overline{)296}$

9. $4\overline{)295}$ 10. $5\overline{)423}$

11. $9\overline{)307}$ 12. $7\overline{)371}$

13. $6\overline{)400}$ 14. $5\overline{)197}$

15. $3\overline{)257}$ 16. $8\overline{)539}$

17. $2\overline{)193}$ 18. $4\overline{)255}$ 19. $7\overline{)119}$ 20. $8\overline{)227}$

21. $9\overline{)700}$ 22. $3\overline{)140}$ 23. $5\overline{)160}$ 24. $6\overline{)176}$ 25. $4\overline{)380}$

26. $462 \div 6$ 27. $134 \div 7$ 28. $338 \div 8$ 29. $372 \div 5$ 30. $464 \div 9$

31. What is 537 divided by 8?

32. Round the dividend to the nearest ten and estimate $719 \div 8$.

33. Al's club received $228 for the aluminum cans they collected. They want to divide it equally among 3 charities. How much does each charity receive?

34. How many cans does Glenda need to collect each day if she wants to collect at least 500 cans in a week?

Think

Space Perception

A sheet is folded as shown and cut along the red line. Draw a picture of what the sheet will look like when it is unfolded.

Math

Dividing: Zeros in the Quotient

Check these papers.

Which paper is correct, Millie's or Vera's? Explain why.

Which paper is correct, Justin's or Emilio's? Explain why.

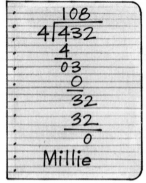

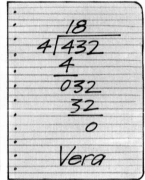

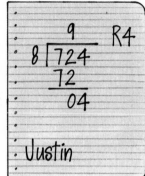

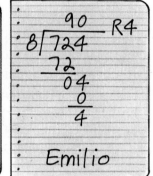

Remember! Every time you bring down a digit, you must divide and write a digit (sometimes 0) in the quotient.

Divide and check.

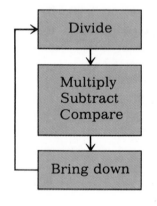

1. 4)363   **2.** 5)402   **3.** 6)965

4. 9)920   **5.** 4)835   **6.** 6)654

7. 3)212   **8.** 5)203   **9.** 7)846   **10.** 8)887   **11.** 2)861

12. 5)523   **13.** 7)724   **14.** 9)910   **15.** 3)615   **16.** 6)645

17. 4)522   **18.** 5)530   **19.** 8)810   **20.** 6)655   **21.** 3)512

22. 5)544   **23.** 9)920   **24.** 7)771   **25.** 4)600   **26.** 6)542

More Practice, page 422, Set D

Problem Solving: Practice

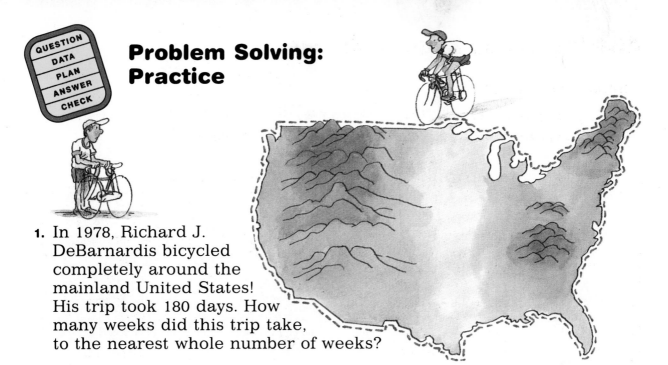

1. In 1978, Richard J. DeBarnardis bicycled completely around the mainland United States! His trip took 180 days. How many weeks did this trip take, to the nearest whole number of weeks?

2. DeBarnardis' trip covered 12,092 mi. A trip taken by John Hathaway covered 50,600 mi. How much longer was Hathaway's trip than DeBarnardis' trip?

3. The record for a bicycle trip across the United States was set by John Marino. He went from Santa Monica, California, to New York City in 13 days, 1 hour (to the nearest hour). How many hours was this?

4. During a 143-day period Ray Reece went "around the world" by bicycle. His trip covered over 13,325 road miles. About how many weeks did his trip take?

5. Tommy Godwin covered an average of almost 1,444 mi per week by bicycle during the year 1939. About how many miles did he travel?

6. The longest bicycle trip on record was made by Walter Stolle. The trip lasted several years and he traveled almost 402 thousand miles. If Stolle used 6 bicycles for equal parts of the total distance, how many thousand miles did he travel on each bicycle?

7. **Try This** Alice, Ben, Dan, Eve, and Fred want to ride in pairs on a "bicycle built for two." How many different rides will be taken if every different possible pair go for a ride? Hint: Make an organized list.

Dividing Larger Numbers

The Museum of Science gave a special showing of American inventions. On the first day the show was open for 7 hours, and 2,212 people visited it. How many people was that per hour?

Since we want to separate 2,212 into 7 equal amounts, we divide.

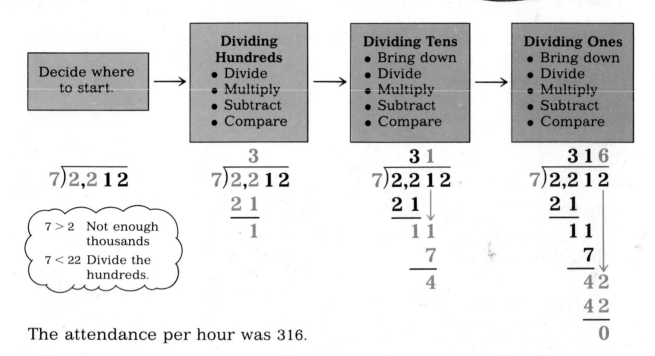

| Decide where to start. | **Dividing Hundreds**
 • Divide
 • Multiply
 • Subtract
 • Compare | **Dividing Tens**
 • Bring down
 • Divide
 • Multiply
 • Subtract
 • Compare | **Dividing Ones**
 • Bring down
 • Divide
 • Multiply
 • Subtract
 • Compare |

$$7\overline{)2{,}2\,1\,2}$$

7 > 2 Not enough thousands
7 < 22 Divide the hundreds.

$$\begin{array}{r} 3 \\ 7\overline{)2{,}2\,1\,2} \\ 2\,1 \\ \hline 1 \end{array}$$

$$\begin{array}{r} 3\,1 \\ 7\overline{)2{,}2\,1\,2} \\ 2\,1 \\ \hline 1\,1 \\ 7 \\ \hline 4 \end{array}$$

$$\begin{array}{r} 3\,1\,6 \\ 7\overline{)2{,}2\,1\,2} \\ 2\,1 \\ \hline 1\,1 \\ 7 \\ \hline 4\,2 \\ 4\,2 \\ \hline 0 \end{array}$$

The attendance per hour was 316.

Other Examples

$$\begin{array}{r} 2\,5\,0 \\ 4\overline{)1{,}0\,0\,0} \\ 8 \\ \hline 2\,0 \\ 2\,0 \\ \hline 0\,0 \\ 0 \\ \hline 0 \end{array}$$

$$\begin{array}{r} 3\,0\,8 \\ 6\overline{)1{,}8\,4\,8} \\ 1\,8 \\ \hline 0\,4\,8 \\ 4\,8 \\ \hline 0 \end{array}$$

$$\begin{array}{r} 8\,6\,0\ \text{R}5 \\ 9\overline{)7{,}7\,4\,5} \\ 7\,2 \\ \hline 5\,4 \\ 5\,4 \\ \hline 0\,5 \\ 0 \\ \hline 5 \end{array}$$

$$\begin{array}{r} 1{,}2\,0\,5\ \text{R}2 \\ 7\overline{)8{,}4\,3\,7} \\ 7 \\ \hline 1\,4 \\ 1\,4 \\ \hline 0\,3\,7 \\ 3\,5 \\ \hline 2 \end{array}$$

Warm Up Divide and check.

1. $3\overline{)2{,}825}$ **2.** $6\overline{)2{,}457}$ **3.** $4\overline{)2{,}560}$ **4.** $8\overline{)9{,}288}$

146

Divide.

1. $4\overline{)\$3.96}$ 2. $3\overline{)\$20.94}$ 3. $6\overline{)\$20.64}$ 4. $8\overline{)\$33.20}$ 5. $5\overline{)\$35.80}$

6. $7\overline{)\$39.62}$ 7. $3\overline{)\$29.37}$ 8. $9\overline{)\$55.62}$ 9. $6\overline{)\$50.58}$ 10. $4\overline{)\$29.52}$

11. $8\overline{)\$51.92}$ 12. $5\overline{)\$20.85}$ 13. $7\overline{)\$65.52}$ 14. $9\overline{)\$52.38}$ 15. $6\overline{)\$46.02}$

16. $3\overline{)\$37.35}$ 17. $5\overline{)\$71.25}$ 18. $4\overline{)\$55.68}$ 19. $6\overline{)\$69.36}$ 20. $8\overline{)\$96.32}$

Which is the better buy, **A** or **B**?

21. T-shirts
   A 3 for $16.47
   B 2 for $11.12

22. Books
   A 4 for $23.04
   B 5 for $29.45

23. Juice
   A 3 cans—$4.77
   B 8 cans—$12.88

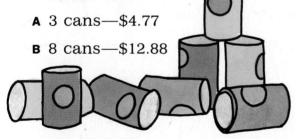

24. Socks
   A 3 pairs—$6.87
   B 8 pairs—$18.00

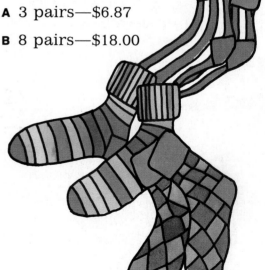

Think

Number Theory

1. Give the remainder when each of these numbers is divided by 7.

   238   239   240   241
   242   243   244

2. Give 6 numbers greater than 280 all of which have a different remainder when divided by 6.

Math

Short Division

Chip scored a total of 5,058 points in 6 tries on an electronic TV game. At this rate, what was the score per try?

Since we want to find the number of points in a try, we divide. We can use a method called **short division**.

Decide where to start.	→	Divide the hundreds. Write the remainder by the tens.	→	Divide the tens. Write the remainder by the ones.	→	Divide the ones.

$$6\overline{)5,058}$$

Not enough thousands
6 < 50   Divide the hundreds.

$$\overset{8}{6\overline{)5,0^2 5 8}}$$

50 ÷ 6 = 8, R2

$$\overset{8\ 4}{6\overline{)5,0^2 5^1 8}}$$

25 ÷ 6 = 4, R1

$$\overset{8\ 4\ 3}{6\overline{)5,0^2 5^1 8}}$$

18 ÷ 6 = 3

Chip scored 843 points per try.

Other Examples

$$\overset{9\ 3\ \text{R1}}{9\overline{)8\ 3^2 8}} \qquad \overset{2\ 3\ 4\ \text{R2}}{3\overline{)7^1 0^1 4}} \qquad \overset{6\ 0\ 3}{7\overline{)4,2\ 2^2 1}} \qquad \overset{1,\ 4\ 1\ 8}{4\overline{)5,^1 6\ 7^3 2}}$$

Warm Up   Divide. Use short division.

1. $8\overline{)675}$
2. $4\overline{)258}$
3. $6\overline{)2,439}$
4. $5\overline{)4,762}$

5. $9\overline{)2,881}$
6. $7\overline{)5,235}$
7. $3\overline{)1,962}$
8. $4\overline{)3,473}$

9. $3\overline{)2,956}$
10. $8\overline{)6,739}$
11. $6\overline{)1,848}$
12. $3\overline{)4,760}$

13. $6\overline{)4,275}$
14. $4\overline{)8,649}$
15. $9\overline{)5,429}$
16. $5\overline{)9,725}$

Divide. Check by multiplying.

1. $3\overline{)168}$ 2. $4\overline{)393}$ 3. $6\overline{)525}$ 4. $7\overline{)448}$ 5. $8\overline{)688}$

6. $6\overline{)1,422}$ 7. $7\overline{)3,532}$ 8. $9\overline{)5,670}$ 9. $2\overline{)311}$ 10. $5\overline{)635}$

11. $3\overline{)2,824}$ 12. $8\overline{)2,448}$ 13. $4\overline{)744}$ 14. $2\overline{)1,080}$ 15. $6\overline{)587}$

16. $9\overline{)3,758}$ 17. $8\overline{)5,384}$ 18. $7\overline{)5,789}$ 19. $6\overline{)6,548}$ 20. $5\overline{)4,380}$

21. $4\overline{)3,035}$ 22. $3\overline{)1,664}$ 23. $2\overline{)12,648}$ 24. $8\overline{)8,424}$ 25. $6\overline{)14,146}$

26. $867 \div 3$  27. $2,465 \div 5$ 28. $3,876 \div 8$

29. $5,076 \div 5$ 30. $3,214 \div 4$ 31. $13,685 \div 9$

32. What is the quotient when 4,638 is divided by 7?

33. Round to the nearest hundred and estimate $5,387 \div 9$.

34. Bruce scored 7,038 points on 6 tries in an electronic game. How many points per try did he score?

35. Judith's all-time high score on her favorite electronic TV game was 9,576. This was 6 times as large as her first score on the game. What was her first score?

Think

Using a Calculator

Find the quotient and remainder for $3,789 \div 8$. Here's how!

Divide. The whole number part is the quotient.

$$473.625$$

$$8\overline{)3,789}$$

Multiply the quotient by the divisor. 473×8

$$3784$$

$$8\overline{)3,789} \quad \begin{array}{r} 473 \\ 3\,784 \end{array}$$

Subtract to find the remainder. $3,789 - 3,784$

$$5$$

$$\begin{array}{r} 473 \text{ R}5 \\ 8\overline{)3,789} \\ 3\,784 \\ \hline 5 \end{array}$$

Try these.

1. $6\overline{)3,638}$ 2. $7\overline{)6,666}$ 3. $4\overline{)3,947}$ 4. $9\overline{)8,000}$

Math

Finding Averages

Veronica and her family took a raft trip on the Colorado River. She kept a record of how far they traveled each day. What was the **average** number of kilometers they traveled each day?

To find the **average** of 4 numbers, we add the numbers and divide the sum by 4.

Day	Kilometers Traveled
Tuesday	30
Wednesday	36
Thursday	25
Friday	37

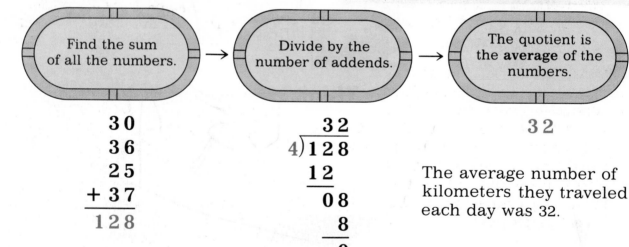

Find the sum of all the numbers. → Divide by the number of addends. → The quotient is the **average** of the numbers.

$$
\begin{array}{r}
30 \\
36 \\
25 \\
+\,37 \\
\hline
128
\end{array}
$$

$$
\begin{array}{r}
32 \\
4\overline{)128} \\
\underline{12} \\
08 \\
\underline{8} \\
0
\end{array}
$$

32

The average number of kilometers they traveled each day was 32.

Find the average of these numbers.

1. 26, 22, 33

2. 19, 30, 26

3. 18, 32, 29, 25

4. 17, 24, 28, 31, 20

5. 34, 21, 17

6. 43, 29, 38, 26, 19

7. 38, 21, 29, 24

8. 17, 24, 34, 27, 18

9. 20, 37, 43, 28

More Practice, page 423, Set D

Problem Solving:
Using Data from a Graph or Table

1. Find the average number of kilometers traveled per day on each of the two kinds of rafts. What is the difference in the averages?

The graph shows the height above sea level (elevation) of some places you might make stops during a raft trip on the Colorado River.

2. What is the average elevation of the four places shown in the graph?

3. What is the average difference in elevation between Lees Ferry and Phantom Ranch, between Phantom Ranch and Mud Baths, and between Mud Baths and Diamond Creek?

4. **DATA BANK** Hoover Dam, on the Colorado River, is the second-highest dam in the United States. How much higher is Hoover Dam than the average height of the seven highest dams in the United States, including Hoover? (See Data Bank, page 412.)

5. **Try This** On a raft trip a group of boaters spent 3 hours on shore for every 2 hours they spent on the river. Their trip lasted 5 days (120 hours). How many hours did they spend on the river? Hint: Make a table.

Raft Trip Distances Traveled Daily (km)				
	Day 1	Day 2	Day 3	Day 4
Oar – driven	25	29	34	36
Motor – driven	48	45	51	52

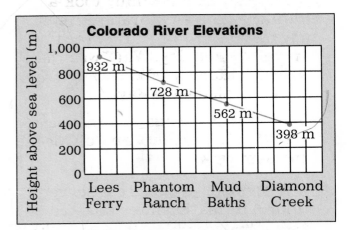

Colorado River Elevations

Hours on shore	3	6	9	12
Hours on the river	2	4	6	8
Total hours	5	10	15	20

QUESTION
DATA
PLAN
ANSWER
CHECK

Problem Solving:
Understanding the Operation

Each problem below can be solved by using one of the four operations (+, −, ×, ÷).

For each problem, give the operation that can be used to solve it.

Add +	**Subtract −**	**Multiply ×**	**Divide ÷**
• Put together, find the total.	• Take away (How many are left?) • Compare (How many more, or less, than?) • Missing amount (How many more are needed?)	• Repeat equal sets, find the total.	• Put into a given number of sets (How many in each set?) • Put into sets of a given size (How many sets?)

1. A member of Congress served for 6 terms. Each term lasted 24 months. How many months did she serve?

2. A certain senate committee must have 24 members present to vote. Only 6 members are present. How many more members are needed?

3. At one meeting 24 senators spoke in favor of a new tax law and 6 senators spoke against it. How many more senators spoke in favor of the law than against the law?

4. One senator served in the Senate for 24 years. Each term lasted 6 years. How many terms did the senator serve?

5. One person served in the House of Representatives for 24 years. Then he served in the Senate for 6 years. How many years did he serve in Congress altogether?

6. A large committee has 24 members. Each member is named to serve on one smaller committee that has 6 members. How many of the smaller committees are there?

7. The president of the Senate decided that only 24 minutes could be used for speeches about a new highway safety law. The first speech about the new law lasted 8 minutes. How many minutes were left for other speeches about the law?

Tell what operation (+, −, ×, or ÷) you could use to solve
each problem if the needed numbers were given.

1. The names of ⦀ states of the
United States begin with the
letter A. The names of ⦀ states
begin with M. How many more
begin with M than with A?

2. There were ⦀ people waiting to
vote. They stood in ⦀ lines, with
the same number in each line.
How many people were in each
line?

3. Alaska's population was ⦀ in
1970. The population was ⦀
greater in 1980. What was the
population of Alaska in 1980?

4. A total of ⦀ presidents of the
United States were born in ⦀
different states. Each state was
the birthplace of the same
number of presidents. How
many were born in each state?

Tell what operations (+, −, ×, ÷)
you could use to solve these
problems.

5. The U.S. Senate has ⦀
members. The House of
Representatives has ⦀ times
that many members and ⦀
more. How many members does
the House have?

6. The population of Phoenix,
Arizona, grew from ⦀ to ⦀ in
⦀ years. What was the average
growth in population each of
those years?

7. The U.S. Congress has ⦀
Senators and ⦀ Representatives.
There are ⦀ more members of
Congress than there are judges
of the U.S. Supreme Court. How
many Supreme Court judges
are there?

8. **Try This** Alabama has three times as many state
representatives as state senators. There are a total
of 140 state representatives and senators. How many
representatives and how many senators are there?

Problem Solving: Use Logical Reasoning

To solve some problems we must think about more than which operations to use. For such problems, we often need a strategy called

Try This Terri, Gwen, Jo, and Elena are roommates at camp. One is from Los Angeles, one from Boston, one from Kansas City, and one from Seattle. Jo is from Kansas City. Gwen is not from Seattle. If Elena is from Los Angeles, where is Terri from?

USE LOGICAL REASONING

Making a table of what you know helps you to reason logically.

First I'll make a table of what I know.

I can use what I know to find more information.

Hmm . . . Now I know Terri must be from Seattle!

	LA	B	KC	S
Terri				
Gwen			no	
Jo			yes	
Elena	yes			

	LA	B	KC	S
Terri	no		no	
Gwen	no		no	no
Jo	no	no	yes	no
Elena	yes	no	no	no

	LA	B	KC	S
Terri	no		no	yes
Gwen	no		no	no
Jo	no	no	yes	no
Elena	yes	no	no	no

Solve.

1. Mel and Dan each have two hobbies. Neither has the same hobby as the other. The hobbies are drawing, collecting rocks, taking photographs, and making model cars. Mel does not collect rocks. Dan does not draw. The boy who draws does not take photographs. Which hobbies does each boy have?

	Mel	Dan
Drawing		
Rocks		
Photos		
Cars		

2. Alice, Dawn, Rick, and George each like one type of music. One likes rock, one jazz, one folk, and one classical music. Alice does not like classical. Rick and George do not like jazz. Dawn likes rock. George dislikes folk music. Who likes which type of music?

Chapter Review-Test

Find the quotients.

1. 540 ÷ 6

2. 2,400 ÷ 8

3. 400 ÷ 5

4. 42,000 ÷ 7

5. 9)7,200

6. 5)3,000

7. 4)280

8. 8)56,000

Estimate the quotients by rounding 3-digit numbers to the nearest ten and 4-digit numbers to the nearest hundred.

9. 4)363

10. 6)538

11. 9)6,275

12. 3)2,447

13. 7)4,896

Divide.

14. 4)38

15. 7)59

16. 3)75

17. 8)97

18. 4)652

19. 5)617

20. 2)86

21. 6)279

22. 4)349

23. 7)336

24. 6)638

25. 5)539

26. 8)2,080

27. 9)3,948

28. 3)$14.04

29. 5)$3.90

Divide. Use Short Division.

30. 3)4,365

31. 4)879

32. 5)43,862

33. 6)21,474

34. What is 5,184 divided by 8?

Solve.

35. Paula received these scores on 5 math tests: 95, 86, 97, 89, 98. What was her average score for these tests?

36. Which is a better buy, 4 rolls of yarn for $10.88 or 5 rolls of yarn for $15.10? How much do you save per roll by choosing the better buy?

Another Look

Steps in Dividing

```
Divide
  ↓
Multiply
Subtract
Compare
  ↓
Bring down
```

$$
\begin{array}{r}
9\ 3\ \text{R7} \\
8\overline{)7\ 5\ 1} \\
7\ 2 \\
\hline
3\ 1 \\
2\ 4 \\
\hline
7
\end{array}
$$

Zeros in the Quotient

$$
\begin{array}{r}
3\ 0 \\
7\overline{)2,1\ 2\ 8} \\
2\ 1 \\
\hline
0\ 2
\end{array}
\quad
\begin{array}{r}
0 \\
7\overline{)2}
\end{array}
$$

Everytime you "bring down," you must write a quotient digit. Sometimes it is 0.

Finding Averages

List of numbers:
19, 25, 21, 27
Find the sum.

$$
\left.
\begin{array}{r}
1\ 9 \\
2\ 5 \\
2\ 1 \\
+\ 2\ 7
\end{array}
\right\} \text{4 addends}
$$

$$
\begin{array}{r}
\hline
9\ 2 \leftarrow \text{Sum}
\end{array}
$$

Divide the sum by the number of addends.

$$
\begin{array}{r}
2\ 3 \leftarrow \text{Average} \\
4\overline{)9\ 2} \\
8 \\
\hline
1\ 2 \\
1\ 2 \\
\hline
0
\end{array}
$$

Divide.

1. $6\overline{)84}$ 2. $3\overline{)702}$

3. $4\overline{)375}$ 4. $7\overline{)429}$

5. $5\overline{)1,170}$ 6. $8\overline{)5,496}$

7. $4\overline{)272}$ 8. $9\overline{)5,076}$

9. $160 \div 5$ 10. $2,067 \div 3$

11. $272 \div 4$ 12. $891 \div 7$

13. $2\overline{)1,004}$ 14. $3\overline{)618}$

15. $4\overline{)2,243}$ 16. $5\overline{)4,002}$

17. $6\overline{)1,024}$ 18. $7\overline{)2,660}$

19. $8\overline{)6,456}$ 20. $9\overline{)2,727}$

Find the average of each set of numbers.

21. 18, 15, 21

22. 36, 41, 23, 72

23. 139, 117, 126, 202

24. 68, 53, 71, 98, 85

25. 306, 415, 392, 511, 361

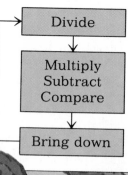

A number that has exactly 2 divisors (the number itself and 1) is called a prime number.

Number Relationships—Prime Numbers

Since the remainder is 0, we say 27 is divisible by 3, and 3 is a divisor of 27.

Make a table for the numbers 2 through 100. Use it to find the prime numbers up to 100. The first 3 rows of this table have been completed as examples.

	2	3	4	5	6	7	8	9	10
11	12	13	14	15	16	17	18	19	20
21	22	23	24	25	26	27	28	29	30
31	32	33	34	35	36	37	38	39	40
41	42	43	44	45	46	47	48	49	50
51	52	53	54	55	56	57	58	59	60
61	62	63	64	65	66	67	68	69	70
71	72	73	74	75	76	77	78	79	80
81	82	83	84	85	86	87	88	89	90
91	92	93	94	95	96	97	98	99	100

1. A number ending in 0, 2, 4, 6, or 8 (an even number) is divisible by 2. Mark an ⊠ through all numbers divisible by 2, except 2.

2. A number is divisible by 3 if the sum of its digits is divisible by 3. (Check this.) Shade in the squares for all numbers divisible by 3, except 3.

3. A number is divisible by 5 if it ends in 5 or 0. Mark a vertical line ⏐ through all numbers divisible by 5, except 5.

4. Mark a horizontal line ⊟ through all numbers divisible by 7, except 7.

5. Since any number up to 100 with a divisor greater than 10 would already be marked out because it also would have a divisor less than 10, we are finished. The numbers with no marks in the table are the **prime numbers**. The other numbers are called **composite numbers**. List the prime numbers up to 100.

159

Cumulative Review

Add.

1. 847
   + 438
   A 1,284
   B 1,209
   C 1,275
   D not given

2. 732
   18
   + 6,953
   A 8,703
   B 7,703
   C 8,603
   D not given

3. $80.75
   + 15.35
   A $96.10
   B $96.00
   C $65.40
   D not given

Subtract.

4. 9,617
   − 7,508
   A 2,109
   B 2,019
   C 2,119
   D not given

5. 4,200
   − 765
   A 3,345
   B 3,435
   C 3,335
   D not given

6. $6.62
   − 1.89
   A $4.73
   B $4.83
   C $4.81
   D not given

Multiply.

7. 9 × 80
   A 810
   B 760
   C 720
   D not given

8. 500
   × 30
   A 15,000
   B 1,500
   C 150,000
   D not given

9. 789
   × 5
   A 39,045
   B 3,945
   C 38,045
   D not given

10. 324
    × 36
    A 11,624
    B 12,624
    C 11,664
    D not given

11. 607
    × 36
    A 38,401
    B 38,142
    C 38,021
    D not given

12. 554
    × 438
    A 242,604
    B 242,654
    C 242,652
    D not given

13. Laverne has $225.75 saved toward her vacation trip. She needs $500 for the trip. How much more does she need to save?

    A $274.25   B $385.35
    C $725.75   D not given

14. Marco plans to take a 2-hour typing lesson 3 days a week. He will take the lessons for 12 weeks. How many hours of lessons will he take in all?

    A 36   B 84
    C 72   D not given

Division: 2-Digit Divisors

José was already on his horse as he watched the distant cloud of dust drawing steadily closer. He knew it must be the pony express rider from the east. It would be José's turn to carry the mail on the next leg of the 3,164-km trip from St. Joseph, Missouri, to San Francisco. About every 20 km along the way he would come to a relay station where a fresh horse was saddled and ready to carry him speedily to the next station. The journey was one that continued nonstop, day and night, for 8 to 10 days. Across hot deserts and through snowy mountains the pony express riders carried the mail on its long trip to California.

Using Division Facts: Mental Math

The principal of Lincoln School needs to rent enough buses to take 480 students and teachers on a field trip. If each bus can hold 60 people, how many buses should the principal rent?

Since each bus holds the same number, we divide.

$$480 \div 60 = ?$$
$$48 \div 6 = 8$$
so $\quad 480 \div 60 = 8$

> We can use division facts to help us find other quotients.

Check:
$60 \times 8 = 480$, so the answer is correct.

The principal should rent 8 buses for the field trip.

Other Examples

$35 \div 5 = 7$
so $\quad 350 \div 50 = 7$

$28 \div 4 = 7$
so $\quad 2,800 \div 40 = 70$

$$1 \overline{)6} = 6$$
so $\quad 10 \overline{)60} = 6$
and $\quad 10 \overline{)600} = 60$

$$7 \overline{)35} = 5$$
so $\quad 70 \overline{)350} = 5$
and $\quad 70 \overline{)3,500} = 50$

Warm Up Divide and check.

1. $42 \div 6$	**2.** $15 \div 5$	**3.** $36 \div 9$	**4.** $3 \overline{)27}$	**5.** $6 \overline{)54}$
$420 \div 60$	$150 \div 50$	$360 \div 90$	$30 \overline{)270}$	$60 \overline{)540}$
6. $32 \div 4$	**7.** $40 \div 8$	**8.** $36 \div 6$	**9.** $1 \overline{)4}$	**10.** $9 \overline{)63}$
$320 \div 40$	$400 \div 80$	$360 \div 60$	$10 \overline{)40}$	$90 \overline{)630}$
$3,200 \div 40$	$4,000 \div 80$	$3,600 \div 60$	$10 \overline{)400}$	$90 \overline{)6,300}$

Divide and check.

1. $60 \div 30$ **2.** $80 \div 10$ **3.** $40 \div 20$ **4.** $90 \div 10$ **5.** $100 \div 50$

6. $210 \div 70$ **7.** $160 \div 80$ **8.** $150 \div 30$ **9.** $180 \div 20$ **10.** $240 \div 40$

11. $180 \div 60$ **12.** $180 \div 90$ **13.** $100 \div 20$ **14.** $120 \div 30$ **15.** $160 \div 40$

16. $300 \div 10$ **17.** $200 \div 20$ **18.** $490 \div 70$ **19.** $320 \div 80$ **20.** $540 \div 90$

21. $30\overline{)1,200}$ **22.** $50\overline{)1,500}$ **23.** $60\overline{)2,400}$ **24.** $70\overline{)5,600}$ **25.** $80\overline{)400}$

26. $10\overline{)200}$ **27.** $90\overline{)2,700}$ **28.** $10\overline{)1,000}$ **29.** $70\overline{)6,300}$ **30.** $80\overline{)4,800}$

31. What is the quotient of 3,000 divided by 60?

Divide each number by 100.

32. 500   **33.** 2,000   **34.** 4,000   **35.** 50,000

36. School buses that hold 40 people each are used to take 240 students and teachers to the museum. How many buses are needed?

37. Madison School rented 20 vans to drive the band to the football game. There are 140 students in the band. How many rode in each van if the same number of students rode in each?

38. Write a story problem about buses that you can solve by using this equation:

$$240 \div 60 = n$$

Think

Estimation

The answer to one of these problems is 585. Use estimation to find which one.

A $\begin{array}{r} 834 \\ -\ 429 \end{array}$ **B** $1,235 \div 20$

C $\begin{array}{r} 195 \\ \times\ \ \ 3 \end{array}$ **D** $\begin{array}{r} 439 \\ +\ 316 \end{array}$

Math

Dividing by Multiples of 10

The stereo set cost $276. The Millers bought it by paying the same amount each week for 30 weeks. About how much was each weekly payment?

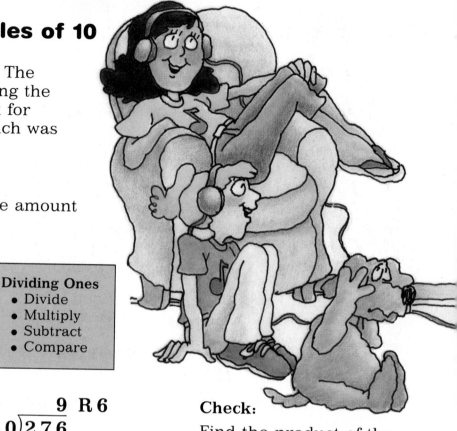

Since they paid the same amount each week, we divide.

Decide where to start.	$\rightarrow$	**Dividing Ones** • Divide • Multiply • Subtract • Compare

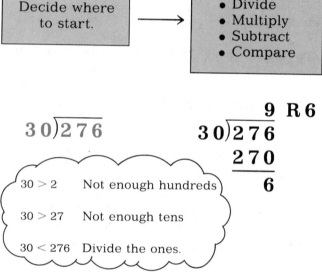

$$30\overline{)276}$$

30 > 2   Not enough hundreds

30 > 27   Not enough tens

30 < 276   Divide the ones.

$$\begin{array}{r} 9 \text{ R}6 \\ 30\overline{)276} \\ 270 \\ \hline 6 \end{array}$$

Check:

Find the product of the quotient and the divisor and add the remainder.

$$\begin{array}{r} 30 \\ \times\ 9 \\ \hline 270 \end{array} \qquad \begin{array}{r} 270 \\ +\ \ 6 \\ \hline 276 \end{array} \checkmark$$

Each weekly payment was about $9.

Other Examples

$$\begin{array}{r} 7 \text{ R}25 \\ 50\overline{)375} \\ 350 \\ \hline 25 \end{array} \qquad \begin{array}{r} 6 \\ 70\overline{)420} \\ 420 \\ \hline 0 \end{array} \qquad \begin{array}{r} 6 \text{ R}14 \\ 80\overline{)494} \\ 480 \\ \hline 14 \end{array}$$

Warm Up   Divide and check.

1. $40\overline{)255}$ **2.** $60\overline{)190}$ **3.** $90\overline{)715}$ **4.** $80\overline{)381}$ **5.** $20\overline{)130}$

Divide and check.

1. $20\overline{)65}$ 2. $40\overline{)180}$ 3. $30\overline{)66}$

4. $50\overline{)184}$ 5. $20\overline{)133}$ 6. $70\overline{)75}$

7. $60\overline{)240}$ 8. $30\overline{)182}$ 9. $40\overline{)98}$

10. $60\overline{)343}$ 11. $30\overline{)266}$ 12. $10\overline{)86}$

13. $40\overline{)281}$ 14. $60\overline{)202}$ 15. $70\overline{)361}$

16. $50\overline{)260}$ 17. $90\overline{)288}$ 18. $60\overline{)555}$

19. $80\overline{)347}$ 20. $70\overline{)430}$ 21. $40\overline{)383}$

22. $799 \div 80$ 23. $583 \div 70$ 24. $803 \div 90$

25. Divide 340 by 40.

26. Find the quotient when 512 is divided by 60.

27. Keiko wants to buy a stereo set that costs $305. She can pay the same amount each week for 50 weeks. Estimate how much each weekly payment will be.

28. Ned is saving $20 a week to buy a tape deck. He has already saved $60. The tape deck costs $220. How many more weeks will it be before he has enough money to buy the tape deck?

Think

History

In 1863 Abraham Lincoln began a famous speech with the words, "*Four score and seven* years ago. . . ." In this line, score means 20.

1. What is the standard number for four score and seven?

2. What was the year four score and seven years before Lincoln gave the speech?

3. Use the word *score* to write the number of years between the year you were born and the year 2040.

Math

Dividing: 1-Digit Quotients

A printer has 235 in. (inches) of paper left on a roll. The paper will be cut into sheets 42 in. long. How many full sheets can he cut from the paper left on the roll?

Since each sheet is the same length, we divide.

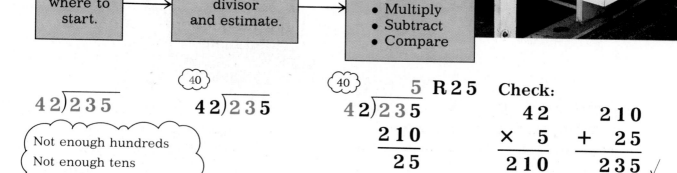

| Decide where to start. | → | Round the divisor and estimate. | → | **Dividing Ones**
• Divide
• Multiply
• Subtract
• Compare |

$$42\overline{)235}$$

Not enough hundreds
Not enough tens
42 < 235 Divide the ones.

$$\overset{40}{42}\overline{)235}$$

$$\overset{40}{42}\overline{)\underset{\underline{210}}{235}}\ \ \overset{5\ R25}{}$$
$$25$$

Check:

$$\begin{array}{r} 42 \\ \times\ 5 \\ \hline 210 \end{array} \qquad \begin{array}{r} 210 \\ +\ 25 \\ \hline 235\ \checkmark \end{array}$$

The printer can cut 5 sheets from the roll.

Other Examples

$$\overset{30}{31}\overline{)\underset{\underline{186}}{195}}\ \overset{6\ R9}{}$$
$$9$$

$$\overset{80}{78}\overline{)\underset{\underline{312}}{321}}\ \overset{4\ R9}{}$$
$$9$$

$$\overset{40}{44}\overline{)\underset{\underline{352}}{352}}\ \overset{8}{}$$
$$0$$

$$\overset{70}{65}\overline{)\underset{\underline{390}}{430}}\ \overset{6\ R40}{}$$
$$40$$

Warm Up Divide and check.

1. $41\overline{)85}$ **2.** $21\overline{)156}$ **3.** $76\overline{)252}$ **4.** $63\overline{)347}$ **5.** $57\overline{)191}$

Divide and check.

1. $22\overline{)66}$
2. $37\overline{)89}$
3. $43\overline{)90}$
4. $51\overline{)162}$
5. $32\overline{)160}$

6. $12\overline{)49}$
7. $26\overline{)78}$
8. $45\overline{)207}$
9. $63\overline{)174}$
10. $82\overline{)328}$

11. $57\overline{)248}$
12. $73\overline{)511}$
13. $88\overline{)225}$
14. $94\overline{)190}$
15. $31\overline{)254}$

16. $77\overline{)277}$
17. $44\overline{)318}$
18. $62\overline{)391}$
19. $49\overline{)112}$
20. $85\overline{)630}$

21. $262 \div 91$
22. $354 \div 68$
23. $600 \div 74$
24. $482 \div 59$
25. $809 \div 81$

26. The printer cut exactly 42 posters from a roll of paper 336 in. long. How long was each poster?

27. A big sheet of colored paper is about 22 in. wide. How many sheets are needed to make one solid row on a bulletin board that is 176 in. wide?

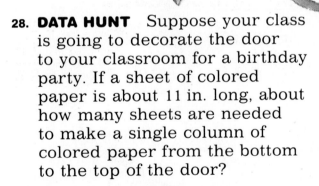

28. **DATA HUNT** Suppose your class is going to decorate the door to your classroom for a birthday party. If a sheet of colored paper is about 11 in. long, about how many sheets are needed to make a single column of colored paper from the bottom to the top of the door?

Skillkeeper

Multiply or divide.

1. $\begin{array}{r} 63 \\ \times\ 7 \end{array}$
2. $\begin{array}{r} 315 \\ \times\ 49 \end{array}$
3. $\begin{array}{r} 608 \\ \times 270 \end{array}$
4. $\begin{array}{r} 6,572 \\ \times\ 368 \end{array}$

5. $265 \div 5$
6. $5,466 \div 6$
7. $4,186 \div 7$

8. $4\overline{)836}$
9. $8\overline{)8,960}$
10. $9\overline{)2,825}$

Changing Estimates

Sometimes your estimated quotient must be changed.

Denise changed her estimate from 5 to 6. Why?

Maynard changed his estimate from 9 to 8. Why?

Decide which estimates must be changed. Give the correct estimates for the ones that need to be changed.

1. $54\overline{)318}$ (50) 6

2. $37\overline{)284}$ (40) 7

3. $65\overline{)335}$ (70) 4

4. $49\overline{)164}$ (50) 3

5. $18\overline{)89}$ 4

6. $83\overline{)490}$ 6

7. $25\overline{)161}$ 5

8. $94\overline{)201}$ 2

9. $29\overline{)268}$ 8

10. $32\overline{)165}$ 5

11. $48\overline{)360}$ 7

12. $35\overline{)302}$ 7

Divide and check.

1. 31)96
2. 20)180
3. 18)161
4. 30)255
5. 14)104

6. 53)315
7. 60)500
8. 29)105
9. 32)275
10. 43)354

11. 22)156
12. 43)330
13. 70)452
14. 51)427
15. 25)169

16. 69)208
17. 56)223
18. 48)304
19. 64)476
20. 86)694

21. 298 ÷ 75
22. 628 ÷ 80
23. 835 ÷ 91
24. 529 ÷ 67
25. 594 ÷ 82

26. 438 ÷ 52
27. 655 ÷ 85
28. 612 ÷ 76
29. 416 ÷ 61
30. 825 ÷ 92

31. A restaurant manager has 144 flowers. She wants to put the same number on each of 24 tables. How many flowers can she put on each table?

32. Write a question that can be answered using the data below. Then solve the problem. The cook in a restaurant needs 285 cartons of milk. There are 30 cartons of milk in each box.

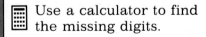
Think

Using a Calculator

Use a calculator to find the missing digits.

1. ? ÷ 21 = 4 R2

2. ? ÷ 40 = 6 R22

3. ? ÷ 37 = 5 R10

★ **4.** 358 ÷ ? = 7 R8

Math

QUESTION
DATA
PLAN
ANSWER
CHECK

Problem Solving:
Using Mental Math

Solve. Use pencil and paper only to write the answer.

1. Mt. St. Helens, in Washington, was 2,550 m high after it erupted. When it erupted, 400 m was blown off the top. How high was Mt. St. Helens before it erupted?

2. Mauna Loa, in Hawaii, is the world's largest active volcano. It erupts an average of once every 4 years. How many times has Mauna Loa erupted in the last 100 years?

5. During the last 1,100 years, Iceland has had a volcano erupt an average of every 5 years. How many eruptions have they had in that time?

6. Mt. St. Helens erupted in 1980. This was the first volcanic eruption in the continental United States since Lassen Peak, in California, erupted in 1921. How many years were there between these eruptions?

3. The top of Mauna Loa is about 4,100 m *above* sea level. Its bottom is 4,500 m *below* sea level. What is the total height of Mauna Loa?

4. Mt. Pelee, in Martinique, erupted in 1902. The lava plug grew 10 m each day. It reached a height of 900 m. How many days did it take the lava plug to reach 900 m?

7. **Try This** The Season Islands have four active volcanoes—Mt. Rumble, Mt. Misty, Mt. Cloudy, and Mt. Shaky. One of the volcanoes is on Spring Island, one on Summer Island, one on Fall Island, and one on Winter Island. Mt. Cloudy is on Fall Island. Mt. Misty is not on Winter Island. If Mt. Shaky is on Summer Island, where is Mt. Rumble? Hint: Use logical reasoning.

Problem Solving: Focus on the Question

Use the answer to the first question to find the answer to the second question.

1. Armando paid $40 for a pair of roller skates and $35 for a special set of outdoor wheels. What was the cost of these items, without tax?
   What was Armando's total bill if the tax was $4.50?

2. The skating coach bought 24 knee pads and 30 elbow pads. How many pads did the coach buy?
   If each pad costs $6, how much did the coach pay before tax was added?

3. Angie paid $2.75 to get into the roller rink and $1.50 to rent skates. How much did it cost Angie to go skating?
   If Angie paid her skating costs with a $5 bill, how much money did she get as change?

4. Wayne paid $50 for skates, $20 for an extra set of wheels, and $15 for a helmet. How much did he pay in all for these items?
   Wayne saved $5 each week to pay for his skating gear. How many weeks did it take him to pay for it?

5. In one race the skaters had to go around the track 20 times. If the total length of the race was 5,000 m, how long was each trip around the track?
   In another race the skaters had to go around the track only 15 times. What was the total length of that race?

6. **Try This** Gloria bought roller skates and a helmet. She gave $15 as a down payment and agreed to pay $12 a month for 6 months. What was the total cost of her skating equipment?

171

Finding Larger Quotients

During 86 working days the mail carrier drove 4,847 km. About how far did she drive each day?

Since we want to find the amount driven each day, we divide.

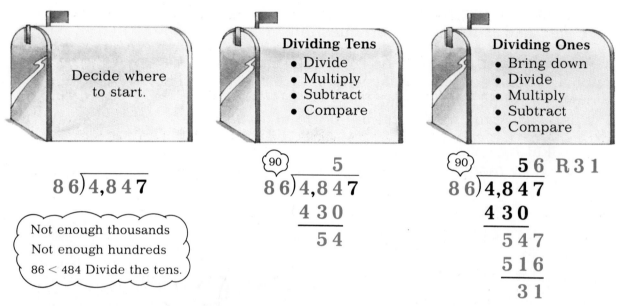

Decide where to start.

$$86\overline{)4,847}$$

Not enough thousands
Not enough hundreds
86 < 484 Divide the tens.

Dividing Tens
• Divide
• Multiply
• Subtract
• Compare

$$\begin{array}{r} \overset{(90)}{5} \\ 86\overline{)4,847} \\ 430 \\ \hline 54 \end{array}$$

Dividing Ones
• Bring down
• Divide
• Multiply
• Subtract
• Compare

$$\begin{array}{r} \overset{(90)}{56} \text{ R31} \\ 86\overline{)4,847} \\ 430 \\ \hline 547 \\ 516 \\ \hline 31 \end{array}$$

The mail carrier drove about 56 km each day.

Other Examples

$$\begin{array}{r} 58 \text{ R3} \\ 41\overline{)2,381} \\ 205 \\ \hline 331 \\ 328 \\ \hline 3 \end{array}$$

$$\begin{array}{r} 435 \text{ R10} \\ 53\overline{)23,065} \\ 212 \\ \hline 186 \\ 159 \\ \hline 275 \\ 265 \\ \hline 10 \end{array}$$

$$\begin{array}{r} 52 \\ 77\overline{)4,004} \\ 385 \\ \hline 154 \\ 154 \\ \hline 0 \end{array}$$

Warm Up Divide and check.

1. $31\overline{)458}$ **2.** $32\overline{)757}$ **3.** $52\overline{)3,796}$ **4.** $23\overline{)14,763}$ **5.** $39\overline{)6,438}$

Remember!

→ Divide
↓
Multiply, subtract, compare
↓
→ Bring down

Divide and check.

1. 68)775   **2.** 44)977   **3.** 21)319   **4.** 24)534   **5.** 45)560

6. 36)1,476   **7.** 50)2,872   **8.** 18)1,574   **9.** 35)1,166   **10.** 53)1,863

11. 82)1,776   **12.** 45)2,000   **13.** 42)10,813   **14.** 83)3,296   **15.** 50)20,900

16. 3,422 ÷ 27   **17.** 5,891 ÷ 76   **18.** 2,335 ÷ 37   **19.** 8,626 ÷ 54   **20.** 5,579 ÷ 54

21. 5,300 ÷ 63   **22.** 32,378 ÷ 67   **23.** 6,549 ÷ 85   **24.** 5,047 ÷ 74   **25.** 41,966 ÷ 96

26. A mail carrier drove 6,912 km in 72 days. What was the average number of kilometers he drove each day?

27. A city mail carrier walked about 3,100 km last year. Estimate how far she walked each week.

Think

Logical Reasoning

Copy each problem and give the missing digits.

1.
```
        ||||| 6 R2
   17) 4 4 |||||
        3 4
        1 0 |||||
        1 ||||| 2
            2
```

2.
```
         4 ||||| R22
   39) 1 6 ||||| 1
       1 ||||| |||||
           ||||| 1
           3 9
           2 |||||
```

3.
```
                6 2
   5 ||||| )||||| 5 3 4
           3 4 |||||
           1 1 4
           ||||| 1 4
                 0
```

Math

Zeros in the Quotient

Gordon and his family took a tour of New England in their camper. They drove a total of 2,592 km in 24 days. What was the average distance they drove each day?

We should divide since we want the average distance.

Decide where to start.	**Dividing Hundreds** • Divide • Multiply • Subtract • Compare	**Dividing Tens** • Bring down • Divide • Multiply • Subtract • Compare	**Dividing Ones** • Bring down • Divide • Multiply • Subtract • Compare

$$24\overline{)2{,}592}$$

24 < 25 Divide the hundreds.

$$\begin{array}{r} 1 \\ 24\overline{)2{,}592} \\ 24 \\ \hline 1 \end{array}$$

Remember! Every time you bring down, you must divide.

$$\begin{array}{r} 10 \\ 24\overline{)2{,}592} \\ 24 \\ \hline 19 \\ 0 \\ \hline 19 \end{array}$$

$$\begin{array}{r} 108 \\ 24\overline{)2{,}592} \\ 24 \\ \hline 19 \\ 0 \\ \hline 192 \\ 192 \\ \hline 0 \end{array}$$

They drove an average of 108 km each day.

Other Examples

$$\begin{array}{r} 105 \\ 40\overline{)4{,}200} \\ 40 \\ \hline 20 \\ 0 \\ \hline 200 \\ 200 \\ \hline 0 \end{array}$$

$$\begin{array}{r} 206 \text{ R18} \\ 72\overline{)14{,}850} \\ 144 \\ \hline 45 \\ 0 \\ \hline 450 \\ 432 \\ \hline 18 \end{array}$$

$$\begin{array}{r} 400 \text{ R5} \\ 56\overline{)22{,}405} \\ 224 \\ \hline 00 \\ 0 \\ \hline 05 \\ 0 \\ \hline 5 \end{array}$$

Warm Up Divide and check.

1. $30\overline{)9{,}065}$ **2.** $42\overline{)8{,}736}$ **3.** $60\overline{)12{,}250}$ **4.** $78\overline{)47{,}270}$ **5.** $56\overline{)22{,}456}$

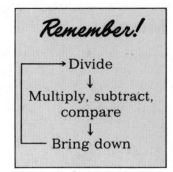
Divide and check.

1. $18\overline{)546}$ **2.** $23\overline{)478}$ **3.** $32\overline{)1,283}$ **4.** $48\overline{)5,113}$ **5.** $37\overline{)3,848}$

6. $52\overline{)6,780}$ **7.** $60\overline{)12,540}$ **8.** $22\overline{)13,308}$ **9.** $56\overline{)16,820}$ **10.** $42\overline{)21,282}$

11. $31\overline{)2,114}$ **12.** $72\overline{)30,275}$ **13.** $91\overline{)6,211}$ **14.** $44\overline{)15,928}$ **15.** $27\overline{)21,854}$

16. $15\overline{)12,144}$ **17.** $82\overline{)3,296}$ **18.** $73\overline{)36,562}$ **19.** $65\overline{)38,763}$ **20.** $85\overline{)40,000}$

21. $47,651 \div 68$ **22.** $33,708 \div 54$ **23.** $65,271 \div 81$ **24.** $59,290 \div 77$

25. Marisa's brother visited Canada for 18 days. He drove 3,600 km. What was the average distance he drove each day?

26. Thad's family spent the entire month of October touring the New England states. They drove 2,688 km during their trip. Estimate the average distance they drove each day.

27. DATA BANK On their vacation the Rays drove from Columbus, Ohio, to Dallas, Texas, by way of St. Louis. They drove through Memphis when they returned to Columbus. They spent 12 days driving. What was the average distance they drove each day? See Data Bank on page 411.

Skillkeeper

Give the product or quotient.

1. 3×4
3×40
3×400

2. 7×8
7×80
7×800

3. $36 \div 9$
$360 \div 9$
$3,600 \div 9$

4. $30 \div 5$
$300 \div 5$
$3,000 \div 5$

Dividing Money

Cheryl bought her father a magazine subscription for his birthday. The cost was $15.84. Her father will get a copy of the magazine each month for 24 months. What is the cost of each copy?

Since each issue costs the same, we divide.

$$
\begin{array}{r}
\$0.66 \\
24\overline{)\$15.84} \\
144 \\
\hline
144 \\
144 \\
\hline
144 \\
144 \\
\hline
0
\end{array}
$$

Check:

$$
\begin{array}{r}
\$0.66 \\
\times\ \ 24 \\
\hline
264 \\
132 \\
\hline
\$15.84\ \checkmark
\end{array}
$$

Remember!

To divide money, divide as with whole numbers and show dollars and cents in the quotient.

Each copy costs $0.66.

Divide and check.

1. $20\overline{)\$1.80}$

2. $48\overline{)\$5.76}$

3. $50\overline{)\$66.50}$

4. $71\overline{)\$74.55}$

5. $87\overline{)\$52.20}$

6. $90\overline{)\$378.00}$

7. $19\overline{)\$42.75}$

8. $52\overline{)\$105.04}$

9. $17\overline{)\$21.08}$

10. $36\overline{)\$34.20}$

11. $43\overline{)\$49.45}$

12. $68\overline{)\$166.60}$

13. $\$63.70 \div 65$

14. $\$780.85 \div 97$

15. $\$331.50 \div 75$

16. $\$537.50 \div 86$

More Practice, page 425, Set A

Using Division: Finding Unit Prices

Use the table at the right for problems 1 through 4.

1. Find the cost for each copy of *Sewing Made Easy*.

2. Find the cost for each copy of *TV View*.

3. Find the cost for each copy of *Movies and Plays*.

4. Justin wants to order *Today's Fisherman* or *Hiking and Camping*. He wants to spend no more than $0.50 for each copy. Which magazine should he buy?

Magazine Subscription Costs		
Name of Magazine	Number of Copies per Year	Cost per Year
Today's Fisherman	12	$6.60
Sewing Made Easy	24	26.40
Hiking & Camping	18	8.10
TV View	52	18.20
Movies and Plays	24	18.00

Find the missing amount for each tag.

5. **Sunday News** — $18.20 for 52 weeks, ___?___ each week

6. **DAILY BULLETIN** — $1.75 a week, ___?___ each day

7. **NAMES IN THE NEWS** — $15.00 for 12 months, ___?___ each month

★ 8. **Weekly Review** — $39.00 for 1 year, ___?___ each week

Problem Solving: Using Estimation

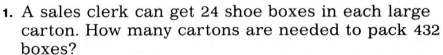

For each problem,
A. estimate the answer.
B. find the exact answer.

1. A sales clerk can get 24 shoe boxes in each large carton. How many cartons are needed to pack 432 boxes?

2. Table tennis balls are sold in packages of 6. The store has 1,176 table tennis balls. How many packages does the store have?

3. Each shelf can hold 12 softball bats. How many shelves are needed for 108 bats?

4. Football shirts are put on tables in stacks of 12 shirts per stack. How many stacks are there if 228 shirts are put on tables?

5. The store manager worked the same number of hours each day for 18 days one month. If the manager worked a total of 198 hours, how many hours did the manager work each day?

6. A school paid $924.00 for 28 pairs of football shoes. What was the average cost of each pair?

7. **Try This** A sales clerk wants to put one pair of sneakers and one pair of stockings in a display window. There are 4 different types of sneakers that the clerk can show and 3 different types of stockings. How many different sneaker-stocking displays can the clerk make?

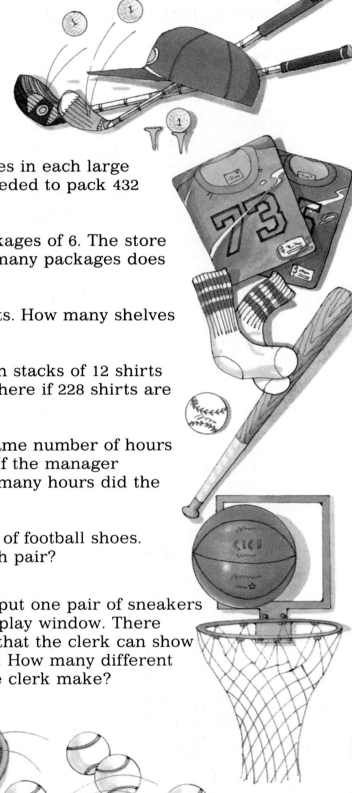

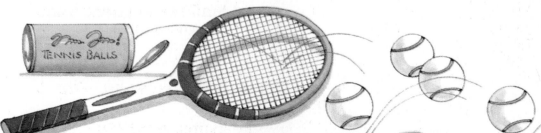

Dividing: Practice

Divide and check.

1. $30\overline{)240}$

2. $40\overline{)252}$

3. $70\overline{)363}$

4. $51\overline{)328}$

5. $87\overline{)368}$

6. $24\overline{)132}$

7. $23\overline{)217}$

8. $55\overline{)441}$

9. $42\overline{)160}$

10. $18\overline{)432}$

11. $36\overline{)1,643}$

12. $81\overline{)4,893}$

13. $50\overline{)15,320}$

14. $26\overline{)1,846}$

15. $72\overline{)40,176}$

16. $64\overline{)6,460}$

17. $44\overline{)17,454}$

18. $93\overline{)6,375}$

19. $58\overline{)41,006}$

20. $67\overline{)59,161}$

21. $32\overline{)2,409}$

22. $56\overline{)11,592}$

23. $49\overline{)4,621}$

24. $62\overline{)10,862}$

25. $28\overline{)8,578}$

26. Find $101.68 divided by 82.

27. Find the quotient when $233.68 is divided by 46.

28. Estimate: $3,545 ÷ 73

29. Estimate: $7,188 ÷ 88

Problem Solving:
Using Data from a Telephone Rate Table

Mr. and Mrs. Zane own a gift shop in Pittsburgh. They make many telephone calls to places outside the United States. Use this telephone rate table for calls from Pittsburgh to solve the problems below.

	First Minute			Each Additional Minute		
	Standard	Discount	Economy	Standard	Discount	Economy
Australia	$4.22	$3.17	$2.53	$1.58	$1.19	$0.95
France	2.37	1.78	1.42	1.33	1.00	0.80
Haiti	1.68	1.26	1.01	1.13	0.85	0.68
Peru	2.77	2.08	1.66	1.18	0.89	0.71
United Kingdom	2.08	1.56	1.25	1.26	0.95	0.76

1. Mrs. Zane called France and Peru at the economy rate and the United Kingdom at the standard rate. Each call lasted 1 minute. What was the total charge for these 3 calls?

2. Mrs. Zane called Australia and talked for 4 minutes at the standard rate. What was the charge for this call?

3. Mr. Zane made 2 calls to France. Each one lasted 2 minutes. One call was at the discount rate and the other at the economy rate. What was the total charge for these 2 calls?

4. How much money would Mrs. Zane save on a 5-minute call to the United Kingdom if she called at the economy rate instead of at the standard rate?

5. **Try This** In May the Zanes made a total of 6 calls to France, Peru, and Australia. They made 3 calls to one country, 2 calls to another country, and just 1 call to the other country. They did not make more than 2 calls to Australia. They made fewer than 3 calls to Peru. If they made more than 1 call to Australia, how many calls did they make to Peru?

Problem Solving: Practice

1. A beef steer eats about 42 lb (pounds) of feed each day. How much feed does it eat in 1 week?

2. A Jersey cow eats about 3,960 lb of grass in a month. About how much grass does it eat in 1 day? (Use 30 days in a month.)

3. A Jersey cow eats about 3,212 lb of feed in one year. It also eats about 4,422 lb of hay. What is the total amount of feed and hay a Jersey cow eats in a year?

4. A Brown Swiss cow gives about 7,040 lb of milk a year. A Jersey cow gives about 5,238 lb of milk a year. How much more milk does a Brown Swiss cow give each year?

5. An average person in the United States drinks about 120 qt (quarts) of milk each year. About how much milk does an average person drink each month?

6. The Wilsons had 570 lb of beef in their freezer. It was enough beef to last for one year. If each person in the family eats an average of 95 lb of beef each year, how many people are in the Wilson family?

7. **Try This** Some chickens and cows are in a barnyard. Altogether there are 10 animals and 28 legs. How many chickens and how many cows are in the barnyard?

Problem Solving: Work Backward

Some problems can be solved most easily by using a strategy called

WORK BACKWARD

Try This Naomi asks her uncle how old he is. He says, "Well, if I add 10 to my age and then double that sum, I get 90."
How old is Naomi's uncle?

It often helps to make a **flowchart** and a **reverse flowchart** for the problem.

I can use what I know to make a flowchart.

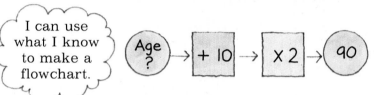

Age ? → + 10 → × 2 → 90

Remember! Adding and subtracting "undo" each other.
Multiplying and dividing "undo" each other.

Now I can work backward using a reverse flowchart.

Age 35 ← − 10 ← ÷ 2 ← 90

Naomi's uncle is 35 years old.

Solve.

1. If Gary multiplies his dog's age by 5 and subtracts 37, he gets 28. How old is his dog?

2. Joyce bought some picture post cards for $0.29 and a ball point pen that cost 3 times as much as the cards. She has $3.18 left. How much money did she have at the start?

Chapter Review-Test

Divide.

1. $70 \div 10$ **2.** $210 \div 30$ **3.** $480 \div 80$ **4.** $4{,}900 \div 70$ **5.** $3{,}200 \div 40$

6. $50\overline{)300}$ **7.** $90\overline{)2{,}700}$ **8.** $70\overline{)560}$ **9.** $60\overline{)5{,}400}$ **10.** $90\overline{)4{,}500}$

Divide and check.

11. $20\overline{)88}$ **12.** $40\overline{)230}$ **13.** $30\overline{)249}$ **14.** $60\overline{)350}$ **15.** $80\overline{)273}$

16. $31\overline{)235}$ **17.** $58\overline{)477}$ **18.** $38\overline{)370}$ **19.** $44\overline{)302}$ **20.** $91\overline{)445}$

21. $72\overline{)5{,}646}$ **22.** $32\overline{)992}$ **23.** $28\overline{)1{,}399}$ **24.** $56\overline{)1{,}193}$ **25.** $25\overline{)8{,}172}$

26. $73\overline{)22{,}693}$ **27.** $86\overline{)35{,}088}$ **28.** $32\overline{)\$16.00}$ **29.** $68\overline{)\$50.32}$ **30.** $75\overline{)\$306.75}$

Solve.

31. The art teacher has 128 straws in the supply room. Each student needs 16 straws for an art project. How many students can do the art project?

32. Ellen bought a bike for $176.80. She paid for it with weekly payments for one year (52 weeks). How much did Ellen pay each week?

33. A salesperson drove about 34,500 km in 46 weeks. What was the average distance the salesperson drove each week?

183

Another Look

Division facts help you
find other quotients!

$$28 \div 7 = 4$$

so $280 \div 70 = 4$

$$\begin{array}{r} 5 \\ 8)\overline{40} \end{array}$$ so $\begin{array}{r} 50 \\ 80)\overline{4,000} \end{array}$

Divide.

1. $480 \div 80$ **2.** $140 \div 20$ **3.** $270 \div 30$

4. $60)\overline{420}$ **5.** $40)\overline{1,600}$ **6.** $50)\overline{2,000}$

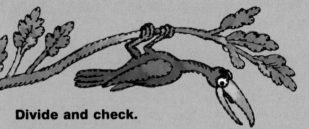

| Decide where to start. | → | Divide the ones. |

$$\begin{array}{r} 5 \text{ R15} \\ 50)\overline{265} \\ 250 \leftarrow 50 \times 5 \quad \text{(multiply)} \\ \overline{15} \leftarrow 15 < 50 \quad \text{(subtract, compare)} \end{array}$$

Divide and check.

7. $30)\overline{200}$ **8.** $40)\overline{372}$ **9.** $70)\overline{195}$

10. $50)\overline{393}$ **11.** $80)\overline{258}$ **12.** $90)\overline{599}$

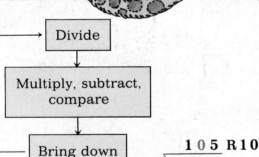

Divide

↓

Multiply, subtract, compare

↓

Bring down

$$\begin{array}{r} 1\ 0\ 5 \text{ R10} \\ 23)\overline{2,4\ 2\ 5} \\ 2\ 3 \\ \hline 1\ 2 \\ 0 \\ \hline 1\ 2\ 5 \\ 1\ 1\ 5 \\ \hline 1\ 0 \end{array}$$

Don't forget
a step!

Divide and check.

13. $22)\overline{176}$ **14.** $48)\overline{250}$

15. $37)\overline{154}$ **16.** $63)\overline{466}$

17. $34)\overline{1,450}$ **18.** $66)\overline{3,432}$

19. $80)\overline{4,581}$ **20.** $24)\overline{10,416}$

21. $43)\overline{25,939}$ **22.** $59)\overline{13,964}$

23. $32)\overline{\$20.16}$ **24.** $92)\overline{\$7.36}$

Enrichment

Number Relationships

When we add or subtract on a clock, we start over when we get to 12.

Examples:
10 o'clock + 5 hours → 3 o'clock
3 o'clock − 5 hours → 10 o'clock

Use the clock to help you give the missing times.

1. 10 o'clock + 7 hours → _?_ o'clock

2. 3 o'clock − 8 hours → _?_ o'clock

3. 6 o'clock − 10 hours → _?_ o'clock

4. 8 o'clock + 7 hours → _?_ o'clock

5. 12 o'clock + 11 hours → _?_ o'clock

6. 2 o'clock − 8 hours → _?_ o'clock

7. 11 o'clock − 14 hours → _?_ o'clock

8. 3 o'clock + 15 hours → _?_ o'clock

9. Rochelle left her house to go fishing at 7 o'clock. She got home 6 hours later. She got home at _?_ o'clock.

10. Aaron arrived in San Diego at 9 o'clock. He had left Sacramento 10 hours earlier. He left Sacramento at _?_ o'clock.

185

Cumulative Review

1. Give the place value of the 3 in the decimal 12.835.

   A three **B** three tenths
   C three hundredths **D** not given

2. Give the decimal for seven hundred fifty-six thousandths.

   A 700.5600 **B** 0.756
   C 0.0756 **D** not given

3. Which sign should go in the ▦?

   0.50 ▦ 0.05

   A > **B** < **C** =

4. Round 3.08 to the nearest tenth.

   A 3.18 **B** 4
   C 3.008 **D** not given

5. Round 2.659 to the nearest whole number.

   A 2 **B** 3
   C 2.7 **D** not given

Add or subtract.

6.   7.526
   + 6.085

   A 13.501
   B 13.511
   C 13.611
   D not given

7.   46.038
   − 6.349

   A 39.789
   B 39.689
   C 42.387
   D not given

Divide.

8. $8\overline{)96}$

   A 12
   B 13
   C 14
   D not given

9. 385 ÷ 6

   A 64 R1
   B 63 R1
   C 64
   D not given

10. $7\overline{)1,435}$

    A 250
    B 25
    C 205
    D not given

11. $3\overline{)12,375}$

    A 4,015
    B 4,025
    C 4,152
    D not given

12. In Chicago one year, there were 8.636 cm of rain in May, 10.16 cm of rain in June, and 10.414 cm of rain in July. What was the total rainfall in those three months?

    A 29.021 cm **B** 29.21 cm
    C 28.021 cm **D** not given

13. One summer, Atlanta, Georgia, had 9.398 cm of rain in June and 12.446 cm of rain in July. How much more rain fell in July?

    A 3.138 cm **B** 3.148 cm
    C 3.048 cm **D** not given

8

Measurement

David's aunt is a nature photographer. She has her own darkroom where she makes her own prints of all the pictures she takes. One Saturday she lets David watch as she works in the darkroom. The room is very small, just 3.2 m long and 2.5 m wide. The only light comes from a small red bulb called a *safelight*. When David's eyes are used to the dim light he watches as his aunt pours a package of chemicals into a tray and mixes them with 828 mL of water. After his aunt finds that the temperature of the liquid is just right (20°C), she dips a special kind of printing paper (15 cm long and 10 cm wide) into the tray. Soon, as if by magic, a picture of a mighty bull moose stands out clearly on the paper.

Length: Meters and Centimeters

The **meter** (m) is the basic unit of length in the metric system.

A meter stick (less than actual size)

End of a meter stick (actual size)

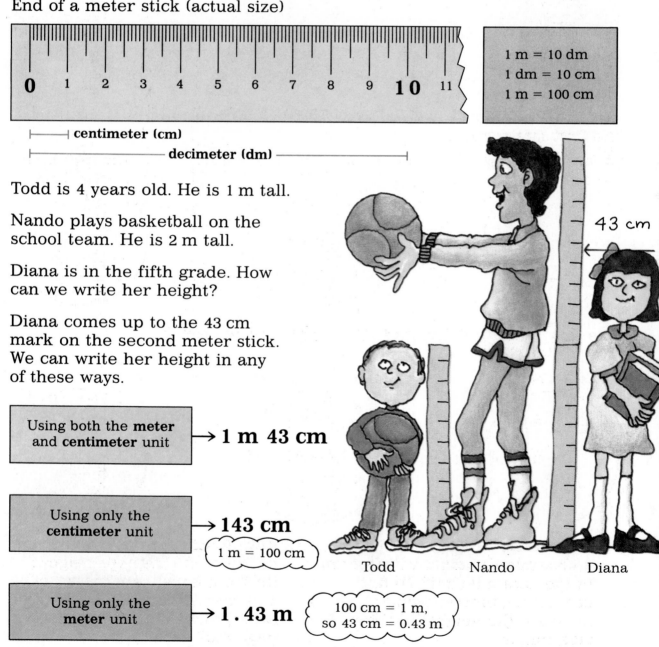

1 m = 10 dm
1 dm = 10 cm
1 m = 100 cm

|—| centimeter (cm)
|————— decimeter (dm) —————|

Todd is 4 years old. He is 1 m tall.

Nando plays basketball on the school team. He is 2 m tall.

Diana is in the fifth grade. How can we write her height?

Diana comes up to the 43 cm mark on the second meter stick. We can write her height in any of these ways.

| Using both the **meter** and **centimeter** unit | → **1 m 43 cm** |

| Using only the **centimeter** unit | → **143 cm** |

1 m = 100 cm

| Using only the **meter** unit | → **1.43 m** |

100 cm = 1 m, so 43 cm = 0.43 m

43 cm

Todd   Nando   Diana

The red mark in each picture shows where the top of
the student's head reaches on the **second meter stick.**
Give each height.

Use both meter and centimeter units to give the heights.
Remember the first meter stick!

1. Jan's height

2. John's height

3. Bob's height

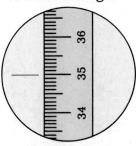

Use only centimeter units to give the heights. Remember
the first meter stick!

4. Maureen's height

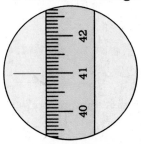

5. Van's height

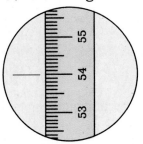

6. Heather's height

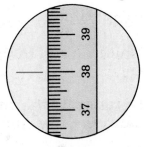

Use only meter units to give the heights. Remember the
first meter stick!

7. Gene's height

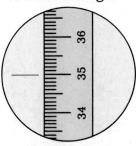

8. Marika's height

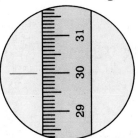

9. Rosalie's height

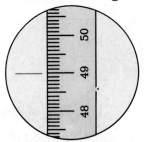

10. DATA HUNT Can you estimate
a classmate's height within 1 dm
of the actual height? To find
out, first estimate, then
measure the heights of three
classmates.

11. DATA BANK How much more
or less is the average height
(to the nearest centimeter) of
6 of your classmates than the
averages given in the table on
page 410?

Length: Centimeters and Millimeters

Sue used this method to measure the amount of rainfall.

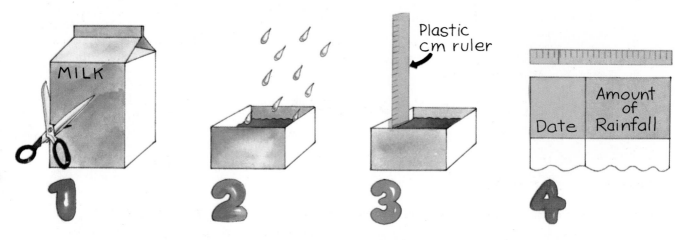

To measure accurately, she wanted to use a smaller unit.

A centimeter is divided into
10 units this size.
This is a **millimeter (mm).**

1 cm = 10 mm
1 m = 1,000 mm

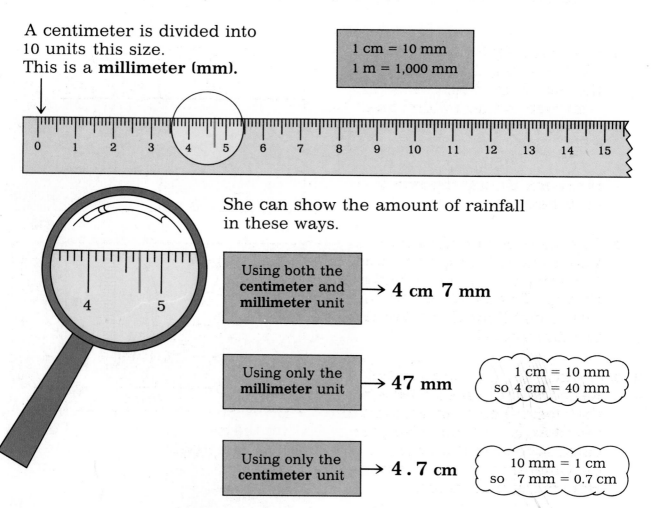

She can show the amount of rainfall
in these ways.

Using both the **centimeter** and **millimeter** unit → **4 cm 7 mm**

Using only the **millimeter** unit → **47 mm**

1 cm = 10 mm
so 4 cm = 40 mm

Using only the **centimeter** unit → **4.7 cm**

10 mm = 1 cm
so 7 mm = 0.7 cm

Show the amount of rainfall for each marking.
Use both centimeter and millimeter units.

1.

2.

3.

Use only millimeter units.

4.

5.

6.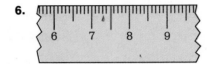

Use only centimeter units.

7.

8.

9.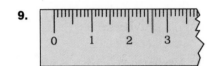

10. Sue made this rainfall table. What was the total rainfall for the month in millimeters? In centimeters and millimeters? In centimeters?

11. What was the average rainfall per week during the month in millimeters?

12. One week it rained every day. Sue made this graph to show the amounts that fell Monday through Friday. What was the total rainfall for these five days in millimeters?

13. A mountain on the island of Kauai is the rainiest place in the world. The average rainfall per year is 1,168 cm. Use your calculator to find how many centimeters this is per day. How many millimeters?

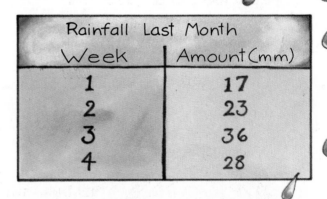

Rainfall Last Month

Week	Amount (mm)
1	17
2	23
3	36
4	28

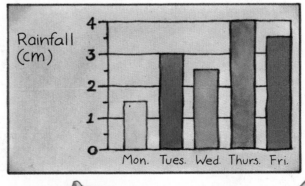

191

Estimating with Metric Units

What size do you need?

First estimate. Then measure
with a measuring tape, or
a string and centimeter ruler.

1. Your hat size
   Estimate: _?_ cm
   Measure: _?_ cm

2. Your collar size
   Estimate: _?_ cm
   Measure: _?_ cm

3. Your watchband size
   Estimate: _?_ cm
   Measure: _?_ cm

4. Your shoe size
   Estimate: _?_ cm
   Measure: _?_ cm

5. Your ring size
   Estimate: _?_ cm
   Measure: _?_ cm

6. Your belt size
   Estimate: _?_ cm
   Measure: _?_ cm

What is your record?

Estimate first, then measure.

1. How far can you step?
   Estimate: _?_ m
   Measure: _?_ m

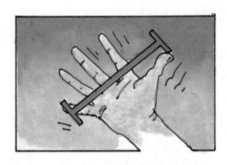

3. How far can you reach?
   Estimate: _?_ m
   Measure: _?_ m

For outside the classroom

5. How far can you jump?
   Estimate: _?_ m
   Measure: _?_ m

2. How high can you reach?
   Estimate: _?_ m
   Measure: _?_ m

4. How far can your fingers reach (your span)?
   Estimate: _?_ cm
   Measure: _?_ cm

6. How far can you throw a ball?
   Estimate: _?_ m
   Measure: _?_ m

193

Length: Kilometers

Carlos and Lita went on a family vacation trip.

They decided to learn as much as they could about the unit of length called a **kilometer (km).**

The odometer in their van looked like this:

km

During their trip they saw signs like these:

San Francisco
100 km

Yosemite
National Park
Headquarters
12 km ahead

In San Francisco, Carlos and Lita used the odometer to measure the distance shown in this picture. They found that it was 1 km. They wrote these notes about the kilometer unit.

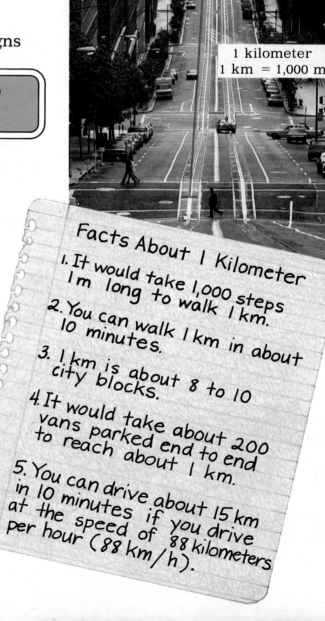

1 kilometer
1 km = 1,000 m

Facts About 1 Kilometer

1. It would take 1,000 steps 1 m long to walk 1 km.

2. You can walk 1 km in about 10 minutes.

3. 1 km is about 8 to 10 city blocks.

4. It would take about 200 vans parked end to end to reach about 1 km.

5. You can drive about 15 km in 10 minutes if you drive at the speed of 88 kilometers per hour (88 km/h).

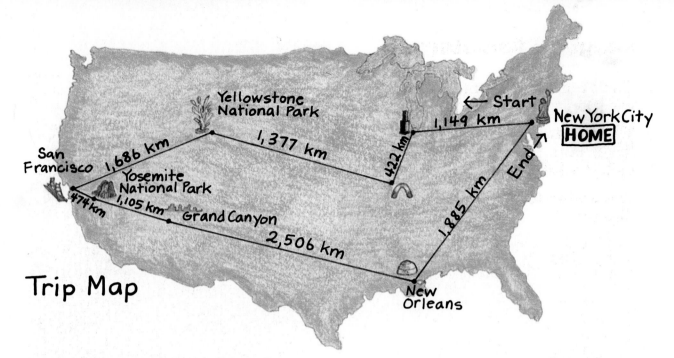

Trip Map

Carlos and Lita wrote these facts about their trip, but they left out the units. Give the correct unit (**centimeter, meter,** or **kilometer**) for each blank.

1. You might travel 88 __?__ in one hour on the freeway.

2. The lake we passed was 8 __?__ wide.

3. The Golden Gate Bridge is between 1 and 2 __?__ long.

4. Old Faithful Geyser reaches a height of 56 __?__.

5. The van key we lost is 6 __?__ long.

6. The St. Louis Arch is 192 __?__ high.

7. The Texas cowboy hat Lita bought is 47 __?__ wide.

8. The Grand Canyon is 29 __?__ wide in some places.

9. The van's front seat is 176 __?__ wide.

10. The nose on the Statue of Liberty is 1.2 __?__ long.

11. Use the map above to find how far the family traveled.

12. Which was longer, the trip from New York to San Francisco, or the trip back to New York? How much longer?

Perimeter

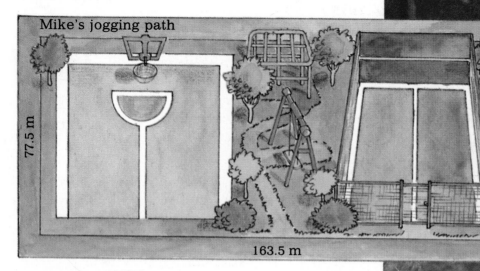

Mike's jogging path

77.5 m

163.5 m

Mike jogs around the small park in his neighborhood. How far does he go every time he runs around the park?

To solve this problem we must find the **distance around** the park. This distance is called the **perimeter** of the park.

To find the perimeter, we add the measures of the sides.

The perimeter of the park is 482 m.

$$
\begin{array}{r}
163.5 \\
77.5 \\
163.5 \\
+77.5 \\
\hline
482.0
\end{array}
$$

Find the perimeter of these regions.

1.

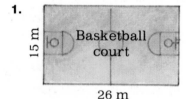

15 m

Basketball court

26 m

2.

219 m

Parking lot

275 m

3.

73.0 m

81.2 m

Baseball field

81.2 m

121.7 m

121.7 m

4. School playground (rectangular)
width: 225 m
length: 187 m

5. Soccer practice field (rectangular)
length: 249.8 m
width: 96.4 m

6. Public garden (rectangular)
length: 1287.6 m
width: 596.9 m

196

Problem Solving: Drawing a Picture

Draw pictures to help you solve the problems.
Example:

Problem

To make a picture frame, we need to know the picture's perimeter. Its width is 46 cm. Its length is twice its width. What is its perimeter?

Solution

We know the width: 46 cm. The length is 2 times the width.
Draw a picture.

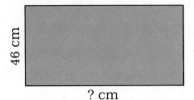

The length is 2 × 46, or 92 cm, so the perimeter is 46 + 92 + 46 + 92, or 276 cm.

1. A rectangular yard is 36.7 m long. The width is 12.9 m less than the length. How many meters of fence are needed to go around the yard?

2. The length of a rectangular playground is 26.5 m more than the width. The width is 137.8 m. What is the perimeter of the playground?

3. The Pentagon Building in Washington, D.C., has 5 equal sides. The distance from one corner of the building to the next is 281 m. What is the perimeter of the building?

4. The width of a rectangular board is 39 cm. The length is 3 times the width. What is the perimeter of the board?

5. A student wants to use yarn to make an outline of a kite. The two longer sides are each 43.5 cm long. The two shorter sides are each 23.5 cm long. How much yarn is needed?

6. The shortest side of a three-sided lot is 36 m. The length of the next-longest side is 12 m greater than this. The longest side is another 12 m greater in length. What is the perimeter of the lot?

7. **Try This** If you double the width of a rectangle and add 24, you find the length of the rectangle. If the length is 96 m, what is the perimeter of the rectangle? Hint: Work backward.

Area

Lori is covering the floor of her room with carpet tiles. How many carpet tiles does she need?

The **area** of the floor is the number of square units (carpet tiles) it takes to cover the floor. We can find the area in two different ways.

Think about square units.

Lori's Floor

9 rows

12 squares in each row

There are 12 squares in each row.
There are 9 rows of squares.
There are 9 x 12, or 108, squares.
The area is 108 square units.

Lori needs 108 carpet tiles.

Use a formula.

Lori's Floor

Width: 9 units

Length: 12 units

Area		length		width
A	$=$	l	$\times$	w
A	$=$	12	$\times$	9
A	$=$	108 square units		

Find the area of each rectangle. The unit is the square meter (m²) or the square centimeter (cm²).

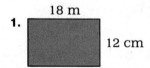

1. 18 m
   12 cm

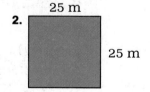

2. 25 m
   25 m

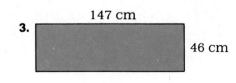

3. 147 cm
   46 cm

4. length: 247 m
   width: 36 m

5. length: 97 cm
   width: 78 cm

6. length: 654 m
   width: 376 m

Problem Solving: Practice

1. Carpet tiles cost $0.37 each. How much will it cost Lori to buy carpet tile for the floor if she needs 108 tiles?

2. A roll of wallpaper is 50 cm wide and 1,000 cm long. What is the area of the paper on the roll?

3. A roll of wallpaper will cover 5 m². The area of one wall is 12 m². How many rolls will she need to buy to paper the wall? (You must buy full rolls.)

4. The wallpaper Lori wants costs $8.95 a roll. How much will it cost for 3 rolls of this wallpaper and a $3.69 smoothing brush?

5. Lori wants to paint the two ends of her room that are shown here. How many square meters of wall must she paint?

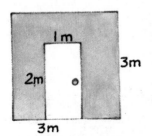 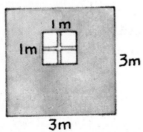

6. Lori wants to buy 2 cans of paint for $3.95 each, a roller kit for $5.69, and an edger for $1.65. What is the total cost?

★ 7. Lori used a drawing on graph paper to help her decide how to arrange the furniture in her room. If each square has an area of 1 square unit, give the area of each piece of furniture in her drawing. You may have to estimate the area of some of the objects.

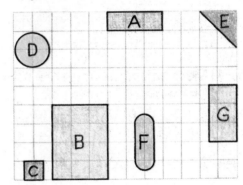

A desk
C night stand
E shelves
G chest of drawers

B bed
D table
F rug

8. **Try This** Lori spent half of her decorating money for paint and wallpaper. Then she spent half of what was left for a new lamp. After that she had $29 left. How much did she have at the start?

Volume

Yolanda works in a sporting goods store. She needs to ship 30 softballs to a school. Will the large box hold that many?

The **volume** of a box is the number of cubic units it contains. We find volume in two ways:

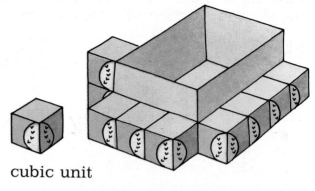

cubic unit

Counting

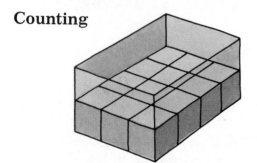

12 cubes in a layer
2 layers
24 cubes in all
Volume = 24 cubic units

Multiplying

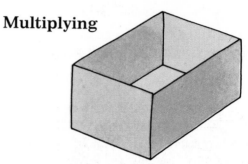

Volume = length × width × height
$V = \underline{4 \times 3} \times \underline{2} = 24$ cubic units

number in   number
a layer   of layers

The large box will not hold 30 small boxes.

Find the volume. The unit is the cubic centimeter (cm³).

1.

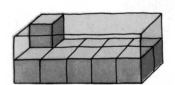

2.

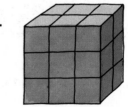

3.

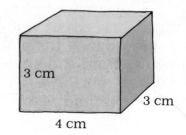

3 cm
3 cm
4 cm

4.

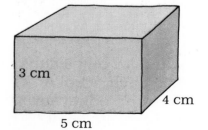

3 cm
4 cm
5 cm

Find the volume. Use the cubic centimeter (cm³) or cubic meter (m³) as the unit of measure.

Sporting goods are delivered by truck or railroad car.

1.

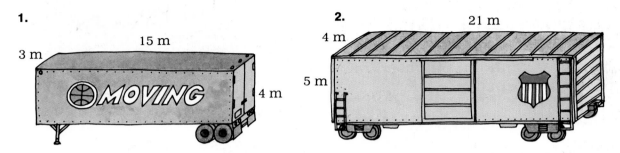

15 m
3 m
4 m

2.

21 m
4 m
5 m

It is important to have the right size boxes for shipping.

3.

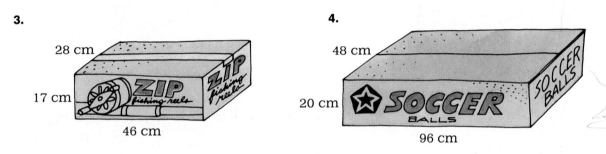

28 cm
17 cm
46 cm

4.

48 cm
20 cm
96 cm

The furnace must be able to give enough heat for the whole building.

5.

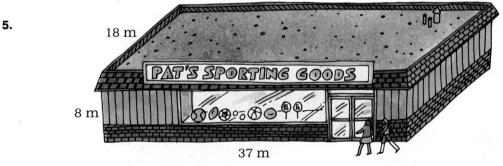

18 m
8 m
37 m

PAT'S SPORTING GOODS

Different kinds of storage space are needed.

6.

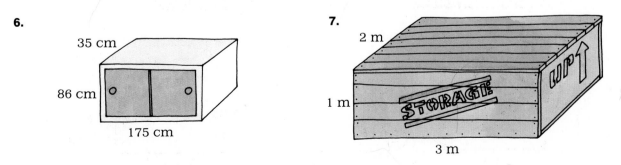

35 cm
86 cm
175 cm

7.

2 m
1 m
3 m

STORAGE

Capacity

Kevin used a 1-liter container to fill his fish tank. He used a 1-milliliter eye dropper to put some special medicine in the water.

The **liter** (L) and the **milliliter** (mL) are units of **capacity**.

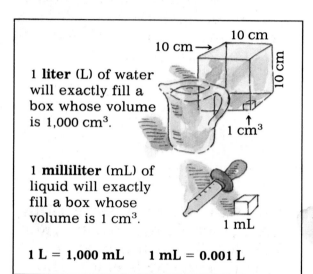

1 **liter** (L) of water will exactly fill a box whose volume is 1,000 cm³.

1 **milliliter** (mL) of liquid will exactly fill a box whose volume is 1 cm³.

1 cm³

1 mL

1 L = 1,000 mL   1 mL = 0.001 L

Choose the best estimate for the capacity of each container.

1.

12 mL
120 mL
1,200 mL

2.

8 L
80 L
800 L

3.

25 mL
250 mL
2,500 mL

Copy and complete the equations.

4. $1,000 \text{ mL} = \text{\:\:\:} \text{L}$

5. $2,000 \text{ mL} = \text{\:\:\:} \text{L}$

6. $8,000 \text{ mL} = \text{\:\:\:} \text{L}$

7. $1 \text{ L} = \text{\:\:\:} \text{mL}$

8. $2 \text{ L} = \text{\:\:\:} \text{mL}$

9. $5 \text{ L} = \text{\:\:\:} \text{mL}$

10. $1 \text{ mL} = \text{\:\:\:} \text{L}$

11. $32 \text{ mL} = \text{\:\:\:} \text{L}$

12. $567 \text{ mL} = \text{\:\:\:} \text{L}$

Problem Solving: Practice

1. Kevin poured 16 L of water into the fish tank. How many milliliters is this?

   How many cubic centimeters is this?

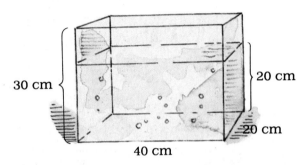

30 cm

20 cm

20 cm

40 cm

2. How many milliliters of water would be in the tank if it were completely filled?

   How many liters is this?

3. One day Kevin added 2 L of water to the tank. He did this by putting 8 cupfuls of water into the tank. How many milliliters of water were in each cupful?

4. Kevin's brother used a bucket to change the water in the tank. Do you think the bucket he used is more likely to hold 10 mL or 10 L? Why?

5. Kevin read that he should have no more than "3 cm of fish" for every 5 L of water in the tank. Suppose he fills the tank so that the water is 25 cm deep. What is the greatest number of 3-cm fish he should put in it?

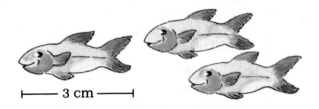

├─── 3 cm ───┤

6. **Try This** Three of Kevin's fish are named Finny, Whiskers, and Bubbles. One fish is blue, one is orange, and one is black. The orange fish often swims at the top of the tank. The black fish spends a lot of time swimming with Finny. Bubbles never swims at the top of the tank. The blue fish always swims alone. What color is each fish? Hint: Use logical reasoning.

Weight

The **kilogram (kg)** unit is used to measure weight.

1 liter of water

1 kg

About 1 kg

About 1 kg

About 1 kg

The **gram (g)** unit is used to measure smaller weights.

1 milliliter of water

1 g

About 1 g

About 1 g

About 1 g

1 kg = 1,000 g   **1 g = 1 thousandth of a kg (0.001 kg)**

If a measurement is given in kilograms,
we can write it in grams.

5 kg: How many grams?

kg	1	2	3	4	5
g	1,000	2,000	3,000	4,000	5,000

Since 1 kg is 1,000 g,
5 kg is **5,000** g.

If a measurement is given in grams,
we can write it in kilograms.

275 g: How many kilograms?

g	1	2	21	22	274	275
kg	0.001	0.002	0.021	0.022	0.274	0.275

Since 1 g is 1 thousandth of a kg,
275 g is 275 thousandths of a kg.

Give each weight in grams.   Give each weight in kilograms.

1. 2 kg   **2.** 23 kg   **3.** 475 kg   **4.** 8 g   **5.** 67 g   **6.** 999 g

Choose the best estimate for the weight of each object.

1.

70 g   70 kg

2.

250 g   250 kg

3.

2 g   2 kg

4.

20 g   20 kg

5.

360 g   3,600 g

6.

3.7 g   3.7 kg

7.

120 kg   1,200 kg

8. The students in Rudy's class held a Guess-the-Weight contest. They guessed the weights of different kinds of balls. Then they weighed each ball to check their guesses. Can you match each kind of ball with its weight in the table below?

A Bowling ball

B Basketball

C Tennis ball

D Baseball

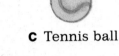

E Table tennis ball

Kind of ball	Weight
?	3 g
?	60 g
?	150 g
?	600 g
?	7 kg

Temperature

Carla used a thermometer to measure some temperatures. The metric unit of temperature is the degree **Celsius (°C)**. She made this temperature graph. (For ⁻10°C, we read "10 degrees Celsius below zero.")

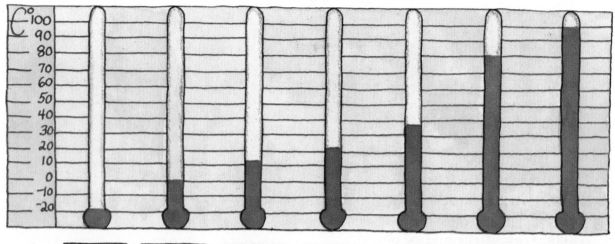

| Inside a Freezer | Crushed Ice | Cold Water | Temperature Room | Body | Hot Soup | Boiling Water |

1. Match each letter on the thermometer at the right with one of the pictures below the graph.

   Example: **A**—Boiling water

Which temperature is the better estimate for each item?

2. Ice cream   ⁻12°C or 12°C

3. Oven temperature—baking cookies   95°C or 195°C

4. Warm bath water   48°C or 84°C

5. High fever   40°C or 90°C

6. Cold day   ⁻2°C or 20°C

7. Inside a refrigerator   5°C or ⁻5°C

Carla measured the temperatures shown below.
Give each temperature.

1. Hot chocolate

2. Frozen yogurt

3. Hot shower

4. Drink with ice cubes

5. Cooking oatmeal

6. Near a light bulb

7. Carla kept a record of the outdoor temperatures for five days at her school. What was the average temperature for the five days?

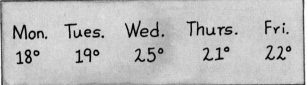

	Mon.	Tues.	Wed.	Thurs.	Fri.
	18°	19°	25°	21°	22°

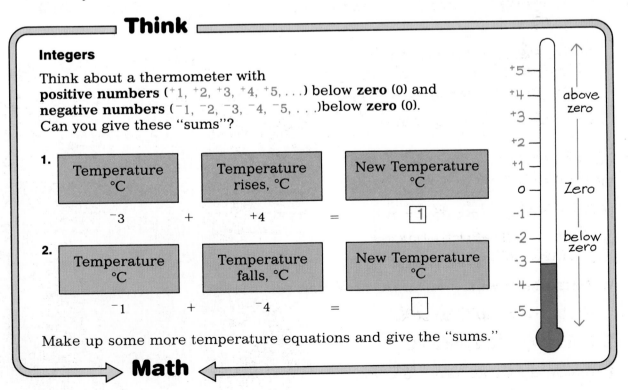

Think

Integers

Think about a thermometer with
positive numbers ($^+1$, $^+2$, $^+3$, $^+4$, $^+5$, ...) below **zero** (0) and
negative numbers ($^-1$, $^-2$, $^-3$, $^-4$, $^-5$, ...) below **zero** (0).
Can you give these "sums"?

1.
Temperature °C	Temperature rises, °C	New Temperature °C
$^-3$	$^+4$	$\boxed{1}$

with: $^-3$ + $^+4$ = $\boxed{1}$

2.
Temperature °C	Temperature falls, °C	New Temperature °C
$^-1$	$^-4$	$\square$

with: $^-1$ + $^-4$ = $\square$

Make up some more temperature equations and give the "sums."

Math

207

Time

Eric made this poster to show how we measure time using a day and smaller units.

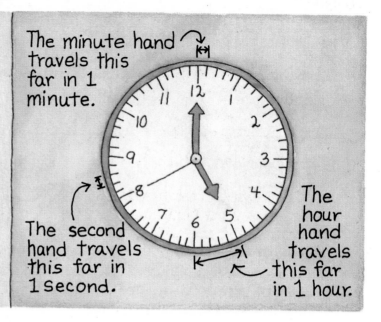

TIME

Units
1 day = 24 hours
1 hour = 60 minutes
1 minute = 60 seconds

Use a.m. to show times after midnight and before noon.

Use p.m. to show times after noon and before midnight.

The minute hand travels this far in 1 minute.

The second hand travels this far in 1 second.

The hour hand travels this far in 1 hour.

Can you answer these questions Eric asked about time?

How many minutes pass while the minute hand goes from

1. 12 to 1?   2. 12 to 3?   3. 12 to 6?

4. 12 to 8?   5. 12 to 9?   6. 12 to 10?

7. 12 to 12?   8. 3 to 6?   9. 4 to 10?

How many hours pass while the hour hand goes from

10. 3 to 8?   11. 10 to 5?   12. 12 past 12 to 12 again?

How many seconds pass while the second hand goes from

13. 12 to 2?   14. 12 to 5?   15. 12 to 12?

Write **a.m.** or **p.m.** for each time. Then tell at which number the minute hand on a clock would be pointing.

16. Breakfast   17. Late show   18. Football game   19. Bedtime
    7:15   12:45   1:20   9:50

Problem Solving: Using Mental Math

Try to solve these problems without pencil and paper.

1. A TV show lasts 1 hour and 30 minutes. It starts at 8:00 p.m. When will it be over?

   Think: 1 hour past 8:00 is 9:00.
   30 minutes past 9:00 is __?__.

2. A plane leaves Chicago at 6:50 a.m. It arrives in New Orleans at 9:05 a.m. How long does the flight take?

   Think: 6:50 to 8:50 is 2 hours.
   8:50 to 9:05 is __?__ minutes.

3. If you start reading at 5:50 p.m. and read for 45 minutes, what time is it when you stop?

4. Jen and her mother left to drive to the lake at 5:45 p.m. They estimated that the drive would take 1 hour and 35 minutes. What time did they expect to reach the lake?

5. Kwang went to sleep at 9:30 p.m. He woke up at 7:15 a.m. How long did he sleep?

6. When Ms. Haskins punched the time clock in the morning it looked like this: 7:56

   When she punched out that evening it looked like this: 4:45

   How long did Ms. Haskins work that day (including lunch time)?

7. **Try This** Beth decided it would take 35 minutes to drive to the airport, 45 minutes to check in, and 1 hour and 10 minutes to eat at the airport restaurant. If her plane takes off at 9:45 p.m., at what time should she leave for the airport?

Time Zones

Lloyd lives in New York. His mother is visiting San Francisco. She wants to call him before he leaves for school at 8:00 a.m. (New York time). At what time in California must his mother make the call?

Because of the earth's shape and rotation, the sun appears in New York while it is still dark in San Francisco.

The **time zone** chart below shows that when it is 8:00 a.m. in New York, it is 5:00 a.m. in California.

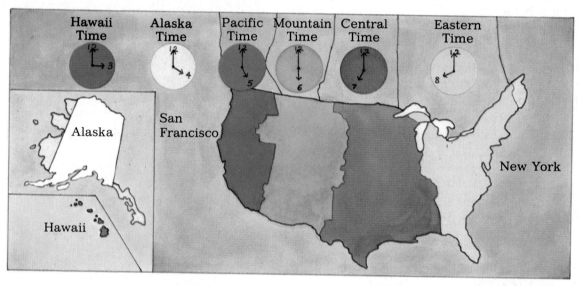

 Suppose it is 12:00 Eastern Time.

1. What is the Central Time?
2. What is the Mountain Time?
3. What is the Pacific Time?
4. What is the Hawaii Time?

 Suppose it is 2:00 Mountain Time.

5. What is the Pacific Time?
6. What is the Central Time?
7. What is the Eastern Time?
8. What is the Alaska Time?

★ 9. A plane left Washington, D.C., at 11 a.m. (Eastern Time) and arrived in Los Angeles at 1:00 p.m. (Pacific Time). How long did the flight take?

Problem Solving: Using Calendar Data

Units
1 year = 365 days (in leap year, 366)
1 year = 52 weeks   1 week = 7 days
1 year = 12 months   1 month = *

* "Thirty days have September, April, June,
    and November.
  And just for fun, all the rest have 31,
    except February.
  February alone doesn't hold the line.
  For 3 years it has 28,
    and in the fourth year, 29."

1. Some school years have 182
   days. How many full weeks is
   this?

2. How many days altogether are
   there in months with 30 days? in
   months with 31 days?

3. A student is 572 weeks old. How
   many years old is the student?

4. If a dog is 156 months old, how
   many years old is it?

5. A **decade** is 10 years. How many
   weeks are there in a decade?

6. A **century** is 100 years. How
   many weeks are there in a
   century?

7. These 3-by-3 squares of numbers
   are taken from the calendar
   above. What is the average of
   the 9 numbers in each square?
   Do you see a pattern? Try this
   with another 3-by-3 square from
   the calendar.

8. **Try This** In how many different
   ways can you fill three blanks
   (_____) with the letters from
   the word for the fifth month of
   the year? Answer the same
   question for two blanks (____).

Problem Solving: Solve a Simpler Problem

Sometimes an answer to a problem can be found by solving a problem like it that has smaller numbers. This strategy is called

SOLVE A SIMPLER PROBLEM

Try This A restaurant has 30 small square tables to be used for a banquet. Each table can seat only one person on each side. If the tables are pushed together to make a long table, how many people can sit at the table?

I don't want to draw a picture for 30 tables. I'll solve simpler problems with 2, 3, and 4 tables and look for a way to solve the more difficult problem.

I see! Two people can sit at each of the 30 tables. Then I can add 2 more people for the ends.

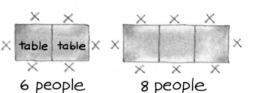

6 people   8 people

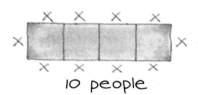

10 people

$$2 \times 30 = 60, \quad 60 + 2 = 62$$

62 people could sit at the long banquet table.

Solve.

1. Jessie bought an old wagon wheel at the flea market. There are 20 spokes in the wheel. How many spaces are between the spokes? Hint: Try 3 spokes.

2. Thalia is planning a business meeting. She wants to use 36 small square tables to make 1 large square table. If each small table can seat only one person on a side, how many people can be seated at the large table? Hint: Try 4 small tables, then 9.

Chapter Review-Test

Write each measure using (A) centimeter units only and (B) meter units only.

1. 1 m 74 cm   **2.** 3 m 42 cm   **3.** 2 m 56 cm   **4.** 5 m 37 cm

Write each measure using (A) millimeter units only (B) centimeter units only.

5. 1 cm 7 mm   **6.** 3 cm 6 mm   **7.** 5 cm 9 mm   **8.** 2 cm 3 mm

9. Estimate the length in centimeters. Then measure the actual length.

Write **cm**, **m**, or **km** to tell which is the correct unit for each blank.

10. A pen is about 14 _?_ long.

11. Chicago is about 1,150 _?_ from New York.

12. The room is about 5 _?_ wide.

Find the perimeter and the area of this rectangular lot.

13. Perimeter: ▓

14. Area: ▓

28 m   56 m

Find the volume and capacity of this box.

15. Volume: ▓ cm³

16. Capacity: ▓ L

24 cm   60 cm   25 cm

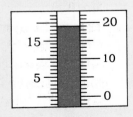

17. Choose the best estimate for the weight.

23 g   23 kg   130 g

18. Give the temperature of the room.

20 15 10 5 0

19. If a musical show starts at 8:30 p.m. and lasts 1 hour and 45 minutes, what time does it end?

213

Another Look

Length
1 kilometer (km) = 1,000 meters (m)
1 m = 100 centimeters (cm) or
        10 decimeters (dm)
1 cm = 10 millimeters (mm)
1 m 36 cm = 1.36 m = 136 cm
1 cm 7 mm = 1.7 cm = 17 mm

Perimeter
How far around?

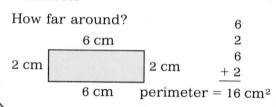

6 cm
2 cm ___ 2 cm
6 cm

```
  6
  2
  6
+ 2
----
perimeter = 16 cm²
```

Area
How many square units?

$A = l \times w$

$A = 6 \times 2$

6 cm   2 cm

Area = 12 cm²

Volume
How many cubic units?

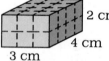

3 cm   4 cm   2 cm

$V = l \times w \times h$
$(4 \times 3) \times 2 = 24$

Volume = 24 cm³

Capacity
1 liter (L) = 1,000 cm³
1 milliliter (mL) = 1 cm³
1 L = 1,000 mL

Weight
1 kilogram (kg) = 1,000 grams (g)

Give the number for each ▦.

1. 100 cm = ▦ m
2. 10 mm = ▦ cm
3. 1,000 m = ▦ km
4. 2 m 75 cm = ▦ m

Find the perimeter.

5.

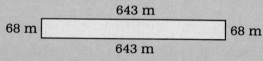

643 m
68 m [_____] 68 m
643 m

6. Rectangle: length, 78 cm; width, 46 cm

Find the area.

7.

49 cm [_____] 146 cm

8. Rectangle: length, 76 m; width, 28 m

Find the volume.

9.

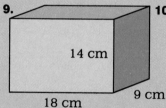

14 cm   18 cm   9 cm

10. Box:
    length, 24 cm
    width, 23 cm
    height, 19 cm

Give the number for each ▦.

11. 1,000 mL = ▦ L
12. 3 kg = ▦ g
13. 1 cm³ = ▦ mL
14. 6 L = ▦ mL
15. 4,000 mL = ▦ L
16. 500 g = ▦ kg

Enrichment

A Calculator Activity

For the problems below, use *only* the keys on your calculator that are also on Alvin's calculator!

Alvin's teacher asked the following question: "What number, multiplied by itself, gives the product 6,084?"

She wrote: "$n \times n = 6{,}084$. Find the number for n using as few multiplications on your calculator as possible."

Can you find n? How many multiplications did you do?

Alvin's Calculator

Find the missing number. Give the number of multiplications you used.

1. $n \times n = 784$

2. $n \times n = 9{,}604$

3. $n \times n = 71{,}824$

4. $n \times n = 4{,}489$

5. $n \times n = 15{,}376$

6. $n \times n = 133{,}225$

The teacher explained that the numbers found for the equations above are called **square roots**. The **square root** of 6,084 is 78.

She wrote: "$\sqrt{6{,}084} = 78$"

If you enter 6,084 in a calculator like Helen's and push the ☑ key, the calculator will show 78.

Helen's Calculator

Find these square roots.

7. $\sqrt{3{,}364} = n$

8. $\sqrt{7{,}056} = n$

9. $\sqrt{24{,}964} = n$

Technology

Using Computer Programs

A computer program gives instructions to a computer. Programs are written using words such as NEW, PRINT, GOTO, and END. Such words tell the computer exactly what to do.

Here is an example of a simple computer program. It will help you review some of the special computer language.

Microcomputers are used in many homes and businesses to keep records, solve problems, and do other tasks.

Computer Program (to be typed into a computer)	Review
NEW	← NEW tells the computer to erase any previous set of instructions.
10 PRINT "THE QUOTIENT OF 36 AND 9 IS"	← PRINT tells the computer to type exactly what is inside the quotation marks (" ").
20 GOTO 40	← GOTO 40 tells the computer to jump to line 40 and follow the instructions there.
30 PRINT 36 * 9	← PRINT, with no quotation marks, tells the computer to type only the value (the result of the computation).
40 PRINT 36/9	← * means multiply. / means divide.
50 END	← END signals the end of the program.

When you type RUN and press RETURN the computer types ⟶ THE QUOTIENT OF 36 AND 9 IS
4

1. What would the RUN be if line 20 were not in the program?

2. What would the RUN be if line 40 read PRINT "36/9"?

Give the RUN for each program in exercises 1–5.

1.
```
NEW
10 PRINT "COMPUTERS MULTIPLY
   AND DIVIDE FIRST."
20 PRINT "THEN THEY ADD
   AND SUBTRACT."
30 PRINT "9 - 4 X 2 = ";
   9 - 4 * 2
40 END
```

2.
```
NEW
10 PRINT "REMEMBER THE"
20 PRINT "BASIC PROPERTIES"
30 PRINT "FOR ZERO?"
40 PRINT "869 + 0 = "; 869 + 0
50 PRINT "869 X 0 = "; 869 * 0
60 END
```

3.
```
NEW
10 PRINT "IF YOU KNOW
   8 X 6 = "; 8 * 6
20 PRINT "THEN YOU KNOW
   6 X 8 = "; 6 * 8
30 PRINT "THIS IS AN EXAMPLE OF"
40 PRINT "THE ORDER PROPERTY."
50 END
```

4.
```
NEW
10 PRINT "AN ODD NUMBER"
20 PRINT "PLUS AN ODD NUMBER"
30 PRINT "IS AN"
40 GOTO 60
50 PRINT "ODD NUMBER."
60 PRINT "EVEN NUMBER."
70 END
```

5.
```
NEW
10 PRINT "COMPUTER PROGRAMS"
20 PRINT "HELP MAKE"
30 GOTO 45
40 PRINT "MATH FUN!"
45 PRINT "MATH INTERESTING!"
50 END
```

6. In exercise 5 change the number in line 30 from 45 to 40. What will the RUN be then?

7. Write a program for this RUN:
```
AN ODD NUMBER
TIMES AN EVEN NUMBER
IS AN EVEN NUMBER!
EXAMPLE: 7 X 6 = 42
```

8. Write a program of your own that uses GOTO. Give its RUN.

217

Cumulative Review

Multiply.

1. 8×900

A 72,000
B 73,000
C 7,300
D not given

2. 900×600

A 45,000
B 450,000
C 540,000
D not given

3.
$$\begin{array}{r} 588 \\ \times \quad 4 \end{array}$$

A 2,532
B 2,352
C 2,523
D not given

4.
$$\begin{array}{r} 8,756 \\ \times \quad 6 \end{array}$$

A 52,526
B 52,536
C 52,506
D not given

5.
$$\begin{array}{r} 603 \\ \times \quad 23 \end{array}$$

A 626
B 13,869
C 1,829
D not given

6.
$$\begin{array}{r} 438 \\ \times \quad 37 \end{array}$$

A 16,206
B 16,236
C 16,266
D not given

Divide.

7. $90\overline{)630}$

A 80
B 7
C 70
D not given

8. $60\overline{)300}$

A 5
B 6
C 50
D not given

9. $720 \div 80$

A 7
B 8
C 9
D not given

Divide and check.

10. $70\overline{)259}$

A 30 R9
B 3 R49
C 34 R9
D not given

11. $32\overline{)672}$

A 21
B 210
C 21 R2
D not given

12. $61\overline{)4,293}$

A 70 R3
B 71 R23
C 70 R23
D not given

13. Ray worked at a part-time job for a year (52 weeks). He earned $38 each week. How much did he earn in a year?

A $1,986   B $1,976
C $266   D not given

14. Ray bought a moped to ride to work. He made 49 weekly payments of $15 each. How much did he pay for his moped?

A $735   B $284
C $635   D not given

218

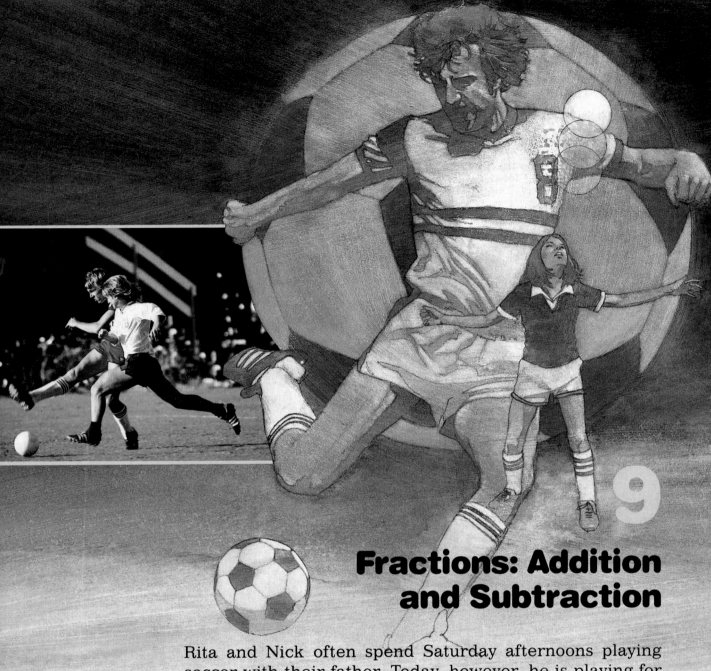

Fractions: Addition and Subtraction

9

Rita and Nick often spend Saturday afternoons playing soccer with their father. Today, however, he is playing for his team, the Suns, in a very important game. Rita and Nick are watching proudly from the stands. As the game begins, Rita looks at her watch and remembers that there are two halves in a game and each half lasts $\frac{3}{4}$ of an hour. She is sure that, if the time between halves is not more than $\frac{1}{2}$ hour, she and Nick will arrive home in time to meet their friends and tell them all about the game. At the end of the first half the game is tied 1 to 1. The score is still tied late in the second half, but just before time runs out the Suns score another goal. The Suns win 2 to 1!

Fractions of Regions

The bulletin board is divided into 4 equal parts. What part of the bulletin board is covered?

3 of 4 equal parts of the **region** are covered. We use a **fraction** to answer the question.

Numerator → $\dfrac{3}{4}$ ← **Denominator**
number of parts covered — number of parts in all

We say: "**Three fourths** of the bulletin board is covered."

Answer the questions and give the fraction.

1.

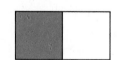

How many equal parts are there?
How many parts are shaded?
▥ of the strip is shaded.

2.

How many equal parts are there?
How many parts are shaded?
▥ of the region is shaded.

Give the fraction of the region.

3.

▥ of the region is shaded.

4.

▥ of the region is shaded.

5.

▥ of the region is shaded.

Write the fractions.

6. two thirds   **7.** one half   **8.** one fifth   **9.** zero fourths

Write the word name for each fraction. Example: $\frac{2}{3} \rightarrow$ two thirds.

10. $\frac{1}{6}$ **11.** $\frac{3}{8}$ **12.** $\frac{7}{10}$ **13.** $\frac{5}{12}$ **14.** $\frac{0}{5}$ **15.** $\frac{1}{9}$

Fractions of Sets

What part of the books are about ways to travel?

2 of the **set** of 5 books are about ways to travel. We use a **fraction**.

number of → **2**
travel
books   **5** ← number of
             books in all

We say: "**Two fifths** of the books are about ways to travel."

Answer the questions and give the fraction.

1.

How many tacks are there in all?
How many tacks are red?
$\frac{\text{▦}}{\text{▥}}$ of the tacks are red.

2.

How many pencils are there in all?
How many pencils are blue?
$\frac{\text{▦}}{\text{▥}}$ of the pencils are blue.

Give the fraction of the set.

3.

$\frac{\text{▦}}{\text{▥}}$ of the map flags
are red.

4.

$\frac{\text{▦}}{\text{▥}}$ of the bookmarks
are yellow.

5.

$\frac{\text{▦}}{\text{▥}}$ of the push pins
are brown.

Write the fractions.

6. one sixth   **7.** three eighths   **8.** zero halves   **9.** seven tenths

Write the word name for each fraction.

10. $\frac{2}{3}$ **11.** $\frac{4}{5}$ **12.** $\frac{0}{6}$ **13.** $\frac{7}{12}$ **14.** $\frac{1}{8}$ **15.** $\frac{3}{4}$

Equivalent Fractions

We can write more than one fraction to tell what part of the tennis balls are yellow.

3 of **4** cans of balls are yellow. $\frac{3}{4}$ of the balls are yellow.

9 of **12** balls are yellow. $\frac{9}{12}$ of the balls are yellow.

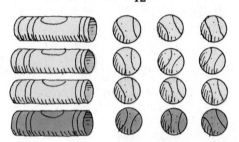

$\frac{3}{4}$ and $\frac{9}{12}$ are **equivalent fractions.** We write: $\frac{3}{4} = \frac{9}{12}$

Equivalent fractions can be found by multiplying the numerator and denominator of a fraction by the same number (not zero).

$$\frac{3}{4} \qquad \frac{3 \times 3}{4 \times 3} \qquad \frac{9}{12}$$

$\frac{9}{12}$ is equivalent to $\frac{3}{4}$.

Other Examples

$$\frac{1}{3} \begin{array}{c} \boxed{\times 3} \\ = \\ \boxed{\times 3} \end{array} \frac{3}{9} \qquad \frac{3}{4} \begin{array}{c} \boxed{\times 5} \\ = \\ \boxed{\times 5} \end{array} \frac{15}{20} \qquad \frac{7}{10} \begin{array}{c} \boxed{\times 10} \\ = \\ \boxed{\times 10} \end{array} \frac{70}{100}$$

Warm Up Find equivalent fractions by multiplying.

1. $\frac{1}{2} \begin{array}{c} \boxed{\times 3} \\ = \\ \boxed{\times 3} \end{array}$

2. $\frac{4}{5} \begin{array}{c} \boxed{\times 2} \\ = \\ \boxed{\times 2} \end{array}$

3. $\frac{1}{3} \begin{array}{c} \boxed{\times 5} \\ = \\ \boxed{\times 5} \end{array}$

4. $\frac{3}{10} \begin{array}{c} \boxed{\times 5} \\ = \\ \boxed{\times 5} \end{array}$

5. $\frac{4}{4} \begin{array}{c} \boxed{\times 3} \\ = \\ \boxed{\times 3} \end{array}$

6. $\frac{2}{3} \begin{array}{c} \boxed{\times 10} \\ = \\ \boxed{\times 10} \end{array}$

Give an equivalent fraction.

1. $\dfrac{1}{4}$ $\boxed{\times 2}$ = $\boxed{\times 2}$ → ▦ ▦

2. $\dfrac{3}{4}$ $\boxed{\times 3}$ = $\boxed{\times 3}$ → ▦ ▦

3. $\dfrac{2}{5}$ $\boxed{\times 4}$ = $\boxed{\times 4}$ → ▦ ▦

4. $\dfrac{1}{10}$ $\boxed{\times 10}$ = $\boxed{\times 10}$ → ▦ ▦

Give the next three equivalent fractions.

$\left(\dfrac{2 \times 2}{5 \times 2}\right)$ $\left(\dfrac{2 \times 3}{5 \times 3}\right)$ $\left(\dfrac{2 \times 4}{5 \times 4}\right)$

Example: $\dfrac{2}{5}$, $\dfrac{▦}{▦}$, $\dfrac{▦}{▦}$, $\dfrac{▦}{▦}$ → $\dfrac{4}{10}$, $\dfrac{6}{15}$, $\dfrac{8}{20}$

5. $\dfrac{1}{2}$, $\dfrac{▦}{▦}$, $\dfrac{▦}{▦}$, $\dfrac{▦}{▦}$

6. $\dfrac{1}{3}$, $\dfrac{▦}{▦}$, $\dfrac{▦}{▦}$, $\dfrac{▦}{▦}$

7. $\dfrac{1}{6}$, $\dfrac{▦}{▦}$, $\dfrac{▦}{▦}$, $\dfrac{▦}{▦}$

8. $\dfrac{2}{3}$, $\dfrac{▦}{▦}$, $\dfrac{▦}{▦}$, $\dfrac{▦}{▦}$

9. $\dfrac{3}{4}$, $\dfrac{▦}{▦}$, $\dfrac{▦}{▦}$, $\dfrac{▦}{▦}$

10. $\dfrac{3}{8}$, $\dfrac{▦}{▦}$, $\dfrac{▦}{▦}$, $\dfrac{▦}{▦}$

★ Give the missing numerator.

Example: $\dfrac{4}{5} = \dfrac{▦}{15}$ $\left(\dfrac{4}{5}\ \boxed{\times 3} = \boxed{\times 3}\ \dfrac{12}{15}\right)$

5 was multiplied by 3 to get 15,
so multiply 4 by 3 to get 12.

11. $\dfrac{2}{3} = \dfrac{▦}{12}$

12. $\dfrac{3}{4} = \dfrac{▦}{12}$

13. $\dfrac{2}{5} = \dfrac{▦}{10}$

14. $\dfrac{1}{2} = \dfrac{▦}{10}$

15. $\dfrac{1}{6} = \dfrac{▦}{30}$

16. $\dfrac{3}{5} = \dfrac{▦}{30}$

17. $\dfrac{1}{3} = \dfrac{▦}{24}$

18. $\dfrac{5}{8} = \dfrac{▦}{24}$

Think

Cross Products

Two fractions are equivalent if (and only if)
their **cross products** are equal.

cross → (3 ⤬ 12) → 5 × 12 = 60
products → (5 ⤬ 20) → 3 × 20 = 60

Since the cross products
are equal, we know that $\dfrac{3}{5} = \dfrac{12}{20}$

1. Check some of exercises 1–18 using cross products.

2. Use cross products to find which pairs of
these fractions are equivalent fractions. $\dfrac{91}{169}$ $\dfrac{99}{187}$ $\dfrac{117}{221}$ $\dfrac{161}{299}$

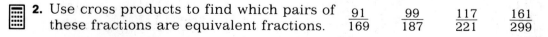

Math

Greatest Common Factor

The idea of the **greatest common factor** of two numbers
will help you find lowest-terms fractions in the next lesson.

What is the greatest common factor of the numerator
and denominator of $\frac{16}{24}$?

List the factors of the two numbers.	→	List the common factors (the numbers that are in both lists).	→	Choose the greatest common factor.

Factors of 16:
1, 2, 4, 8, 16

1, 2, 4, 8

8

Factors of 24:
1, 2, 3, 4, 6, 8, 12, 24

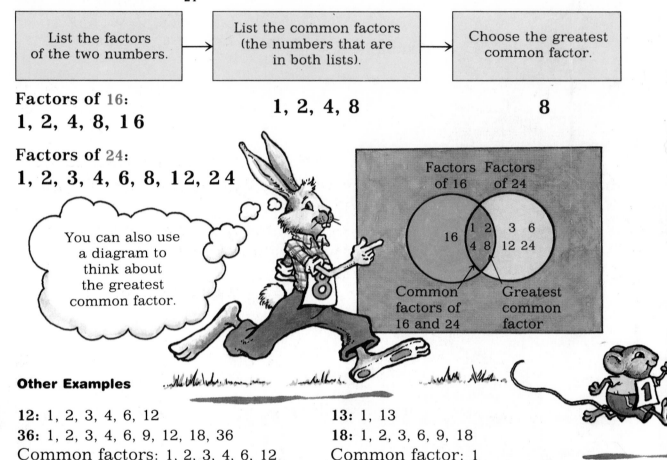

You can also use a diagram to think about the greatest common factor.

Factors of 16   Factors of 24

16   1 2 4 8   3 6 12 24

Common factors of 16 and 24

Greatest common factor

Other Examples

12: 1, 2, 3, 4, 6, 12
36: 1, 2, 3, 4, 6, 9, 12, 18, 36
Common factors: 1, 2, 3, 4, 6, 12
Greatest common factor: 12

13: 1, 13
18: 1, 2, 3, 6, 9, 18
Common factor: 1
Greatest common factor: 1

Warm Up

1. List the factors of 28.
   List the factors of 42.
   List the common factors of 28 and 42.
   Give the greatest common factor of 28 and 42.

2. List the factors of 27.
   List the factors of 18.
   List the common factors of 27 and 18.
   Give the greatest common factor of 27 and 18.

List the factors of each number. Then give the greatest common factor.

1. 9 12	**2.** 8 20	**3.** 9 15	**4.** 7 13	**5.** 10 14	**6.** 9 27
7. 40 50	**8.** 20 25	**9.** 16 24	**10.** 15 18	**11.** 15 25	**12.** 8 14
13. 18 24	**14.** 9 10	**15.** 18 30	**16.** 10 30	**17.** 3 21	**18.** 15 21
19. 9 21	**20.** 8 18	**21.** 7 8	**22.** 16 36	**23.** 10 15	**24.** 20 50

Try a shortcut

★ **A** List only the factors of the smaller number.

B Choose those that are also factors of the other number.

C The largest factor of both numbers is the greatest common factor.

Example:

15 → <u>1</u>, 3, <u>5</u>, 15; greatest common factor, 5
20

25. 12 15	**26.** 18 45	**27.** 28 16	**28.** 42 18	**29.** 15 21	**30.** 18 32
31. 24 40	**32.** 36 42	**33.** 15 24	**34.** 16 12	**35.** 14 21	**36.** 18 27

★ **37.** Find the greatest common factor of 12, 18, and 27.

Skillkeeper

Give the measures in centimeters.

Give the measures in meters.

Give the measures in milliliters.

1. 2 m **2.** 50 mm

3. 3 km **4.** 600 cm

5. 800 cm^3 **6.** 4 L

7. How many grams is 5 kg?

8. How many kilograms is 10,000 g?

9. Give the perimeter and area of a rectangular field 47 m long and 24 m wide.

10. What is the volume of a box 15 cm long, 12 cm wide, and 4 cm high?

Lowest-Terms Fractions

In Esperanza's class 16 out of 24, or $\frac{16}{24}$, of all the children have birthdays during the school year. To show this more simply, we write $\frac{16}{24}$ as a **lowest-terms fraction**.

The numerator and denominator are called **terms** of a fraction.

A fraction is in **lowest terms** when the greatest common factor of both terms is 1.

We can divide both terms by any common factor and keep on dividing until we find the lowest-terms fraction.

OR

We can divide both terms by the **greatest common factor** to find the lowest-terms fraction.

$$\frac{16 \div 2}{24 \div 2} = \frac{8}{12} \rightarrow \frac{8 \div 4}{12 \div 4} = \frac{2}{3}$$

Lowest-terms fraction

$$\frac{16 \div 8}{24 \div 8} = \frac{2}{3}$$

Lowest-terms fraction

$\frac{16}{24}$ reduced to lowest terms is $\frac{2}{3}$.

Other Examples

$$\frac{2}{6} \xrightarrow[\div 2]{\div 2} \frac{1}{3}$$

$$\frac{70}{100} \xrightarrow[\div 10]{\div 10} \frac{7}{10}$$

$$\frac{15}{25} \xrightarrow[\div 5]{\div 5} \frac{3}{5}$$

Warm Up   Reduce to lowest terms.

1. $\frac{12}{30} \xrightarrow[\div 6]{\div 6}$ ▥▥

2. $\frac{9}{27} \xrightarrow[\div 9]{\div 9}$ ▥▥

3. $\frac{28}{40} \xrightarrow[\div 4]{\div 4}$ ▥▥

4. $\frac{9}{24}$

5. $\frac{7}{10}$

6. $\frac{8}{12}$

7. $\frac{5}{15}$

8. $\frac{9}{12}$

9. $\frac{27}{45}$

Is the fraction in lowest terms? Write **yes** or **no**.
(Do not reduce.)

1. $\frac{1}{5}$ 2. $\frac{2}{6}$ 3. $\frac{5}{10}$ 4. $\frac{3}{12}$ 5. $\frac{12}{18}$ 6. $\frac{4}{9}$

7. $\frac{3}{8}$ 8. $\frac{6}{8}$ 9. $\frac{9}{15}$ 10. $\frac{8}{20}$ 11. $\frac{6}{13}$ 12. $\frac{6}{18}$

Reduce to lowest terms.

13. $\frac{6}{8}$ 14. $\frac{9}{12}$ 15. $\frac{18}{45}$ 16. $\frac{3}{15}$ 17. $\frac{12}{20}$ 18. $\frac{8}{20}$

19. $\frac{3}{24}$ 20. $\frac{12}{15}$ 21. $\frac{2}{18}$ 22. $\frac{4}{6}$ 23. $\frac{35}{42}$ 24. $\frac{8}{14}$

25. $\frac{24}{40}$ 26. $\frac{4}{12}$ 27. $\frac{20}{30}$ 28. $\frac{36}{42}$ 29. $\frac{6}{10}$ 30. $\frac{18}{24}$

31. $\frac{18}{27}$ 32. $\frac{25}{75}$ 33. $\frac{10}{16}$ 34. $\frac{75}{100}$ 35. $\frac{25}{100}$ 36. $\frac{4}{50}$

Write the lowest-terms fraction.

37. On Monday $\frac{3}{24}$ of the students were absent.

38. A class birthday party took $\frac{24}{60}$ of an hour.

39. Jerry spent $\frac{6}{8}$ of his money for a present.

40. Janice finished only $\frac{16}{40}$ of her math problems during class.

41. Each of these fractions has a simple lowest-terms fraction. Find the lowest-terms fractions.

$\frac{6,381}{57,429}$ $\frac{3,942}{15,768}$ $\frac{5,823}{17,469}$ $\frac{6,729}{13,458}$

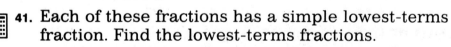

Think

Shape Perception

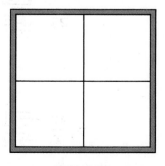

Can you trace this picture of a window and color exactly half of the large square so that the uncolored half is still a square?

Hint: What part of this square is shaded?

Math

Comparing and Ordering Fractions

Eleanor practiced $\frac{2}{3}$ of an hour. Ann practiced $\frac{3}{4}$ of an hour. Who practiced longer?

Here are two ways to compare the fractions:

Using a region

 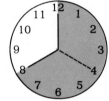

$\frac{3}{4}$ of an hour $> \frac{2}{3}$ of an hour

Using a number line

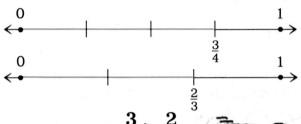

$\frac{3}{4} > \frac{2}{3}$

We can also compare fractions by finding **equivalent fractions** with a **common denominator.**

Look at the denominators.	→	Write equivalent fractions with a common denominator.	→	Compare the numerators.	→	The fractions compare the same way the numerators compare.

$\frac{3}{4}$

$\frac{2}{3}$

Not the same

$\frac{3}{4} = \frac{9}{12}$

$\frac{2}{3} = \frac{8}{12}$

Common denominator (the same)

$9 > 8$

$\frac{9}{12} > \frac{8}{12}$

so $\frac{3}{4} > \frac{2}{3}$

Warm Up Give the correct sign ($>$, $<$, or $=$) for each 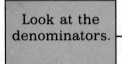.

1. $\left.\begin{array}{l} \frac{1}{2} = \frac{4}{8} \\[4pt] \frac{3}{8} = \frac{3}{8} \end{array}\right\}$ $\frac{1}{2}$ ◍ $\frac{3}{8}$

2. $\left.\begin{array}{l} \frac{2}{3} = \frac{10}{15} \\[4pt] \frac{4}{5} = \frac{12}{15} \end{array}\right\}$ $\frac{2}{3}$ ◍ $\frac{4}{5}$

3. $\left.\begin{array}{l} \frac{6}{8} = \frac{18}{24} \\[4pt] \frac{9}{12} = \frac{18}{24} \end{array}\right\}$ $\frac{6}{8}$ ◍ $\frac{9}{12}$

4. $\frac{1}{2}$ ◍ $\frac{3}{7}$

5. $\frac{10}{12}$ ◍ $\frac{5}{6}$

6. $\frac{4}{5}$ ◍ $\frac{3}{4}$

7. $\frac{5}{8}$ ◍ $\frac{2}{3}$

Give the correct sign (>, <, or =) for each ◖.

1. $\frac{1}{5}$ ◖ $\frac{1}{4}$ **2.** $\frac{3}{4}$ ◖ $\frac{5}{6}$

3. $\frac{1}{2}$ ◖ $\frac{2}{3}$ **4.** $\frac{4}{5}$ ◖ $\frac{5}{8}$

5. $\frac{7}{8}$ ◖ $\frac{7}{10}$ **6.** $\frac{3}{10}$ ◖ $\frac{9}{30}$

7. $\frac{1}{3}$ ◖ $\frac{1}{2}$ **8.** $\frac{5}{6}$ ◖ $\frac{7}{8}$

9. $\frac{7}{12}$ ◖ $\frac{2}{3}$ **10.** $\frac{7}{10}$ ◖ $\frac{3}{4}$ **11.** $\frac{1}{4}$ ◖ $\frac{1}{3}$ **12.** $\frac{3}{5}$ ◖ $\frac{2}{3}$ **13.** $\frac{1}{3}$ ◖ $\frac{3}{8}$

14. $\frac{1}{5}$ ◖ $\frac{20}{100}$ **15.** $\frac{8}{10}$ ◖ $\frac{79}{100}$ **16.** $\frac{4}{5}$ ◖ $\frac{3}{4}$ **17.** $\frac{5}{8}$ ◖ $\frac{2}{3}$ **18.** $\frac{5}{12}$ ◖ $\frac{1}{3}$

Compare the fractions two at a time. Then give them in order from the least to the greatest.

19. $\frac{1}{2}, \frac{3}{8}, \frac{2}{5}$ **20.** $\frac{5}{8}, \frac{3}{5}, \frac{2}{3}$ **21.** $\frac{3}{4}, \frac{2}{3}, \frac{7}{12}$

22. Jennifer's clarinet lesson lasted $\frac{7}{10}$ of an hour. Howard's piano lesson lasted $\frac{4}{5}$ of an hour. Whose lesson lasted longer?

Think

Fraction Comparison

Cross products can help you compare fractions.

First $\quad$ (4) ✕ (5) → $5 \times 5 = 25 \quad \frac{4}{5}$ > $\frac{5}{8}$
Second $\;$ (5) ✕ (8) → $4 \times 8 = 32$

Since the first cross product is greater, the first fraction is greater than the second.

1. Check some of exercises 1–18 by using cross products.

2. Which fraction in each pair is greater?

$\frac{371}{480} \quad \frac{242}{357} \qquad \frac{155}{195} \quad \frac{174}{213} \qquad \frac{398}{987} \quad \frac{2,310}{5,733}$

Math

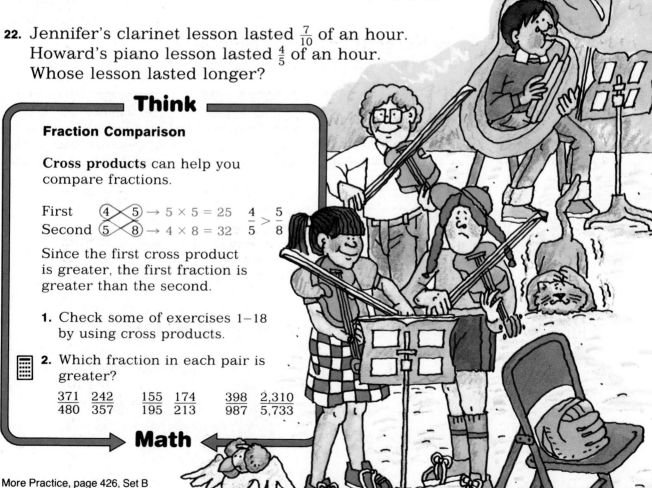

More Practice, page 426, Set B

Problem Solving: Practice

Carol Martin is an apprentice carpenter. She likes to work with tools and see a building grow. She goes to carpentry school two nights a week, and will soon be a carpenter.

Here are some problems she should be able to solve.

1. A house 55 ft long and 35 ft wide is to be built on a lot 94 ft wide and 125 ft long. What is the area in square feet of the house? Of the lot? Of the yard?

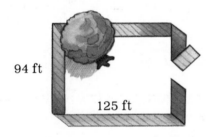

94 ft

125 ft

2. Which will drill a larger hole, a $\frac{3}{8}$-inch bit or a $\frac{7}{16}$-inch bit?

3. A 77-inch board must be cut into fourths. If a total of 1 inch is lost in cutting and sanding, how long will each finished piece be?

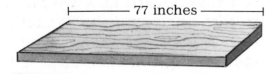

77 inches

4. Sometimes boards are bolted together to give more strength. A $\frac{5}{8}$-inch wrench was too small for a nut. Is the next larger size a $\frac{13}{16}$-inch wrench or a $\frac{3}{4}$-inch wrench?

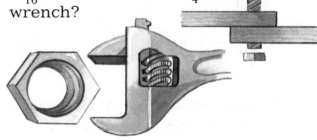

5. A 72-inch board and a 36-inch board were nailed together to make one longer board. There was a 12-inch overlap. How long was the new, longer board?

├── 12 in. ──┤ Overlap

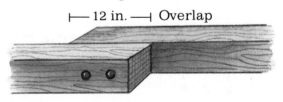

6. **Try This** It takes 1 minute to saw through a board. How long would it take to cut a board into 25 pieces? Hint: Solve a simpler problem.

Problem Solving: Using Estimation

Choose the best estimate.

1. About how full is the jar of nails?

$\frac{1}{2}$ $\frac{2}{3}$ $\frac{9}{10}$

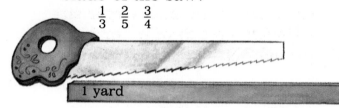

2. About what part of a yard is the blade of the saw?

$\frac{1}{3}$ $\frac{2}{5}$ $\frac{3}{4}$

3. About what part of the whole board is the shorter piece?

$\frac{1}{4}$ $\frac{2}{5}$ $\frac{3}{4}$

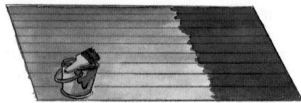

4. About what part of the floor has been painted?

$\frac{1}{2}$ $\frac{1}{3}$ $\frac{1}{6}$

5. About what part of a foot is the screwdriver?

$\frac{5}{6}$ $\frac{7}{12}$ $\frac{3}{4}$

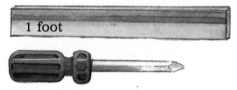

6. About what size (in inches) is the wrench opening?

$\frac{5}{8}$ $\frac{3}{8}$ $\frac{3}{4}$

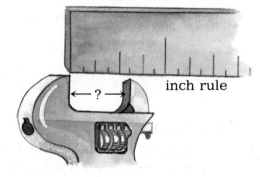

7. **Try This** A carpenter wants to saw a 6-ft board into two parts so that one part is half as long as the other part. How many inches long will each part be?

231

Adding and Subtracting Fractions: Common Denominators

Jason drew this map to show some friends how to get to the campground at the park. How far is it from the park entrance to the campground along Lake Road and Rocky Road?

We want to find the total distance, so we add.

Look at the denominators.	→	Add the numerators.	→	Write the sum over the denominator.

$$\frac{5}{10} + \frac{4}{10}$$

Same

$$5 + 4 = 9$$

$$\frac{5}{10} + \frac{4}{10} = \frac{9}{10}$$

It is $\frac{9}{10}$ mile to the campground along Lake Road and Rocky Road.

Other Examples

Subtract the numerators.

$$\frac{4}{5} - \frac{1}{5} = \frac{3}{5}$$

Write the difference over the denominator.

$$\begin{array}{r} \frac{1}{6} \\ + \frac{2}{6} \\ \hline \frac{3}{6} = \frac{1}{2} \end{array}$$

$$\begin{array}{r} \frac{11}{12} \\ - \frac{7}{12} \\ \hline \frac{4}{12} = \frac{1}{3} \end{array}$$

Warm Up   Add or subtract.

1. $\frac{3}{8} + \frac{4}{8}$

2. $\begin{array}{r} \frac{3}{10} \\ + \frac{5}{10} \\ \hline \end{array}$

3. $\begin{array}{r} \frac{5}{6} \\ - \frac{1}{6} \\ \hline \end{array}$

4. $\frac{9}{10} - \frac{4}{10}$

5. $\begin{array}{r} \frac{5}{12} \\ + \frac{4}{12} \\ \hline \end{array}$

6. $\begin{array}{r} \frac{7}{8} \\ - \frac{3}{8} \\ \hline \end{array}$

Add. Reduce sums to lowest terms.

1. $\frac{1}{3} + \frac{1}{3}$ **2.** $\frac{3}{5} + \frac{1}{5}$ **3.** $\frac{1}{10} + \frac{7}{10}$ **4.** $\frac{3}{8} + \frac{3}{8}$

5. $\begin{array}{r} \frac{1}{8} \\ + \frac{3}{8} \\ \hline \end{array}$ **6.** $\begin{array}{r} \frac{5}{10} \\ + \frac{3}{10} \\ \hline \end{array}$ **7.** $\begin{array}{r} \frac{2}{4} \\ + \frac{1}{4} \\ \hline \end{array}$ **8.** $\begin{array}{r} \frac{5}{12} \\ + \frac{1}{12} \\ \hline \end{array}$ **9.** $\begin{array}{r} \frac{2}{6} \\ + \frac{2}{6} \\ \hline \end{array}$ **10.** $\begin{array}{r} \frac{7}{12} \\ + \frac{3}{12} \\ \hline \end{array}$

Subtract. Reduce differences to lowest terms.

11. $\frac{2}{3} - \frac{1}{3}$ **12.** $\frac{5}{12} - \frac{1}{12}$ **13.** $\frac{4}{5} - \frac{2}{5}$ **14.** $\frac{9}{10} - \frac{3}{10}$

15. $\begin{array}{r} \frac{13}{15} \\ - \frac{4}{15} \\ \hline \end{array}$ **16.** $\begin{array}{r} \frac{7}{8} \\ - \frac{5}{8} \\ \hline \end{array}$ **17.** $\begin{array}{r} \frac{11}{12} \\ - \frac{4}{12} \\ \hline \end{array}$ **18.** $\begin{array}{r} \frac{15}{16} \\ - \frac{9}{16} \\ \hline \end{array}$ **19.** $\begin{array}{r} \frac{8}{10} \\ - \frac{4}{10} \\ \hline \end{array}$ **20.** $\begin{array}{r} \frac{9}{12} \\ - \frac{6}{12} \\ \hline \end{array}$

Add or subtract. Reduce to lowest terms.

21. $\begin{array}{r} \frac{3}{8} \\ + \frac{2}{8} \\ \hline \end{array}$ **22.** $\begin{array}{r} \frac{5}{6} \\ - \frac{1}{6} \\ \hline \end{array}$ **23.** $\begin{array}{r} \frac{5}{12} \\ + \frac{4}{12} \\ \hline \end{array}$ **24.** $\begin{array}{r} \frac{7}{10} \\ + \frac{2}{10} \\ \hline \end{array}$ **25.** $\begin{array}{r} \frac{13}{16} \\ - \frac{9}{16} \\ \hline \end{array}$ **26.** $\begin{array}{r} \frac{10}{12} \\ - \frac{2}{12} \\ \hline \end{array}$

27. What is the sum of $\frac{3}{8}$ and $\frac{4}{8}$?

28. What is $\frac{4}{12}$ more than $\frac{7}{12}$?

29. How much greater is $\frac{7}{8}$ than $\frac{5}{8}$?

30. How much less is $\frac{1}{4}$ than $\frac{3}{4}$?

31. Bobbi went $\frac{3}{10}$ mile on one road and $\frac{4}{10}$ mile on another. How far did she travel?

32. Look at the map on page 232. If Angelo went from the park entrance to Moose Lake, how far would he travel?

Think

Space Perception

Suppose that the patterns below have been folded to form cubes.

What face will be opposite
1. the blue face?
2. the red face?

What face will be opposite
3. the red face?
4. the green face?

Math

Improper Fractions to Mixed Numbers

The picture shows that $\frac{7}{2}$ (seven halves) can be renamed as $3\frac{1}{2}$ (three and one half). $\frac{7}{2}$ is an **improper fraction**. $3\frac{1}{2}$ is a **mixed number**.

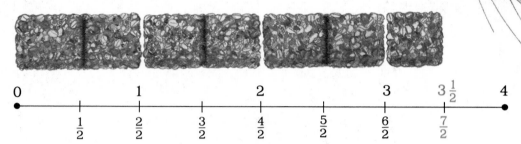

We can use the idea that $\frac{7}{2}$ means $7 \div 2$ or $2\overline{)7}$ to write $\frac{7}{2}$ as a mixed number.

Divide the numerator by the denominator.	→	Write the quotient as the whole number part.	→	Write the remainder over the divisor as the fraction part.

$\frac{7}{2}$ $\begin{array}{r} 3 \\ 2\overline{)7} \\ \underline{6} \\ 1 \end{array}$ ← Number of wholes

← Number of halves

$3\,\frac{\text{█}}{\text{█}}$

$3\frac{1}{2}$

Other Examples

$\frac{11}{4} = 2\frac{3}{4}$ $\begin{array}{r} 2 \text{ R3} \\ 4\overline{)11} \\ \underline{8} \\ 3 \end{array}$

$\frac{12}{3} = 4$ $\begin{array}{r} 4 \\ 3\overline{)12} \\ \underline{12} \\ 0 \end{array}$

Rename as a whole number or mixed number.
Reduce the fraction part to lowest terms.

1. $\frac{8}{2}$ 2. $\frac{10}{3}$ 3. $\frac{9}{2}$ 4. $\frac{15}{4}$ 5. $\frac{18}{3}$ 6. $\frac{13}{10}$

7. $\frac{17}{5}$ 8. $\frac{4}{3}$ 9. $\frac{5}{5}$ 10. $\frac{20}{4}$ 11. $\frac{23}{6}$ 12. $\frac{33}{8}$

13. $\frac{27}{3}$ 14. $\frac{25}{8}$ 15. $\frac{28}{6}$ 16. $\frac{46}{10}$ 17. $\frac{17}{3}$ 18. $\frac{24}{5}$

Mixed Numbers to Improper Fractions

How many grapefruit halves can you make
from $4\frac{1}{2}$ grapefruit?

The picture shows 4 whole grapefruit and $\frac{1}{2}$ of a
grapefruit, or $4\frac{1}{2}$ grapefruit. Each grapefruit has
2 halves $\left(\frac{2}{2}\right)$, so we can also say there are $\frac{9}{2}$ grapefruit.

We can use the method below to write $4\frac{1}{2}$ as an
improper fraction.

Multiply the whole number by the denominator.	→	Add the numerator to the product.	→	Write the sum over the denominator.

$4\frac{1}{2}$ $2 \times 4 = 8$ $8 + 1 = 9$ $\frac{9}{2}$

You can make 9 grapefruit halves $\left(\frac{9}{2}\right)$.

Other Examples

$$2\frac{3}{4} = \frac{11}{4}$$
$(4 \times 2) + 3 = 11$

$$1\frac{7}{10} = \frac{17}{10}$$
$(10 \times 1) + 7 = 17$

$$15\frac{1}{2} = \frac{31}{2}$$
$(2 \times 15) + 1$

Rename each mixed number as an improper fraction.

1. $3\frac{1}{2}$ **2.** $4\frac{1}{5}$ **3.** $2\frac{1}{4}$ **4.** $6\frac{2}{3}$ **5.** $4\frac{1}{3}$ **6.** $8\frac{1}{5}$

7. $2\frac{3}{4}$ **8.** $7\frac{5}{6}$ **9.** $11\frac{1}{4}$ **10.** $12\frac{2}{5}$ **11.** $6\frac{3}{10}$ **12.** $15\frac{1}{3}$

13. $24\frac{1}{2}$ **14.** $8\frac{4}{5}$ **15.** $9\frac{3}{8}$ **16.** $20\frac{3}{5}$ **17.** $8\frac{1}{10}$ **18.** $25\frac{1}{4}$

Least Common Multiple (Denominator)

The idea of **least common multiple** of two numbers will help you find the **least common denominator** of two fractions. You will use this idea to add fractions on page 238.

What is the least common multiple of the denominators of the fractions $\frac{5}{6}$ and $\frac{3}{8}$?

List some multiples of each number. (Do not list zero.)	List the common multiples (the numbers in both lists).	Choose the smallest of these common multiples.

Multiples of 6:
6, 12, 24, 30, 36, 42, 48   **24, 48**   **24**

Multiples of 8:
8, 16, 24, 32, 40, 48

The **least common multiple** of 6 and 8 is 24.
The **least common denominator** of $\frac{5}{6}$ and $\frac{3}{8}$ is 24.

Other Examples

$\frac{1}{4} \longrightarrow$ 4, 8, 12
$\frac{3}{8} \longrightarrow$ 8, 16, 24
The least common denominator is 8.

$\frac{2}{5} \longrightarrow$ 5, 10, 15, 20
$\frac{3}{4} \longrightarrow$ 4, 8, 12, 16, 20
The least common denominator is 20.

Warm Up Find the least common denominator of each pair of fractions.

1. $\frac{2}{3}$ 2. $\frac{1}{3}$ 3. $\frac{3}{4}$ 4. $\frac{3}{8}$ 5. $\frac{5}{6}$ 6. $\frac{3}{4}$

    $\frac{3}{4}$ $\frac{1}{5}$ $\frac{1}{12}$ $\frac{5}{10}$ $\frac{7}{10}$ $\frac{1}{5}$

Find the least common denominator of each pair of fractions.

1. $\frac{1}{2}$ 2. $\frac{2}{5}$ 3. $\frac{1}{4}$ 4. $\frac{2}{3}$ 5. $\frac{5}{8}$
   $\frac{2}{3}$ $\frac{5}{10}$ $\frac{1}{2}$ $\frac{5}{6}$ $\frac{7}{16}$

6. $\frac{3}{10}$ 7. $\frac{3}{8}$ 8. $\frac{3}{8}$ 9. $\frac{1}{2}$ 10. $\frac{7}{8}$
   $\frac{5}{16}$ $\frac{7}{10}$ $\frac{7}{12}$ $\frac{5}{6}$ $\frac{4}{5}$

11. $\frac{1}{2}$ 12. $\frac{1}{5}$ 13. $\frac{3}{8}$ 14. $\frac{3}{10}$ 15. $\frac{5}{6}$
    $\frac{3}{5}$ $\frac{1}{6}$ $\frac{1}{2}$ $\frac{86}{100}$ $\frac{3}{4}$

★ A Start a list of multiples of the larger number.

B Check each number in the list to see if it is also a multiple of the smaller number.

C The smallest number that is a multiple of both numbers is the least common multiple.

Use the shortcut to find the least common denominator of each pair of fractions.

16. $\frac{1}{8}$ 17. $\frac{2}{3}$ 18. $\frac{3}{5}$ 19. $\frac{1}{4}$ 20. $\frac{5}{6}$
    $\frac{5}{6}$ $\frac{3}{4}$ $\frac{1}{6}$ $\frac{5}{12}$ $\frac{9}{10}$

★ 21. Find the least common multiple of 6, 8, and 10.

Skillkeeper

Give an equivalent fraction.

1. $\frac{1}{3}$ 2. $\frac{1}{5}$ 3. $\frac{3}{4}$ 4. $\frac{1}{2}$ 5. $\frac{3}{8}$

Give the lowest-terms fraction.

6. $\frac{4}{8}$ 7. $\frac{3}{9}$ 8. $\frac{6}{10}$ 9. $\frac{3}{12}$ 10. $\frac{4}{6}$

Give the correct sign (>, <, or =) for each ▦.

11. $\frac{2}{3}$ ▦ $\frac{3}{8}$ 12. $\frac{5}{12}$ ▦ $\frac{4}{6}$ 13. $\frac{3}{4}$ ▦ $\frac{12}{16}$ 14. $\frac{7}{8}$ ▦ $\frac{13}{16}$

Adding Fractions: Unlike Denominators

Connie's corn plant grew $\frac{1}{4}$ inch on Monday and $\frac{3}{8}$ inch on Tuesday. How much did it grow during the two days?

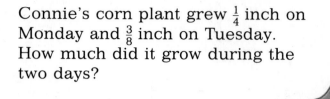

Since we want to find the plant's total growth for two days, we add.

Look at the denominators.	Find the least common denominator.	Write equivalent fractions with this denominator.	Add the fractions.

$\frac{1}{4}$

$+\frac{3}{8}$ — Not the same

Multiples of 4: 4, 8
Multiples of 8: 8

$\frac{1}{4} = \frac{2}{8}$

$+\frac{3}{8} = \frac{3}{8}$

$\frac{2}{8}$

$+\frac{3}{8}$

$\frac{5}{8}$

The plant grew $\frac{5}{8}$ inch in two days.

Other Examples

$\frac{1}{2} = \frac{3}{6}$

$+\frac{1}{3} = \frac{2}{6}$

$\frac{5}{6}$

$\frac{2}{3} = \frac{8}{12}$

$+\frac{3}{4} = \frac{9}{12}$

$\frac{17}{12} = 1\frac{5}{12}$

Rename

$\frac{3}{8} = \frac{9}{24}$

$+\frac{5}{6} = \frac{20}{24}$

$\frac{29}{24} = 1\frac{5}{24}$

Warm Up   Add.

1. $\frac{1}{8}$
$+\frac{3}{4}$

2. $\frac{1}{3}$
$+\frac{1}{5}$

3. $\frac{3}{4}$
$+\frac{1}{12}$

4. $\frac{3}{4}$
$+\frac{2}{5}$

5. $\frac{2}{3}$
$+\frac{1}{4}$

6. $\frac{3}{8}$
$+\frac{5}{10}$

Add.

1. $\dfrac{1}{4}$
$+\dfrac{1}{5}$

2. $\dfrac{2}{5}$
$+\dfrac{3}{10}$

3. $\dfrac{1}{2}$
$+\dfrac{3}{8}$

4. $\dfrac{4}{5}$
$+\dfrac{1}{2}$

5. $\dfrac{3}{4}$
$+\dfrac{1}{2}$

6. $\dfrac{1}{2}$
$+\dfrac{2}{3}$

7. $\dfrac{3}{4}$
$+\dfrac{1}{3}$

8. $\dfrac{5}{6}$
$+\dfrac{1}{2}$

9. $\dfrac{1}{4}$
$+\dfrac{2}{3}$

10. $\dfrac{1}{6}$
$+\dfrac{3}{8}$

11. $\dfrac{3}{4}$
$+\dfrac{5}{8}$

12. $\dfrac{3}{5}$
$+\dfrac{2}{3}$

13. $\dfrac{5}{8}$
$+\dfrac{3}{10}$

14. $\dfrac{7}{8}$
$+\dfrac{7}{16}$

15. $\dfrac{7}{8}$
$+\dfrac{4}{5}$

16. $\dfrac{9}{10}$
$+\dfrac{3}{100}$

17. $\dfrac{3}{10}$
$+\dfrac{9}{20}$

18. $\dfrac{3}{10}$
$+\dfrac{49}{100}$

19. $\dfrac{9}{100}$
$+\dfrac{9}{10}$

20. $\dfrac{13}{50}$
$+\dfrac{37}{100}$

21. $\dfrac{1}{8} + \dfrac{3}{4}$

22. $\dfrac{1}{2} + \dfrac{7}{10}$

23. $\dfrac{1}{3} + \dfrac{1}{5}$

24. $\dfrac{2}{3} + \dfrac{1}{8}$

25. What is $\dfrac{1}{2}$ more than $\dfrac{2}{3}$?

26. What is the sum of $\dfrac{5}{6}$ and $\dfrac{5}{8}$?

27. Connie spent $\dfrac{3}{4}$ hour making the planter box and $\dfrac{1}{3}$ hour getting dirt and planting the seed. How much time did she spend?

28. List the data not needed. Then solve.

A plant is $3\dfrac{1}{4}$ inches tall. It grows $\dfrac{7}{8}$ inch in one week and $\dfrac{3}{4}$ inch the next. How much does it grow in two weeks?

Think

Discovering a Pattern

Give the next three fractions in each pattern.

1. $\dfrac{1}{2}, \dfrac{1}{4}, \dfrac{1}{8}, \dfrac{1}{16},$ ▓, ▓, ▓

2. $\dfrac{2}{4}, \dfrac{5}{4}, \dfrac{8}{4}, \dfrac{11}{4},$ ▓, ▓, ▓

3. $\dfrac{1}{2}, \dfrac{2}{3}, \dfrac{3}{4}, \dfrac{4}{5}, \dfrac{5}{6}, \dfrac{6}{7},$ ▓, ▓, ▓

Math

Subtracting Fractions: Unlike Denominators

Mindy had $\frac{7}{8}$ yard of material. She used $\frac{2}{3}$ yard to make a sleeveless blouse. How much material did she have left over?

Since some of the material is taken away from the original piece, we subtract.

Look at the denominators.		Find the least common denominator.		Write equivalent fractions with this denominator.		Subtract the fractions.

$\frac{7}{8}$ ⌐ Not the
$-\frac{2}{3}$ ⌐ same

Multiples of 8:
8, 16, 24

Multiples of 3:
3, 6, 9, 12,
15, 18, 21, 24

$\frac{7}{8} = \frac{21}{24}$

$-\frac{2}{3} = \frac{16}{24}$

$\frac{21}{24}$

$-\frac{16}{24}$

$\frac{5}{24}$

Mindy had $\frac{5}{24}$ yard of material left over.

Other Examples

$\frac{3}{4} = \frac{6}{8}$
$-\frac{3}{8} = \frac{3}{8}$
$\quad\quad \frac{3}{8}$

$\frac{7}{10} = \frac{7}{10}$
$-\frac{1}{2} = \frac{5}{10}$
$\quad\quad \frac{2}{10} = \frac{1}{5}$

$\frac{1}{3} = \frac{4}{12}$
$-\frac{1}{4} = \frac{3}{12}$
$\quad\quad \frac{1}{12}$

Warm Up Subtract.

1. $\frac{1}{3}$
$-\frac{1}{5}$

2. $\frac{3}{4}$
$-\frac{3}{8}$

3. $\frac{7}{8}$
$-\frac{5}{6}$

4. $\frac{4}{5}$
$-\frac{1}{10}$

5. $\frac{7}{10}$
$-\frac{39}{100}$

Subtract.

1. $\frac{2}{3}$
$-\frac{1}{2}$

2. $\frac{1}{2}$
$-\frac{1}{5}$

3. $\frac{3}{8}$
$-\frac{1}{4}$

4. $\frac{2}{3}$
$-\frac{1}{4}$

5. $\frac{1}{3}$
$-\frac{1}{12}$

6. $\frac{7}{10}$
$-\frac{1}{5}$

7. $\frac{7}{8}$
$-\frac{1}{2}$

8. $\frac{2}{3}$
$-\frac{1}{6}$

9. $\frac{3}{5}$
$-\frac{3}{10}$

10. $\frac{3}{8}$
$-\frac{1}{6}$

11. $\frac{9}{10}$
$-\frac{5}{6}$

12. $\frac{17}{100}$
$-\frac{1}{10}$

13. $\frac{7}{12}$
$-\frac{1}{4}$

14. $\frac{3}{4}$
$-\frac{1}{3}$

15. $\frac{15}{16}$
$-\frac{7}{8}$

16. $\frac{11}{12}$
$-\frac{3}{8}$

17. $\frac{19}{20}$
$-\frac{3}{4}$

18. $\frac{3}{4}$
$-\frac{5}{10}$

19. $\frac{9}{10}$
$-\frac{87}{100}$

20. $\frac{87}{100}$
$-\frac{3}{4}$

21. $\frac{3}{4} - \frac{2}{3}$

22. $\frac{1}{6} - \frac{1}{8}$

23. $\frac{4}{5} - \frac{3}{10}$

24. $\frac{83}{100} - \frac{7}{10}$

25. What is the difference of $\frac{3}{5}$ and $\frac{1}{3}$?

26. What is $\frac{4}{5}$ less than $\frac{7}{8}$?

27. Dave had $\frac{5}{6}$ yard of cloth. He used $\frac{3}{4}$ yard. How much did he have left?

28. Supply the additional data needed and solve the problem. Graciela bought some material. She used $\frac{1}{3}$ yd. How much was left over?

Think

Logical Reasoning

Complete this fraction Magic Square.

Each row, column, and diagonal must have the same sum.

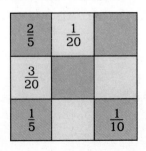

Math

Problem Solving:
Using Data from a Fact List

Facts About the Earth's Surface

$\frac{18}{25}$ of the surface is **water.**

The remaining part is **land.**

How much of the land can produce food?

$\frac{1}{50}$ is grassland. $\frac{1}{10}$ grows food crops.

$\frac{2}{10}$ might someday be useful.

$\frac{1}{5}$ is too mountainous.

$\frac{4}{25}$ is too cold.

$\frac{8}{25}$ has soil too dry or too poor.

1. What part of the earth's surface is land?
   Is this more than or less than $\frac{1}{3}$?

2. Is the part of the earth's surface that is covered by water more than or less than $\frac{3}{4}$? How much more or less?

3. What part of the land area is either grassland or grows food crops?

4. What part of the land area is too mountainous or has soil too dry or too poor?

5. What part of the land area is too mountainous or is too cold?

6. Which is greater, the amount of land area that might someday be useful or the amount of land area that is too cold? How much greater?

7. About 18,000 years ago, $\frac{3}{10}$ of the earth's land was covered by ice. How much more is this than the part that is now too cold to produce food?

8. The Sahara Desert covers about $\frac{3}{50}$ of the earth's land area. This is about the same as the part covered by the United States. How much less is this than the part that has soil too dry or too poor?

9. The Pacific Ocean covers about $\frac{1}{3}$ of the earth's surface. The Atlantic Ocean covers about $\frac{1}{6}$. What part of the earth's surface is covered by other bodies of water?

10. **Try This** A plane carrying 14 passengers is forced to land in a desert, and they need to walk for help. Each person can carry enough food and water for 3 days, but it will take 4 days to get help. What is the least number of people that would have to start out in order for one person to get help?

Problem Solving: Find a Pattern

To solve this problem you might first try the strategies Solve a Simpler Problem, Draw a Picture, and Make a Table. Then it might help to use a strategy called

Try This Each of 8 friends takes a "bicycle built for two" ride with everyone else. How many bike rides do they take?

FIND A PATTERN

Here's how!

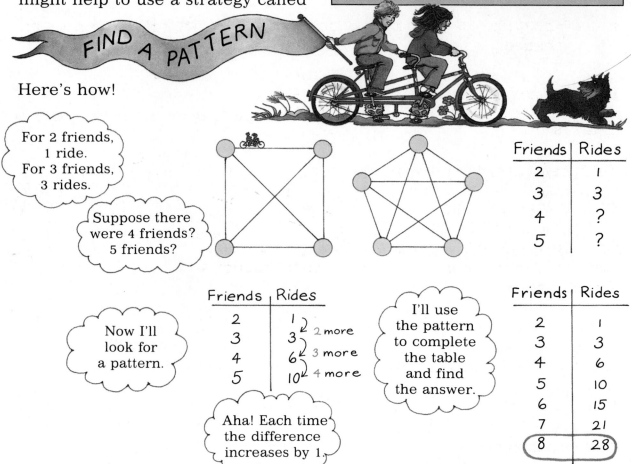

For 2 friends, 1 ride.
For 3 friends, 3 rides.

Suppose there were 4 friends? 5 friends?

Friends	Rides
2	1
3	3
4	?
5	?

Now I'll look for a pattern.

Friends	Rides
2	1
3	3
4	6
5	10

2 more
3 more
4 more

I'll use the pattern to complete the table and find the answer.

Friends	Rides
2	1
3	3
4	6
5	10
6	15
7	21
8	28

Aha! Each time the difference increases by 1.

For 8 friends there are 28 rides.

Solve.

1. Each of 8 friends says "Hello" to everyone else at a party. How many hellos are spoken? (Note: When 2 friends meet, there are 2 hellos.)

2. It takes 1 block to make 1 step, 3 blocks to make 2 steps, and so on. How many steps can be made with 36 blocks?

Chapter Review-Test

Write the fraction for each 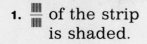.

 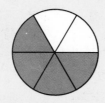 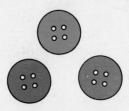

1. 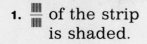 of the strip is shaded.

2. 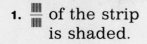 of the region is shaded.

3. 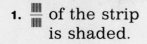 of the buttons are blue.

Find the missing numerators.

4. $\frac{3}{4} = \frac{\text{▦}}{8}$

5. $\frac{1}{3} = \frac{\text{▦}}{12}$

6. $\frac{3}{8} = \frac{\text{▦}}{24}$

7. $\frac{2}{5} = \frac{\text{▦}}{10}$

Find the next two equivalent fractions.

8. $\frac{1}{2}, \frac{\text{▦}}{\text{▦}}, \frac{\text{▦}}{\text{▦}}$

9. $\frac{2}{3}, \frac{\text{▦}}{\text{▦}}, \frac{\text{▦}}{\text{▦}}$

10. $\frac{1}{4}, \frac{\text{▦}}{\text{▦}}, \frac{\text{▦}}{\text{▦}}$

Give the greatest common factor of the numerator and the denominator. Then reduce each fraction to lowest terms.

11. $\frac{10}{15}$

12. $\frac{18}{24}$

13. $\frac{27}{36}$

14. $\frac{48}{60}$

Write >, <, or = for each ◖◗.

15. $\frac{3}{5} \, ◖◗ \, \frac{3}{4}$

16. $\frac{7}{16} \, ◖◗ \, \frac{3}{8}$

17. $\frac{6}{10} \, ◖◗ \, \frac{9}{15}$

Add or subtract.

18. $\frac{3}{5} + \frac{4}{5}$

19. $\frac{7}{10} + \frac{2}{10}$

20. $\frac{5}{6} - \frac{1}{6}$

21. $\frac{3}{8} - \frac{2}{8}$

22. $\frac{3}{4} + \frac{2}{3}$

23. $\frac{1}{5} + \frac{3}{8}$

24. $\frac{5}{6} - \frac{3}{4}$

25. $\frac{5}{8} - \frac{1}{6}$

Solve.

26. A carpenter used $\frac{3}{4}$ of a sheet of plywood for one project. Then he used $\frac{1}{2}$ of another sheet. How many sheets of plywood did he use?

27. About $\frac{1}{8}$ of the land area on earth is desert. About $\frac{1}{10}$ of the land area grows food crops. How much greater is the part that is desert?

Another Look

Equivalent Fractions

$$\frac{2}{3} \boxed{\begin{array}{c}\times 2\\=\\\times 2\end{array}} \frac{4}{6}$$

$$\frac{2}{3} \boxed{\begin{array}{c}\times 3\\=\\\times 3\end{array}} \frac{6}{9}$$

$$\frac{2}{3} \boxed{\begin{array}{c}\times 4\\=\\\times 4\end{array}} \frac{8}{12}$$

We find equivalent fractions by multiplying.

$$\frac{10}{15} \boxed{\begin{array}{c}\div 5\\=\\\div 5\end{array}} \frac{2}{3}$$

We **reduce** to **lowest terms** by dividing by the greatest common factor.

Comparing Fractions

$$\frac{3}{4} > \frac{5}{8} \qquad \frac{5}{8} < \frac{3}{4}$$

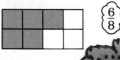

$$\left(\frac{6}{8}\right)$$

Adding (Subtracting) Fractions

$$\frac{3}{8} + \frac{5}{6}$$

8, 16, 24   6, 12, 18, 24

$$\frac{9}{24} + \frac{20}{24} = \frac{29}{24} = 1\frac{5}{24}$$

The least common denominator is 24.

Give the next three equivalent fractions.

1. $\frac{1}{4}$, ▦, ▦, ▦

2. $\frac{2}{5}$, ▦, ▦, ▦

Give the missing numerators.

3. $\frac{1}{12} = \frac{▦}{24}$

4. $\frac{5}{6} = \frac{▦}{18}$

5. $\frac{3}{8} = \frac{▦}{32}$

Reduce to lowest terms.

6. $\frac{20}{25}$

7. $\frac{12}{32}$

8. $\frac{8}{48}$

9. $\frac{27}{36}$

Write >, <, or = for each ▦.

10. $\frac{4}{5}$ ▦ $\frac{5}{8}$

11. $\frac{3}{4}$ ▦ $\frac{5}{6}$

12. $\frac{1}{3}$ ▦ $\frac{1}{2}$

13. $\frac{4}{6}$ ▦ $\frac{2}{3}$

14. $\frac{3}{5}$ ▦ $\frac{3}{4}$

15. $\frac{5}{5}$ ▦ $\frac{5}{8}$

16. $\frac{2}{6}$ ▦ $\frac{3}{8}$

17. $\frac{6}{8}$ ▦ $\frac{9}{16}$

Add or subtract.

18. $\frac{3}{10} + \frac{5}{10}$

19. $\frac{5}{8} - \frac{3}{8}$

20. $\frac{4}{5} - \frac{3}{10}$

21. $\frac{7}{8} + \frac{3}{4}$

22. $\frac{3}{4} + \frac{2}{5}$

23. $\frac{1}{3} + \frac{4}{5}$

24. $\frac{5}{6} - \frac{1}{8}$

25. $\frac{3}{8} - \frac{1}{5}$

Estimation of Area

On the graph paper below, the area of each small square ☐ is 1.

1. Match these fractions with the areas covered in squares A, B, C, and D:

   $\frac{1}{3}$ $\frac{1}{2}$ $\frac{1}{8}$ $\frac{4}{5}$

   Check your answers against the upside-down answers at the bottom of the page.

2. Estimate the area covered by the hand below.

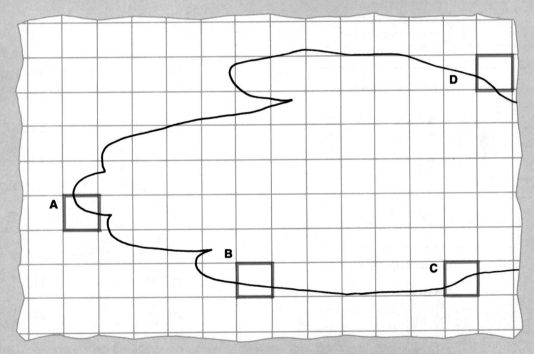

3. Trace the outline of one of your hands on centimeter graph paper. Estimate its area.

4. Trace the outline of the bottom of one of your shoes on graph paper. Estimate its area.

$\frac{4}{5}$B $\frac{1}{8}$D $\frac{1}{2}$C $\frac{1}{3}$A

Cumulative Review

Divide.

1. 7)91
  - **A** 14
  - **B** 13
  - **C** 12 R1
  - **D** none of these

2. 6)168
  - **A** 26
  - **B** 27
  - **C** 28
  - **D** none of these

3. 215 ÷ 3
  - **A** 73
  - **B** 75
  - **C** 71
  - **D** none of these

4. 4,032 ÷ 8
  - **A** 540
  - **B** 504
  - **C** 54
  - **D** none of these

5. 9)8,107
  - **A** 900 R7
  - **B** 900 R3
  - **C** 90 R7
  - **D** none of these

6. 8)5,784
  - **A** 724
  - **B** 723
  - **C** 732
  - **D** none of these

7. 3)2,396
  - **A** 789 R2
  - **B** 7098 R2
  - **C** 798 R6
  - **D** none of these

8. 10 cm is the same length as ▦ mm.
  - **A** 1000
  - **B** 10
  - **C** 100
  - **D** none of these

9. Find the perimeter.

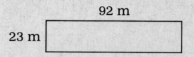

  - **A** 320 m
  - **B** 230 m
  - **C** 115 m
  - **D** none of these

10. Find the area.

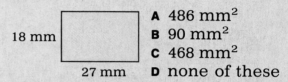

  - **A** 486 mm²
  - **B** 90 mm²
  - **C** 468 mm²
  - **D** none of these

11. Find the volume.

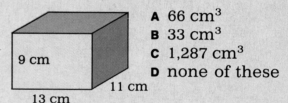

  - **A** 66 cm³
  - **B** 33 cm³
  - **C** 1,287 cm³
  - **D** none of these

12. 3,000 cm³ is the same as ▦ L.
  - **A** 10
  - **B** 3
  - **C** 30
  - **D** none of these

13. Kim jogged around a rectangular field 337 meters long and 225 meters wide. How far did she jog in 1 lap around the field?
  - **A** 1,124 m
  - **B** 925 m
  - **C** 562 m
  - **D** none of these

14. What is the volume of a box 9 cm by 8 cm by 7 cm?
  - **A** 405 cm³
  - **B** 504 cm³
  - **C** 540 cm³
  - **D** none of these

10
Larger Fractions

When Sarah opened the gift from her grandfather, she wondered what it was. It looked like a plain piece of paper with fancy printing on it. Her mother explained that it was a share of Safe-T-Skates Company stock. If the company earned enough money from its sales, the value of its stock would rise and Sarah's share would be worth more money. Sarah and her mother began to check the business pages of the newspaper every day to see if the value of Safe-T-Skates stock had gone up or down. One day, Sarah found in small print "Safe-T-Skates $+\frac{7}{8}$." The closing price was $32\frac{1}{2}$. The value of the share of stock then was $1\frac{1}{4}$ dollars more than it was when her grandfather gave it to her.

Adding and Subtracting Mixed Numbers

Jean estimated and then measured the capacity of two containers. What is the actual total capacity of the containers?

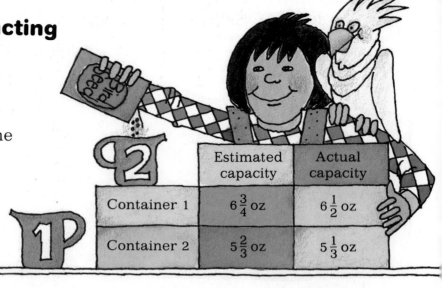

	Estimated capacity	Actual capacity
Container 1	$6\frac{3}{4}$ oz	$6\frac{1}{2}$ oz
Container 2	$5\frac{2}{3}$ oz	$5\frac{1}{3}$ oz

To find the total capacity, we add.

Look at the denominators.	Find equivalent fractions with a common denominator.	Add or subtract the fractions.	Add or subtract the whole numbers.

$6\frac{1}{2}$ ← Not the same

$+ 5\frac{1}{3}$ ←

$6\frac{1}{2} = 6\frac{3}{6}$

$+ 5\frac{1}{3} = 5\frac{2}{6}$

$6\frac{3}{6}$

$+ 5\frac{2}{6}$

$\frac{5}{6}$

$6\frac{3}{6}$

$+ 5\frac{3}{6}$

$11\frac{5}{6}$

The two containers can hold a total of $11\frac{5}{6}$ oz (ounces).

Other Examples

$6\frac{3}{4} = 6\frac{3}{4}$
$- 6\frac{1}{2} = 6\frac{2}{4}$
$\frac{1}{4}$

$26\frac{3}{5} = 26\frac{12}{20}$
$+ 15\frac{1}{4} = 15\frac{5}{20}$
$41\frac{17}{20}$

$37\frac{4}{5} = 37\frac{8}{10}$
$- 24\frac{1}{2} = 24\frac{5}{10}$
$13\frac{3}{10}$

$12\frac{3}{8}$
$+ 7\frac{1}{8}$
$19\frac{4}{8} = 19\frac{1}{2}$

Warm Up   Add or subtract. Reduce to lowest terms.

1. $8\frac{3}{8}$
   $+ 4\frac{1}{2}$

2. $3\frac{1}{8}$
   $+ 7\frac{3}{8}$

3. $11\frac{5}{6}$
   $- 4\frac{2}{3}$

4. $32\frac{3}{4}$
   $- 15\frac{1}{2}$

5. $42\frac{7}{10}$
   $- 12\frac{1}{5}$

Add or subtract. Reduce to lowest terms.

1. $3\frac{1}{5}$
$+\ 2\frac{3}{5}$

2. $8\frac{1}{6}$
$+\ 2$

3. $21\frac{7}{10}$
$+\ 19\frac{1}{5}$

4. $43\frac{3}{4}$
$+\ 34\frac{1}{5}$

5. $6\frac{1}{6}$
$+\ 8\frac{1}{3}$

6. $9\frac{2}{4}$
$-\ 3\frac{2}{8}$

7. $12\frac{7}{8}$
$-\ 3\frac{1}{8}$

8. $14\frac{5}{6}$
$-\ 11\frac{4}{6}$

9. $38\frac{7}{10}$
$-\ 24\frac{1}{2}$

10. $26\frac{4}{5}$
$-\ 12\frac{1}{2}$

11. $35\frac{2}{3}$
$+\ 1\frac{1}{12}$

12. $20\frac{1}{6}$
$+\ 40\frac{1}{4}$

13. $8\frac{3}{10}$
$+\ 62\frac{1}{4}$

14. $20\frac{5}{8}$
$-\ 14\frac{3}{16}$

15. $67\frac{5}{8}$
$-\ 14\frac{1}{3}$

16. $82\frac{2}{5}$
$+\ 34\frac{3}{8}$

17. $24\frac{2}{3}$
$-\ 13\frac{1}{6}$

18. $30\frac{1}{4}$
$+\ 41\frac{2}{5}$

19. $58\frac{1}{6}$
$+\ 69\frac{1}{5}$

20. $48\frac{7}{10}$
$-\ 14\frac{1}{2}$

21. $8\frac{1}{3} + 7\frac{1}{6}$

22. $14\frac{1}{8} + 16\frac{2}{5}$

23. $42\frac{1}{2} - 26\frac{1}{5}$

24. How much greater is $64\frac{2}{3}$ than $18\frac{3}{5}$?

25. Find the sum of $11\frac{2}{5}$ and $16\frac{1}{4}$.

26. Barry estimated that a small pail held $3\frac{3}{4}$ qt. He then measured and found that the actual amount it held was $3\frac{9}{10}$ qt. How much more or less was his estimate than the actual amount?

27. Art poured $4\frac{1}{4}$ qt of water into a fish bowl. He added another $\frac{1}{2}$ qt and then the bowl was full. How much water did it hold?

28. Make up a question for this story. Then find the answer.

Lisa estimated that a container could hold $5\frac{1}{3}$ qt of liquid. The actual amount it could hold was $\frac{1}{2}$ qt more than she had estimated.

Think

Discovering a Pattern

Find the pattern and complete the last four equations.

$1 \times 8 + 1 = 9$
$12 \times 8 + 2 = 98$
$123 \times 8 + 3 = 987$
$\text{▥} \times 8 + 4 = 9{,}876$
$\text{▥} \times 8 + \text{▥} = \text{▥}$
$\text{▥} \times 8 + \text{▥} = \text{▥}$
$\text{▥} \times 8 + \text{▥} = \text{▥}$

Math

Problem Solving: Using Estimation

You can estimate with mixed numbers by rounding each mixed number to the nearest whole number. Here are the rules for rounding fractions.

For the problems on this page, find the best estimate by rounding. Then find the exact answer.

Rules

- Round **down** if the fraction part is less than $\frac{1}{2}$. $5\frac{2}{5} \to 5$

- Round **up** if the fraction part is greater than or equal to $\frac{1}{2}$. $5\frac{3}{5} \to 6$

Example

Lisa jogged $4\frac{3}{4}$ miles on Saturday and $6\frac{1}{10}$ miles on Sunday. How far did she jog over the weekend?

- **A** 10 miles
- **B** 11 miles
- **C** 12 miles

Estimate:

$4\frac{3}{4}$ is about 5.

$6\frac{1}{10}$ is about 6.

$5 + 6 = 11$, so

B is the best estimate.

Exact:

$$4\frac{3}{4} = 4\frac{15}{20}$$
$$+ \ 6\frac{1}{10} = 6\frac{2}{20}$$
$$\overline{\phantom{+ \ 6\frac{1}{10} =}\ 10\frac{17}{20} \text{ miles}}$$

1. Earl jogs from home to school and back home. The school is $3\frac{1}{8}$ miles from his home. How far does he jog?

   A 6 miles   **B** 7 miles   **C** 8 miles

2. Jackie rode her bike $12\frac{1}{10}$ miles Friday and $22\frac{4}{5}$ miles Saturday. How far did she ride those two days?

   A 34 miles   **B** 35 miles   **C** 36 miles

3. Inga rides her bike $7\frac{5}{8}$ miles to her school. Her younger brother rides $4\frac{1}{2}$ miles to his school. How much farther does Inga ride?

   A 3 miles   **B** 4 miles   **C** 5 miles

4. Susan jogged $7\frac{1}{4}$ miles Monday and $9\frac{3}{5}$ miles Tuesday. How far did she jog in all on those days?

   A 15 miles   **B** 16 miles   **C** 17 miles

5. Dick jogged $8\frac{3}{4}$ laps around the track before school. He jogged $12\frac{7}{8}$ laps after school. How many more laps did he jog after school than before school?

   A 3   **B** 4   **C** 5

6. **Try This** On Monday there was 1 person jogging on the school track. On Tuesday 3 more people began jogging, for a total of 4. On Wednesday 5 more people began jogging, and on Thursday 7 more began. If the pattern continued, how many people were jogging on Sunday?

Renaming Mixed Numbers

When we add mixed numbers, we sometimes get a mixed number that needs to be renamed. We rename this mixed number when its fraction part is an improper fraction.

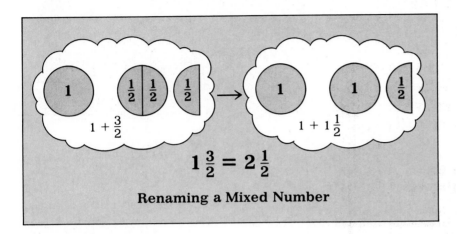

$$1\frac{3}{2} = 2\frac{1}{2}$$

Renaming a Mixed Number

Other Examples

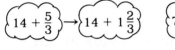 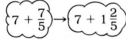 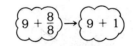

$$14\frac{5}{3} = 15\frac{2}{3} \qquad 7\frac{7}{5} = 8\frac{2}{5} \qquad 9\frac{8}{8} = 10$$

Rename each mixed number. Keep the denominator the same.

1. $4\frac{5}{3} = 5\frac{\text{▥}}{3}$ **2.** $6\frac{3}{2} = 7\frac{\text{▥}}{2}$ **3.** $9\frac{7}{4} = 10\frac{\text{▥}}{4}$

4. $7\frac{8}{5} = 8\frac{\text{▥}}{5}$ **5.** $12\frac{5}{3} = 13\frac{\text{▥}}{3}$ **6.** $3\frac{7}{6} = 4\frac{\text{▥}}{\text{▥}}$

7. $5\frac{14}{10} = 6\frac{\text{▥}}{\text{▥}}$ **8.** $8\frac{12}{8} = 9\frac{\text{▥}}{\text{▥}}$ **9.** $14\frac{6}{5} = 15\frac{\text{▥}}{\text{▥}}$

10. $23\frac{7}{4} = 24\frac{\text{▥}}{\text{▥}}$ **11.** $10\frac{7}{6}$ **12.** $26\frac{14}{8}$

13. $42\frac{15}{10}$ **14.** $16\frac{10}{6}$ **15.** $9\frac{5}{3}$

16. $42\frac{5}{4}$ **17.** $77\frac{7}{5}$ **18.** $92\frac{3}{2}$

19. $10\frac{12}{10}$ **20.** $99\frac{6}{4}$ **21.** $36\frac{4}{3}$

Adding Mixed Numbers: Renaming Sums

The Wealth of Health juice stand sold $1\frac{3}{4}$ cases of pineapple juice on Saturday and $2\frac{1}{2}$ cases on Sunday. How many cases of pineapple juice did the stand sell that weekend?

Since we want to find the total of two numbers, we add.

Look at the denominators.	→	Find equivalent fractions with a common denominator.	→	Add the fractions.	→	Add the whole numbers.

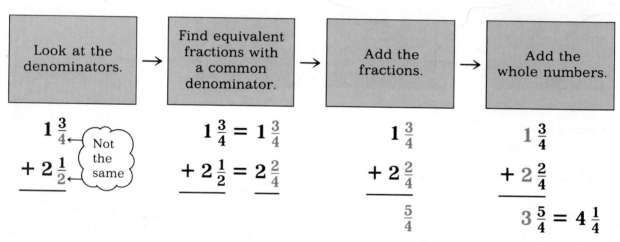

$1\frac{3}{4}$ ← Not the same

$+2\frac{1}{2}$ ← Not the same

$1\frac{3}{4} = 1\frac{3}{4}$

$+2\frac{1}{2} = 2\frac{2}{4}$

$1\frac{3}{4}$

$+2\frac{2}{4}$

$\frac{5}{4}$

$1\frac{3}{4}$

$+2\frac{2}{4}$

$3\frac{5}{4} = 4\frac{1}{4}$

That weekend $4\frac{1}{4}$ cases of pineapple juice were sold.

Other Examples

$5\frac{5}{8} = 5\frac{5}{8}$

$+2\frac{3}{4} = 2\frac{6}{8}$

$7\frac{11}{8} = 8\frac{3}{8}$

$32\frac{4}{5} = 32\frac{12}{15}$

$+17\frac{2}{3} = 17\frac{10}{15}$

$49\frac{22}{15} = 50\frac{7}{15}$

$7\frac{1}{2} = 7\frac{10}{20}$

$5\frac{4}{5} = 5\frac{16}{20}$

$+2\frac{3}{4} = 2\frac{15}{20}$

$14\frac{41}{20} = 16\frac{1}{20}$

Warm Up Add. Reduce the sums to lowest terms.

1. $4\frac{4}{5}$
   $+2\frac{3}{5}$

2. $5\frac{5}{6}$
   $+8\frac{1}{3}$

3. $9\frac{3}{4}$
   $+14\frac{5}{6}$

4. $34\frac{5}{6}$
   $+25\frac{4}{5}$

5. $8\frac{3}{4}$
   $5\frac{1}{3}$
   $+6\frac{1}{6}$

Add. Reduce the sums to lowest terms.

1. $3\frac{2}{3}$
$+ 6\frac{2}{3}$

2. $8\frac{5}{6}$
$+ 2\frac{4}{6}$

3. $11\frac{5}{7}$
$+ 7\frac{6}{7}$

4. $4\frac{7}{12}$
$+ 8\frac{5}{6}$

5. $19\frac{1}{2}$
$+ 2\frac{3}{4}$

6. $5\frac{5}{8}$
$+ 6\frac{3}{4}$

7. $3\frac{7}{10}$
$+ 5\frac{1}{2}$

8. $9\frac{2}{3}$
$+ 2\frac{5}{6}$

9. $11\frac{1}{2}$
$+ 12\frac{1}{2}$

10. $6\frac{5}{12}$
$+ 9\frac{5}{6}$

11. $67\frac{3}{5}$
$+ 27\frac{7}{20}$

12. $33\frac{7}{8}$
$+ 8\frac{1}{6}$

13. $41\frac{5}{6}$
$+ 25\frac{6}{7}$

14. $42\frac{7}{10}$
$+ 31\frac{41}{100}$

15. $46\frac{5}{6}$
$+ 64\frac{7}{8}$

16. $92\frac{3}{5}$
$88\frac{3}{5}$
$+ 9\frac{3}{5}$

17. $27\frac{1}{4}$
$46\frac{3}{4}$
$+ 50\frac{1}{2}$

18. $27\frac{1}{2}$
$18\frac{5}{8}$
$+ 12\frac{1}{4}$

19. $48\frac{1}{10}$
$65\frac{3}{5}$
$+ 74\frac{1}{2}$

20. $40\frac{4}{5}$
$23\frac{5}{6}$
$+ 8\frac{10}{15}$

21. Find the sum of $9\frac{4}{5}$ and $8\frac{7}{10}$.

22. Ned sold $1\frac{3}{4}$ cases of juice on Saturday. On Sunday he sold $2\frac{1}{3}$ cases. How many cases did he sell over the weekend?

23. Jill worked $4\frac{1}{2}$ hours Friday and $4\frac{1}{2}$ hours Saturday. Sunday she worked $2\frac{3}{4}$ hours. How long did she work these three days?

24. Make up the **missing data.** Then solve the problem.

Kimber worked at the stand $5\frac{1}{2}$ hours on Wednesday. Altogether how many hours did she work Wednesday and Thursday?

Skillkeeper

Divide.

1. $240 \div 60$
2. $3,500 \div 70$
3. $480 \div 80$
4. $6,300 \div 90$
5. $30\overline{)250}$
6. $40\overline{)325}$
7. $21\overline{)158}$
8. $51\overline{)426}$
9. $32\overline{)2,336}$
10. $83\overline{)3,290}$

Problem Solving: Practice

QUESTION
DATA
PLAN
ANSWER
CHECK

Solve.

1. A butcher mixed $2\frac{3}{4}$ pounds of lean meat and $\frac{2}{3}$ pounds of fatty meat to make some ground beef. What was the weight of the ground beef?

2. Ground beef sells for $1.89 per pound. The store sold 37 pounds of ground beef. How many dollars worth of ground beef were sold?

3. A steak weighed $2\frac{1}{2}$ pounds. After the fat was trimmed off, it weighed $2\frac{1}{4}$ pounds. What was the weight of the fat that was trimmed off?

4. Two chickens were packaged together for an order. One chicken weighed $2\frac{3}{4}$ pounds. The other weighed $2\frac{1}{2}$ pounds. What was the total weight of the order?

5. Grocery bags are packaged in bundles of 25. If a box contains 1,875 bags, how many bundles are in the box?

6. During one day, the store sold $249.60 worth of beef, $194.85 worth of poultry, and $110.25 worth of dairy products. How much more money was taken in for beef than for poultry?

7. **Try This** Mario ordered a sandwich and a drink at the grocery store lunch counter. He paid $2.25. What sandwich and drink combinations could Mario have ordered?

MENU

Sandwiches		Drinks	
Ham	$1.75	Large juice	$0.85
Roast beef	$1.85	Small juice	$0.60
Chicken	$1.50	Large milk	$0.75
Corned beef	$1.60	Small milk	$0.50

More Renaming Mixed Numbers

When we subtract mixed numbers, we often need to rename one of them by changing its fraction part to an improper fraction.

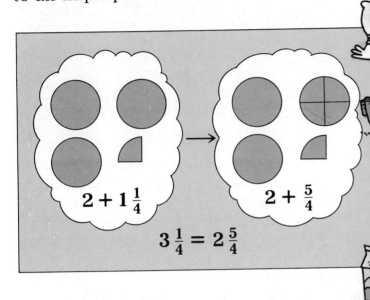

$2 + 1\frac{1}{4}$ → $2 + \frac{5}{4}$

$$3\frac{1}{4} = 2\frac{5}{4}$$

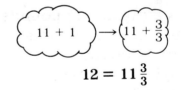

Other Examples

$6 + 1\frac{3}{4}$ → $6 + \frac{7}{4}$

$$7\frac{3}{4} = 6\frac{7}{4}$$

$4 + 1\frac{2}{5}$ → $4 + \frac{7}{5}$

$$5\frac{2}{5} = 4\frac{7}{5}$$

$11 + 1$ → $11 + \frac{3}{3}$

$$12 = 11\frac{3}{3}$$

Rename each mixed number.

1. $8\frac{1}{4} = 7\frac{\text{▓}}{4}$

2. $1\frac{2}{3} = \frac{\text{▓}}{3}$

3. $2\frac{4}{5} = 1\frac{\text{▓}}{5}$

4. $4\frac{1}{6} = 3\frac{\text{▓}}{6}$

5. $18\frac{5}{8} = 17\frac{\text{▓}}{8}$

6. $6\frac{2}{3} = 5\frac{\text{▓}}{3}$

7. $4\frac{3}{8} = 3\frac{\text{▓}}{8}$

8. $10 = 9\frac{\text{▓}}{6}$

9. $22\frac{1}{2} = 21\frac{\text{▓}}{2}$

10. $30\frac{3}{4} = 29\frac{\text{▓}}{4}$

11. $13\frac{3}{5} = \text{▓}\frac{\text{▓}}{5}$

12. $29 = \text{▓}\frac{\text{▓}}{6}$

13. $42\frac{1}{5} = \text{▓}\frac{\text{▓}}{5}$

14. $32\frac{1}{3} = \text{▓}\frac{\text{▓}}{3}$

15. $24\frac{1}{10} = \text{▓}\frac{\text{▓}}{10}$

16. $36\frac{3}{4} = \text{▓}\frac{\text{▓}}{4}$

17. $55\frac{5}{6} = \text{▓}\frac{\text{▓}}{6}$

18. $31\frac{7}{10} = \text{▓}\frac{\text{▓}}{10}$

19. $46 = 45\frac{\text{▓}}{8}$

20. $71 = 70\frac{\text{▓}}{4}$

Subtracting Mixed Numbers

A woman from East Germany set a new Olympic shot-put record in 1980 with a throw of 73 feet $6\frac{1}{4}$ inches. In 1977, a woman from Czechoslovakia held the world record of 73 feet $2\frac{3}{4}$ inches. How many inches farther was the new Olympic record?

Since we want to compare the distances, we should subtract.

Look at the denominators.	→	Rename if necessary.	→	Subtract the fractions.	→	Subtract the whole numbers.

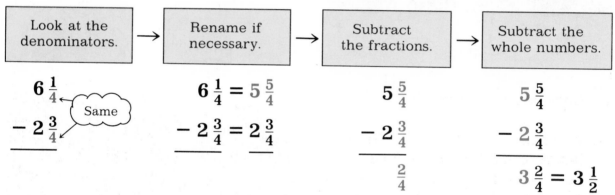

$$6\frac{1}{4}$$
$$-2\frac{3}{4}$$
Same

$$6\frac{1}{4} = 5\frac{5}{4}$$
$$-2\frac{3}{4} = 2\frac{3}{4}$$

$$5\frac{5}{4}$$
$$-2\frac{3}{4}$$
$$\frac{2}{4}$$

$$5\frac{5}{4}$$
$$-2\frac{3}{4}$$
$$3\frac{2}{4} = 3\frac{1}{2}$$

The new Olympic record was $3\frac{1}{2}$ inches farther.

Other Examples

$$8\frac{5}{8} = 7\frac{13}{8}$$
$$-4\frac{7}{8} = 4\frac{7}{8}$$
$$3\frac{6}{8} = 3\frac{3}{4}$$

$$14 = 13\frac{3}{3}$$
$$-12\frac{2}{3} = 12\frac{2}{3}$$
$$1\frac{1}{3}$$

$$80\frac{1}{5} = 79\frac{6}{5}$$
$$-42\frac{3}{5} = 42\frac{3}{5}$$
$$37\frac{3}{5}$$

Warm Up   Subtract. Reduce answers to lowest terms.

1. $6\frac{1}{3}$
   $-3\frac{2}{3}$

2. $11\frac{3}{5}$
   -6

3. 11
   $-6\frac{3}{5}$

4. $23\frac{7}{10}$
   $-4\frac{9}{10}$

5. $170\frac{1}{6}$
   $-95\frac{5}{6}$

Subtract. Reduce answers to lowest terms.

1. $5\frac{1}{5}$
$-\ 2\frac{3}{5}$

2. $7\frac{5}{6}$
$-\ 4\frac{5}{6}$

3. $9\frac{2}{3}$
$-\ 8\frac{1}{3}$

4. 6
$-\ 3\frac{3}{4}$

5. $10\frac{3}{5}$
$-\ 4$

6. $8\frac{3}{8}$
$-\ 2\frac{7}{8}$

7. 4
$-\ 2\frac{4}{5}$

8. $11\frac{7}{10}$
$-\ 5\frac{4}{10}$

9. $24\frac{3}{4}$
$-\ 14\frac{3}{4}$

10. $33\frac{5}{6}$
$-\ 3\frac{1}{6}$

11. $67\frac{2}{5}$
$-\ 45\frac{3}{5}$

12. $54\frac{3}{4}$
$-\ 26$

13. $75\frac{3}{8}$
$-\ 6\frac{5}{8}$

14. $40\frac{3}{10}$
$-\ 20\frac{7}{10}$

15. $124\frac{4}{6}$
$-\ 31\frac{1}{6}$

16. $44\frac{2}{4}$
$-\ 33\frac{3}{4}$

17. $25\frac{3}{5}$
$-\ 15\frac{4}{5}$

18. 74
$-\ 63\frac{1}{3}$

19. $87\frac{4}{7}$
$-\ 46$

20. $42\frac{5}{8}$
$-\ 21\frac{7}{8}$

21. Subtract $18\frac{2}{5}$ from $32\frac{4}{5}$.

22. A school record for the high jump was 6 feet $5\frac{2}{4}$ inches. A new record was set at 6 feet $7\frac{1}{4}$ inches. How many inches higher was the new record?

23. Sara Simeoni, from Italy, set a world high jump record in 1978 with a jump of 6 feet 7 inches. She set a new Olympic record in 1980 of 6 feet $5\frac{1}{2}$ inches. How many inches higher was her world record?

24. DATA BANK In a recent school track meet, Greg Sloan set a new pole vault record. How much less than the old record height were the jumps made by Coe, Chin, and Ould? (See Data Bank page 409.)

Think

Logical Reasoning

Complete this magic square.

The numbers in each row, column, and diagonal must have the same sum.

$1\frac{3}{4}$	0	$1\frac{1}{4}$
$\frac{3}{4}$		$\frac{1}{4}$

Math

More Subtracting Mixed Numbers

A flight from New York to Los Angeles lasts $5\frac{1}{2}$ hours.
A flight from Chicago to Los Angeles lasts $3\frac{3}{4}$ hours.
How much longer is the flight from New York than the
flight from Chicago?

We subtract since we want to compare flight times.

Look at the denominators.	Find equivalent fractions with a common denominator.	Rename if necessary. Subtract the fraction.	Subtract the whole number.

$$5\frac{1}{2} \quad \text{Not the same}$$
$$-\,3\frac{3}{4}$$

$$5\frac{1}{2} = 5\frac{2}{4}$$
$$-\,3\frac{3}{4} = 3\frac{3}{4}$$

$$5\frac{2}{4} = 4\frac{6}{4}$$
$$-\,3\frac{3}{4} = 3\frac{3}{4}$$
$$\frac{3}{4}$$

$$4\frac{6}{4}$$
$$-\,3\frac{3}{4}$$
$$1\frac{3}{4}$$

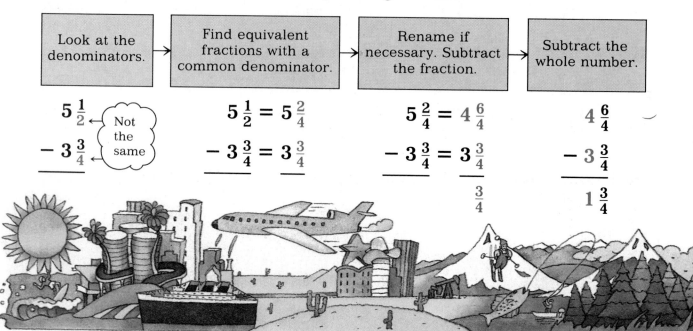

The flight from New York is $1\frac{3}{4}$ hours longer.

Other Examples

$$28\frac{3}{4} = 28\frac{6}{8} = 27\frac{14}{8}$$
$$-\,13\frac{7}{8} = 13\frac{7}{8} = 13\frac{7}{8}$$
$$14\frac{7}{8}$$

$$12\frac{1}{3} = 12\frac{2}{6} = 11\frac{8}{6}$$
$$-\,9\frac{5}{6} = 9\frac{5}{6} = 9\frac{5}{6}$$
$$2\frac{3}{6} = 2\frac{1}{2}$$

$$14 \quad\;\; = 13\frac{10}{10}$$
$$-\,3\frac{3}{10} = \;\; 3\frac{3}{10}$$
$$10\frac{7}{10}$$

Warm Up Subtract. Reduce answers to lowest terms.

1. $9\frac{2}{3}$
   $-\,6\frac{5}{6}$

2. $7\frac{2}{5}$
   $-\,3\frac{7}{10}$

3. $11\frac{3}{4}$
   $-\,5\frac{3}{8}$

4. 16
   $-\,4\frac{1}{3}$

5. $23\frac{1}{6}$
   $-\,9\frac{5}{12}$

Subtract. Reduce answers to lowest terms.

1. $6\frac{1}{5}$
$-\,3\frac{5}{10}$

2. $8\frac{1}{4}$
$-\,3\frac{3}{4}$

3. $10\frac{1}{3}$
$-\,4\frac{2}{3}$

4. 22
$-\,9\frac{5}{8}$

5. $32\frac{1}{6}$
$-\,10\frac{5}{12}$

6. $47\frac{5}{8}$
$-\,11\frac{1}{4}$

7. $41\frac{1}{2}$
$-\,27\frac{1}{10}$

8. $86\frac{1}{3}$
$-\,38\frac{3}{4}$

9. $60\frac{1}{6}$
$-\,7\frac{4}{5}$

10. $52\frac{3}{8}$
$-\,27\frac{4}{5}$

11. $93\frac{4}{10}$
$-\,23$

12. $73\frac{5}{6}$
$-\,26\frac{7}{8}$

13. $68\frac{3}{4}$
$-\,37\frac{9}{10}$

14. $62\frac{1}{5}$
$-\,30\frac{1}{3}$

15. 24
$-\,7\frac{3}{8}$

16. Find the difference between $16\frac{4}{5}$ and $26\frac{1}{10}$.

17. Subtract $47\frac{2}{3}$ from $67\frac{2}{5}$.

18. The flying time from St. Louis to Kansas City is $\frac{3}{4}$ hour. The driving time is $5\frac{1}{4}$ hours. How much less time does it take to go by plane?

19. A jet plane takes $1\frac{3}{4}$ hours to fly from Pittsburgh to Atlanta. A propeller-driven plane takes $2\frac{1}{2}$ hours. How many **minutes** shorter is the jet trip?

20. DATA HUNT Find the driving time and the flying time (to the nearest quarter of an hour) between a city near your home and another city. How much faster is the flight than the drive?

Adding and Subtracting Mixed Numbers, Whole Numbers, and Fractions

Holly likes to walk for exercise. Last week she took her exercise walks on 3 days. On Monday she walked $4\frac{1}{2}$ miles, and on Wednesday she walked 3 miles. On Friday she only walked $1\frac{3}{4}$ miles. How far did Holly walk last week?

Since we want the total distance, we add.

Look at the denominators.	→	Find equivalent fractions with a common denominator.	→	Add or subtract the fractions.	→	Add or subtract the whole numbers.

$$4\frac{1}{2} \quad \text{Not the same}$$
$$3$$
$$+\,1\frac{3}{4}$$

$$4\frac{1}{2} = 4\frac{2}{4}$$
$$3\ \ = 3$$
$$+\,1\frac{3}{4} = 1\frac{3}{4}$$

$$4\frac{2}{4}$$
$$3$$
$$+\,1\frac{3}{4}$$
$$\overline{\frac{5}{4}}$$

$$4\frac{2}{4}$$
$$3$$
$$+\,1\frac{3}{4}$$
$$\overline{8\frac{5}{4} = 9\frac{1}{4}}$$

Holly walked $9\frac{1}{4}$ miles last week.

Other Examples

$$6\frac{3}{4}$$
$$-\,3$$
$$\overline{3\frac{3}{4}}$$

$$\frac{5}{6} = \frac{25}{30}$$
$$+\,3\frac{1}{5} = 3\frac{6}{30}$$
$$\overline{3\frac{31}{30} = 4\frac{1}{30}}$$

$$8\ \ = 7\frac{3}{3}$$
$$-\,4\frac{2}{3} = 4\frac{2}{3}$$
$$\overline{3\frac{1}{3}}$$

$$16\ \ = 15\frac{5}{5}$$
$$-\ \ \frac{4}{5} = \ \ \frac{4}{5}$$
$$\overline{15\frac{1}{5}}$$

Warm Up Add or subtract. Reduce answers to lowest terms.

1. $\frac{3}{4}$
    $+\,6\frac{5}{8}$

2. 23
    $-\,4\frac{7}{10}$

3. $30\frac{4}{5}$
    $-\,12\frac{5}{6}$

4. $9\frac{3}{5}$
    $+\ \ \frac{9}{10}$

5. $12\frac{1}{2}$
    $\frac{1}{4}$
    $+\ \ \frac{7}{8}$

Add or subtract. Reduce answers to lowest terms.

1. $9\frac{1}{3}$
$+\ 4\frac{1}{6}$

2. $6\frac{7}{8}$
$-\ \ \frac{2}{4}$

3. 12
$-\ 7\frac{1}{5}$

4. $14\frac{2}{5}$
$+\ \ 8$

5. $26\frac{5}{6}$
$+\ 14\frac{1}{6}$

6. $32\frac{1}{3}$
$-\ 16\frac{5}{15}$

7. 62
$+\ 34\frac{4}{12}$

8. $\frac{9}{12}$
$+\ \ \frac{3}{8}$

9. 48
$-\ 31\frac{7}{10}$

10. 28
$-\ \ 2\frac{5}{8}$

11. $37\frac{2}{3}$
$+\ 68\frac{3}{5}$

12. $\frac{21}{4}$
$+\ \ \frac{55}{8}$

13. $\frac{13}{8} - \frac{2}{3}$

14. $26\frac{4}{8} + 4 + \frac{3}{5}$

15. $73 - 6\frac{3}{8}$

16. $13\frac{4}{5} + 20\frac{2}{3} + 10$

17. Find the sum of $42\frac{6}{8}$ and $24\frac{6}{12}$.

18. Find the difference of $38\frac{2}{3}$ and $27\frac{5}{6}$.

19. Linda wants to walk 14 miles each week. The first six days of the week she walked a total of $11\frac{1}{4}$ miles. How many miles does she need to walk the seventh day?

20. On Monday Alberto walked 4 miles. On Tuesday he walked $\frac{3}{4}$ mile farther than he walked on Monday. What was the total distance Alberto walked on Monday and Tuesday?

Problem Solving:
Using Data from an Advertisement

SEWING CENTER FABRIC SALE

PATIO PRINT $1\frac{1}{4}$-yard pieces	$3.70	**BLUE DENIM** $\frac{3}{4}$-yard pieces	$4.00
VELVET $1\frac{5}{8}$-yard pieces	$12.95	**SATIN** $\frac{7}{8}$-yard pieces	$2.80
BALL FRINGE 2-yard pieces	$1.80	**RUFFLED LACE** 3-yard pieces	$4.11
PLAID $2\frac{1}{2}$-yard pieces	$8.65	**CANVAS** $2\frac{3}{4}$-yard pieces	$13.50

LAST TWO DAYS

Use the data in the advertisement to help you solve the problems.

1. Mrs. Tenney bought 2 of the $1\frac{5}{8}$-yard velvet pieces. How many yards of material did she buy?

2. Tracey wants to make 2 pillow covers. She needs $\frac{3}{4}$ of a yard for one cover and $\frac{3}{8}$ of a yard for the other. Can she make both covers from one patio print piece?

3. Kristy wants to buy 3 of the $\frac{7}{8}$-yard satin pieces. How much will they cost?

4. Mr. Ishida needs $1\frac{5}{8}$ yards of plaid. If he buys 1 of the plaid pieces, how much extra material will he have?

5. Tanya needed only $\frac{3}{4}$ yard of the ball fringe, but she bought a whole piece of the fringe. How much more ball fringe than she needed did she buy?

6. Rose needs $2\frac{11}{16}$ yards of canvas for a yard chair. Must she buy more than 1 piece of canvas?

7. Jack bought 1 piece of patio print, 1 piece of plaid, and 1 piece of blue denim. How much did he spend?

8. Curt bought 1 piece of plaid. He gave the clerk a $20 bill. How much change should the clerk give him?

9. Leslie is covering some small pillows with velvet. She needs $\frac{3}{4}$ yard for one pillow, $\frac{1}{2}$ yard for another, and $\frac{1}{3}$ yard for another. If she buys 1 piece of velvet, will she have enough to cover all three pillows?

10. Denine needed 8-inch lengths of ruffled lace. How many 8-inch lengths could she cut from 1 piece of the lace? (Remember: 1 yard = 36 inches)

11. Try This The Sewing Center had 7 sewing classes last month. Just 1 person attended the first class, but 3 attended the second, and 6 attended the third. If this pattern continued, how many people attended the last class?

Problem Solving: Using the Strategies

Use one or more of the **strategies** listed to solve each problem below.

CHOOSE THE OPERATIONS

GUESS AND CHECK

DRAW A PICTURE

MAKE A TABLE

MAKE AN ORGANIZED LIST

USE LOGICAL REASONING

WORK BACKWARD

SOLVE A SIMPLER PROBLEM

FIND A PATTERN

1. A basketball team played 25 games. They won 3 more games than they lost. How many games did they win?

2. There are 3 classroom jobs to be done: cleaning erasers, passing out books, and collecting papers. Carmen, Jodi, and Jeremy volunteer. The teacher wants to assign one job to each of the three students. How many different ways can the teacher assign the jobs?

3. Pete and Ernie started reading their books on the same day. Pete read 6 pages a day and Ernie read 4 pages a day. How many more pages had Pete read than Ernie after 6 days?

4. A train can hold 100 people. One person gets on at the first stop, 2 get on at the second stop, 4 get on at the third stop, and so on. If this pattern continues (and no one gets off the train), after what stop will the train be full?

Chapter Review-Test

Add or subtract. Reduce answers to lowest terms.

1. $5\frac{1}{5}$
$+ 2\frac{2}{5}$

2. $6\frac{3}{4}$
$- 3\frac{1}{4}$

3. $9\frac{3}{8}$
$+ 6\frac{1}{2}$

4. $12\frac{4}{5}$
$- 7\frac{3}{10}$

5. $8\frac{1}{4}$
$+ 5\frac{2}{3}$

Give the missing numerators to complete the renaming.

6. $6\frac{5}{3} = 7\frac{\text{||||}}{3}$

7. $5\frac{3}{2} = 6\frac{\text{||||}}{2}$

8. $12\frac{9}{8} = 13\frac{\text{||||}}{8}$

9. $24\frac{7}{4} = 25\frac{\text{||||}}{4}$

Add. Reduce answers to lowest terms.

10. $7\frac{1}{6}$
$+ 3\frac{2}{6}$

11. $5\frac{3}{4}$
$+ 4\frac{3}{8}$

12. $12\frac{1}{2}$
$+ 23\frac{1}{3}$

13. $42\frac{4}{5}$
$+ 21\frac{2}{3}$

14. $64\frac{5}{6}$
$+ 17\frac{1}{4}$

Give the missing numerators to complete the renaming.

15. $24\frac{3}{4} = 23\frac{\text{||||}}{4}$

16. $9\frac{1}{3} = 8\frac{\text{||||}}{3}$

17. $15\frac{4}{5} = 14\frac{\text{||||}}{5}$

18. $33 = 32\frac{\text{||||}}{8}$

Subtract. Reduce answers to lowest terms.

19. $9\frac{4}{5}$
$- 2\frac{3}{5}$

20. $7\frac{2}{3}$
$- 6\frac{1}{6}$

21. $28\frac{3}{4}$
$- 16\frac{2}{5}$

22. $83\frac{1}{3}$
$- 63\frac{2}{3}$

23. $74\frac{1}{4}$
$- 24\frac{5}{6}$

Add or subtract. Reduce answers to lowest terms.

24. $6 - 3\frac{2}{5}$

25. $12\frac{5}{6} - \frac{3}{5}$

26. $\frac{9}{5} + 2\frac{1}{5}$

27. $\frac{4}{3} + \frac{4}{4}$

Solve.

28. On her first try Natalie long-jumped 16 feet $4\frac{1}{2}$ inches. On her second try she jumped 16 feet $8\frac{1}{4}$ inches. How much longer was the second jump?

29. Larry rode his bike $12\frac{1}{2}$ miles. Then he had a flat tire and had to walk $6\frac{3}{4}$ miles. How far did he travel in all?

Another Look

Adding or subtracting

$$5\frac{3}{5} = 5\frac{9}{15}$$

Find the common denominator. $\frac{3}{5} = \frac{9}{15}$

$$-2\frac{4}{15} = 2\frac{4}{15}$$

$$3\frac{5}{15} = 3\frac{1}{3}$$

Reduce to lowest terms. $\frac{5}{15} = \frac{1}{3}$

Renaming after adding

$$12\frac{2}{3}$$

$$+\ 7\frac{2}{3}$$

$$19\frac{4}{3} = 20\frac{1}{3}$$ $19 + \frac{4}{3}$ or $19 + 1\frac{1}{3}$

Renaming before subtracting

$8 + 1\frac{1}{4}$ or $8 + \frac{5}{4}$

$$9\frac{1}{4} = 8\frac{5}{4}$$

$$-2\frac{3}{4} = 2\frac{3}{4}$$

$$6\frac{2}{4} = 6\frac{1}{2}$$

Reduce

Add or subtract. Reduce to lowest terms.

1. $6\frac{1}{2}$
$+\ 2\frac{1}{3}$

2. $5\frac{1}{4}$
$+\ 6\frac{1}{2}$

3. $9\frac{2}{3}$
$-\ 3\frac{1}{6}$

4. $8\frac{4}{5}$
$-\ 1\frac{1}{5}$

5. $12\frac{3}{8}$
$+\ 14\frac{1}{4}$

6. $14\frac{5}{6}$
$-\ 5\frac{3}{8}$

Add. Rename the sums.

7. $7\frac{3}{4}$
$+\ 7\frac{3}{4}$

8. $6\frac{2}{3}$
$+\ 5\frac{5}{6}$

9. $8\frac{7}{10}$
$+\ 9\frac{4}{5}$

10. $15\frac{3}{8}$
$+\ 17\frac{5}{8}$

11. $21\frac{1}{6}$
$+\ 12\frac{4}{6}$

12. $14\frac{3}{4}$
$+\ 15\frac{5}{6}$

Rename and subtract.

13. $4\frac{3}{5}$
$-\ 2\frac{4}{5}$

14. $8\frac{3}{10}$
$-\ 6\frac{7}{10}$

15. $10\frac{3}{8}$
$-\ 9\frac{5}{8}$

16. $14\frac{2}{5}$
$-\ \frac{4}{5}$

17. 12
$-\ 4\frac{5}{6}$

18. $33\frac{1}{8}$
$-\ 23\frac{3}{8}$

Add or subtract.

19. $5\frac{1}{4}$
$-\ 3\frac{1}{2}$

20. $11\frac{3}{8}$
$+\ 16\frac{3}{4}$

21. $24\frac{1}{8}$
$-\ \frac{3}{4}$

Enrichment

Logical Reasoning

Find the missing numbers.

1.
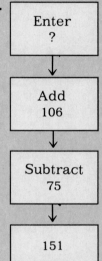

Enter ?
→ Add 106
→ Subtract 75
→ 151

2.
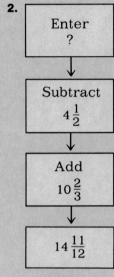

Enter ?
→ Subtract $4\frac{1}{2}$
→ Add $10\frac{2}{3}$
→ $14\frac{11}{12}$

3.
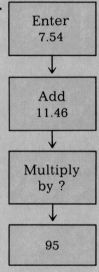

Enter 7.54
→ Add 11.46
→ Multiply by ?
→ 95

4.
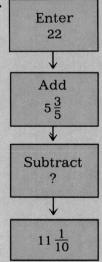

Enter 22
→ Add $5\frac{3}{5}$
→ Subtract ?
→ $11\frac{1}{10}$

5.
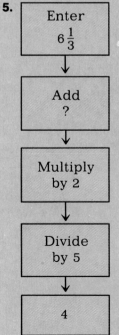

Enter $6\frac{1}{3}$
→ Add ?
→ Multiply by 2
→ Divide by 5
→ 4

6.
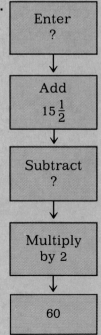

Enter ?
→ Add $15\frac{1}{2}$
→ Subtract ?
→ Multiply by 2
→ 60

Cumulative Review

Divide.

1. $630 \div 90$
A 80
B 7
C 70
D not given

2. $80\overline{)240}$
A 30
B 4
C 40
D not given

Divide and check.

3. $40\overline{)182}$
A 40 R2
B 4 R22
C 40 R22
D not given

4. $73\overline{)223}$
A 3 R4
B 30 R4
C 30 R3
D not given

5. $35\overline{)1439}$
A 41 R4
B 31 R4
C 41 R3
D not given

6. $68\overline{)20,558}$
A 302 R28
B 303 R22
C 302 R22
D not given

7. $43\overline{)\$139.32}$
A $3.23
B $3.24
C $3.32
D not given

Which signs should go in the ●?

8. $\frac{5}{8}$ ● $\frac{10}{16}$
A $>$ B $<$ C $=$

9. $\frac{4}{5}$ ● $\frac{2}{3}$
A $>$ B $<$ C $=$

10. $\frac{5}{7}$ ● $\frac{3}{4}$
A $>$ B $<$ C $=$

Add or subtract.

11. $\frac{5}{8} + \frac{2}{8}$
A $\frac{3}{8}$ B $\frac{7}{8}$ C $\frac{6}{8}$ D not given

12. $\frac{9}{10} - \frac{3}{5}$
A $\frac{6}{15}$ B $\frac{3}{10}$ C $\frac{6}{10}$ D not given

13. Tony ate $\frac{3}{8}$ of a melon and Luis ate $\frac{1}{4}$ of the melon. What fraction of the melon did they eat altogether?
A $\frac{1}{8}$ B $\frac{4}{12}$ C $\frac{5}{8}$ D not given

14. Nelda wanted $\frac{1}{3}$ cup of milk for her cereal. She had only $\frac{1}{6}$ cup. How much more milk did she need?
A $\frac{3}{6}$ B $\frac{1}{6}$ C $\frac{1}{9}$ D not given

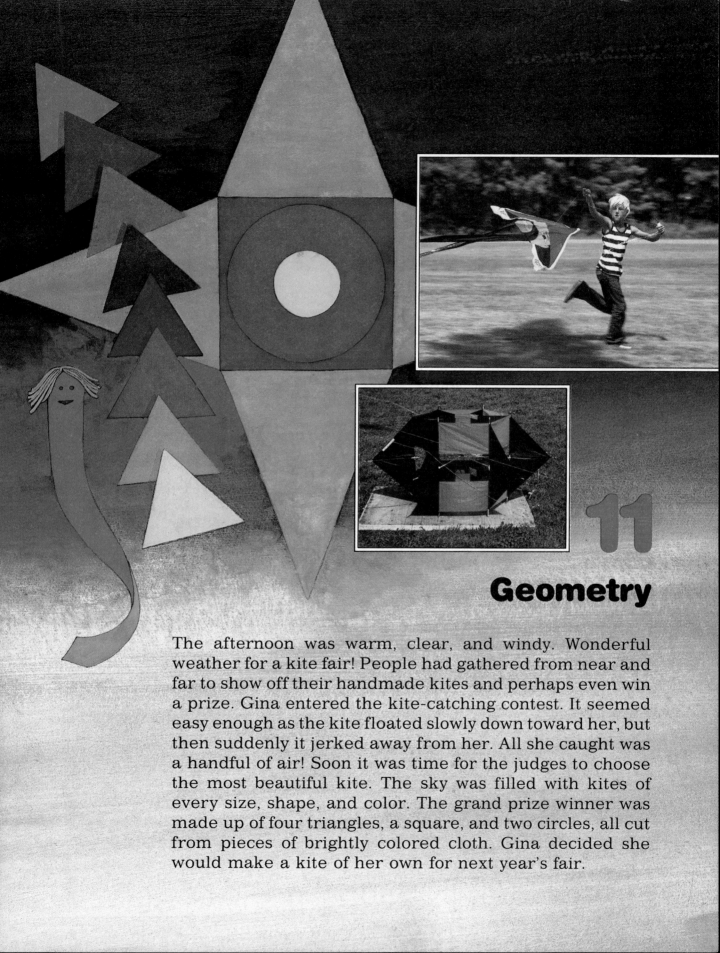

11

Geometry

The afternoon was warm, clear, and windy. Wonderful weather for a kite fair! People had gathered from near and far to show off their handmade kites and perhaps even win a prize. Gina entered the kite-catching contest. It seemed easy enough as the kite floated slowly down toward her, but then suddenly it jerked away from her. All she caught was a handful of air! Soon it was time for the judges to choose the most beautiful kite. The sky was filled with kites of every size, shape, and color. The grand prize winner was made up of four triangles, a square, and two circles, all cut from pieces of brightly colored cloth. Gina decided she would make a kite of her own for next year's fair.

Points, Lines, and Segments

Leon's photography club had a photo contest. Prizes were given for the best pictures of "Geometry in Our World." Some of the photos are used below to suggest some basic geometric ideas.

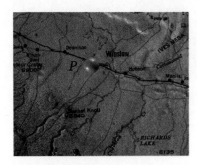

A pin showing a location on a map suggests a **point.**
We write: P
We say: "point P"

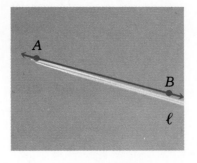

The trail of a jet plane, which seems unending in both directions, suggests a **line.**
We write: $\overleftrightarrow{AB}$ or ℓ
We say: "line AB" or "line ℓ"

The edge of a box suggests a part of a line called a **segment.**
We write: $\overline{AB}$
We say: "segment AB"

The diagonal boards on a fence suggest **intersecting lines.**
We write: ℓ intersects m
We say: "Line ℓ intersects line m."

The railroad tracks suggest **parallel lines.**
We write: $j \parallel k$
We say: "Line j is parallel to line k."

The two strings that form square corners suggest **perpendicular lines.**
We write: $r \perp s$
We say: "Line r is perpendicular to line s."

Write the name for each figure.

1. 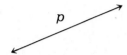 $\cdot A$

2.  P Q

3. X ————————— Y

4.  p

5. 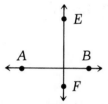 N M

6. 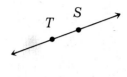 T S

Use ∥, ⊥, or **intersects** to write a statement about each pair of lines.

Example:
R S
C D

$\overleftrightarrow{RS} \parallel \overleftrightarrow{CD}$

7.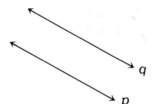
E
A B
F

8.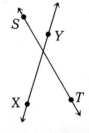
q
p

9.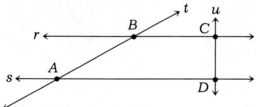
S Y
X T

Use the figure below for exercises 10–12.

t u
r B C
s A D

10. Name a pair of parallel lines.

11. Name a pair of perpendicular lines.

12. Name the point where line r intersects line u.

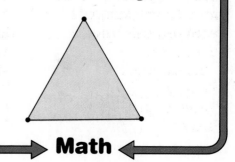

Think

Guess and Check

Can you arrange 7 dots so that you can draw straight lines through 6 different sets of 3 dots? Hint: Start with 3 dots at the corners of a triangle.

Math

Rays and Angles

This picture of a bicycle suggests several important geometric ideas. The beam of the bike light suggests a **ray**. A ray is a part of a line and has only one end point.

We write: $\overrightarrow{PQ}$

We say: "ray PQ"

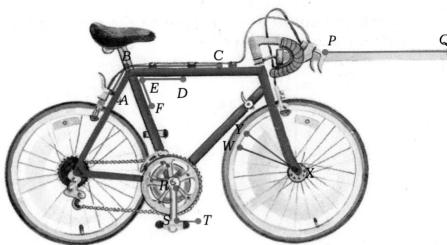

An **angle** is two rays with the same end point.

We write: $\angle ABC$ (or $\angle CBA$ or $\angle B$)

We say: "angle ABC"

B is called the **vertex** of the angle. $\overrightarrow{BA}$ and $\overrightarrow{BC}$ are **sides** of the angle.

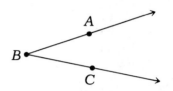

Here are three special kinds of angles.

A right angle

An **acute angle** is less than a right angle.

An **obtuse angle** is greater than a right angle.

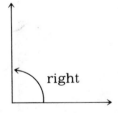

right

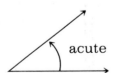

acute

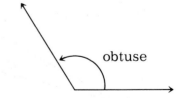

obtuse

Name an example of each of these kinds of angles in the picture at the top of the page.

1. right angle   **2.** acute angle   **3.** obtuse angle

274

Name the angle in each picture. Then tell if the angle is
right, **acute**, or **obtuse.**

1.

2.

3.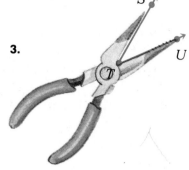

4.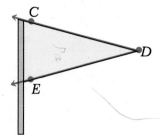

5.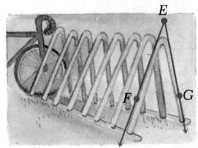

6.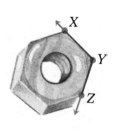

7. Give three different names for this angle.

8. What is the vertex of the angle?

9. Name two sides of the angle.

10. Do you think the angle is acute, right, or obtuse? (Use a square corner to check.)

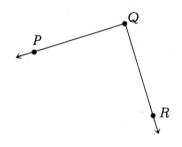

★ 11. Name 6 different angles in this figure.

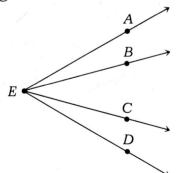

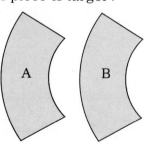
275

Measuring Angles

To find out how much
the wind would slow down
an airplane, an airplane
designer might want to
know the measure of
these angles.

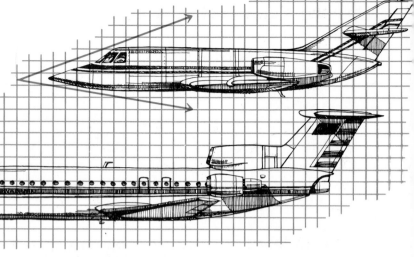

The basic unit of angle measure is a **degree.**
We can use a **protractor** to find angle measures.
The protractor below is marked with 180 degree
units. What is the measure of ∠*BAC*?

1 degree (1°)

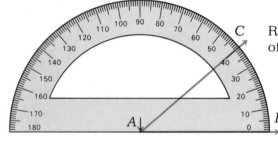

Read the measure
of the angle.

Place the zero edge
on one side of the angle.

Place the arrow on the vertex of the angle.

The measure of ∠*BAC* is 40°.

Give the measure of these angles.

1.

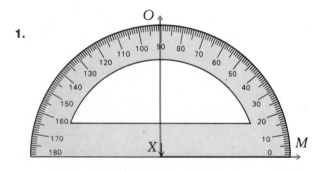

2.

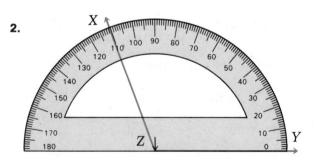

Which kind of angle (acute, right, obtuse) has
the given measure?

3. 90°

4. less than 90°

5. greater than 90°

276

Give the measure of each angle.

1.

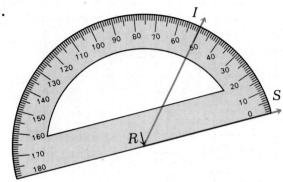

2.

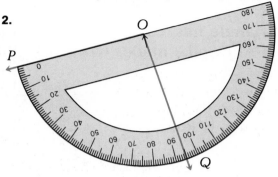

First **estimate** the measure of each angle. Then use a protractor to check your estimate. Trace the angle and draw longer sides if necessary.

3.

4.

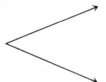

5.

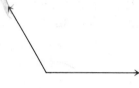

6.

7.

8.

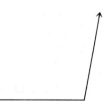

★ **9.** Use a protractor to draw angles with measures 20°, 80°, 105°, and 165°.

Skillkeeper

Write **cm, m,** or **km** to tell which is the correct unit for each blank.

1. A jumbo jet is about 71 __?__ long.

2. A notebook is about 30 __?__ wide.

3. A bicycle wheel is about 1 __?__ in diameter.

4. Lake Erie is about 386 __?__ long.

Triangles

A **triangle** has 3 **sides** ($\overline{AB}$, $\overline{BC}$, and $\overline{AC}$) and 3 **angles** ($\angle A$, $\angle B$, and $\angle C$).

We write: $\triangle ABC$
We say: "triangle ABC"

Look at the SIDES.

| All 3 sides the same length | At least 2 sides the same length | No sides the same length |

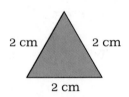

2 cm   2 cm

2 cm

Equilateral

2 cm   2 cm

1 cm

Isosceles

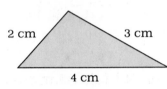

2 cm   3 cm

4 cm

Scalene

Look at the ANGLES.

All 3 angles the same measure | At least 2 angles the same measure | No angles the same measure

60°

60°   60°

Equilateral

30°

75°   75°

Isosceles

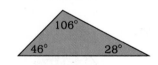

106°

46°   28°

Scalene

An isosceles or a scalene triangle with a right angle is called a **right triangle.**

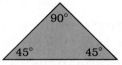

90°

45°   45°

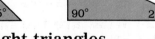

65°

90°   25°

Right triangles

Find the sum of the measures of the three angles of the triangles above for which angle measures are given.

Complete this statement: The sum of the measures of the angles of any triangle is __?__.

Use letters to name each triangle. Tell whether it is
equilateral, isosceles, or **scalene.**

1.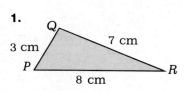

3 cm · 7 cm · 8 cm

2.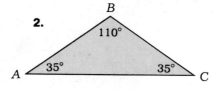

110° · 35° · 35°

3.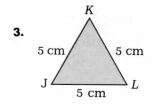

5 cm · 5 cm · 5 cm

4.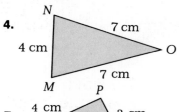

N · 7 cm · 4 cm · O · 7 cm · M · P

5.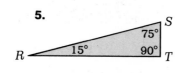

S · 75° · 15° · 90° · R · T

6.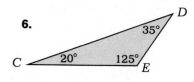

D · 35° · 20° · 125° · C · E

7.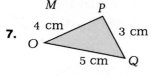

4 cm · P · 3 cm · O · 5 cm · Q

8.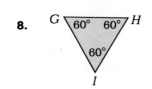

G · 60° · 60° · H · 60° · I

9.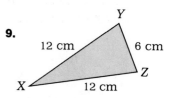

Y · 12 cm · 6 cm · X · 12 cm · Z

10. Which triangles above are right triangles?

In each triangle, find the measure of the third angle.
Example: The sum of the measures of all the angles is 180°.

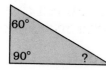

60° · 90° · ?

$$\begin{array}{r} 90° \\ + \ 60° \\ \hline 150° \end{array} \qquad \begin{array}{r} 180° \\ - 150° \\ \hline 30° \end{array}$$

The measure of the
third angle is 30°.

11.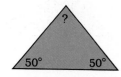

? · 50° · 50°

12.

? · 60° · 60°

13.

32° · 43° · ?

★ **14.** Only one of the angles in an
isosceles triangle has measure
72°. What are the measures of
the other angles of the
triangle?

279

Quadrilaterals

A **quadrilateral** has four sides ($\overline{AB}$, $\overline{BC}$, $\overline{CD}$, and $\overline{AD}$) and four angles ($\angle A$, $\angle B$, $\angle C$, and $\angle D$).

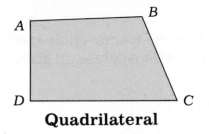

Quadrilateral

Four types of quadrilaterals have been made below by putting together all seven pieces of the famous tangram puzzle. Another quadrilateral, called a rhombus, cannot be made with all the pieces. Study the properties of each quadrilateral.

Square

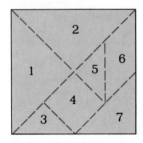

All sides the same length
All angles right angles

Rectangle

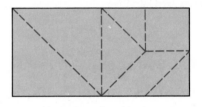

Two pairs of sides the same length
All right angles

Parallelogram

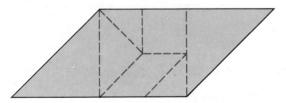

Two pairs of sides the same length
Two pairs of parallel sides

Trapezoid

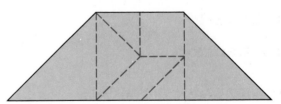

One pair of parallel sides

Rhombus

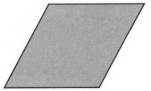

All sides the same length

Write **square, rectangle, parallelogram, rhombus,** or
trapezoid to describe each quadrilateral below.

1.    **2.** 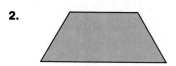   **3.**

4. 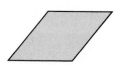   **5.** 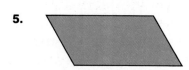   **6.**

7.    **8.**   **9.**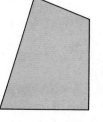

Which of these strips could you
use to form these quadrilaterals?

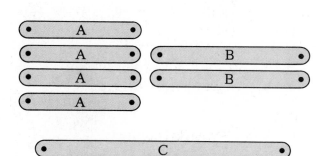

10. a rectangle

11. a square

12. a parallelogram

13. a rhombus

14. a trapezoid

Which quadrilateral has

15. all sides the same length and
four right angles?

16. only one pair of parallel sides?

17. four right angles, but not all
sides the same length?

Think

Puzzle Logic

Trace four copies of this
quadrilateral and cut them out.

Put the four pieces together
to make
1. a square.
2. a parallelogram.
3. a square with a
   small square
   hole in it.

Math

Other Polygons

Triangles and quadrilaterals are simple closed figures formed by line segments. Such figures are called **polygons.** Objects in our world suggest other important polygons.

Fire Hydrant Nut	Honeycomb	Stop Sign

Pentagon—5 sides	**Hexagon**—6 sides	**Octagon**—8 sides

Write **pentagon, hexagon,** or **octagon** to describe each figure.

1.   **2.**   **3.**    **4.**

5.    **6.**   **7.**   **8.**

9. A **regular polygon** has all sides the same length and all angles the same measure. Which of the polygons in exercises 1-8 appear to be regular?

10. What kind of triangle is a regular polygon?

11. What quadrilateral is a regular polygon?

★ **12.** A **diagonal** is a segment (not a side) connecting two vertices of a polygon.

How many different diagonals does a pentagon have?

vertex

diagonal

vertex

Problem Solving:
Using Data from a Picture

Use the data from the pictures as needed
to solve each problem.

1. How many meters of fence are
   needed to go around the field?

2. What is the area of the field?

25 m

35 m

3. What is the difference in the
   altitudes of the two airplanes?

8,229 m   10,668 m

4. How long did it take the train to
   go from City A to City B?

45 km/h

City A   1,035 km   City B

5. How much farther is a trip from
   San Antonio through Austin to
   Houston than a trip from San
   Antonio directly to Houston?

Austin

132 km   237 km

San Antonio   315 km   Houston

6. How much too small is the
   wrench for the nut? Give the
   difference in width.

2.2 cm   1.6 cm

★ 7. Write and solve a problem for
   this picture.

⟵ 186 km ⟶   ⟵ 259 km ⟶

City D   623 km   City E

8. **Try This** What is the greatest
   number of roads that can go
   through 8 cities if each road
   goes through two of the cities?
   Hint: Look for a pattern.

Cities	Picture	Roads
2		1
3		3
4		6

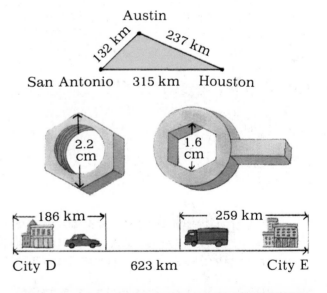
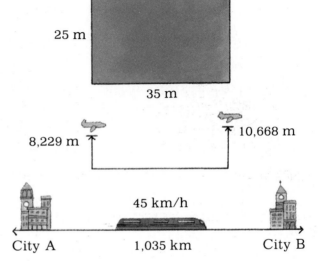

Circles

This wallpaper design can be made by drawing circles with a compass.

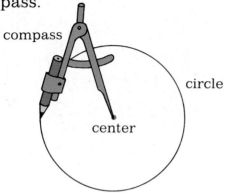

compass

circle

center

When the compass metal tip is on the **center** of the circle, the pencil marks points of the **circle.**

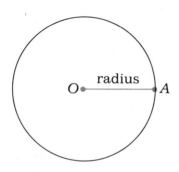

Any segment from the center to a point of the circle is a **radius** of the circle.

Any segment containing two points of the circle and the center is a **diameter** of the circle.

The diameter is double the radius. The radius is the diameter divided by 2. Give the diameter or the radius.

1.

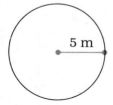

5 m

diameter = ▯ m

2.

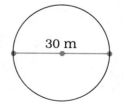

30 m

radius = ▯ m

3.

12 m

diameter = ▯ m

Measure the diameter or radius shown in red.
Double or divide by 2 to find the other.

1.

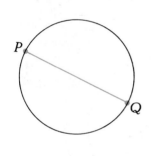

diameter: ⫿⫿⫿ cm
radius:　 ⫿⫿⫿ cm

2.

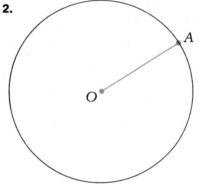

radius:　 ⫿⫿⫿ cm
diameter: ⫿⫿⫿ cm

3.

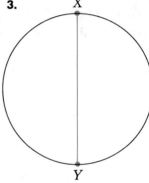

diameter: ⫿⫿⫿ cm
radius:　 ⫿⫿⫿ cm

Use a compass and centimeter ruler to draw a circle with

4. radius 6 cm.　　**5.** radius 3 cm.　　**6.** diameter 4 cm.　　**7.** diameter 8 cm.

Think

Compass Designs

These two designs were made using only a compass. Can you make them?

Make other designs of your own. Color them in an interesting way.

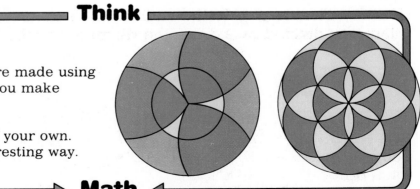

Math

Congruent Figures

Cutting out pattern pieces that are the same size and shape suggests the idea of congruent figures.

Congruent Segments

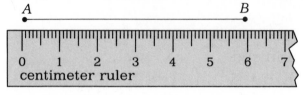

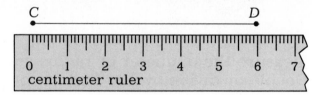

Two segments that have the same length are **congruent** to each other.
We write: $\overline{AB} \cong \overline{CD}$
We say: "Segment AB is congruent to segment CD."

Congruent Angles

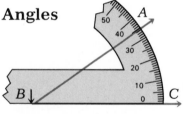

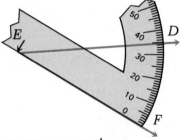

Two angles that have the same measure are **congruent** to each other.
We write: $\angle ABC \cong \angle DEF$

Congruent Polygons

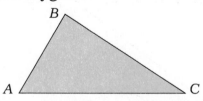

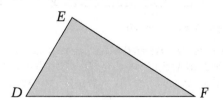

Two polygons that have matching angles congruent ($\angle A \cong \angle D$, $\angle B \cong \angle E$, $\angle C \cong \angle F$) and matching sides congruent ($\overline{AB} \cong \overline{DE}$, $\overline{BC} \cong \overline{EF}$, $\overline{AC} \cong \overline{DF}$) are **congruent** to each other.
We write: $\triangle ABC \cong \triangle DEF$

1. Which pairs of segments are congruent?

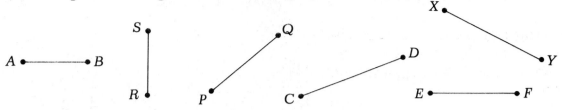

2. Which pairs of angles are congruent? Use your protractor. You may need to trace and extend the rays.

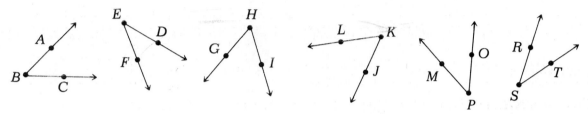

3. Which figures are congruent? Trace a figure and turn it, flip it, or slide it if necessary to see whether it matches another figure.

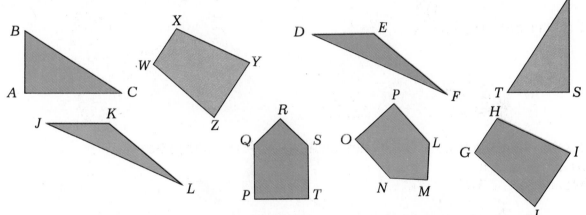

Think

Shape Perception

Trace and cut out four congruent copies of this "bird." Put the four "birds" together to form a square.

Math

Similar Figures

Graph paper was used to make a larger picture of the small animal. The two pictures suggest the idea of similar figures.

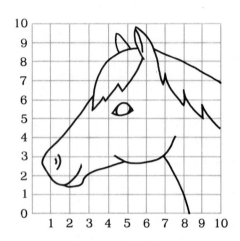

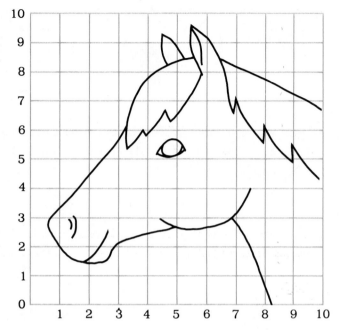

Similar polygons have the same shape, but not necessarily the same size.

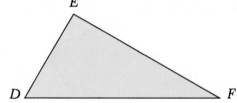

△ABC is similar to △DEF. We write: △ABC ~ △DEF

We say: "Triangle ABC is similar to triangle DEF."

Which two polygons in each row are similar?

1.

2.

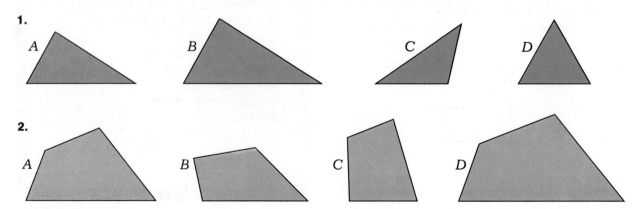

Are the figures similar? Write **yes** or **no**.

1.
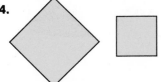

2.
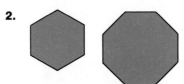

3.
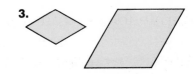

4.
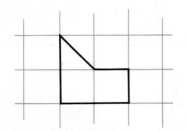

5.

6.

7. Three pairs of similar triangles are shown below. Use the symbol ~ to tell which pairs are similar.

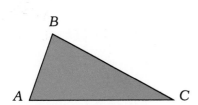

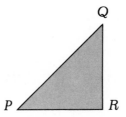

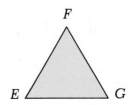

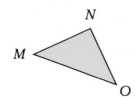

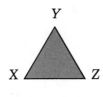

8. Copy this figure on graph paper. Then draw a similar figure on the graph paper with sides 4 times as long.

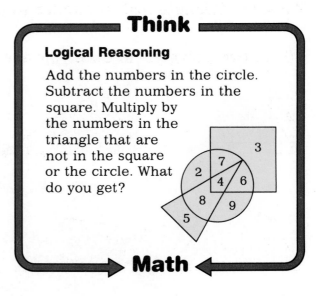

Think

Logical Reasoning

Add the numbers in the circle. Subtract the numbers in the square. Multiply by the numbers in the triangle that are not in the square or the circle. What do you get?

Math

289

Symmetric Figures

Bernie followed these steps to make a symmetric figure.

Fold a piece
of paper.

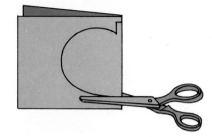

Make a cut that starts
and ends on the fold.

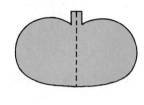

Unfold the piece
that was cut out.

A figure that can be folded so that the two halves match
exactly is a **symmetric figure**. The fold line is a **line of
symmetry** of the figure.

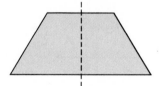

This trapezoid
has one line
of symmetry.

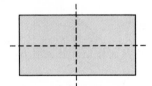

This rectangle
has two lines
of symmetry.

This parallelogram
has no lines
of symmetry.

Tell what each symmetric figure will be when cut out
and unfolded.

1.

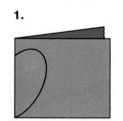

2.

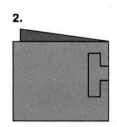

3.

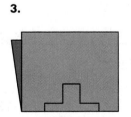

4.

Give the number of lines of symmetry for each
geometric shape. Trace and fold the shape if necessary.

1.

Isosceles triangle

2.

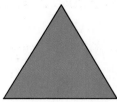

Equilateral triangle

3.

Kite-shaped
quadrilateral

4.

Rhombus

5.

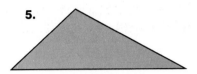

Scalene triangle

6.

Square

7. How many lines of symmetry
does each letter have?

A H S T X

★ **8.** Fold a square piece of paper three times as shown.
Cut off the corner where all folds intersect. What shape
is formed? How many lines of symmetry does it have?

First fold

Second fold

Diagonal
fold

Skillkeeper

Rename each mixed number.

1. $9\frac{4}{3} = 10\frac{}{3}$

2. $12\frac{7}{6} = 13\frac{}{6}$

3. $11\frac{17}{12} = 12\frac{}{12}$

4. $20\frac{4}{5} = 19\frac{}{5}$

5. $3\frac{7}{10} = 2\frac{}{10}$

6. $1\frac{5}{8} = \frac{}{8}$

7. Find the sum of $\frac{2}{10}$ and $\frac{5}{6}$.

8. Subtract $\frac{1}{4}$ from $\frac{7}{8}$.

Graphing Points and Figures

Graphing Points

The picture shows how to **graph the point** that has **coordinates** (5,3). Use graph paper. Start at (0,0). Go **over** 5 and **up** 3. Mark the point.

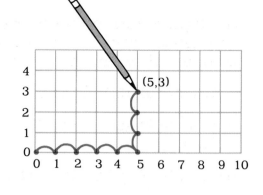

Give the coordinates of each of these points.

1. M	**2.** N	**3.** I	**4.** L
5. G	**6.** B	**7.** K	**8.** A
9. F	**10.** O		

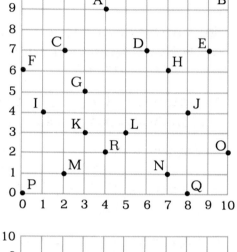

Give the letter of the point for each pair of coordinates.

11. (0,0)	**12.** (8,4)	**13.** (8,0)	**14.** (7,6)
15. (6,7)	**16.** (9,7)	**17.** (2,7)	**18.** (4,2)

Graphing Figures

This figure shows the parallelogram that is formed when the following points are graphed and connected in order:

(7,8) → (6,5) → (1,5) → (2,8) → (7,8)

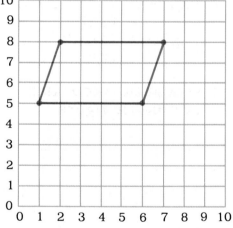

Warm Up Graph each set of points. Connect the points in order to form a geometric figure.

1. (1,3), (3,8), (5,2), (1,3)

2. (7,5), (5,9), (1,7), (3,3), (7,5)

3. (1,1), (1,3), (6,3), (6,1), (1,1)

4. (1,6), (5,10), (9,6), (7,1), (3,1), (1,6)

5. (3,4), (3,7), (6,9), (9,7), (9,4), (6,2), (3,4)

6. (3,9), (6,9), (8,7), (8,4), (6,2), (3,2), (1,4), (1,7), (3,9)

The figures formed by connecting these points are **symmetric figures.** Graph each figure and draw its line (or lines) of symmetry.

1. (1,2), (3,9), (5,2), (1,2)

2. (4,8), (10,8), (9,4), (5,4), (4,8)

3. (3,9), (8,9), (9,7), (8,5), (3,5), (4,7), (3,9)

4. (7,1), (9,3), (9,6), (3,6), (3,3), (5,1), (7,1)

5. (1,5), (6,10), (9,7), (4,2), (1,5)

6. (2,1), (1,6), (2,9), (4,9), (5,6), (4,1), (2,1)

The pairs of figures formed by connecting the points below are either **congruent** or **similar.** Graph each figure and write ≅ or ~.

7. Figure A: (1,1), (1,7), (4,1), (1,1)
Figure B: (4,3), (4,9), (7,3), (4,3)

8. Figure A: (1,1), (1,3), (3,1), (1,1)
Figure B: (2,3), (2,9), (8,3), (2,3)

9. Figure A: (2,1), (3,3), (6,3), (7,1), (2,1)
Figure B: (3,5), (2,7), (7,7), (6,5), (3,5)

10. Figure A: (6,1), (2,7), (6,7), (10,1), (6,1)
Figure B: (7,6), (5,9), (7,9), (9,6), (7,6)

11. Graph the other half of this symmetric figure.

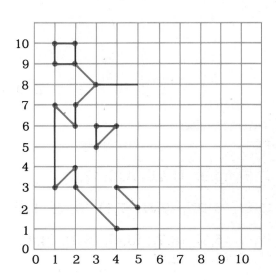

===== Think =====

Riddle Puzzle

Answer the riddle. Then use the Code Graph to check your answer.

Riddle
What can you serve, but never eat?

Answer
(1,6)
(6,3)(5,8)(0,4)(0,4)(3,5)(4,0)
(2,2)(1,6)(8,5)(8,5)!

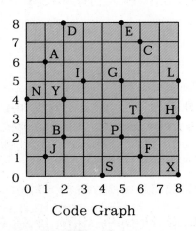

Code Graph

➡ **Math** ⬅

293

Space Figures

The gift box is a real world model of a **space figure** called a **cube**.
A **face**, a **vertex**, and an **edge** of the cube are shown in red.

Gift box

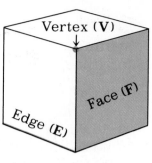

Cube

Some other space figures are shown below. Try to name a real world object that is shaped like the figure.

1.

Sphere

2.

Cylinder

3.

Cone

Give the number of faces, edges, and vertices.

4.

Triangular prism
||||| faces
||||| vertices
||||| edges

5.

Rectangular prism
||||| faces
||||| vertices
||||| edges

6.

Hexagonal prism
||||| faces
||||| vertices
||||| edges

7.

Triangular pyramid
||||| faces
||||| vertices
||||| edges

8.

Rectangular pyramid
||||| faces
||||| vertices
||||| edges

9.

Hexagonal pyramid
||||| faces
||||| vertices
||||| edges

★ **10.** Add the number of faces and vertices in each figure in exercises 4 through 9. By how much does this sum differ from the number of edges? Do you see a pattern?

Problem Solving: Practice

1. The cup shaped like a cylinder holds 3 times as much as the cup shaped like a cone. If the cone-shaped cup holds 198 mL, how much does the other cup hold?

2. A basketball weighs about 624 g. A soccer ball weighs about 228 g less than a basketball. About how much does a soccer ball weigh?

3. A tent floor is 4 m long and 3 m wide. If twice the area of the floor is needed to set up the tent, how many square meters of ground are needed to set it up?

4. The Great Pyramid in Egypt has a square bottom that is 228 m on each side. A football field (including end zones) is 110 m by 48 m. Does the pyramid cover more area or less area than 10 football fields? How much more or less?

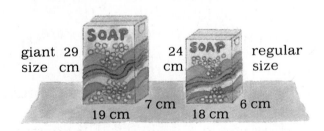

5. How much greater is the volume of the giant size box than the volume of the regular size box?

6. **Try This** Marie drew a star whose "points" were isosceles triangles. Each of the two angles with the same measure is twice as large as the third angle. What are the measures of the three angles?

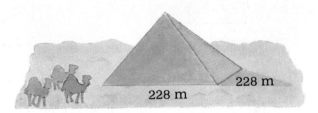

Problem Solving: Using the Strategies

Use one or more of the strategies listed to solve each problem below.

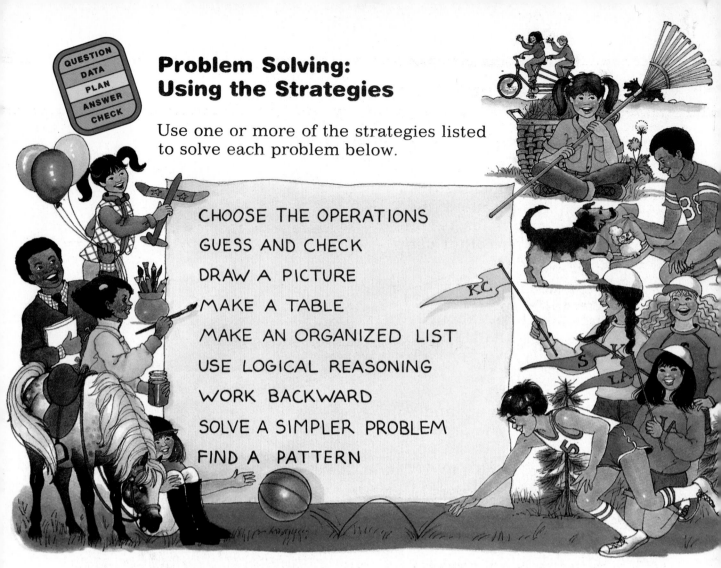

CHOOSE THE OPERATIONS

GUESS AND CHECK

DRAW A PICTURE

MAKE A TABLE

MAKE AN ORGANIZED LIST

USE LOGICAL REASONING

WORK BACKWARD

SOLVE A SIMPLER PROBLEM

FIND A PATTERN

1. Takio gets 36 pictures from each roll of film she uses. She can paste 9 pictures on each page of her new picture album. Her album has 48 pages. How many rolls of film will she need before she has enough pictures to fill the album?

2. Gail dropped a special rubber ball from the top of a wall 16 m high. Each time the ball bounced, it bounced up $\frac{1}{2}$ as high as it fell. Gail caught the ball when the bounce was 1 m high. Find the total distance the ball traveled.

3. It is 1,362 km from Bloomton to Clinton. It is 997 km from Clinton to Ridgeville. Ridgeville is on the highway between Bloomton and Clinton. How far is it from Bloomton to Ridgeville?

4. Some of Chet's friends had a picnic in the park. After the picnic, half of them went to a movie. Then 7 of those who remained went swimming and 3 went home. This left 4 to play tennis. How many were at the picnic at the beginning?

Chapter Review-Test

Write the name for each figure in items 1-4.

1. •————————•
    E   F

2. •
    Y

3. •————————→
    P   Q

4.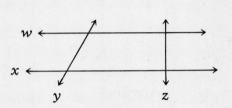
    M   N

Use the drawing at the right for items 5 and 6.

5. Name a pair of parallel lines.

6. Name a pair of intersecting lines that are *not* perpendicular.

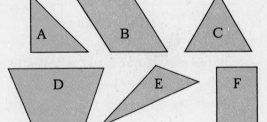

Use a protractor to measure each angle. Tell whether the angle is **acute**, **right**, or **obtuse**.

7.

8.

9.

Use the figures at the right for items 10-14.

10. Which figure is a scalene triangle?

11. Which figure is a trapezoid?

12. Which figure has all right angles?

13. Which figure is an isosceles triangle?

14. In which figure are all sides and all angles equal?

Use the circle for items 15 and 16.

15. Name a diameter of the circle.

16. Give the measure of the radius.

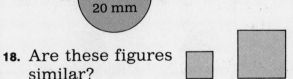

17. Are these figures congruent?

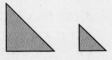

18. Are these figures similar?

19. How many lines of symmetry does a square have?

20. Give the number of
faces: ▦
edges: ▦
vertices: ▦

21. Greta mowed a section of lawn 12 m long and 8 m wide. Then she mowed an area 68 m². What was the total area she mowed?

Another Look

Some Basic Ideas

A •———————• B C •———————• D

Segment AB Ray CD

$\overline{AB}$ $\overrightarrow{CD}$

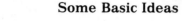
Parallel lines
‖

Perpendicular lines
⊥

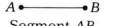   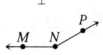

Acute angle ∠ABC Right angle ∠PQR Obtuse angle ∠MNP

Some Polygons

No sides ≅ (congruent) At least 2 sides ≅ All sides ≅

Scalene triangle Isosceles triangle Equilateral triangle

Square Rectangle Parallelogram

Trapezoid Rhombus

Circles

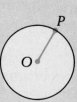

A •——O——• B

$\overline{AB}$—diameter

$\overline{OB}$—radius

diameter = 2 × radius

Match.

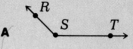

1. $\overleftrightarrow{RS} \perp \overleftrightarrow{TU}$

A

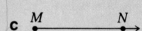

2. right angle

B

3. $\overleftrightarrow{RS} \parallel \overleftrightarrow{TU}$

C

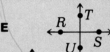

4. $\overline{MN}$

D

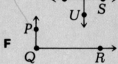

5. obtuse angle

E

6. $\overrightarrow{MN}$

F

What kind of triangle is it?

7.   8.   9.

Name the polygon.

10.   11.

12.   13.

14. Measure the length of radius OP.

15. What is the diameter of the circle?

Coordinate Geometry (Transforming Figures)

Terry graphed the figure shown. Then he used this rule to change the coordinates:

Add 5 to each black number.
Add 6 to each red number.

$(1,1) \rightarrow (6,7)$ Graph these new
$(2,4) \rightarrow (7,10)$ coordinates to see
$(3,1) \rightarrow (8,7)$ how the figure
                             was changed.

Draw Terry's new figure.

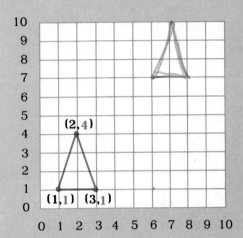

Val graphed the figure shown. Then she used this rule to change the coordinates:

Switch the numbers.

$(5,2) \rightarrow (2,5)$
$(5,4) \rightarrow (4,5)$
$(9,4) \rightarrow (4,9)$

What did Val's new figure look like?

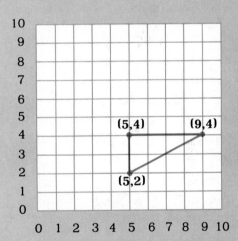

Larry graphed the figure shown. Then he used this rule to change the coordinates:

Multiply all numbers by 3.

Show what Larry's new figure looked like.

Graph a figure. Then make up a rule for changing the coordinates. Show the new figure.

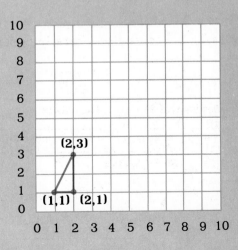

Cumulative Review

1. The distance 2 m 23 cm is the same as ___?___ cm.

   A 2.23 cm   B 223 cm
   C 22.3 cm   D not given

2. What is the perimeter of a rectangle 176 cm long and 49 cm wide?

   A 8,624 cm³   B 225 cm
   C 450 cm   D not given

3. Find the area.

   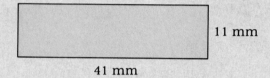
   11 mm
   41 mm

   A 52 mm²   B 104 mm²
   C 208 mm²   D not given

4. Find the volume of a box that is 17 cm long, 23 cm wide, and 14 cm high.

   A 5,474 cm³   B 54 cm³
   C 118 cm³   D not given

Give the missing number.

5. 10 mL = ___?___ cm³

   A 10   B 1
   C 100   D not given

6. 6 L = ___?___ mL

   A 60   B 600
   C 6,000   D not given

7. 2 kg = ___?___ g

   A 2,000   B 200
   C 20   D not given

Add or subtract.

8. $9\frac{3}{4}$
   $+ 2\frac{1}{8}$

   A $11\frac{5}{8}$ B $11\frac{7}{8}$
   C $11\frac{2}{8}$ D not given

9. $12\frac{4}{5}$
   $- 3\frac{1}{10}$

   A $9\frac{7}{10}$ B $9\frac{3}{10}$
   C $9\frac{3}{5}$ D not given

10. $5\frac{2}{3}$
    $+ 9\frac{1}{2}$

    A $15\frac{3}{5}$ B $14\frac{1}{6}$
    C $15\frac{1}{6}$ D not given

11. $7\frac{2}{7}$
    $- 4\frac{5}{7}$

    A $3\frac{4}{7}$ B $2\frac{4}{7}$
    C $11\frac{4}{7}$ D not given

12. $18\frac{1}{10}$
    $+ 3\frac{9}{10}$

    A $21\frac{9}{10}$ B $15\frac{1}{10}$
    C $14\frac{1}{10}$ D not given

13. Mona rode her horse $18\frac{1}{2}$ laps around the track on Saturday and $15\frac{2}{3}$ laps on Sunday. How many laps did she ride altogether on those two days?

    A $34\frac{1}{6}$ B $34\frac{2}{3}$
    C $33\frac{2}{3}$ D not given

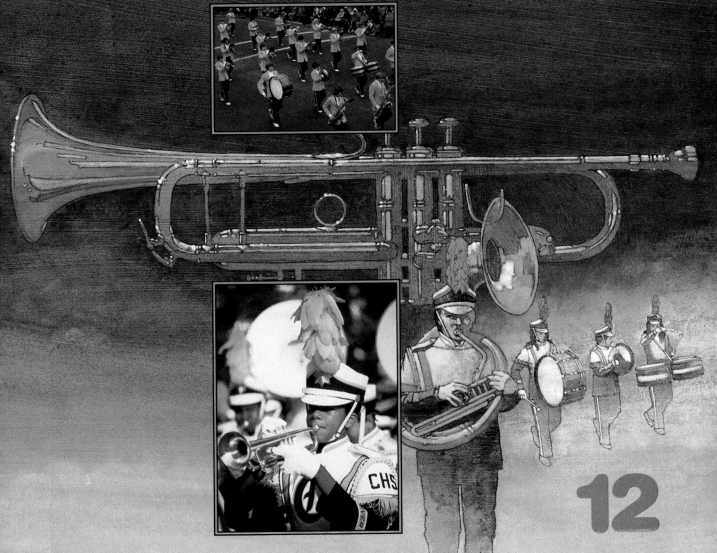

Fractions: Multiplication and Division

12

All summer long Ethan played his trombone for $1\frac{1}{2}$ or more hours every day. His goal was to become good enough by September to win a place in his school's marching band. Only 96 of the school's best musicians were chosen for the band, so Ethan felt both proud and lucky when he learned that he was chosen to play in the brass section. This part of the band was made up of all the different kinds of horns. One third of all the band members were in this part of the band. For Ethan the high point of the year was the first football game when the band marched onto the field in their bright gold and black uniforms and played the school song.

Finding a Fraction of a Number

Mindy drew these pictures to show data she collected about the 18 children in her class.

$\frac{1}{3}$ of the children wear glasses.

$\frac{1}{3}$ of 18 is 6.

To find $\frac{1}{3}$ of a number, divide the number by 3.

$\frac{2}{3}$ of the children are boys.

$\frac{2}{3}$ of 18 is 12.

To find $\frac{2}{3}$ of a number, find $\frac{1}{3}$ and multiply by 2.

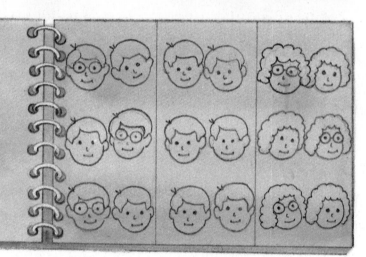

Find the fraction of each number. Use pictures if necessary.

1. $\frac{1}{2}$ of 8

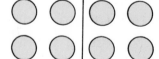

2. $\frac{1}{4}$ of 12

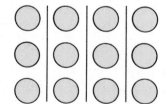

3. $\frac{3}{4}$ of 12

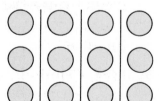

4. $\frac{1}{2}$ of 16

5. $\frac{1}{3}$ of 24

6. $\frac{2}{3}$ of 24

7. $\frac{2}{3}$ of 9

8. $\frac{1}{4}$ of 20

9. $\frac{3}{4}$ of 20

10. $\frac{1}{2}$ of 18

11. $\frac{2}{3}$ of 15

12. $\frac{1}{10}$ of 50

60 **minutes** in one **hour**	4 **quarts** in one **gallon**	12 **eggs** in one **dozen**

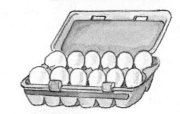

How many minutes are in	How many quarts are in	How many eggs are in
1. $\frac{1}{2}$ of an hour?	4. $\frac{1}{2}$ of a gallon?	7. $\frac{1}{2}$ of a dozen?
2. $\frac{1}{4}$ of an hour?	5. $\frac{1}{4}$ of a gallon?	8. $\frac{1}{4}$ of a dozen?
3. $\frac{3}{4}$ of an hour?	6. $\frac{3}{4}$ of a gallon?	9. $\frac{2}{3}$ of a dozen?

16 **ounces** in one **pound**	36 **inches** in one **yard**	5,280 **feet** in one **mile**

How many ounces are in	How many inches are in	How many feet are in
10. $\frac{1}{2}$ of a pound?	14. $\frac{1}{2}$ of a yard?	18. $\frac{1}{2}$ of a mile?
11. $\frac{1}{4}$ of a pound?	15. $\frac{1}{4}$ of a yard?	19. $\frac{1}{4}$ of a mile?
12. $\frac{3}{4}$ of a pound?	16. $\frac{2}{3}$ of a yard?	20. $\frac{3}{4}$ of a mile?
13. $\frac{3}{8}$ of a pound?	17. $\frac{3}{4}$ of a yard?	21. $\frac{2}{5}$ of a mile?

22. Of the 18 students in Mindy's class $\frac{5}{6}$ have pets. How many of the students in Mindy's class have pets?

23. Mrs. Goodwin described her class as "two dozen good eggs." If $\frac{3}{4}$ of the class helped in the school cleanup project, how many students helped?

Think

Guess and Check

You may use any of these symbols as many times as necessary:

+   −   ×   ÷   ( )   —   9

1. Write a symbol for 10 that has three 9s in it.
2. Write a symbol for 10 that has five 9s in it.
3. Write a symbol for 100 that has four 9s in it.

Math

Multiplying Fractions

Chet covered $\frac{3}{4}$ of the bulletin board with large sheets of white paper.

Then he made a math poster on $\frac{2}{3}$ of the white paper.

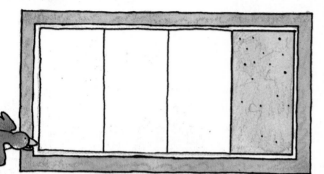

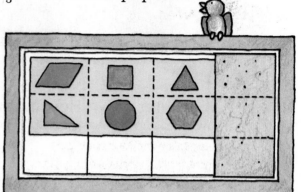

$\frac{2}{3}$ of $\frac{3}{4}$ of the bulletin board is covered by the poster. What fraction of the board is this?

Since we want to find $\frac{2}{3}$ of $\frac{3}{4}$, we multiply.

Multiply the numerators.	→	Multiply the denominators.

$$\frac{2}{3} \times \frac{3}{4} = \frac{6}{} \qquad \frac{2}{3} \times \frac{3}{4} = \frac{6}{12} = \frac{1}{2}$$

Other Examples

$$\frac{1}{2} \times \frac{1}{4} = \frac{1 \times 1}{2 \times 4} = \frac{1}{8} \qquad \frac{3}{4} \times \frac{5}{2} = \frac{3 \times 5}{4 \times 2} = \frac{15}{8} = 1\frac{7}{8} \qquad \frac{2}{3} \times 5 = \frac{2}{3} \times \frac{5}{1} = \frac{10}{3} = 3\frac{1}{3}$$

Warm Up Multiply.

1. $\frac{1}{2} \times \frac{1}{5}$

2. $\frac{1}{4} \times \frac{1}{3}$

3. $\frac{3}{5} \times \frac{2}{3}$

4. $\frac{1}{3} \times \frac{2}{3}$

5. $\frac{3}{4} \times 6$

6. $8 \times \frac{1}{3}$

7. $\frac{3}{10} \times \frac{7}{10}$

8. $\frac{1}{2} \times \frac{1}{10}$

Multiply. Write the product in lowest terms.

1. $\frac{1}{4} \times \frac{2}{5}$
2. $\frac{3}{8} \times \frac{2}{5}$
3. $\frac{1}{2} \times \frac{3}{4}$
4. $\frac{6}{1} \times \frac{3}{4}$

5. $\frac{3}{2} \times \frac{1}{4}$
6. $\frac{1}{3} \times \frac{5}{8}$
7. $\frac{5}{6} \times \frac{1}{2}$
8. $9 \times \frac{2}{3}$

9. $\frac{2}{3} \times \frac{3}{8}$
10. $\frac{1}{5} \times \frac{3}{10}$
11. $16 \times \frac{5}{8}$
12. $\frac{3}{4} \times \frac{4}{3}$

13. $\frac{2}{5} \times 12$
14. $8 \times \frac{9}{10}$
15. $\frac{3}{4} \times \frac{3}{4}$
16. $\frac{3}{4} \times 10$

17. $\frac{2}{5} \times \frac{9}{3}$
18. $\frac{3}{10} \times 20$
19. $\frac{5}{6} \times \frac{3}{5}$
20. $15 \times \frac{2}{3}$

21. Emilia used $\frac{1}{4}$ of $\frac{2}{3}$ of a bulletin board for announcements. What part of the bulletin board did she use?

22. This problem has some unneeded data. Choose the data that is needed. Then solve the problem.

Jim put maps on $\frac{2}{3}$ of $\frac{4}{5}$ of a bulletin board. Jo put designs on $\frac{1}{5}$ of the bulletin board. What part was used for maps?

23. Jo had $\frac{1}{2}$ of a bottle of glue. She used $\frac{3}{4}$ of it. What part of the bottle was left?

Skillkeeper

Add or subtract. Reduce answers to lowest terms.

1. $8\frac{3}{5}$
$- 1\frac{1}{3}$

2. $12\frac{1}{2}$
$- 2\frac{5}{6}$

3. $8\frac{1}{6}$
$+ 4\frac{5}{6}$

4. $47\frac{1}{6}$
$+ 14\frac{1}{3}$

5. $9 - 1\frac{1}{8}$
6. $\frac{3}{2} + \frac{5}{2}$
7. $3\frac{1}{4} - 1\frac{1}{3}$

8. $4\frac{3}{8} + 2\frac{3}{4}$
9. $15\frac{1}{3} - 6\frac{1}{12}$
10. $2\frac{1}{4} + 5\frac{4}{5}$

More Practice, page 430, Set B

Problem Solving: Practice

Many people work together to produce a daily newspaper. Reporters, editors, photographers, artists, printers, and many others play an important part in making a good newspaper arrive on time.

Solve these problems to find out more about how newspapers are produced.

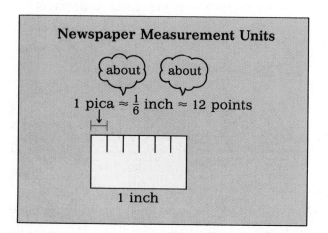

Newspaper Measurement Units

about   about

1 pica ≈ $\frac{1}{6}$ inch ≈ 12 points

1 inch

1. How many picas are in 1 inch?

2. How many points are in 1 inch?

3. A point is what fraction of an inch?

4. A standard column in a newspaper is about 13 picas wide. How many inches is this?

5. A front page headline letter is on a rectangular piece of metal 84 points high. About how high is this in inches?

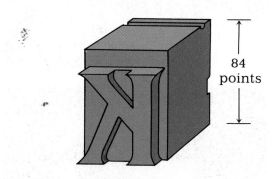

84 points

6. One newspaper company has two tanks of ink that, together, last 6 weeks. One tank holds 2,200 gallons and the other holds 2,500 gallons. About how many gallons of ink are used each day?

7. Some typesetting machines have discs that move 75 miles per hour. They can set type at a rate of 37 words per second. How many words can they set in one minute?

8. A total of 40 people work in the editorial department of a local newspaper. If $\frac{5}{8}$ of these people are news reporters, how many news reporters are there in the department?

9. A roll of newsprint contains $\frac{11}{2}$ miles of paper. During the first hour the press was running, $\frac{3}{4}$ of the roll was used. How many miles of paper were used?

10. DATA BANK What country has about $\frac{1}{4}$ as many newspapers as the United States? About $\frac{1}{7}$ as many? About $\frac{1}{10}$ as many? (See Data Bank, page 411.)

11. Try This The average newspaper story takes up 12 column-inches of space. (The number of column-inches is found by multiplying the number of columns wide by the number of inches long.) One layout possibility for the 12 column-inches story is 4 columns wide and 3 inches long. How many other layouts are possible using only whole numbers of inches?

Multiplying Mixed Numbers

An assembly line turns out an average of $2\frac{1}{2}$ trucks per hour. At this rate how many trucks does the line turn out during a $5\frac{1}{2}$-hour period?

Since the same number is turned out each hour, we multiply.

Write the mixed numbers as improper fractions.	→	Multiply the fractions.

$$2\frac{1}{2} \times 5\frac{1}{2} = \frac{5}{2} \times \frac{11}{2} \qquad \frac{5}{2} \times \frac{11}{2} = \frac{55}{4} = 13\frac{3}{4}$$

The assembly line turns out an average of $13\frac{3}{4}$ trucks during a $5\frac{1}{2}$-hour period.

Other Examples

$$3\frac{1}{3} \times 1\frac{3}{4} = \frac{10}{3} \times \frac{7}{4} = \frac{70}{12} = 5\frac{5}{6} \qquad \frac{1}{3} \times 3\frac{2}{5} = \frac{1}{3} \times \frac{17}{5} = \frac{17}{15} = 1\frac{2}{15}$$

$$2\frac{1}{4} \times 5 = \frac{9}{4} \times \frac{5}{1} = \frac{45}{4} = 11\frac{1}{4} \qquad 5 \times 4\frac{3}{8} = \frac{5}{1} \times \frac{35}{8} = \frac{175}{8} = 21\frac{7}{8}$$

Warm Up Multiply.

1. $2\frac{1}{2} \times 1\frac{1}{4}$

2. $3\frac{1}{3} \times 1\frac{2}{5}$

3. $2\frac{1}{5} \times 1\frac{1}{2}$

4. $1\frac{3}{8} \times 6$

5. $\frac{2}{3} \times 3\frac{1}{2}$

6. $4\frac{1}{5} \times 2\frac{2}{3}$

7. $8 \times 2\frac{3}{4}$

8. $5\frac{1}{2} \times \frac{1}{3}$

9. $3\frac{4}{5} \times 2\frac{3}{8}$

10. $2\frac{1}{6} \times 1\frac{5}{8}$

11. $3\frac{2}{3} \times 2\frac{4}{5}$

12. $1\frac{5}{6} \times 3\frac{7}{8}$

Multiply.

1. $1\frac{1}{3} \times 2\frac{1}{2}$

2. $2\frac{1}{3} \times 1\frac{1}{4}$

3. $\frac{3}{4} \times 1\frac{1}{2}$

4. $5 \times 1\frac{2}{5}$

5. $2\frac{1}{5} \times 1\frac{1}{4}$

6. $10 \times 2\frac{1}{2}$

7. $1\frac{1}{3} \times \frac{2}{3}$

8. $2\frac{1}{8} \times \frac{1}{4}$

9. $1\frac{3}{4} \times 1\frac{2}{3}$

10. $8\frac{1}{2} \times 4$

11. $1\frac{2}{3} \times 12$

12. $2\frac{1}{2} \times 1\frac{3}{4}$

13. $3\frac{1}{4} \times 2\frac{1}{2}$

14. $4\frac{1}{3} \times 2\frac{2}{5}$

15. $5\frac{1}{8} \times \frac{1}{4}$

16. $9 \times 2\frac{2}{3}$

17. $1\frac{4}{5} \times 2\frac{1}{2}$

18. $2\frac{3}{8} \times 1\frac{1}{4}$

19. $3\frac{1}{2} \times 6$

20. $2\frac{1}{3} \times \frac{5}{6}$

21. $1\frac{5}{8} \times 1\frac{1}{4}$

22. $2\frac{1}{2} \times 3\frac{3}{4}$

23. $4\frac{5}{6} \times \frac{1}{3}$

24. $8 \times 2\frac{3}{4}$

25. $2\frac{3}{10} \times 1\frac{1}{5}$

26. $3\frac{5}{8} \times 4\frac{1}{4}$

27. $2\frac{3}{8} \times 6\frac{1}{3}$

28. $5\frac{1}{4} \times 3\frac{7}{10}$

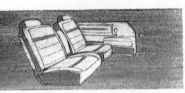

29. If an assembly line turns out an average of $3\frac{1}{4}$ trucks each hour, what is the number of trucks turned out during a $7\frac{1}{2}$-hour period?

30. This problem contains some unneeded data. Choose the data you need and solve the problem. An assembly line turns out an average of $2\frac{3}{4}$ cars an hour. This is 1 car every 22 minutes. At this rate how many cars will be turned out in $6\frac{1}{4}$ hours?

31. The first automatic assembly line for cars was built in Detroit in 1955. It turned out 1 engine every $2\frac{1}{2}$ minutes. How long did it take to turn out 24 engines? How many engines did it turn out in 8 hours?

Skillkeeper

Round each decimal to the nearest whole number.

1. 5.4

2. 3.70

3. 0.5

4. 2.49

5. 4.09

6. 5.504

Round decimals to the nearest whole number and estimate the product or quotient.

7. 6×6.893

8. 3.4×3.58

9. 9.99×5.05

10. 6.3×7.5

11. $15.8 \div 4$

12. $24.35 \div 5.90$

13. $80.81 \div 8.61$

14. $35.6 \div 9.46$

Problem Solving:
Using Data from a Recipe

Gingerbread

$1\frac{3}{4}$ c whole wheat flour

$\frac{1}{2}$ c white flour

$\frac{1}{2}$ tsp salt

1 tsp baking soda

2 tsp baking powder

1 tbsp grated ginger root

2 eggs, beaten

$\frac{1}{3}$ c melted butter

1 c molasses

$\frac{3}{4}$ c hot water

- Stir flour, salt, baking soda, baking powder, and ginger root together in one bowl.

- Stir the eggs, butter, molasses, and hot water together in another bowl.

- Mix together all of the ingredients. Place the mixture in greased baking pan.

- Bake at 325°F for 35 minutes.

- Makes 12 pieces.

1. Tammy wants to make $2\frac{1}{2}$ times as much gingerbread as the recipe makes. How much whole wheat flour should she use? How much white flour should she use?

2. A box of raisins costs $1.29. What is the cost of 3 boxes?

3. What is the total amount of flour called for by the recipe?

4. For a bake sale, Jamie wants to make 4 times the amount that the recipe makes. How many pieces will he make?

5. Nan used a different recipe that called for $1\frac{1}{2}$ times as much butter as the recipe given above. How much butter did she use?

6. Fred's mother has 87 recipes in one box and twice as many recipes in another box. What is the total number of recipes in the two boxes?

7. **DATA HUNT** Find a recipe for your favorite dessert. How much of each item would you use to make $2\frac{1}{2}$ times as much as the given recipe?

8. **Try This** The recipe cards in Mr. Woo's recipe box were numbered in order. The product of the numbers on two recipes next to each other was 6,162. What were the numbers on the recipes?

Problem Solving: Mental Math

QUESTION DATA PLAN ANSWER CHECK

The **multiplication-addition** property tells us that we can **multiply** parts of a number and **add** the partial products to find the answer. It helps us solve problems mentally.

No pens or pencils please!

4 × 10 is 40, and 4 × 7 is 28, so 4 × 17 is 68.

4×2 is 8, and $4 \times \frac{1}{2}$ is 2, so $4 \times 2\frac{1}{2}$ is 10.

17 loaves of bread. 4 cups of flour for each. How many cups of flour?

Work $2\frac{1}{2}$ hours a day for 4 days a week. Work how many hours a week?

Solve mentally.

1. Mr. Frank sold 24 books for $3 each. How much money did he receive?

2. Ann cut 6 pieces of ribbon for a customer. Each piece was $2\frac{1}{2}$ yards long. How many yards did she cut in all?

3. A job pays time and a half for overtime. (This means $1\frac{1}{2}$ times regular pay.) If the regular pay rate is $4 per hour, how much is the overtime pay per hour?

4. Omar helped 28 customers in the morning. He helped 9 in the afternoon. How many customers did he help in all?

5. Lon rides his bike to work 4 days each week. The distance he rides each day is $3\frac{1}{2}$ miles. How many miles does he ride each week?

6. **Try This** Job A pays $1 the first day, $2 the second day, $4 the third day, and so on. Job B pays $2,000 each day. Which job pays more for 15 days work? How much more?

Dividing Fractions

How many people can you serve with 4 chicken pies if each person gets $\frac{1}{2}$ of a pie?

Since we want to know how many halves are in 4, we divide.

Product   Factor   Factor

$$4 \div \frac{1}{2} = 8$$

Check: $\overset{F}{8} \times \overset{F}{\frac{1}{2}} = \overset{P}{4}$

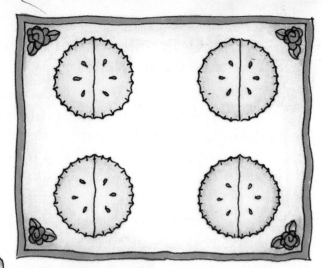

There are 8 halves in 4.

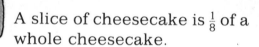

A slice of cheesecake is $\frac{1}{8}$ of a whole cheesecake.

If you have $\frac{3}{4}$ of a cheesecake, how many slices do you have?

Since we want to know how many eighths are in $\frac{3}{4}$, we divide.

$$\overset{P}{\frac{3}{4}} \div \overset{F}{\frac{1}{8}} = \overset{F}{6}$$

Check: $\overset{F}{6} \times \overset{F}{\frac{1}{8}} = \overset{P}{\frac{6}{8}} = \frac{3}{4}$

There are 6 eighths in $\frac{3}{4}$.

Warm Up

1. How many fifths are in 2?

$$2 \div \frac{1}{5} = n$$

Check your answer.

2. How many sixths are in $\frac{1}{2}$?

$$\frac{1}{2} \div \frac{1}{6} = n$$

Check your answer.

312

Find the quotients. Check by multiplying.

1.

How many fourths are in 2?

$2 \div \frac{1}{4} = n$

2.

How many thirds are in 3?

$3 \div \frac{1}{3} = n$

3. How many halves are in 2?

$2 \div \frac{1}{2} = n$

4. How many fourths are in 3?

$3 \div \frac{1}{4} = n$

5.

How many fourths are in $\frac{1}{2}$?

$\frac{1}{2} \div \frac{1}{4} = n$

6.

How many sixths are in $\frac{2}{3}$?

$\frac{2}{3} \div \frac{1}{6} = n$

7. How many eighths are in $\frac{1}{2}$?

$\frac{1}{2} \div \frac{1}{8} = n$

8. How many eighths are in $\frac{1}{4}$?

$\frac{1}{4} \div \frac{1}{8} = n$

★ **9.** Find $3 \div \frac{1}{2}$. Then find $3 \times \frac{2}{1}$. How do the answers compare? Does this work for the quotients in exercises 1–8?

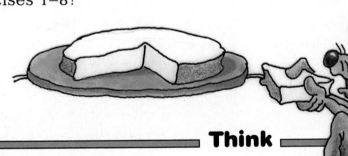

Think

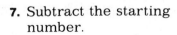

Discovering a Pattern

Follow the directions and try this with at least 5 different numbers.

What do you discover?

1. Choose an even number.

2. Multiply by $\frac{1}{2}$.

3. Add 15.

4. Multiply by $\frac{1}{5}$.

5. Multiply by 10.

6. Subtract 17.

7. Subtract the starting number.

Math

Applied Problem Solving

Your water bill is very costly. You want to reduce the amount of water you use. You need to decide whether you should take showers or baths.

Some Things to Consider

- You have no more than 10 minutes to take a shower or a bath in the morning.

- A shower uses 2 L of water every 10 seconds.

- Water flows into the bathtub at a rate of 2 L every 6 seconds. It takes 6 minutes to fill the tub.

- You prefer baths, but you do not mind showers.

Some Questions to Answer

1. How much water does a 6-minute shower use? A 10-minute shower?

2. How much water does it take to fill the tub?

What Is Your Decision?

Will you take showers or baths? Why?

Find the fraction of each number.

1. $\frac{1}{2}$ of 14   **2.** $\frac{1}{4}$ of 24   **3.** $\frac{2}{3}$ of 12   **4.** $\frac{3}{10}$ of 50

Multiply. Reduce answers to lowest terms.

5. $\frac{1}{3} \times \frac{1}{4}$ **6.** $\frac{3}{5} \times \frac{4}{3}$ **7.** $\frac{3}{4} \times 6$ **8.** $\frac{2}{5} \times \frac{3}{8}$

9. $\frac{2}{3} \times \frac{3}{8}$ **10.** $\frac{4}{5} \times \frac{3}{4}$ **11.** $3 \times \frac{2}{3}$ **12.** $\frac{3}{4} \times 8$

13. $\frac{2}{5} \times \frac{1}{3}$ **14.** $7 \times \frac{1}{7}$ **15.** $\frac{4}{7} \times \frac{3}{8}$ **16.** $\frac{2}{3} \times 6$

Find the products.

17. $2\frac{1}{3} \times 1\frac{1}{3}$ **18.** $3\frac{1}{2} \times 1\frac{3}{4}$ **19.** $\frac{1}{4} \times 3\frac{2}{5}$ **20.** $6 \times 4\frac{4}{5}$

21. $3\frac{3}{8} \times 4\frac{1}{3}$ **22.** $6\frac{1}{8} \times 4\frac{1}{2}$ **23.** $3\frac{2}{3} \times 7$ **24.** $4\frac{1}{3} \times 2\frac{7}{10}$

Divide.

25. How many $\frac{1}{3}$s are in 2?

$2 \div \frac{1}{3} = n$

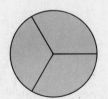 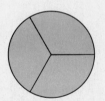

26. How many $\frac{1}{8}$s are in $\frac{3}{4}$?

$\frac{3}{4} \div \frac{1}{8} = n$

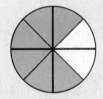

Solve.

27. A column in a newspaper is $2\frac{1}{4}$ inches wide. How wide is an ad that uses 8 columns?

28. A sauce recipe calls for $\frac{2}{3}$ cup of cheese. If you want to make $\frac{1}{2}$ as much sauce, how much cheese should you use?

Another Look

Multiplying Fractions

$$\frac{3}{4} \times \frac{2}{5} = \frac{3 \times 2}{4 \times 5} = \frac{6}{20} = \frac{3}{10}$$

Multiply the numerators.
Multiply the denominators.

$$\frac{3}{4} \times 15 = \frac{3}{4} \times \frac{15}{1} = \frac{45}{4} = 11\frac{1}{4}$$

Write the whole number as a fraction.

$$4\overline{)45}\ \ 11\frac{1}{4}$$

Multiply.

1. $\frac{2}{3} \times \frac{4}{5}$ 2. $\frac{1}{2} \times \frac{3}{4}$ 3. $\frac{3}{5} \times \frac{3}{8}$

4. $\frac{4}{5} \times \frac{3}{2}$ 5. $\frac{1}{4} \times \frac{2}{3}$ 6. $\frac{2}{5} \times \frac{3}{10}$

7. $\frac{1}{3} \times 12$ 8. $\frac{3}{4} \times 20$ 9. $9 \times \frac{1}{2}$

10. $\frac{1}{5} \times 35$ 11. $12 \times \frac{2}{3}$ 12. $17 \times \frac{3}{5}$

Multiplying Mixed Numbers

$(2 \times 3) + 1 = 7$

$$2\frac{1}{3} \times 3\frac{4}{5} = \frac{7}{3} \times \frac{19}{5} = \frac{133}{15} = 8\frac{13}{15}$$

$(3 \times 5) + 4 = 19$

13. $1\frac{1}{2} \times 3\frac{1}{4}$ 14. $1\frac{2}{3} \times 3\frac{1}{5}$

15. $4\frac{1}{8} \times 1\frac{3}{4}$ 16. $5\frac{1}{3} \times \frac{3}{4}$

17. $3\frac{1}{2} \times 2\frac{1}{3}$ 18. $\frac{3}{8} \times 2\frac{1}{4}$

19. $1\frac{3}{4} \times 3$ 20. $1\frac{1}{6} \times 2\frac{2}{3}$

21. $2\frac{1}{3} \times \frac{1}{4}$ 22. $\frac{4}{5} \times 1\frac{1}{2}$

Enrichment

Estimation with Fractions

Riddle

Why did the owner buy new tires for his car and then never use it again?

To solve the riddle:

1. Copy the Message-Maker Box.
2. Estimate the answer to each problem and look for that answer in the Message-Maker Box.
3. Each time you find an answer to a problem write the letter of that problem above the answer.

> **Rules for Rounding a Mixed Number to the Nearest Whole Number**
>
> - When the fraction part is less than $\frac{1}{2}$, round down.
>
> $$3\frac{3}{8} \to 3$$
>
> - When the fraction part is equal to or greater than $\frac{1}{2}$, round up.
>
> $$3\frac{2}{4} \to 4 \qquad 3\frac{5}{8} \to 4$$

A Cost per ounce: $4\frac{5}{8}$ cents
How many cents will 12 ounces cost?

B Rope: $99\frac{1}{2}$ feet long
How many $4\frac{3}{4}$-foot lengths can be cut from it?

D Bag of salt: 630 ounces
How many $9\frac{1}{4}$-ounce boxes can be filled from it?

E Rectangular picture:
$6\frac{3}{4}$ inches long, $4\frac{3}{8}$ inches wide
What is its area?

H Car trip: 150 miles in $3\frac{1}{4}$ hours
What is the average number of miles per hour?

I Board: 36 inches long
How many pieces $5\frac{7}{8}$ inches long can be cut from it?

N One-way trip: $8\frac{1}{2}$ miles
How many miles if you take 4 round trips? (Be careful!)

R Picking fruit: $4\frac{3}{4}$ baskets per hour
How many baskets are picked in $8\frac{1}{4}$ hours?

T 2 gallons →

How many gallons? →

Gas Gauges

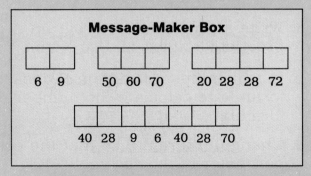

Message-Maker Box

6	9		50	60	70		20	28	28	72

40	28	9	6	40	28	70

Technology

Using Variables in Computer Programs

It is often useful to use a letter of the alphabet to stand for a number in a computer program. Such a letter is called a number **variable**.

Space scientists use computers to help them keep track of space flights.

Study these sample programs.

Computer Program A

```
10 LET A = 240
20 LET B = 60
30 PRINT A/B
40 END
```

The letter A has a value of 240.

Computer Program B

```
10 PRINT "COMPUTERS CAN USE
   FORMULAS."
20 LET L = 24
30 LET W = 16
40 LET A = L * W
50 PRINT "THE RECTANGLE'S AREA
   IS "; A
```

RUN of the Program

```
40
```

RUN

```
COMPUTERS CAN USE FORMULAS.
THE RECTANGLE'S AREA IS 384
```

---

1. Write a program like Program A that finds the product 35 times 45. Use X and Y as variables.

2. In which line of Program B does the computer use a formula to calculate the number for a letter? What formula?

3. Change Program B so that the computer will find the perimeter of the rectangle.

318

Give the RUN for each program in exercises 1–5.

1. ```
10 LET A = 144
20 LET B = 16
30 PRINT "A PLUS B = "; A + B
40 PRINT "A MINUS B = "; A - B
50 PRINT "A TIMES B = "; A * B
60 PRINT "A DIVIDED BY B = ";
   A/B
70 END
```

2. ```
10 PRINT "COMPUTERS CAN FIND
   AVERAGES."
20 LET M = 324
30 LET N = 468
40 LET P = 279
50 LET A = (M + N + P)/3
60 PRINT "THE AVERAGE OF"
70 PRINT "THE THREE NUMBERS
   IS "; A
80 END
```

3. ```
10 PRINT "MULTIPLY A NUMBER"
20 PRINT "BY 3 AND ADD 5."
30 LET N = 9
40 LET R = 3 * N + 5
50 PRINT "WHEN THE NUMBER"
60 PRINT "IS "; N; "THE RESULT
   IS "; R
70 END
```

4. ```
10 LET S = 16
20 LET P = 3 * S
30 PRINT "THE PERIMETER (IN CM)"
40 PRINT "OF AN EQUILATERAL"
50 PRINT "TRIANGLE WITH SIDE"
60 PRINT "LENGTH (IN CM) = "; S;
   "IS "; P
70 END
```

5. ```
10 LET N = 25
20 PRINT "THE NUMBER IS "; N
30 PRINT "THE DOUBLE OF THE
   NUMBER IS "
40 GOTO 70
50 PRINT 3 * N
60 GOTO 100
70 PRINT 2 * N
80 PRINT "THE TRIPLE OF THE
   NUMBER IS "
90 GOTO 50
100 END
```

6. How would you change the program in exercise 2 to find the average of 78, 64, and 47?

7. How would you change the program in exercise 4 to find the perimeter of a square with side length 24?

★ 8. Write a short program that uses a number variable.
```

Cumulative Review

Which sign should go in the ?

1. $\frac{3}{8}$ $\frac{3}{9}$ **A** $>$ **B** $<$ **C** $=$

2. $\frac{6}{8}$ $\frac{12}{16}$ **A** $>$ **B** $<$ **C** $=$

3. $\frac{1}{10}$ $\frac{1}{20}$ **A** $>$ **B** $<$ **C** $=$

Add or subtract.

4. $\frac{3}{9} + \frac{4}{9}$ **A** $\frac{1}{9}$ **B** $\frac{9}{7}$

          C $\frac{7}{9}$ **D** not given

5. $\frac{3}{8} + \frac{1}{4}$ **A** $\frac{4}{8}$ **B** $\frac{5}{8}$

          C $\frac{4}{12}$ **D** not given

6. $\frac{6}{7} - \frac{4}{7}$ **A** $\frac{10}{7}$ **B** $\frac{2}{7}$

          C $\frac{10}{14}$ **D** not given

7. $\frac{7}{15} - \frac{2}{5}$ **A** $\frac{5}{15}$ **B** $\frac{6}{15}$

          C $\frac{1}{15}$ **D** not given

8. What is the measure of this angle?

   A 45°   **B** 90°

   C 120°   **D** not given

9. What kind of angle is this?

   A obtuse   **B** right

   C acute   **D** not given

Use these triangles for items 10-12.

M   N   O

10. Which triangle is a scalene triangle?

   A M   **B** N

   C O   **D** not given

11. Which triangle is an equilateral triangle?

   A N   **B** M

   C O   **D** not given

12. Which triangle is an isosceles triangle?

   A N   **B** O

   C M   **D** not given

13. Toni mowed $\frac{1}{3}$ of a field on Wednesday. On Thursday she mowed $\frac{1}{6}$ of the field. What fraction of the field did she mow in those two days?

   A $\frac{2}{3}$ **B** $\frac{2}{6}$

   C $\frac{1}{2}$ **D** not given

14. Mack used $\frac{3}{4}$ of the water in the watering can on a fern and $\frac{1}{8}$ of the water on a geranium. What fraction of the water was left?

   A $\frac{2}{3}$ **B** $\frac{1}{4}$

   C $\frac{3}{8}$ **D** not given

Decimals: Multiplication and Division

Mr. Field's fifth grade class is in the business of making note cards. The cards are sold in a large downtown store. The store has a shop where things made by the city's school children are shown and sold. When any of the note cards are sold, 0.25 of the money goes to the class, 0.5 goes to the store to cover its costs, and 0.25 goes to the girl or boy who made the cards. This means that the child who made the cards receives $0.25 for every dollar's worth that is sold. When the first note cards were ready for sale, the class went to the store to help arrange them in a showcase. While the children were still there, the first set of their note cards was sold to a happy customer!

Estimating Decimal Products and Quotients: Mental Math

Carol multiplied 8.72 × 6.14 on a calculator. Does the product shown seem reasonable?

We can round decimals to the nearest whole number to estimate the product.

$$8.72 \times 6.14$$
$$\downarrow \qquad \downarrow$$
$$9 \quad \times \quad 6 \quad = 54$$

The product on the calculator is about 54, so it seems reasonable.

Michael divided 36.022 by 8.68 on a calculator. Does the quotient shown seem reasonable?

We can round the decimals to the nearest whole number to estimate the quotient.

$$36.022 \div 8.68$$
$$\downarrow \qquad \downarrow$$
$$36 \quad \div \quad 9 \quad = 4$$

The quotient on the calculator is about 4, so it seems reasonable.

Warm Up Estimate the products.

1. 9.3 × 4.78 2. 7.89 × 3.94

3. 1.89 × 3.5 4. 7.08 × 6.74

Estimate the quotients.

5. 24.37 ÷ 6.14 6. 35.98 ÷ 3.82

7. 53.742 ÷ 8.9 8. 72.46 ÷ 7.992

Round each decimal to the nearest whole number and estimate the product. If the given calculator product seems reasonable, write **R**. If not, write **NR**.

1. 3.87×4.09

$$15.8283$$

2. 4.23×8.76

$$370.548$$

3. 0.968×6.45

$$6.2436$$

4. 12.7×3.21

$$407.67$$

5. 4.38×7.75

$$33.945$$

6. 2.98×5.84

$$17.4032$$

7. 9.013×6.872

$$7.859336$$

8. 15.386×1.89

$$29.07954$$

9. 43.28×3.14

$$135.8992$$

Round each decimal to the nearest whole number and estimate the quotient. If the given calculator quotient seems reasonable, write **R**. If not, write **NR**. (Only the first five digits of each quotient are shown.)

10. $41.98 \div 7.16$

$$6.8631$$

11. $16.43 \div 3.98$

$$4.1281$$

12. $19.997 \div 5.08$

$$0.3936$$

13. $62.76 \div 6.84$

$$9.1754$$

14. $48.11 \div 6.43$

$$2.8564$$

15. $26.50 \div 2.84$

$$9.3309$$

16. $99.87 \div 20.142$

$$4.9582$$

17. $49.441 \div 6.57$

$$0.7525$$

Think

Discovering a Pattern

Do you see a pattern in these equations?

$0.1089 \times 9 = n$
$0.10989 \times 9 = n$
$0.109989 \times 9 = n$

Give the next two equations.

Math

Multiplying Decimals

The doctor at the animal hospital needs to give a young rabbit 0.2 mg (milligram) of medicine for each kilogram of its weight. If the rabbit weighs 0.9 kg, how much medicine should the doctor give it?

Since the same amount is given for each kilogram of weight, we multiply.

Multiply as with whole numbers.	→	Write the product so it has as many decimal places as the sum of the decimal places in the factors.

$$\begin{array}{r} 0.2 \\ \times\, 0.9 \\ \hline 18 \end{array}$$

$$\begin{array}{r} 0.2 \leftarrow 1 \text{ decimal place} \\ \times\, 0.9 \leftarrow 1 \text{ decimal place} \\ \hline 0.18 \leftarrow 2 \text{ decimal places} \end{array}$$

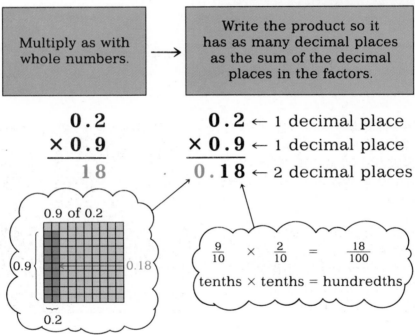

0.9 of 0.2

0.9 ← → 0.18

0.2

$$\frac{9}{10} \times \frac{2}{10} = \frac{18}{100}$$

tenths × tenths = hundredths

The doctor should give the rabbit 0.18 mg of medicine.

Other Examples

$$\begin{array}{r} 8.3\,2 \leftarrow 2 \text{ decimal places} \\ \times\quad 0.4 \leftarrow 1 \text{ decimal place} \\ \hline 3.3\,2\,8 \leftarrow 3 \text{ decimal places} \end{array}$$

$$\begin{array}{r} 0.0\,7\,3 \leftarrow 3 \text{ places} \\ \times\qquad 8 \leftarrow 0 \text{ places} \\ \hline 0.5\,8\,4 \leftarrow 3 \text{ places} \end{array}$$

$$\begin{array}{r} 5.3 \leftarrow 1 \text{ place} \\ \times\, 1.4 \leftarrow 1 \text{ place} \\ \hline 2\,1\,2 \\ 5\,3 \\ \hline 7.4\,2 \leftarrow 2 \text{ places} \end{array}$$

Warm Up Multiply.

1.	2.	3.	4.	5.
0.8	5.8	0.046	9.67	0.76
× 0.7	× 0.4	× 7	× 1.8	× 9.3

324

Multiply.

1. 3.4 × 1.2	**2.** 0.7 × 0.4	**3.** 5.23 × 4	**4.** 1.32 × 0.7	**5.** 1.6 × 5.3
6. 0.56 × 5	**7.** 1.38 × 6	**8.** 3.2 × 1.4	**9.** 38 × 5.3	**10.** 0.95 × 20
11. 6.8 × 0.9	**12.** 0.72 × 3.8	**13.** 1.04 × 36	**14.** 9.6 × 0.85	**15.** 16.4 × 0.7
16. 39 × 0.07	**17.** 3.8 × 10	**18.** 4.06 × 8.2	**19.** 5.43 × 6.8	**20.** 3.72 × 4.1

21. 15 × 0.06

22. 3.12 × 4

23. 0.68 × 1.4

24. First estimate, then find the product: 4.7 × 6.3

25. First estimate, then find the product: 8.5 × 7.92

26. Irina's dog weighs 15.7 kg. She needs to give it 1.5 mg of medicine for each kilogram of its weight. How much medicine should she give it?

27. A 12-year-old horse needs 2.35 mg of medicine for every kilogram of its weight. If it weighs 479.4 kg, how much medicine does it need?

Skillkeeper

Subtract.

1. $7\frac{1}{3}$ $-3\frac{2}{3}$	**2.** 9 $-4\frac{1}{5}$	**3.** $13\frac{3}{8}$ $-2\frac{5}{8}$	**4.** $11\frac{2}{5}$ $-4\frac{3}{5}$	**5.** $12\frac{1}{2}$ -3
6. $4\frac{1}{4}$ $-2\frac{1}{3}$	**7.** $11\frac{1}{2}$ $-3\frac{5}{8}$	**8.** 6 $-3\frac{5}{6}$	**9.** $8\frac{1}{3}$ $-5\frac{3}{4}$	**10.** $14\frac{2}{5}$ $-7\frac{7}{10}$

More Multiplying Decimals

A person who walks slowly might travel 6 km per hour (km/h). A fast snail might travel 0.008 times as fast. How fast does the snail travel?

Since the snail travels 0.008 times as fast, we multiply.

$$
\begin{array}{r}
0.008 \leftarrow 3\text{ places} \\
\times \quad\quad 6 \leftarrow 0\text{ places} \\
\hline
0.048 \leftarrow 3\text{ places}
\end{array}
$$

Sometimes you need to write more zeros in the product to have the correct number of decimal places.

The snail travels 0.048 km per hour.

Other Examples

$$
\begin{array}{r}
0.09 \\
\times \quad 0.6 \\
\hline
0.054
\end{array}
\qquad
\begin{array}{r}
0.2 \\
\times\, 0.04 \\
\hline
0.008
\end{array}
\qquad
\begin{array}{r}
0.003 \\
\times \quad 2 \\
\hline
0.006
\end{array}
\qquad
\begin{array}{r}
37 \\
\times\, 0.002 \\
\hline
0.074
\end{array}
$$

Warm Up Write the product with the decimal point in the correct place. Write extra zeros when necessary.

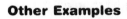

1. $\begin{array}{r} 0.3 \\ \times\, 0.3 \\ \hline 9 \end{array}$
2. $\begin{array}{r} 0.05 \\ \times\, 0.3 \\ \hline 15 \end{array}$
3. $\begin{array}{r} 1.5 \\ \times\, 0.4 \\ \hline 60 \end{array}$
4. $\begin{array}{r} 6.2 \\ \times\, 0.01 \\ \hline 62 \end{array}$
5. $\begin{array}{r} 0.008 \\ \times\quad 7 \\ \hline 56 \end{array}$

Multiply.

6. $\begin{array}{r} 0.2 \\ \times\, 0.3 \end{array}$
7. $\begin{array}{r} 5.03 \\ \times\, 0.7 \end{array}$
8. $\begin{array}{r} 0.02 \\ \times\, 0.1 \end{array}$
9. $\begin{array}{r} 24 \\ \times\, 0.002 \end{array}$
10. $\begin{array}{r} 0.009 \\ \times\quad 6 \end{array}$

Multiply.

1. $\begin{array}{r} 0.06 \\ \times\ 0.8 \\ \hline \end{array}$	**2.** $\begin{array}{r} 2.6 \\ \times\ 0.04 \\ \hline \end{array}$	**3.** $\begin{array}{r} 0.9 \\ \times\ 0.06 \\ \hline \end{array}$	**4.** $\begin{array}{r} 0.18 \\ \times\ 0.5 \\ \hline \end{array}$	**5.** $\begin{array}{r} 0.12 \\ \times\ 0.6 \\ \hline \end{array}$
6. $\begin{array}{r} 1.2 \\ \times\ 0.06 \\ \hline \end{array}$	**7.** $\begin{array}{r} 7.4 \\ \times\ 0.05 \\ \hline \end{array}$	**8.** $\begin{array}{r} 0.94 \\ \times\ 0.2 \\ \hline \end{array}$	**9.** $\begin{array}{r} 0.02 \\ \times\ 0.4 \\ \hline \end{array}$	**10.** $\begin{array}{r} 4.5 \\ \times\ 2.7 \\ \hline \end{array}$
11. $\begin{array}{r} 424 \\ \times\ 0.006 \\ \hline \end{array}$	**12.** $\begin{array}{r} 0.67 \\ \times\ 10 \\ \hline \end{array}$	**13.** $\begin{array}{r} 40 \\ \times\ 0.06 \\ \hline \end{array}$	**14.** $\begin{array}{r} 0.009 \\ \times\ 8 \\ \hline \end{array}$	**15.** $\begin{array}{r} 1.28 \\ \times\ 0.7 \\ \hline \end{array}$
16. $\begin{array}{r} 63.4 \\ \times\ 7.2 \\ \hline \end{array}$	**17.** $\begin{array}{r} 0.013 \\ \times\ 6 \\ \hline \end{array}$	**18.** $\begin{array}{r} 7.45 \\ \times\ 2.3 \\ \hline \end{array}$	**19.** $\begin{array}{r} 27 \\ \times\ 0.002 \\ \hline \end{array}$	**20.** $\begin{array}{r} 136 \\ \times\ 0.01 \\ \hline \end{array}$

21. 0.05×0.3

22. 0.4×0.02

23. 0.011×9

24. 0.3×0.001

25. $0.4 \times 6 \times 0.002$

26. $5 \times 0.02 \times 0.103$

27. An average-size beetle might be 3 cm long, but the minute beetle is only 0.004 times this long. How long is the minute beetle?

28. Write a question for this data. Then solve the problem. A coat hanger wire is 0.2 cm thick. A human hair is 0.02 times as thick as the wire.

29. One leaf of a book is 0.006 cm thick and one front or back cover is 0.35 cm thick. Find how many centimeters of shelf space are needed for three books that have 475 leaves each.

Skillkeeper

Multiply.

1. $3 \times \frac{1}{4}$

2. $\frac{1}{2} \times \frac{1}{3}$

3. $\frac{2}{5} \times \frac{1}{6}$

4. $\frac{5}{8} \times 2$

5. $\frac{1}{4} \times \frac{3}{5}$

6. $\frac{2}{3} \times \frac{5}{6}$

7. $5 \times \frac{2}{5}$

8. $\frac{3}{4} \times \frac{1}{3}$

9. $4 \times 1\frac{1}{2}$

10. $\frac{3}{8} \times 2\frac{1}{4}$

11. $1\frac{1}{3} \times 2\frac{1}{2}$

12. $3\frac{1}{5} \times 1\frac{1}{4}$

QUESTION
DATA
PLAN
ANSWER
CHECK

Problem Solving: Practice

Read the facts. Then solve the problems.

The **circumference** of a full-size bike wheel (the distance around it) is about 2.15 m. When the wheel goes around once, you travel 2.15 m.

The **gear ratio** tells how many times the wheels go around each time the pedals go around once. If the gear ratio is 3, the wheels go around 3 times as the pedals go around once.

10-Speed Bike	
Gear	Gear Ratio
Highest (speed 10)	3.7
Lowest (speed 1)	1.4

Gear ratio	×	Wheel circumference (m)	=	Distance traveled (m) as pedals go around once

1. How far do you travel in highest gear as the pedals go around once?

2. How far do you travel in lowest gear as the pedals go around once?

3. How much farther do you travel in highest gear than in lowest gear as the pedals go around once?

4. How far do you travel in highest gear as the pedals go around 25 times?

5. If the pedals go around once in highest gear and once in lowest gear, how far do you travel?

6. Round the circumference to the nearest whole number and estimate how many times the bike wheel goes around as the bike travels 126 km.

7. **Try This** Jill's bike travels 5 m for every 2 times the pedals go around. How many times must the pedals go around as the bike travels 40 m? Hint: Make a table.

Problem Solving:
Using Data from a Catalog

When you order from a catalog, you must fill out an order form like the one shown here.

Item	How many	Price each	Total price
Tent Repair Kit	1	$ 3.95	
Air Mattress	4	12.69	
Flashlight	2	7.45	
Lantern Battery	3	2.58	
Total for goods			
Tax (0.05 × total)			
Postage		$2.75	
Amount Enclosed			

1. Find the "Total price" for each item on the order form. Then find the total amount you should enclose. Do not forget to include the tax! (Round to the nearest cent.)

2. A family ordered 4 sleeping bags. Each bag cost $23.95. They also ordered a camp stove for $37.50. The postage was $1.87. How much money should they send with their order, including tax?

3. A backpack and a frame cost $39.87 (tax included) if they are ordered from a catalog. The postage cost is $1.49. The same items cost $45.24 (tax included) in a local store. How much do you save by ordering from the catalog?

4. **DATA HUNT** What would you choose if you were given $100 and could order any 3 or more items you wished from a department store catalog? Use a catalog and calculate the amount you must enclose for the items you choose. Include tax if necessary.

5. **Try This** The total cost of two catalog items is $11.85. The more expensive item costs two times as much as the less expensive item. How much does the less expensive item cost?

Dividing Decimals

Lee, David, and Barb had a garage sale. They made $23.85 from the sale and shared it equally. How much money did each person get?

To find the amount for 1 of 3 equal shares, we divide.

Divide the whole number part.	→	Place the decimal point. Divide the tenths.	→	Divide the hundredths.

$$\begin{array}{r} 7 \\ 3\overline{)23.85} \\ 21 \\ \hline 2 \end{array}$$

Think about dividing **dollars.** Each gets 7, 2 extra.

$$\begin{array}{r} 7.9 \\ 3\overline{)23.85} \\ 21 \\ \hline 28 \\ 27 \\ \hline 1 \end{array}$$

Think about dividing **dimes.** 2 dollars, 8 dimes → 28 dimes. Each gets 9, 1 extra.

$$\begin{array}{r} 7.95 \\ 3\overline{)23.85} \\ 21 \\ \hline 28 \\ 27 \\ \hline 15 \\ 15 \\ \hline 0 \end{array}$$

Think about dividing **pennies.** 1 dime, 5 pennies → 15 pennies. Each gets 5, 0 extra.

Each person got $7.95.

Other Examples

$$\begin{array}{r} 24.14 \\ 3\overline{)72.42} \\ 6 \\ \hline 12 \\ 12 \\ \hline 04 \\ 3 \\ \hline 12 \\ 12 \\ \hline 0 \end{array}$$

$$\begin{array}{r} 0.537 \\ 2\overline{)1.074} \\ 10 \\ \hline 07 \\ 6 \\ \hline 14 \\ 14 \\ \hline 0 \end{array}$$

$$\begin{array}{r} 0.164 \\ 6\overline{)0.984} \\ 6 \\ \hline 38 \\ 36 \\ \hline 24 \\ 24 \\ \hline 0 \end{array}$$

Warm Up Divide. Check your answers.

1. $3\overline{)8.52}$ **2.** $2\overline{)1.672}$ **3.** $4\overline{)98.48}$ **4.** $5\overline{)0.875}$ **5.** $3\overline{)24.36}$

Divide.

1. $2\overline{)3.16}$ 2. $3\overline{)1.095}$ 3. $4\overline{)18.48}$ 4. $5\overline{)41.5}$ 5. $6\overline{)14.94}$

6. $4\overline{)7.28}$ 7. $3\overline{)73.08}$ 8. $7\overline{)16.8}$ 9. $5\overline{)23.25}$ 10. $4\overline{)2.348}$

11. $2\overline{)1.888}$ 12. $5\overline{)15.6}$ 13. $3\overline{)20.4}$ 14. $4\overline{)217.2}$ 15. $6\overline{)14.88}$

16. $8\overline{)0.984}$ 17. $9\overline{)34.56}$ 18. $7\overline{)3.822}$ 19. $5\overline{)31.45}$ 20. $4\overline{)0.852}$

21. $1.12 \div 2$ 22. $25.92 \div 3$ 23. $48.15 \div 5$

24. $157.44 \div 6$ 25. $0.572 \div 4$ 26. $194.4 \div 3$

27. What is the quotient when 35.46 is divided by 3?

28. First estimate, then find the quotient: $35.8 \div 4$

29. Four clubs working together made $338.76 from paper they sold for recycling. If they shared the earnings, how much did each club receive?

30. Gardiner School held a White Elephant Sale after school on the last 3 Thursdays and Fridays in May. The total sales were $233.70. What was the average amount of their sales each day?

Think

Fraction → Decimal

$\frac{3}{4}$ means $3 \div 4$,

So $\frac{3}{4} = 0.75$.

$\dfrac{0.75}{4\overline{)3.}}$

Write extra zeros as needed.

Divide to find decimals for these fractions. Use a calculator to check your work.

$\dfrac{1}{2}, \dfrac{1}{4}, \dfrac{1}{5}, \dfrac{1}{8}, \dfrac{2}{5}, \dfrac{3}{5}, \dfrac{4}{5}, \dfrac{3}{8}, \dfrac{5}{8}, \dfrac{7}{8}$

Math

Dividing Decimals: Working with Zeros

Mrs. Perez is a bank teller. She helps bank customers cash checks, make deposits, and complete other bank business. She earns $40.36 for 8 hours work. How much does she earn per hour (to the nearest cent)?

To find the amount earned per hour, we divide.

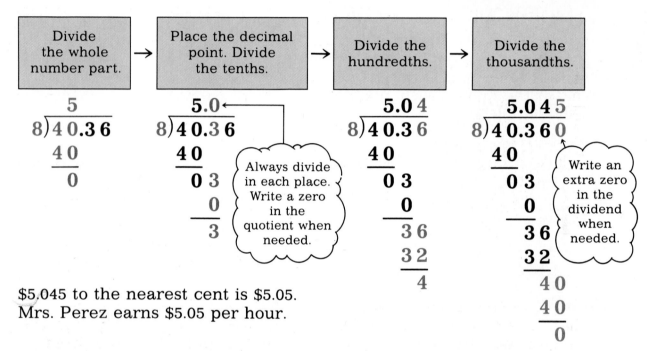

| Divide the whole number part. | → | Place the decimal point. Divide the tenths. | → | Divide the hundredths. | → | Divide the thousandths. |

$$\begin{array}{r} 5 \\ 8\overline{)40.36} \\ 40 \\ \hline 0 \end{array}$$

$$\begin{array}{r} 5.0 \\ 8\overline{)40.36} \\ 40 \\ \hline 03 \\ 0 \\ \hline 3 \end{array}$$

Always divide in each place. Write a zero in the quotient when needed.

$$\begin{array}{r} 5.04 \\ 8\overline{)40.36} \\ 40 \\ \hline 03 \\ 0 \\ \hline 36 \\ 32 \\ \hline 4 \end{array}$$

$$\begin{array}{r} 5.045 \\ 8\overline{)40.360} \\ 40 \\ \hline 03 \\ 0 \\ \hline 36 \\ 32 \\ \hline 40 \\ 40 \\ \hline 0 \end{array}$$

Write an extra zero in the dividend when needed.

$5.045 to the nearest cent is $5.05.
Mrs. Perez earns $5.05 per hour.

Other Examples

$$\begin{array}{r} 0.408 \\ 3\overline{)1.224} \\ 12 \\ \hline 02 \\ 0 \\ \hline 24 \\ 24 \\ \hline 0 \end{array}$$

$$\begin{array}{r} 0.007 \\ 4\overline{)0.028} \\ 28 \\ \hline 0 \end{array}$$

$$\begin{array}{r} 0.062 \\ 5\overline{)0.310} \\ 30 \\ \hline 10 \\ 10 \\ \hline 0 \end{array}$$

Write an extra zero as needed when dividing.

Warm Up Divide. Check your answers.

1. $2\overline{)12.04}$ 2. $3\overline{)0.084}$ 3. $5\overline{)31.035}$ 4. $6\overline{)0.054}$ 5. $4\overline{)0.3}$

6. $7\overline{)2.114}$ 7. $5\overline{)0.045}$ 8. $6\overline{)0.534}$ 9. $3\overline{)12.618}$ 10. $5\overline{)0.37}$

Divide.

1. $3\overline{)0.624}$ 2. $5\overline{)1.82}$ 3. $4\overline{)0.156}$

4. $6\overline{)17.184}$ 5. $2\overline{)1.622}$ 6. $4\overline{)0.032}$

7. $5\overline{)27.01}$ 8. $6\overline{)6.354}$ 9. $7\overline{)0.042}$

10. $8\overline{)5.672}$ 11. $3\overline{)38.4}$ 12. $2\overline{)47.4}$

13. $5\overline{)0.24}$ 14. $8\overline{)0.608}$ 15. $9\overline{)9.954}$

16. $7\overline{)163.94}$ 17. $6\overline{)40.698}$ 18. $4\overline{)0.396}$

19. $5\overline{)10.045}$ 20. $3\overline{)18.021}$ 21. $2\overline{)2.212}$

22. $6\overline{)0.534}$ 23. $4\overline{)106.72}$ 24. $3\overline{)6.204}$

25. $12.111 \div 3$ 26. $4.032 \div 4$

27. First estimate then find the quotient:
$54.12 \div 8.8$

28. A bank file clerk earns $32.72 for 8 hours work. How much does he earn per hour?

29. A bank worker earns time and a half for overtime work. If the person's regular hourly salary is $4.26, how much would his or her overtime salary be per hour?

30. **DATA BANK** What are the hourly earnings (to the nearest cent) of persons in the three kinds of work that are most interesting to you? (See Data Bank, page 412.)

Think

Logical Reasoning

Can you follow these rules and exchange positions of the red and black checkers?

1. Reds move only to the left.

2. Blacks move only to the right.

3. A checker can slide one place to a empty space.

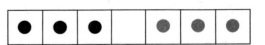

4. You can jump one checker of a different color if you can land in an empty space.

5. You cannot jump a same-color checker.

Math

Problem Solving:
Using Data from Advertisements

Solve.

1. Are the oranges cheaper at Bill's or at MaxiMart? How much cheaper?

2. Which brand of soup costs less per can? How much less?

3. How much per roll are paper towels at each of these markets? How much less would 15 rolls of towels cost at the cheaper price?

4. Which paper plates should you buy to save money? (Hint: How much does each plate cost?) How much will you save per plate?

5. What does each Hillfarm egg cost? What does a Quality egg cost? How much do you save when buying a dozen of the cheaper eggs?

6. **DATA BANK** How much more would it cost to get your total daily protein needs by eating frankfurters than by eating peanut butter? (See Data Bank, page 410.)

7. **Try This** One roll of paper towels contains 8 m² of paper and costs $1.28. Another brand of the same quality contains 6 m² of paper. How much would the second roll need to cost in order for the two rolls to be equally good buys?

Bill's Market
ORANGES
5 for $1.95

MAXIMART
ORANGES
3 for $1.29

Bell's Soup
3 cans for $1.14

Mom SOUP
2 cans for $0.82

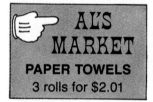

AL'S MARKET
PAPER TOWELS
3 rolls for $2.01

Hi-Value Grocery
Paper Towel Special
5 rolls–$3.15

PICNIC SPECIAL
PAPER PLATES
6 packages–$2.16
(12 per package)

Cookout Bargain!
PAPER PLATES
8 packages–$3.20
(16 per package)

3 DOZEN
Hillfarm Eggs
$2.52

2 Dozen
Quality Eggs
$1.92

334

Problem Solving:
Using Data from a Blueprint

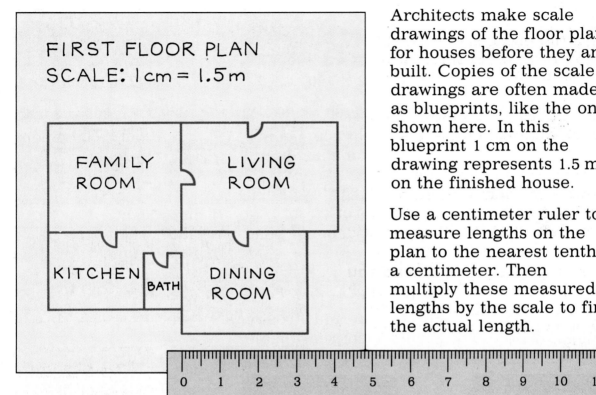

FIRST FLOOR PLAN
SCALE: 1 cm = 1.5 m

FAMILY ROOM

LIVING ROOM

KITCHEN

BATH

DINING ROOM

Architects make scale drawings of the floor plans for houses before they are built. Copies of the scale drawings are often made as blueprints, like the one shown here. In this blueprint 1 cm on the drawing represents 1.5 m on the finished house.

Use a centimeter ruler to measure lengths on the plan to the nearest tenth of a centimeter. Then multiply these measured lengths by the scale to find the actual length.

Actual length of dining room: $1.5 \times 3.3 = 4.95$ m

1. How wide is the dining room?

2. What are the actual dimensions (length and width) of the living room?

3. What are the actual dimensions of the family room?

4. To find how much baseboard to use, the builder needs to know the perimeter of the rooms. What is the actual perimeter of the kitchen?

5. The carpet layer needs to know the area of rooms in order to decide how much carpeting will be needed for each room. What is the actual area of the family room?

6. **Try This** The perimeter of a rectangular room is 17 m. The length of the room is 1.5 m greater than the width. What is the width of the room?

Multiplying and Dividing
by Multiples of 10: Mental Math

Jack multiplied 3.142 by 10, 100, and 1,000 on a calculator. Do the products seem reasonable?

3.142 × 10
↓
3 × 10 = 30

About 30. Seems reasonable.

3.142 × 100
↓
3 × 100 = 300

About 300. Seems reasonable.

3.142 × 1,000
↓
3 × 1,000 = 3,000

About 3,000. Seems reasonable.

The products above suggest these short cuts:

To **multiply** by ⎰10⎱ move the decimal point ⎰1 place right⎱
              ⎨100⎬   ⎨2 places right⎬
              ⎩1,000⎭   ⎩3 places right⎭

Megan divided 5,978.6 by 10, 100, and 1,000 on a calculator. Do the quotients seem reasonable?

5,978.6 ÷ 10
↓
6,000 ÷ 10 = 600

About 600. Seems reasonable.

5,978.6 ÷ 100
↓
6,000 ÷ 100 = 60

About 60. Seems reasonable.

5,978.6 ÷ 1,000
↓
6,000 ÷ 1,000 = 6

About 6. Seems reasonable.

The quotients above suggest these short cuts:

To **divide** by ⎰10⎱ move the decimal point ⎰1 place left⎱
           ⎨100⎬   ⎨2 places left⎬
           ⎩1,000⎭   ⎩3 places left⎭

Multiply or divide.

1. 7.623 × 10   **2.** 7.623 × 100   **3.** 7.623 × 1,000   **4.** 100 × 4.38

5. 3,842.3 ÷ 10   **6.** 3,842.3 ÷ 100   **7.** 3,842.3 ÷ 1,000   **8.** 5.7 ÷ 10

Changing Metric Units

After an object is measured using a certain unit, we can **multiply by multiples of 10** to give its measure in a smaller unit.

1 cm = 10 mm
1 m = 100 cm
1 km = 1,000 m
1 L = 1,000 mL
1 kg = 1,000 g

Examples:

shoe length, 28.3 **cm** → 28.3 × 10, or 283 **mm**

person's height, 1.96 **m** → 1.96 × 100, or 196 **cm**

lake's length, 2.4 **km** → 2.4 × 1,000, or 2,400 **m**

jar's capacity 0.875 **L** → 0.875 × 1,000, or 875 **mL**

book's weight, 1.124 **kg** → 1.124 × 1,000, or 1,124 **g**

Give the number for each ▥.

1. fork, 14.3 cm; ▥ mm **2.** belt, 0.68 m; ▥ cm **3.** trail, 3.4 km; ▥ m

4. pail, 2.42 L; ▥ mL **5.** ribbon, 2.56 m; ▥ cm **6.** meat, 1.542 kg; ▥ g

After an object is measured using a certain unit, we can **divide by multiples of 10** to give its measure in a larger unit.

10 mm = 1 cm
100 cm = 1 m
1,000 m = 1 km
1,000 mL = 1 L
1,000 g = 1 kg

Examples:

bolt, 72 **mm** → 72 ÷ 10, or 7.2 **cm**

bat, 96 **cm** → 96 ÷ 100, or 0.96 **m**

field, 836 **m** → 836 ÷ 1,000, or 0.836 **km**

glass, 265 **mL** → 265 ÷ 1,000, or 0.265 **L**

apple, 287 **g** → 287 ÷ 1,000, or 0.287 **kg**

Give the number for each ▥.

7. pen, 167 mm; ▥ cm **8.** ski, 170 cm; ▥ m **9.** runway, 1,255 m; ▥ km

10. vase, 787 mL; ▥ L **11.** melon, 2,475 g; ▥ kg **12.** fishing rod, 165 cm; ▥ m

Applied Problem Solving

You live in Chicago, and you are planning a 2-week vacation in San Francisco. Should you fly or drive?

Some Things to Consider

- You will be staying with friends in San Francisco. You will not need a hotel room while you are there.

- A round-trip airline ticket costs $418.00.

- You will need a car for 7 days in San Francisco. You can rent one for $42.00 a day.

- You will spend about $20 for gas and oil for your own car or for the rented car while you are in San Francisco.

- Your driving time to San Francisco and back to Chicago will be 8 days. You will have to stay in motels 6 nights.

- Gas and oil will cost about $43.75 a day during your drive to San Francisco and back to Chicago.

- A motel room will cost about $45.00 a night.

Some Questions to Answer

1. What will your total expenses be if you drive? What will they be if you fly and rent a car?

2. Compare the total costs of the two trips. Is one much more expensive, or are they about the same?

What Is Your Decision?

Will you fly or drive? Why?

Chapter Review-Test

Round to the nearest whole number and estimate the product or quotient.

1. 3.78 × 4.14
2. 6.27 × 8.79
3. 5.86 × 7.98
4. 2.073 × 8.75

5. 24.36 ÷ 8.34
6. 41.58 ÷ 5.99
7. 63.47 ÷ 8.57
8. 44.98 ÷ 4.64

Multiply.

9.
```
   7.46
×  0.7
```
10.
```
   0.8
× 0.9
```
11.
```
  0.085
×     9
```
12.
```
   6.4
× 2.3
```
13.
```
   8.78
×  4.5
```

14.
```
  0.007
×     6
```
15.
```
   0.07
×  0.8
```
16.
```
   0.4
× 0.08
```
17.
```
  0.003
×     7
```
18.
```
      89
× 0.004
```

Divide.

19. 4)49.28
20. 3)7.29
21. 6)1.416
22. 5)0.835

23. 7)2.128
24. 9)0.054
25. 8)0.456
26. 2)12.816

Find the products.

27. 3.42 × 10
28. 8.674 × 100
29. 9.63 × 1000
30. 100 × 7.4

Find the quotients.

31. 86.7 ÷ 10
32. 364.2 ÷ 100
33. 873.64 ÷ 1000
34. 7.6 ÷ 100

35. 8.6 km = ▒ m
36. 9 kg = ▒ g
37. 123 cm = ▒ m
38. 2,643 mL = ▒ L

39. Which juice costs less per can?

A
3 cans for $3.36

B
4 cans for $4.72

40. A restaurant sells whole submarine sandwiches and half submarine sandwiches. How much would 9.5 submarine sandwiches cost at $1.85 per sandwich?

Another Look

Estimating

$6.3\,7 \times 4.5$ ←

⬇   ⬇

$6 \quad \times \quad 5 \quad = 3\,0$

Round up when 5 or more.

$2\,6.7\,4 \div 9.0\,7$

⬇   ⬇

$2\,7 \quad \div \quad 9 \quad = 3$

Multiplying

$7\,4.6$ ← 1 place
$\times \quad 0.3$ ← 1 place
$\overline{2\,2.3\,8}$ ← 2 places

0.7 ← 1 place
$\times\,0.0\,9$ ← 2 places
$\overline{0.0\,6\,3}$ ← 3 places

Be sure to write a zero.

Special Products and Quotients

$4.7\,3\,2 \times 1\,0 \quad = \quad 4\,7.3\,2$

$4.7\,3\,2 \times 1\,0\,0 \quad = \quad 4\,7\,3.2$

$4.7\,3\,2 \times 1,0\,0\,0 = \quad 4,7\,3\,2.$

$8\,7\,5.6 \div 1\,0 \quad = \quad 8\,7.5\,6$

$8\,7\,5.6 \div 1\,0\,0 \quad = \quad 8.7\,5\,6$

$8\,7\,5.6 \div 1,0\,0\,0 = 0.8\,7\,5\,6$

Estimate the product or quotient.

1.	5.23	**2.**	0.963	**3.**	8.91
	× 6.87		× 4.3		× 0.75

4. $31.97 \div 7.68$ **5.** $55.55 \div 6.83$

6. $39.71 \div 4.501$ **7.** $48.38 \div 7.85$

Multiply.

8.	9.45	**9.**	6.4	**10.**	0.07
	× 0.8		× 3.7		× 0.5
11.	43	**12.**	9.46	**13.**	3.76
	× 0.002		× 2.3		× 2.8
14.	1.08	**15.**	0.057	**16.**	3.02
	× 0.09		× 0.34		× 0.75

Find the product or quotient.

17. 3.47×10 **18.** 2.365×100

19. $4.578 \times 1,000$ **20.** $3.2 \div 10$

21. $456.2 \div 100$ **22.** $3,457.3 \div 1,000$

Enrichment

Finding and Using Patterns

Square B below is a **magic square** because the sum of the numbers in each row, column, and diagonal is the same magic sum. Here is how this 4-by-4 magic square is made.

- Start with the numbers in order, as shown in square A.
- Exchange numbers as shown by the arrows to get magic square B.

1. What is the magic sum for square B?

2. Start with a different number and make your own 4-by-4 magic square.

3. What is the magic sum for square C?

A

3	4	5	6
7	8	9	10
11	12	13	14
15	16	17	18

B

18	4	5	15
7	13	12	10
11	9	8	14
6	16	17	3

C

87.12	10.89	65.34
32.67	54.45	76.23
43.56	98.01	21.78

→

D

7.1	0.8	5.3
2.6	4.4	6.2
3.5	8.0	1.7

4. What pattern was used to make square D from square C?

5. Is square D a magic square?

6. Find some other squares that can be made from square D and see if they are magic squares.

Cumulative Review

Add or subtract.

1. $10\frac{3}{5}$
$+\ 2\frac{1}{3}$

A $12\frac{4}{8}$ **B** $12\frac{14}{15}$
C $12\frac{4}{15}$ **D** not given

2. $17\frac{2}{7}$
$-\ 8\frac{3}{7}$

A $9\frac{6}{7}$ **B** $8\frac{6}{7}$
C $9\frac{5}{7}$ **D** not given

3. $4\frac{3}{4}$
$+2\frac{1}{6}$

A $6\frac{5}{6}$ **B** $6\frac{5}{12}$
C $7\frac{1}{6}$ **D** not given

4. $40\frac{1}{6}$
$+16\frac{5}{6}$

A 57 **B** $56\frac{5}{6}$
C 56 **D** not given

5. $9\frac{8}{9}$
$-4\frac{2}{3}$

A $4\frac{2}{9}$ **B** $5\frac{1}{3}$
C $5\frac{2}{9}$ **D** not given

6. $21\frac{1}{3}$
$-\ \frac{2}{3}$

A $20\frac{1}{3}$ **B** $21\frac{2}{3}$
C $20\frac{2}{3}$ **D** not given

7. 24
$-16\frac{3}{7}$

A $8\frac{4}{7}$ **B** $7\frac{4}{7}$
C $8\frac{3}{7}$ **D** not given

8. $17\frac{1}{3}$
$+15\frac{3}{4}$

A $32\frac{1}{3}$ **B** 33
C $33\frac{1}{12}$ **D** not given

Multiply.

9. $\frac{1}{6} \times \frac{1}{2}$

A $\frac{1}{8}$ **B** $\frac{2}{8}$
C $\frac{1}{12}$ **D** not given

10. $\frac{1}{8} \times 7$

A $\frac{7}{8}$ **B** $\frac{8}{8}$
C $1\frac{7}{8}$ **D** not given

11. $9\frac{1}{3} \times 30$

A 300 **B** 372
C 280 **D** not given

12. $2\frac{1}{4} \times 1\frac{1}{2}$

A $3\frac{1}{8}$ **B** $3\frac{3}{4}$
C $3\frac{1}{3}$ **D** not given

13. Scott picked $3\frac{1}{3}$ baskets of pears. Joanna picked $\frac{3}{4}$ of a basket more than Scott. How many baskets of pears did she pick?

A $3\frac{1}{12}$ **B** $4\frac{1}{12}$
C $3\frac{11}{12}$ **D** not given

14. Sandy needs $3\frac{3}{4}$ packages of yarn to knit one scarf. How much yarn does she need for 5 scarfs?

A $18\frac{2}{3}$ **B** $18\frac{3}{4}$
C $18\frac{3}{5}$ **D** not given

Graphing and Data

The seal pup looked sick and very weak when Karen found it on a lonely beach one day in June. She took it to the Marine Mammal Center, where the young harbor seal would receive the proper care and food. The Center was like a hospital for animals that were sick or too young to get along on their own. Karen was afraid that it would be many months before the seal pup was healthy enough and large enough to be set loose in the harbor again. Even though the pup was almost a month old when Karen found it, it weighed only 16 pounds. She visited the Center every month and recorded the seal's weight each time: 20 pounds in July, 34 pounds in August, 44 pounds in September, 50 pounds in October. By the time Karen visited the Center in November the seal's weight was 55 pounds. Now it was healthy and big enough to return to its ocean home.

Thinking About Graphs

Graphs help us answer questions by showing data in pictures. **Bar graphs, pictographs, circle graphs,** and **line graphs** are types of graphs.

Answer the questions about these graphs.

1. Which subject is liked by the most students?

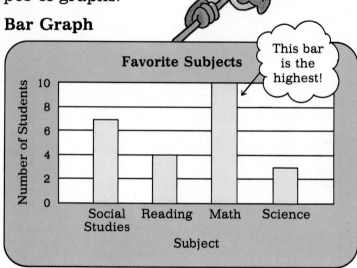

Bar Graph

Favorite Subjects

This bar is the highest!

Number of Students

Social Studies   Reading   Math   Science

Subject

Pictograph

Number of Students in Three Classes

Mr. Wilson

Mrs. Mendez

Mrs. Thomas

This class has the most

= 5 students

2. Which class has the most students?

3. Which type of TV show is liked by the most students?

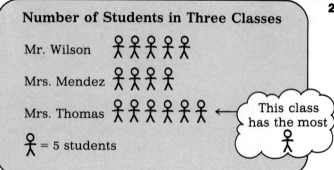

Circle Graph

Favorite TV Shows of 100 Students

This part is the biggest.

Comedy 20

Police 40

News 15

Sports 25

Line Graph

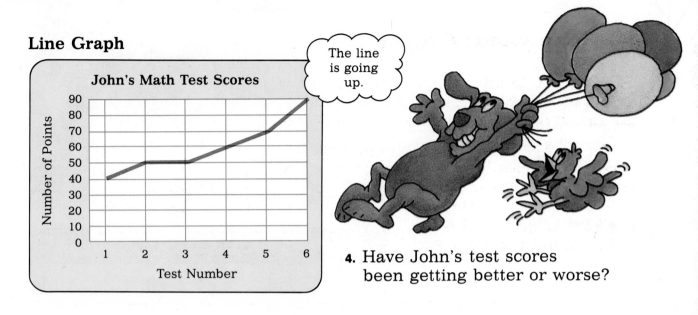

John's Math Test Scores

(Line graph: y-axis "Number of Points" from 0 to 90 by 10s, x-axis "Test Number" from 1 to 6)

The line is going up.

4. Have John's test scores been getting better or worse?

Use the graphs on page 344 and above to answer the questions below.

All graphs should have a **title**.

1. What is the title of the bar graph?

2. What is the title of the pictograph? Number of Students in

3. What is the title of the circle graph? Favorite TV shows of 100

4. What is the title of the line graph?

Each part of a graph should have a **label**.

5. What do social studies, reading, math, and science represent in the bar graph?

6. What are the teachers' names in the pictograph?

7. What are the labels for each section in the circle graph?

8. What do the numbers 1, 2, 3, 4, 5, and 6 represent in the line graph?

All graphs should have a **number scale**.

9. In the bar graph, what numbers are used to show how many students like each subject best?

10. What does each $\overset{\circ}{\curlywedge}$ stand for in the pictograph?

11. Does each section in the circle graph have a number to show how many? What are the numbers?

Think

Magic Square

Copy and complete this magic square. Each row, column, and diagonal must have the same sum.

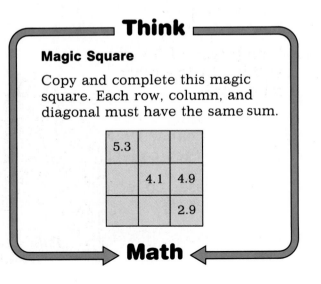

5.3		
	4.1	4.9
		2.9

Math

Bar Graphs

The fifth grade classes at McKinley School have 3 class projects each year. They use **bar graphs** to show the results of their projects.

Use the bar graph to the right to answer these questions.

1. What is the title of the graph?

2. How many fifth grade classrooms took part in the project?

3. Which class sold the greatest amount? What was the amount of their sales?

4. Which class sold the smallest amount? What was the amount of their sales?

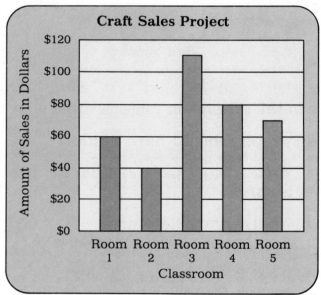

Use the bar graph for the aluminum can project to answer these questions.

5. Which class collected the largest amount of aluminum cans? How much did they collect?

6. Which class collected the smallest amount of aluminum cans? How much did they collect?

7. Which classes collected less than 25 kg?

8. Which classes collected more than 30 kg?

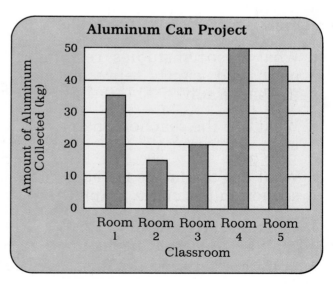

Use the bar graph below for exercises 9 through 12.

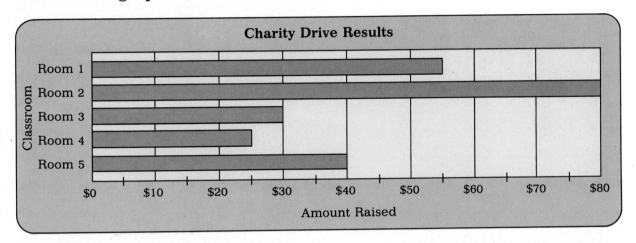

Charity Drive Results

9. What amount does the mark between $30 and $40 on the number scale represent?

10. About how much more did Room 2 raise than Room 1?

11. Which class raised about half as much money as Room 2?

12. Copy and complete this table. Find the total amount of money earned in the Charity Drive.

Room	1	2	3	4	5	Total
Amount Raised	$55	▦	$30	▦	▦	▦

Skillkeeper

Multiply.

1. 0.7
   × 0.6

2. 0.021
   ×   8

3. 3.8
   × 4.5

4. 0.007
   ×   0.5

5.   47
   × 0.009

Find the product or quotient.

6. 2.79×10

7. 6.472×100

8. $9.3 \div 100$

9. $79.1 \div 10$

Pictographs

Sheila's social studies class used an almanac to find some data about cities and states. They used **pictographs** to show their data.

Number of Clear Days in One Year

Phoenix	☼☼☼☼☼☼☼☼☼☼☼
Reno	☼☼☼☼☼☼☼☼☼
San Diego	☼☼☼☼☼☼◖
Kansas City	☼☼☼☼☼☼
Houston	☼☼☼☼☼
New York	☼☼☼☼◖
Miami	☼☼☼
Anchorage	☼☼

☼ = 20 clear days

Use the data in the graph above to answer these questions.

1. What is the title of the pictograph?

2. How many clear days does ☼ represent?

3. How many clear days does ◖ represent?

4. Which city had the most clear days? How many did it have?

5. Which city had the fewest clear days? How many did it have?

6. How many more clear days did San Diego have than Houston?

348

Use the pictograph on state populations for exercises
7 through 10.

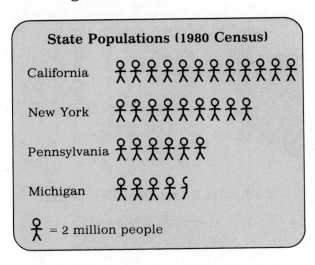

State Populations (1980 Census)

California

New York

Pennsylvania

Michigan

☖ = 2 million people

7. How many people does one ☖ represent?

8. How many people does one ⸓ represent?

9. Write the population for each state, according to the graph.

10. Suppose a state had a population of 8 million. How many ☖ would be shown for that state?

Use the pictograph on airports for exercises 11–14.

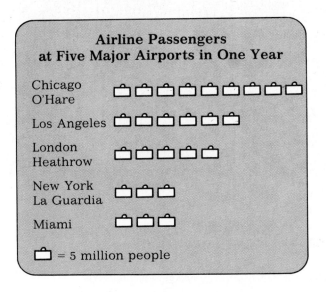

**Airline Passengers
at Five Major Airports in One Year**

Chicago O'Hare

Los Angeles

London Heathrow

New York La Guardia

Miami

🧳 = 5 million people

11. Which airport was the busiest? How many passengers did it have according to the graph?

12. About how many more passengers went through Chicago than through Los Angeles?

13. Which two airports had the same number of passengers according to the graph?

14. How many 🧳 would be shown for an airport that had 35 million passengers?

Think

Guess and Check

Arrange these tags in pairs so that all pairs have the same sum.

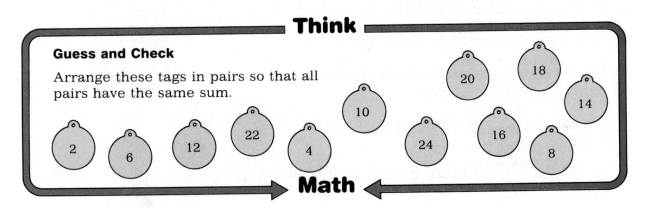

2   6   12   22   4   10   24   16   20   18   8   14

Math

Circle Graphs

Tanya works in a bookstore. She used circle graphs to show some data she collected.

Solve these problems about the sports books circle graph.

1. Which types of sports books had the greatest sales?

2. For which sport were 9 books sold last month?

3. What do you think should be the sum of the numbers in the circle graph? Add to check your answer.

4. Name two other kinds of books that could be included in the "others" section.

100 Sports Books Sold Last Month

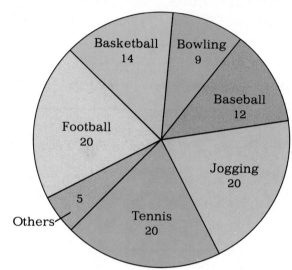

Solve these problems about how Tanya uses her time at the bookstore.

5. Which activity takes up the greatest fraction of Tanya's time?

6. Which activity takes up the smallest fraction of her time?

7. What do you think the sum of the fractions in the graph should be? Add to check your guess.

8. Suppose Tanya works 8 hours and uses that time as shown in the graph. How many hours does she spend stocking shelves?

How My Working Day Is Spent

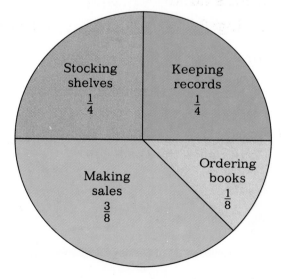

Solve these problems about the store's sales.

9. Which item has the greatest fraction of the sales?

10. Which item has the smallest fraction of the sales?

11. What is the sum of the fractions in the circle graph?

12. Can you tell from the graph the total amount of sales for the month?

Use the data in the table below to solve the problems about the incomplete circle graph

Fractional Parts of Store's Sales by Departments

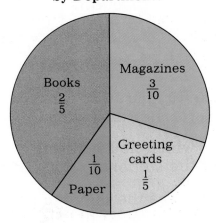

30 Animal Books Sold Last Week				
Dogs	Fish	Cats	Horses	Others
卌卌 卝	卌	卌 |||	|||	||
12	5	8	3	2

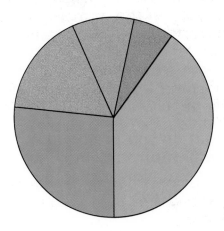

13. What is the color of the circle graph part that shows sales of books about

    A dogs?   B cats?   C fish?

14. What fraction of the books sold last week were about fish? dogs?

15. What fraction of the books sold were about dogs or cats?

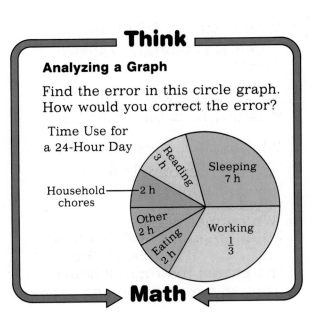

Line Graphs

Ned's science class collected data about weather. They drew **line graphs** to show their data.

Use the temperature line graph for exercises 1 through 5.

1. For which hours during the day did the students collect data?

2. What was the high temperature of the day according to the graph?

3. Between what hours was the temperature increasing? Decreasing?

4. About what time in the morning was the temperature about 10°?

5. What do you predict the temperature might be at 5:00 p.m., lower than or higher than 16°C?

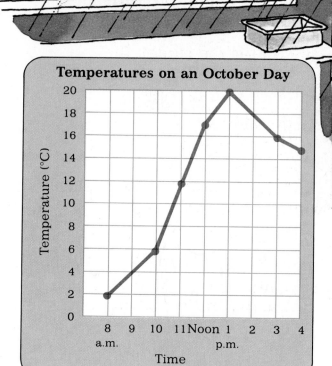

Use the rainfall line graph for exercises 6 through 10.

6. What was the total rainfall in June?

7. Which months had 85 mm of rain?

8. Which two months had the greatest amount of precipitation?

9. Which month had 87 mm of precipitation?

10. What was the total rainfall for the six months?

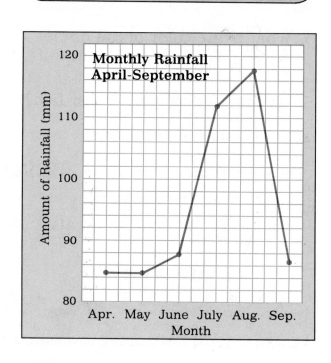

Use the temperature graph for exercises 11–17.

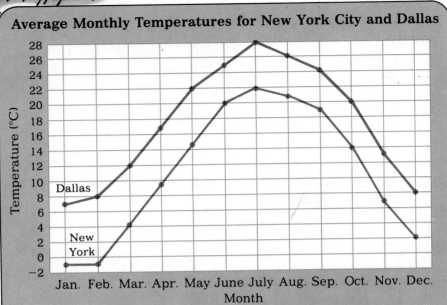

Average Monthly Temperatures for New York City and Dallas

Temperature (°C)

Jan. Feb. Mar. Apr. May June July Aug. Sep. Oct. Nov. Dec.
Month

Dallas

New York

11. Which city has the higher average monthly temperatures?

12. Which is the warmest month in Dallas? In New York?

13. Are the two lines about the same distance apart at each month?

14. About how many degrees warmer is Dallas than New York in March?

15. For which months is the average monthly temperature in Dallas 20°C or higher?

16. For which months is the average monthly temperature in New York 20°C or higher?

★ **17.** How many degrees higher is the average February temperature in Dallas than in New York?

18. **DATA BANK** What is the average of the monthly rainfalls for the summer months (June, July, August) in Charleston? How much greater is this than the average for those months in Peoria? See Data Bank, page 412.

Skillkeeper

Give the next three equivalent fractions.

1. $\frac{1}{3}$, ▥, ▥, ▥

2. $\frac{2}{5}$, ▥, ▥, ▥

3. $\frac{1}{6}$, ▥, ▥, ▥

4. $\frac{7}{8}$, ▥, ▥, ▥

Give the missing numerators.

5. $\frac{3}{4} = \frac{▥}{12}$

6. $\frac{2}{5} = \frac{▥}{15}$

7. $\frac{2}{3} = \frac{▥}{33}$

8. $\frac{3}{8} = \frac{▥}{48}$

9. $\frac{7}{10} = \frac{▥}{20}$

Making Graphs

Copy and complete the **bar graph** about the use of electricity in five households. Use the data in the table.

Kilowatt-Hours Used in One Year	
(1 kilowatt-hour = 1,000 watts × 1 hour)	
Family	Kilowatt-hours
Davis	27,000
Li	46,000
Conrad	49,000
Jacobs	24,000
Grasso	35,000

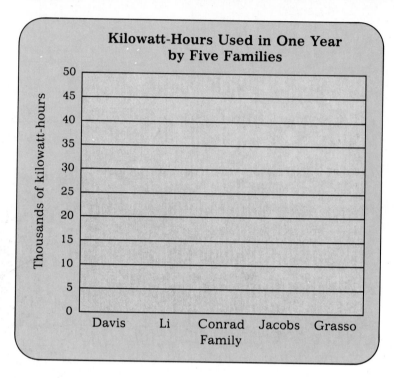

Copy and complete the **pictograph** about magazine sales. Use the data in the table.

Room 1	Room 2	Room 3	Room 4
60	120	80	70

Room 1

Room 2

Room 3

Room 4

📖 = 20 magazines

Questions to think about:

1. What is a good title for the pictograph?

2. If 📖 stands for 20 magazines, what picture would you use to represent 10 magazines?

3. What pictures do you need to draw for the number of magazines sold by each class?

Copy and complete the **circle graph** about fish catches.

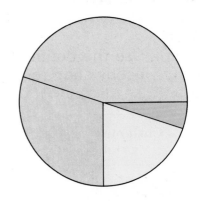

Name of Lake	Long Neck	Williams	Big Bend	Lemon
Number of fish caught in a week	45	30	20	5

Questions to think about:

1. What would be a good title for the graph?

2. What labels are needed on each section in the circle?

3. What numbers are needed on each section of the graph?

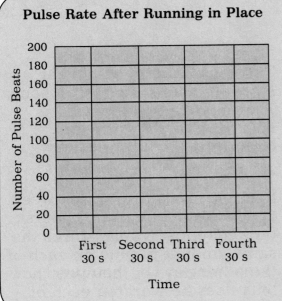

Pulse Rate After Running in Place

Number of Pulse Beats

200
180
160
140
120
100
80
60
40
20
0

First 30 s · Second 30 s · Third 30 s · Fourth 30 s

Time

DATA HUNT Run in place for 1 minute. Then take your pulse for 2 minutes. Copy and complete the table below to show the number of beats for each 30-second period. Then copy and complete the line graph using your data.

First 30 seconds	Second 30 seconds	Third 30 seconds	Fourth 30 seconds

QUESTION
DATA
PLAN
ANSWER
CHECK

Problem Solving:
Using Data from Graphs

Use the double bar graph about the
hobby shop to solve problems 1 through 6.

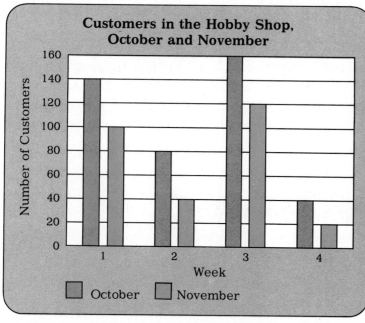

Customers in the Hobby Shop, October and November

Number of Customers (vertical axis): 0, 20, 40, 60, 80, 100, 120, 140, 160

Week (horizontal axis): 1, 2, 3, 4

■ October □ November

1. Which week's total number of
   customers for the two months
   was greatest?

2. Which week's total number of
   customers was the least?

3. Which month had the greater
   total number of customers? How
   many more customers were
   there in that month?

4. What was the average number
   of customers for the first week
   of these two months?

5. About how many more
   customers came into the shop
   during the third week in
   October than during the third
   week in November?

6. The customers in November
   spent an average of $12.50 each.
   About how much money was
   spent in the hobby shop in
   November?

7. **Try This**   Juan works in a
   hobby shop 25 hours each week.
   He works 15 of these 25 hours
   on weekends. If Juan works the
   same amount of time on each of
   the other days of the week, how
   long does he work on each of
   those days?

Problem Solving: Practice

Solve these other problems about the shop.

1. Glenda bought a model railroad engine for $22.95, a passenger car for $4.49, and some railroad track for $8.75. What was the total cost of these items without tax?

2. Brett bought a set of oil paints and brushes last year for $24.95. This year the same kind of paint set sells for $31.50. How much less did the set cost last year?

3. Wendy wants to buy 12 metal frames for some photographs she took. The frames cost $3.79 each. How much will Wendy need to spend not counting tax?

Use the bar graph for problems 4 through 6.

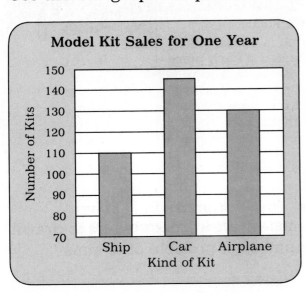

Model Kit Sales for One Year

Number of Kits — Kind of Kit: Ship, Car, Airplane

4. About how many of each kind of model kit were sold?

5. A model ship kit costs $12.96. How much money did the shop take in on model ship sales during the year?

6. A model airplane kit sells for $9.65 and a model car kit sells for $8.29. Did the shop take in more money on model airplanes or on model cars? How much more?

Items on Sale	
Giant photo album	$ 6.95
Model sailboat kit	7.75
Needlepoint kit	18.05
Beaded belt kit	6.50
Kite kit	4.50

7. **Try This** Andrea bought 3 of the items that were on sale at the hobby shop. She gave the clerk $20 and received $0.80 change. What did she buy?

357

Probability

The teacher needed one student for a special job. Teresa, Jane, Jeff, Bob, and Steve volunteered. To be fair, the teacher placed the names of the five students in a box and drew one name. What is the **probability** of drawing Teresa's name?

Important Fact!
Each name is **equally likely** to be selected if each piece of paper is the same, the pieces of paper are mixed well, and the choice is made without looking.

There is **1** chance in **5** that Teresa's name will be drawn.

We can show the probability of drawing Teresa's name as a fraction.

The probability of drawing Teresa's name $= \dfrac{1}{5}$ ← Outcomes where Teresa's name is drawn
← Total number of possible outcomes

Answer these probability questions.

1. What is the probability of drawing Jane's name?

2. What is the probability of drawing Jeff's name?

3. What is the probability of drawing Bob's name?

4. What is the probability of drawing a girl's name?

5. What is the probability of drawing Bruce's name?

Suppose you toss a penny and it lands on the desk.

1. What are the possible outcomes?

2. Is each outcome equally likely?

3. What is the probability of getting heads?

4. What is the probability of getting tails?

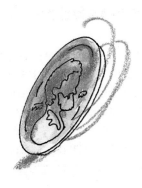

Suppose you toss a cube that has the letters A, B, C, D, E, and F on its faces. The outcome is the letter that appears on top after a toss.

5. What are the possible outcomes?

6. Is each outcome equally likely?

7. What is the probability of getting a B? a C? a D?

8. What is the probability of getting a 7?

Suppose you use this spinner for a game.

9. What are the possible outcomes if you do not count landing on a line?

10. What is the probability of landing on red? blue? yellow?

11. What is the probability of landing on red or yellow?

Think

More Probability

Suppose you toss two pennies. What is the probability that both pennies will come up heads?

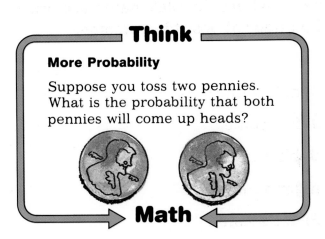

Math

More Probability

The fifth grade classes made a giant spinner for the school fair. What is the probability of winning?

There are 20 numbers altogether. 4 of the numbers are 6s. → There are **4** chances out of **20** to be a winner.

The **probability** of winning $= \dfrac{4}{20}$ or $\dfrac{1}{5}$

Answer these questions about the spinner.

1. What is the probability of losing?

2. What is the probability of spinning a 1?

3. What is the probability of spinning a 3?

4. What is the probability of spinning an even number?

5. What is the probability of spinning an odd number?

Solve these.

1. Suppose these 4 cards are turned over and shuffled. What is the probability of getting a ★ if you pick one card?

2. The letters in the word ARITHMETIC are placed in a hat and one letter is pulled out. What is the probability of getting a vowel? a consonant?

Suppose you spin two spinners like these. One outcome could be a 2 on the first spinner and a 1 on the second spinner, or (2,1).

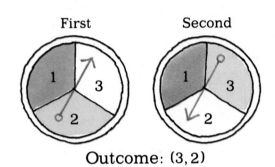

First   Second

Outcome: (3, 2)

3. What are the 9 possible outcomes?

4. What is the probability of getting the pair (2,1)?

5. What is the probability of getting a 1 on one spinner and a 2 on the other?

6. What is the probability of getting a pair with both numbers the same?

★ 7. Are the chances of getting heads the same with a penny as with a nickel? Copy and complete these tables by tossing coins.

Number of heads	Number of tails	Total tosses
⦀⦀⦀	⦀⦀⦀	

Number of heads	Number of tails	Total tosses
⦀⦀⦀	⦀⦀⦀	

Think

Predicting

Sarah tossed a penny 4 times. She got heads each time. If she is using a regular penny, what is the probability she will get heads on the next toss? (Remember what you know about probability!)

Math

361

Applied Problem Solving

You want to earn enough money from a paper route to buy a video game system for your family. Will you be able to pay for it by New Year's Day?

Some Things to Consider

- You can start your paper route on November 1.

- The route has 50 customers.

- You will make an average of $0.50 per customer each week.

- When you buy the video system, you get 1 game tape free. You want to buy 2 extra game tapes.

- A video game system costs $159. Extra game tapes cost $29 each.

- You would like to have some money left over for Christmas.

Some Questions to Answer

1. How much money can you make in 1 week on your paper route? In 1 month (use 4 weeks)? How many weeks do you have before New Year's Day?

2. How much will a video game system and 2 extra game tapes cost? Will you make enough money? If so, how much will you have left over?

What Is Your Decision?

Will you buy the system and extra tapes for New Year's Day? What else might you do?

Chapter Review-Test

Use the graphs to answer the questions.

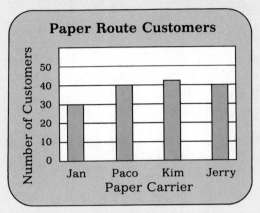

Paper Route Customers

1. Which paper carrier has the most customers?

2. How many more customers does Paco have than Jan?

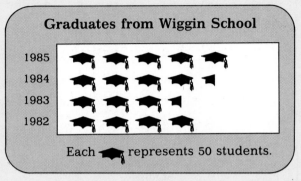

Graduates from Wiggin School

Each 🎓 represents 50 students.

3. How many students does each 🎓 represent? each ◀ ?

4. How many students graduated in 1984?

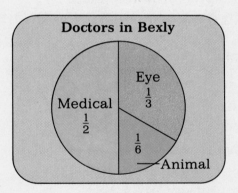

Doctors in Bexly

Medical $\frac{1}{2}$ Eye $\frac{1}{3}$ $\frac{1}{6}$ Animal

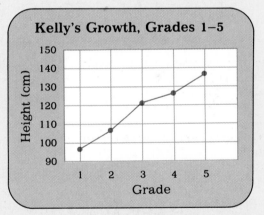

Kelly's Growth, Grades 1–5

5. What is the sum of the fractions in the graph?

6. If Bexly has 24 doctors in all, how many are eye doctors?

7. Between which grades did Kelly's height change the most?

8. How much did Kelly grow from Grade 1 to Grade 5?

Solve these problems.

9. Suppose you toss a cube with the numbers 1, 2, 3, 4, 5, and 6 on its faces. What is the probability that the top face will be a number less than 3?

10. Denny collected $2.25 each from 5 customers on his paper route. What was the total amount he collected?

Another Look

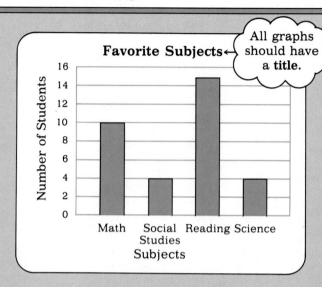

Favorite Subjects ← All graphs should have a **title**.

Bar Graphs

1. Which subject was selected by the most students?

2. How many students selected math?

3. Which subjects were selected by the same number of students?

Rainy Days per Year

Cleveland
Boston
Tampa

🌂 = 20 days ← All graphs should have a **number scale**.

Pictographs

4. What does each 🌂 stand for?

5. What does each 🌂 stand for?

6. How many rainy days did Boston have?

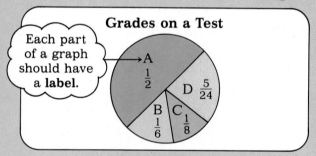

Grades on a Test

Each part of a graph should have a **label**.

A $\frac{1}{2}$ D $\frac{5}{24}$ B $\frac{1}{6}$ C $\frac{1}{8}$

Circle Graphs

7. What is the sum of the fractions?

8. What fraction of the class got a C or a D?

9. If 24 students took the test, how many got an A?

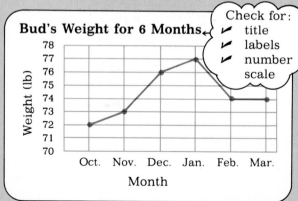

Bud's Weight for 6 Months ← Check for:
✔ title
✔ labels
✔ number scale

Line Graphs

10. During which month did Bud weigh the most?

11. How much did Bud weigh in March?

12. Did Bud's weight increase or decrease between October and January?

Enrichment

Coordinate Geometry

Each player should make a grid like the one below. Then follow these directions for playing Hit or Miss:

1. Place circles on the grid at 3 different points where lines intersect. Do not show your partner where you put your circles.

2. Decide who goes first. Player 1 names a pair of numbers, trying to guess where Player 2's circles are located.

3. If a circle is located at the point named, Player 2 must say, "Hit." If a circle is not at the place called, Player 2 must say, "Miss."

4. Take turns and continue play until all 3 circles for one player have been "Hit."

Play this game with a partner.

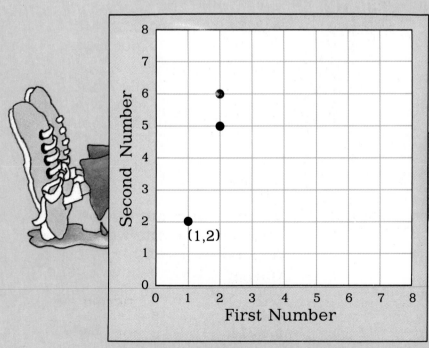

(1,2)

Cumulative Review

1. Which is **not** a name for this angle?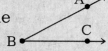

   A ∠ABC **C** ∠B
   B ∠CAB **D** not given

2. What kind of angle is this?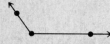

   A right **C** acute
   B obtuse **D** not given

Use these polygons for items 3–5.

3. Which polygon is a rhombus?

   A F **B** I
   C H **D** not given

4. Which polygon is a rectangle?

   A G **B** I
   C H **D** not given

5. Which polygon is a trapezoid?

   A H **B** I
   C F **D** not given

Use these triangles for items 6 and 7.

6. Which triangles are congruent?

   A Q, R **B** Q, U
   C Q, S **D** not given

7. Which triangles are similar?

   A T, U **B** S, T
   C R, S **D** not given

Estimate the product.

8. $\begin{array}{r} 0.976 \\ \times\ \ \ 6.9 \\ \hline \end{array}$

   A 7
   B 6
   C 10
   D not given

Multiply or divide.

9. $\begin{array}{r} 4.5 \\ \times\ 6.3 \\ \hline \end{array}$

   A 27.35
   B 28.35
   C 24.15
   D not given

10. $\begin{array}{r} 0.97 \\ \times\ 0.05 \\ \hline \end{array}$

   A 0.485
   B 0.00485
   C 0.0485
   D not given

11. 8.448×100

   A 84.48 **C** 8448.0
   B 844.8 **D** not given

12. $236.4 \div 10$

   A 2364.0 **C** 0.2364
   B 2.364 **D** not given

13. If the average daily rainfall in a city is 0.121 cm, what would be the total rainfall for a month that has 31 days?

   A 37.51 cm **B** 3.751 cm
   C 30.751 cm **D** not given

14. To find out about how much she makes in one week, Dee divided her monthly salary of $980 by 4. About how much does Dee earn in one week?

   A $225 **B** $245
   C $254 **D** not given

Ratio and Percent

One part of Jim's job as a forester is very lonely. That is when he must sit alone at the top of a lookout tower watching for fires. By day, he looks for smoke, and at night, for a red glow. Whenever he spots a fire, Jim must act quickly. First he uses his map to find exactly where the blaze is. The scale on the map tells him that every 1 cm stands for 3 km, so he can figure out just how far away the blaze is. Then he phones the nearest firefighter station and reports the facts about the fire. Within minutes, teams of firefighters will be on their way to try to put out the blaze before much of the forest has burned.

Ratio

A **ratio** is used to compare two quantities.

The ratio of odd-numbered cars to even-numbered cars is **2 to 3**.

We also write this ratio as the fraction $\frac{2}{3}$.

The ratio of even-numbered cars to odd-numbered cars is 3 to 2, or $\frac{3}{2}$.

Here are some other examples of uses of ratios.

RACES TODAY
SPECIAL
TICKET PRICES
!2 FOR $9!

LUCKY
RING TOSS
3 OUT OF EVERY 5
PLAYERS ARE
WINNERS!

FAIRGROUNDS MAP
LIVESTOCK   MIDWAY   RACE GROUNDS
ARTS & CRAFTS
SCALE: 3cm → 50m

We say: The ratio of **tickets to dollars** is **2 to 9**.

We write: $\frac{2}{9}$

We say: The ratio of **winners to all players** is **3 to 5**.

We write: $\frac{3}{5}$

We say: The ratio of **centimeters to meters** is **3 to 50**.

We write: $\frac{3}{50}$

Warm Up   Write each ratio as a fraction.

1. 2 out of every 3 people at the races are regular fans.

The ratio of	regular fans —to— all customers	is	$\frac{|||||}{|||||}$.

2. Midway ride tickets were on sale at 8 for $5.

The ratio of	tickets —to— dollars	is	$\frac{|||||}{|||||}$.

3. The ratio of cows to sheep in the livestock show is 5 to 1.

4. The ratio of adults to children at the fair is 2 to 5.

STATE FAIR NEWS

Write each ratio as a fraction.

1. 3 out of every 4 hats sold at the hat stand are red.

The ratio of	red hats —to— is all hats	$\frac{||||}{||||}$.

2. The winner of today's race averaged 8 laps in 3 minutes.

The ratio of	laps —to— is minutes	$\frac{||||}{||||}$.

3. The camera stand sells film with 24 pictures per roll.

The ratio of	pictures —to— is rolls	$\frac{||||}{||||}$.

4. State fair pennants: 2 for $7

The ratio of	pennants —to— is dollars	$\frac{||||}{||||}$.

5. 3 of every 5 cats in the cat show have long hair.

cats with long hair →
cats → $\frac{||||}{||||}$

6. The Ferris wheel goes completely around 15 times in 2 minutes.

times around → $||||$
minutes → $||||$

7. State fair season tickets are on sale at 2 for $21.

tickets → $||||$
dollars → $||||$

8. A race car traveled 9 km in 2 minutes.

km → $||||$
minutes → $||||$

9. You can park in the fairgrounds parking lot 7 hours for $2. What is the ratio of hours to dollars?

Think

Estimating Area

Estimate the ratio of the area of parking lot A to the area of parking lot B.

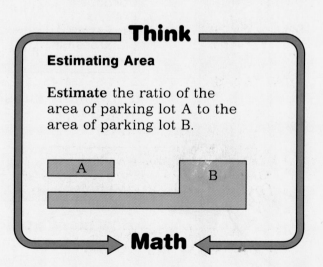

Math

369

Making and Using Ratio Tables

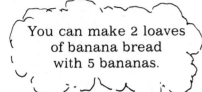

You can make 2 loaves of banana bread with 5 bananas.

We can make **ratio tables** by finding equivalent fractions.

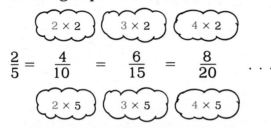

$$\frac{2}{5} = \frac{4}{10} = \frac{6}{15} = \frac{8}{20} \quad \cdots$$

Loaves	2	4	6	?	?	?
Bananas	5	10	15	?	?	?

The ratios in the table are called **equal ratios.** We can use ratio tables to help solve problems.

Problem: How many loaves can be made with 30 bananas?

Loaves	2	4	6	8	10	12
Bananas	5	10	15	20	25	30

Answer: 12 loaves   Use this column

Copy and complete each ratio table. Then use it to answer the question.

1.

Scoops of mix	3	6	9	12
Glasses of lemonade	8	16	▦	▦

How many cups can be made with 12 scoops?

2.

Apples	1	▦	▦	▦
Muffins	6	▦	▦	▦

How many apples are needed for 24 muffins?

3.

Cups of pancake mix	4	▦	▦	▦
Cups of milk	3	▦	▦	▦

How many cups of milk are needed for 16 cups of mix?

4.

Eggs	2	▦	▦	▦
Waffles	9	▦	▦	▦

How many eggs are needed for 36 waffles?

Problem Solving: Using Data from a Ratio Table

Exercising and Calories

Solve these problems. Complete the ratio tables as needed.

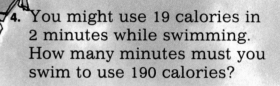

1. A person walking slowly uses 5 calories every 2 minutes. How many calories are used during a 10-minute walk?

Calories	5	▦	▦	▦	▦
Minutes	2	4	6	8	10

2. When bicycling, you use about 20 calories in 3 minutes. How many calories would you use during a 15-minute ride?

Calories	20	▦	▦	▦	▦
Minutes	3	6	9	12	15

3. If you use 30 calories for every 20 minutes you watch TV, how many minutes must you watch to use 150 calories?

Calories	30	▦	▦	▦	▦
Minutes	20	40	60	80	100

4. You might use 19 calories in 2 minutes while swimming. How many minutes must you swim to use 190 calories?

Calories	19	▦	▦	▦	▦	▦
Minutes	2	4	6	8	18	20

5. A person playing tennis might use 15 calories every 2 minutes. How many calories would be used in 20 minutes?

Calories	15	▦	▦	▦	▦	▦
Minutes	2	4	6	8	10	20

6. **Try This** Al, Beth, and Carol all have different kinds of jobs. One of them is an artist, one is a photographer, and one is an editor. The one who is a photographer loves to play tennis, the editor is Al's sister, Al is Beth's grandson, and jogging is Al's only form of exercise. Who is in each occupation? (Hint: Use logical reasoning.)

Using Equal Ratios

In Marcia's class 2 out of every 3 students live in an apartment building. There are 27 students in the class. How many live in apartments?

Since the ratio 2 to 3 is given, we use 27 to form an equal ratio.

Write an equation with equal ratios.	→	Find the multiplier.	→	Multiply to solve the equation.

Students living in apartments

$$\frac{2}{3} = \frac{n}{27}$$

All students

$$\frac{2}{3} = \frac{n}{27}$$

3×9

$2 \times 9 = 18$

$$\frac{2}{3} = \frac{n}{27}$$

$$n = 18$$

In Marcia's class 18 students live in apartments.

Other Examples

$$\frac{3}{5} = \frac{n}{20}$$
$5 \times 4 = 20$
$3 \times 4 = 12$
$n = 12$

$$\frac{4}{3} = \frac{n}{24}$$
$3 \times 8 = 24$
$4 \times 8 = 32$
$n = 32$

$$\frac{2}{1} = \frac{n}{36}$$
$1 \times 36 = 36$
$2 \times 36 = 72$
$n = 72$

Warm Up Solve the equations.

1. $\frac{1}{4} = \frac{n}{28}$

$4 \times 7 = 28$

2. $\frac{2}{5} = \frac{n}{35}$

$5 \times 7 = 35$

3. $\frac{3}{8} = \frac{n}{32}$

$8 \times 4 = 32$

4. $\frac{3}{10} = \frac{n}{40}$

$10 \times 4 = 40$

5. $\frac{2}{3} = \frac{n}{18}$

$3 \times 6 = 18$

6. $\frac{3}{4} = \frac{n}{20}$

$4 \times 5 = 20$

7. $\frac{1}{5} = \frac{n}{30}$

$5 \times 6 = 30$

8. $\frac{5}{3} = \frac{n}{12}$

$3 \times 4 = 12$

Solve the equations.

1. $\frac{1}{3} = \frac{n}{24}$

2. $\frac{2}{5} = \frac{n}{25}$

3. $\frac{3}{4} = \frac{n}{28}$

4. $\frac{5}{2} = \frac{n}{16}$

5. $\frac{2}{1} = \frac{n}{5}$

6. $\frac{1}{4} = \frac{n}{28}$

7. $\frac{9}{10} = \frac{n}{50}$

8. $\frac{5}{8} = \frac{n}{48}$

9. $\frac{3}{8} = \frac{n}{56}$

10. $\frac{5}{6} = \frac{n}{48}$

11. $\frac{7}{8} = \frac{n}{72}$

12. $\frac{3}{10} = \frac{n}{90}$

Solve the problem.
Use the equation to help you.

13. In Akim's class 2 out of every 5 students have younger sisters or brothers. There are 30 students in the class. How many students have younger sisters or brothers?

$$\frac{2}{5} = \frac{n}{30} \quad \begin{matrix} \leftarrow \text{ students with younger} \\ \text{sisters or brothers} \\ \leftarrow \text{ students} \end{matrix}$$

Write and solve an equation for each problem.

14. There are 28 students in Tad's class. 3 out of every 4 of them play a musical instrument. How many students play a musical instrument?

15. In Room 36, 2 out of every 9 students wear braces on their teeth. If there are 36 students in Room 36, how many of them wear braces on their teeth?

Think

Solving Equations

> When two ratios are equal the cross products are equal.
>
> $\frac{2}{3} \bowtie \frac{4}{6}$ → $3 \times 4 = 12$
> $2 \times 6 = 12$

Solve → $\frac{2}{3} = \frac{n}{12}$

1. Find the cross products.
$3 \times n = 2 \times 12$
$3 \times n = 24$

2. Divide to find n. → $n = 24 \div 3$
$n = 8$

Solve these.

1. $\frac{2}{5} = \frac{n}{15}$

2. $\frac{3}{4} = \frac{n}{24}$

3. $\frac{5}{3} = \frac{n}{12}$

Math

Percents and Ratios

What is the ratio of dots inside the loop to all dots in the square?

First estimate, then count to check your estimate.

The ratio of dots inside the loop to all dots is 56 to 100.

We say: "56 percent of the dots are inside."

We write: **56%** (read "fifty-six percent")

Percent means **per one hundred**, or **hundredths.** We use percent when we want to compare a number with 100.

Warm Up Give the ratios and percents.

100 Dots

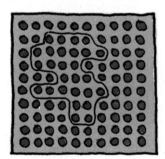

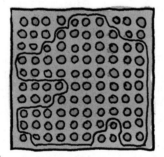

1. Ratio: ⫽/⫽   **2.** Ratio: ⫽/⫽   **3.** Ratio: ⫽/⫽

Percent: ⫽⫽%   Percent: ⫽⫽%   Percent: ⫽⫽%

Write each ratio as a percent.

4. 38 to 100   **5.** 8 to 100   **6.** 99 to 100   **7.** 50 to 100

8. $\frac{17}{100}$ **9.** $\frac{45}{100}$ **10.** $\frac{9}{100}$ **11.** $\frac{83}{100}$ **12.** $\frac{71}{100}$

Write each percent as a ratio in fraction form.

13. 15%   **14.** 96%   **15.** 11%   **16.** 64%   **17.** 5%

Write each ratio as a percent.

1. 3 to 100

2. 17 to 100

3. 25 to 100

4. 59 to 100

5. 12 to 100

6. 50 to 100

7. 75 to 100

8. 10 to 100

9. $\frac{5}{100}$

10. $\frac{16}{100}$

11. $\frac{33}{100}$

12. $\frac{98}{100}$

13. $\frac{100}{100}$

14. $\frac{32}{100}$

15. $\frac{20}{100}$

16. $\frac{3}{100}$

17. $\frac{49}{100}$

18. $\frac{1}{100}$

Write each percent as a ratio.

19. 30%

20. 76%

21. 84%

22. 20%

23. 5%

24. 15%

25. 35%

26. 52%

27. 60%

28. 39%

29. 7%

30. 19%

31. 99%

32. 100%

33. 16%

What is the percent?

34. 31 out of 100

35. 54 per hundred

36. a ratio of 17 to 100

37. 66 out of every 100 people in the U.S. read a newspaper each day. What percent is this?

38. In a recent poll, 46 out of every 100 people named television as their favorite leisure pastime. What percent is this?

★ **39.** Out of every 100 Americans 18 play a musical instrument. What percent play no musical instrument?

Skillkeeper

Find the products or quotients.

1. $\begin{array}{r} 1.45 \\ \times\ 0.3 \\ \hline \end{array}$

2. $\begin{array}{r} 0.06 \\ \times\ 0.8 \\ \hline \end{array}$

3. $\begin{array}{r} 1.2 \\ \times\ 7.3 \\ \hline \end{array}$

4. $\begin{array}{r} 0.09 \\ \times\ \ 7 \\ \hline \end{array}$

5. $\begin{array}{r} 4.6 \\ \times\ 0.03 \\ \hline \end{array}$

6. 8.23×10

7. 6.47×100

8. $1.36 \times 1,000$

9. $73.6 \div 10$

10. $133.9 \div 100$

11. $37.8 \div 1,000$

Percents and Decimals

Here are two facts about hobbies of people in the United States.

Write the decimal as a percent. Write the percent as a decimal.

Hobbies

0.39 of the people do craft work.
18% of the people play a musical instrument.

Decimal **0.39** *(39 hundredths)*

↓

Percent **39**%   39% of the people do craft work.

Percent **18**% *(18 hundredths)*

↓

Decimal **0.18**   0.18 of the people play a musical instrument.

Other Examples

$0.06 = 6\%$ $13\% = 0.13$

$0.4 = 0.40 = 40\%$ $1\% = 0.01$

$1.00 = 100\%$ $60\% = 0.60 \text{ or } 0.6$

$100\% = 1.00 \text{ or } 1$

Write a percent for each decimal.

1. 0.15	**2.** 0.29	**3.** 0.75	**4.** 0.62	**5.** 0.20
6. 0.50	**7.** 0.3	**8.** 0.7	**9.** 0.04	**10.** 0.08
11. 0.10	**12.** 1.00	**13.** 0.98	**14.** 0.01	**15.** 0.8

Write a decimal for each percent.

16. 31%	**17.** 17%	**18.** 48%	**19.** 67%	**20.** 94%
21. 40%	**22.** 10%	**23.** 80%	**24.** 100%	**25.** 25%
26. 3%	**27.** 4%	**28.** 12%	**29.** 1%	**30.** 99%

More Practice, page 432, Set C

Percents as Fractions

Painting and drawing are also popular hobbies. Almost 25% of the people in the United States paint or draw.

Write the percent as a fraction.

Percent	25%	Percent means per hundred.
↓		
Fraction	$\frac{25}{100}$	
↓		
Lowest-terms fraction	$\frac{1}{4}$	$25\% = \frac{1}{4}$

Almost $\frac{1}{4}$ of the people in the United States paint or draw.

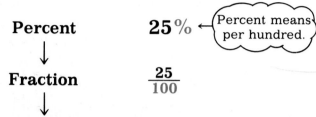

Other Examples

$$50\% = \frac{50}{100} = \frac{1}{2} \qquad 37\% = \frac{37}{100}$$

$$5\% = \frac{5}{100} = \frac{1}{20} \qquad 70\% = \frac{70}{100} = \frac{7}{10}$$

Write a fraction in lowest terms for each percent.

1. 75%	**2.** 20%	**3.** 45%	**4.** 24%	**5.** 60%
6. 10%	**7.** 4%	**8.** 40%	**9.** 31%	**10.** 68%
11. 50%	**12.** 80%	**13.** 17%	**14.** 1%	**15.** 15%
16. 2%	**17.** 35%	**18.** 28%	**19.** 53%	**20.** 30%
21. 85%	**22.** 97%	**23.** 90%	**24.** 3%	**25.** 95%

Fractions as Percents

Joan found that 18 out of 24, or $\frac{3}{4}$, of the students in her class have a dog or a cat as a pet. What percent of the class is this?

Fraction $\frac{3}{4}$

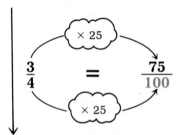

$\frac{3}{4} = \frac{75}{100}$ $\times 25$

Find an equivalent fraction with 100 as its denominator.

Percent   **75**%

In Joan's class 75% of the students have a dog or cat as a pet.

Other Examples

$\frac{1}{5} = \frac{1 \times 20}{5 \times 20} = \frac{20}{100} = 20\%$ $\frac{2}{25} = \frac{2 \times 4}{25 \times 4} = \frac{8}{100} = 8\%$

Write a percent for each fraction.

1. $\frac{1}{2}$ 2. $\frac{3}{5}$ 3. $\frac{1}{4}$ 4. $\frac{9}{10}$ 5. $\frac{1}{20}$ 6. $\frac{7}{10}$

7. $\frac{36}{50}$ 8. $\frac{2}{5}$ 9. $\frac{7}{25}$ 10. $\frac{11}{20}$ 11. $\frac{1}{10}$ 12. $\frac{17}{20}$

13. $\frac{4}{5}$ 14. $\frac{24}{25}$ 15. $\frac{49}{50}$ 16. $\frac{3}{10}$ 17. $\frac{19}{20}$ 18. $\frac{4}{10}$

★ To find the nearest whole percent for *any* fraction, follow these steps:

- Divide to find a decimal.
- Round the decimal to the nearest hundredth.
- Write the rounded decimal as a percent.

Give these fractions as percents.

19. $\frac{5}{8}$ 20. $\frac{2}{3}$ 21. $\frac{5}{6}$ 22. $\frac{7}{16}$

$\frac{3}{8} = 3 \div 8$

$0.375 \longrightarrow 0.38$

About 38%

More Practice, page 432, Set D

Problem Solving: Practice

Solve.

1. Jody bought a scratching post and 3 catnip mice. What was the total cost (not including tax)?

2. Cal bought a Fleas-Away Dog Collar and a Leather Bone. The tax on these items was $0.18. How much change should he get back from a $10 bill?

3. What is the average cost of the 3 kinds of **collars** listed in the ad?

4. The total sales by the pet store during this 6-day sale were $3,588. What was the average amount of sales per day?

5. A catnip mouse usually sells for $0.74. What is the total amount saved by buying 3 mice at the sale price?

6. The pet store received an average of 3 telephone calls every 10 minutes during the sale. How many calls is this per hour?

SALE

Puss and Pooch Pet Store

Fleas-Away Dog Collars	$2.29
Fleas-Away Cat Collars	1.88
Night-Glow Pet Collars	3.30
Cat's Meow Scratching Posts	4.75
Leather Doggie Bones	1.24
Catnip Mice	0.59

6 days only

★ **7.** The price of each item during this sale was 80% of its regular price. At a later sale, the price was 75% of the regular price. How much greater is the fraction for 80% than the fraction for 75%?

8. Try This Kathy spent half of her money on a Purrfect Rest Kitty Bed. She then spent $8.75 for a book on pet care. She had $12 left. How much money did she have before buying these items?

Finding a Percent of a Number

Sandra asked 120 students in her school about their favorite weekend activities. She showed the results of her poll in this circle graph. How many students like bicycling best?

Since we want to find how many of the 120 students like bicycling best, we need to find 15% of 120.

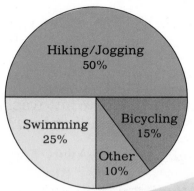

Hiking/Jogging 50%

Swimming 25%

Bicycling 15%

Other 10%

15% of 120

$$
\begin{array}{r}
1\,2\,0 \\
\times\,0.1\,5 \\
\hline
6\,0\,0 \\
1\,2\,0\,0 \\
\hline
1\,8.0\,0
\end{array}
$$

> First write a **decimal** for the **percent.** Then multiply.

Bicycling is liked best by 18 students.

Other Examples

> Use a shortcut for some of these problems! Since 25% = $\frac{1}{4}$, 25% of 24 is $\frac{1}{4}$ of 24, or 6.

25% of 24

$$
\begin{array}{r}
2\,4 \\
\times\,0.2\,5 \\
\hline
1\,2\,0 \\
4\,8\,0 \\
\hline
6.0\,0
\end{array}
$$

50% of 86

$$
\begin{array}{r}
8\,6 \\
\times\,0.5\,0 \\
\hline
4\,3.0\,0
\end{array}
$$

13% of 174

$$
\begin{array}{r}
1\,7\,4 \\
\times\,0.1\,3 \\
\hline
5\,2\,2 \\
1\,7\,4\,0 \\
\hline
2\,2.6\,2
\end{array}
$$

Find the percent of each number.

1. 10% of 60   2. 25% of 28   3. 50% of 96   4. 12% of 50

5. 75% of 24   6. 15% of 516   7. 16% of 150   8. 6% of 135

9. 30% of 60   10. 20% of 125   11. 15% of 40   12. 3% of 800

More Practice, page 432, Set E

Problem Solving: Using Percent

Solve. Use the circle graph on page 380 for problems 1, 2, and 3.

1. How many students like swimming best?

2. How many like hiking or jogging best?

3. How many students like activities other than hiking, jogging, or swimming?

4. Teresa asked 40 students to complete a question sheet about their favorite records. 90% of the students returned the sheet. How many returned the sheet? How many did not return it?

5. Sam read that 14% of all people are left-handed. How many of the 350 students in his school could he predict to be left-handed?

6. Jenny answered 85% of the 60 items on a test correctly. She took the test again and answered 95% correctly. How many more questions did she answer correctly the second time?

7. Carlos sells an average of $80 worth of greeting cards each month. The card company lets him keep 16% of the money taken in. How much does he earn in 6 months?

8. **Try This** Ann, Bob, Cathy, and Don have favorite weekend activities. One likes hiking, one swimming, one bicycling, and one softball. Cathy and Don do not enjoying bicycling. Bob always chooses hiking as his favorite. Don dislikes swimming. What is each person's favorite weekend activity?

Applied Problem Solving

You want to redo the walls of your room. Should you paint the walls and put up posters, or should you wallpaper them?

Some Things to Consider

- The cost of equipment for each job is about the same. You can get free help to do either job.
- If you use posters, you would like to put up 6. Posters cost $5 each.
- If you paint, the walls will need 2 coats.
- A liter of paint costs $4 and will cover 8 m².
- A roll of wallpaper costs $13. You will be able to use about 2.8 m² of paper out of each roll.
- Your room is 4 m long, 3.5 m wide, and 2.5 m high.
- The area of the door and window together is 3 m².

Some Questions to Answer

1. What is the area of the walls, not including the door and window?

2. If you paint, how many liters of paint will be needed? What will be the total paint cost? What will be the total cost for the paint and posters?

3. If you use wallpaper, how many rolls will you need? What will be the total cost for wallpaper?

What Is Your Decision?

Will you use paint and posters, or wallpaper?

Chapter Review-Test

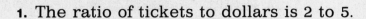

Write each ratio as a fraction.

1. The ratio of tickets to dollars is 2 to 5.

2. The ratio of red cars to all cars is 3 to 8.

3. Copy and complete the ratio table. Then solve the problem.

   3 pictures on every 4 pages

Pictures	3	6	▩	▩	▩
Pages	4	▩	▩	▩	▩

   How many pages are needed for 12 pictures?

Solve the equations.

4. $\frac{2}{3} = \frac{n}{12}$

5. $\frac{1}{5} = \frac{n}{20}$

6. $\frac{4}{3} = \frac{n}{15}$

7. $\frac{7}{10} = \frac{n}{80}$

Write the ratio as a percent.

8. 17 to 100

9. 96 to 100

10. 8 to 100

11. 50 to 100

Write the percent as a ratio in fraction form.

12. 7%

13. 50%

14. 32%

15. 86%

16. 10%

Write the decimal as a percent.

17. 0.15

18. 0.95

19. 1.00

Write the percent as a decimal.

20. 66%

21. 25%

22. 1%

Write the lowest-terms fraction.

23. 10%

24. 40%

25. 75%

Write the fraction as a percent.

26. $\frac{79}{100}$

27. $\frac{4}{5}$

28. $\frac{1}{2}$

Find the percent of each number.

29. 10% of 80

30. 50% of 240

31. 20% of 60

32. 25% of 200

33. In a class of 24 students, 3 out of 4 have a pet at home. What percent of the students have a pet at home?

Ratio Table

5 rides for $2

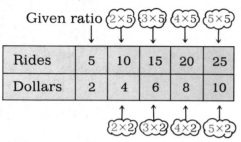

Given ratio

Rides	5	10	15	20	25
Dollars	2	4	6	8	10

How many rides do you get for $8?

Equal Ratios

$$\frac{3}{4} = \frac{n}{20}$$

$\times 5$

Since $20 = 4 \times 5$
we know $n = 3 \times 5$, or 15.

$$\frac{37}{100} = 37\%$$

Percent means per hundred.

Copy and complete the ratio table. Then solve the problem.

1. 3 post cards for 25¢

Post cards	3	||||| ||||| ||||| |||||
Cents	25	50	75	100	125

How many post cards can you buy for 125¢?

2. 2 hours to hike 15 km

Hours	2	||||| ||||| ||||| |||||
Kilometers	15	||||| ||||| ||||| |||||

How many hours does it take to hike 75 km?

Solve the equations.

3. $\frac{2}{3} = \frac{n}{9}$ **4.** $\frac{3}{5} = \frac{n}{15}$ **5.** $\frac{5}{6} = \frac{n}{24}$

6. $\frac{3}{8} = \frac{n}{32}$ **7.** $\frac{4}{3} = \frac{n}{27}$ **8.** $\frac{5}{8} = \frac{n}{40}$

9. $\frac{6}{5} = \frac{n}{40}$ **10.** $\frac{7}{12} = \frac{n}{72}$ **11.** $\frac{8}{15} = \frac{n}{90}$

Write each ratio as a percent. Write each percent as a ratio.

12. $\frac{63}{100}$ **13.** $\frac{94}{100}$ **14.** $\frac{7}{100}$

15. 25%   **16.** 33%   **17.** 99%

Mental Math

Try the **Lightning Method**
for multiplying two 2-digit numbers!

Try 45 × 23.

Multiply ones × ones.	→	Multiply tens × ones and add.	→	Multiply tens × tens and add.

$$\begin{array}{r} 2\,3 \\ \times\,4\,5 \\ \hline 5 \end{array}$$

$$\begin{array}{r} 2\,3 \\ \times\,4\,5 \\ \hline 3\,5 \end{array}$$

$$\begin{array}{r} 2\,3 \\ \times\,4\,5 \\ \hline 1{,}0\,3\,5 \end{array}$$

5 × 3 = 15
Remember the **1**.

4 × 3 = 12
5 × 2 = 10
Add the 1. + 1
$\overline{\quad 23}$
Remember the **2**.

4 × 2 = 8
Add the 2. + 2
$\overline{\quad 10}$

Do these for practice.
Use pencils for answers only.

1. 24
 × 43

2. 52
 × 26

3. 43
 × 32

4. 34
 × 26

5. 54
 × 35

6. 61
 × 27

Cumulative Review

Multiply.

1. $\frac{3}{8} \times \frac{1}{4}$ A $\frac{3}{32}$ B $\frac{4}{32}$
   C $\frac{4}{12}$ D not given

2. $\frac{2}{3} \times \frac{4}{5}$ A $\frac{6}{8}$ B $\frac{10}{12}$
   C $\frac{8}{15}$ D not given

3. $45 \times \frac{2}{5}$ A 90 B 18
   C $17\frac{2}{5}$ D not given

4. $6 \times 3\frac{2}{3}$ A 22 B 21
   C $20\frac{2}{3}$ D not given

5. $2\frac{1}{4} \times 1\frac{2}{3}$ A $4\frac{1}{4}$ B $3\frac{3}{4}$
   C $3\frac{7}{12}$ D not given

6. $4 \times 3\frac{1}{3}$ A $13\frac{2}{3}$ B $14\frac{1}{3}$
   C $\frac{5}{6}$ D not given

7. $2\frac{1}{5} \times 3$ A $5\frac{2}{5}$ B $\frac{11}{15}$
   C $6\frac{3}{5}$ D not given

8. $5 \times 2\frac{1}{2}$ A $12\frac{1}{2}$ B 25
   C $7\frac{1}{2}$ D not given

9. $1\frac{2}{3} \times 1\frac{1}{5}$ A $2\frac{3}{8}$ B $\frac{11}{15}$
   C 2 D not given

10. $6 \times 2\frac{1}{3}$ A $8\frac{1}{3}$ B 14
    C 42 D not given

Use this graph for items 11–12.

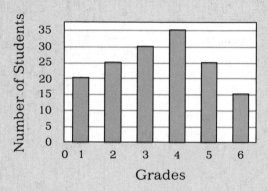

11. Which two grades have the same number of students?
    A 4 and 5 B 2 and 3
    C 2 and 5 D not given

12. Which grade has 15 students more than Grade 1?
    A 3 B 5
    C 4 D not given

Use this graph for items 13–14.

May Weather

Sunny Cloudy Rainy

13. What was the weather like the least number of days?
    A sunny B cloudy
    C rainy D not given

14. Sunny days made up what fraction of the month?
    A $\frac{1}{2}$ B $\frac{1}{6}$
    C $\frac{1}{3}$ D not given

16

Measurement

The old paint in the halls of Wilson School had become dark and dull. It was time to brighten things up a bit. The fifth grade class was chosen to do a mural (wall painting) to cover a wall that was 10 feet high and 21 feet long. First they decided that the subject of their picture would be dinosaurs. Then they drew many different dinosaur pictures on art paper. After the wall was covered with a base coat of white paint, they traced their drawings onto the wall. Next, they painted in a background of swamps and strange plants. Last of all, everyone joined in the fun of painting the dinosaurs. Now the hall looks like a scene from the times when dinosaurs roamed the world.

Length: Inches and Feet

The **inch (in.)** is a customary unit of length.

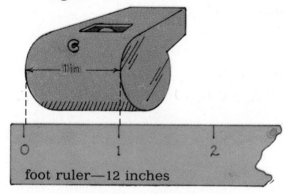

foot ruler—12 inches

The whistle is 1 inch wide.

1 ft = 12 in.

The **foot (ft)** is a longer customary unit of length.

The shoe of a basketball player might be about 1 foot long.

The heights of players on a high school basketball team might be given using both feet and inches. If a player is **5 feet 10 inches** tall, we sometimes write **5'10"**.

Player	Height
K. Glynn	5'10"
D. Otto	5'11"
L. Gover	6'1"
D. Ha	5'6"
M. Lopez	5'8"

We use parts of an inch to make more accurate measurements.

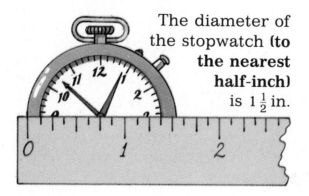

The diameter of the stopwatch **(to the nearest half-inch)** is $1\frac{1}{2}$ in.

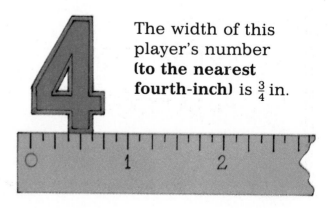

The width of this player's number **(to the nearest fourth-inch)** is $\frac{3}{4}$ in.

Which unit would you use? Write **inches** or **feet**.

1. Very tall player: 7 _?_
2. Shoe string length: 28 _?_
3. Basketball basket height: 10 _?_

4. Long basketball shot: 30 _?_
5. Basketball diameter: 9 _?_
6. Backboard width: 54 _?_

Complete.

Example: 4 ft = |||| in.   4 × 12 = 48, so 4 ft = 48 in.

7. 3 ft = |||| in.
8. 6 ft = |||| in.
9. 2 ft = |||| in.
10. 12 ft = |||| in.

Complete.

Example: 36 in. = |||| ft   36 ÷ 12 = 3, so 36 in. = 3 ft

11. 24 in. = |||| ft
12. 72 in. = |||| ft
13. 240 in. = |||| ft
14. 60 in. = |||| ft

15. Give the height in **inches** of each player listed in the table on page 388.
    Example: 5'10"   Since 5' = 60 in., 5'10" = 70 in.

16. Find the width of your desk top to the **nearest inch.**

17. Find the length of your pencil to the **nearest half inch.**

18. Find the length of a paper clip to the **nearest fourth inch.**

Think

Roman Numeral Puzzles

These toothpick equations use Roman numerals. None of the equations are correct as they now stand. Make each equation correct by moving one, and only one, toothpick.

Example: I — I = III   Solution: I + I = II

Try These!

1. IV — I = V
2. IX — V = VI
3. X + IV = V
4. VI — IV = XI
5. XL + X = II
6. LV — X = XIV

Math

Length: Yards and Miles

The **yard (yd)** is a customary unit of length.

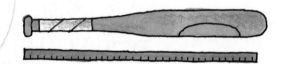

Yardstick

A baseball bat is about a yard long.

1 yd = 3 ft = 36 in.

The **mile (mi)** is a customary unit of length used for measuring longer distances.

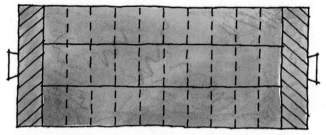

15 football fields laid end to end would be about 1 mile long.

1 mi = 1,760 yd = 5,280 ft

Which unit would you use? Write **inches, feet, yards,** or **miles.**

1. An airplane might fly 7 _?_ high.

2. An automobile is about 14 _?_ long.

3. A long step might be about 36 _?_ long.

4. A football field, including end zones, is 120 _?_ long.

5. The Amazon River is 3,912 _?_ long.

6. A city bus might be about 10 _?_ long.

Complete.

7. 6 yd = ▥ ft

8. 2 yd = ▥ in.

9. 5 mi = ▥ ft

10. 24 ft = ▥ yd

11. 100 yd = ▥ ft

12. 10 yd = ▥ in.

13. 144 in. = ▥ yd

14. 220 yd = ▥ ft

15. 10 ft = ▥ in.

16. To change from yards to feet, multiply by ▥.

17. To change from yards to inches, multiply by ▥.

18. To change from feet to yards, divide by ▥.

19. To change from inches to yards, divide by ▥.

20. To change from miles to feet, multiply by ▥.

Problem Solving: Length and Perimeter

QUESTION · DATA · PLAN · ANSWER · CHECK

Solve.

1. A rectangular sports field is 165 yd long and 96 yd wide. What is the perimeter of the field (the distance around the field)?

2. Some of the events at a track meet were a $\frac{1}{2}$-mile run, a $\frac{1}{4}$-mi run, and a $\frac{1}{8}$-mi run. How many yards long is each of these distances?

3. The middle-grades record for the high jump is 5 ft. Carl jumped 51 inches. How many inches less than the record was Carl's jump?

4. A rectangular field is 1 mi long and $\frac{1}{2}$-mi wide. What is the perimeter of the field in yards?

5. Maria threw the shot 34 ft. Lucia threw it 13 yd 2 ft. Who threw it farther? How much farther?

6. A recent record for the two-hour walk was 17 mi 881 yd. If each step was 1 yd long, how many steps were taken during the walk?

7. **DATA HUNT** How many yards would you run if you ran around the perimeter of your school yard 4 times?

8. **DATA BANK** What is the greatest difference (in seconds) between one record-setting time and the next for the 1-mile run? (See Data Bank, page 412.)

9. **Try This** Five girls ran the 100-yard dash. Ann came in last. Beth was ahead of Cathy. If Cathy was ahead of Dora and Janel was just behind Dora, who came in third? Hint: Draw a picture.

Estimating with Customary Units

Check your size!

First estimate. Then measure
with a measuring tape or
with a string and an inch ruler.

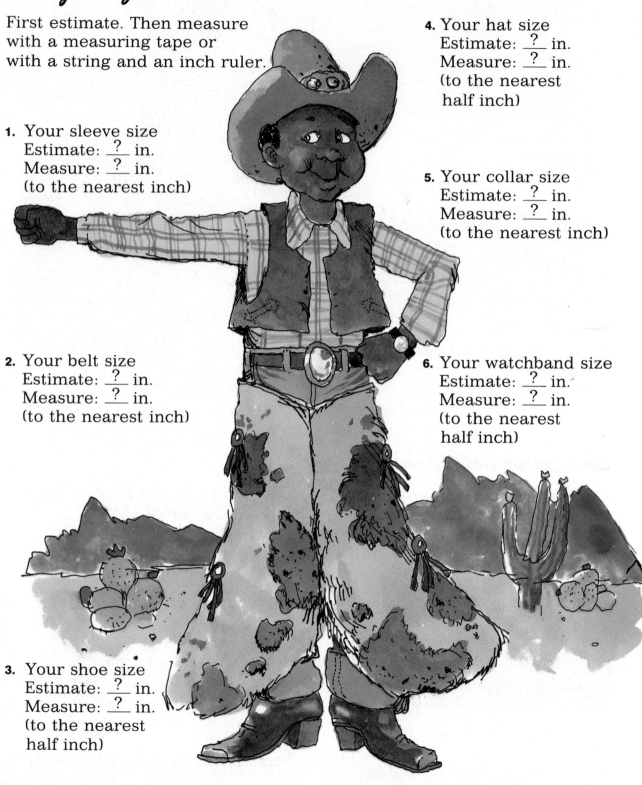

1. Your sleeve size
Estimate: _?_ in.
Measure: _?_ in.
(to the nearest inch)

2. Your belt size
Estimate: _?_ in.
Measure: _?_ in.
(to the nearest inch)

3. Your shoe size
Estimate: _?_ in.
Measure: _?_ in.
(to the nearest
half inch)

4. Your hat size
Estimate: _?_ in.
Measure: _?_ in.
(to the nearest
half inch)

5. Your collar size
Estimate: _?_ in.
Measure: _?_ in.
(to the nearest inch)

6. Your watchband size
Estimate: _?_ in.
Measure: _?_ in.
(to the nearest
half inch)

What is your record?

Estimate first, then measure.

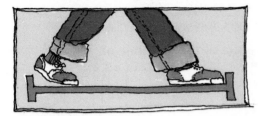

1. How far can you step?
Estimate: __?__ ft __?__ in.
Measure: __?__ ft __?__ in.

2. How high can you reach?
Estimate: __?__ yd __?__ in.
Measure: __?__ yd __?__ in.

3. How far can you reach?
Estimate: __?__ ft __?__ in.
Measure: __?__ ft __?__ in.

4. How high can your fingers
reach (your span)?
Estimate: __?__ in.
Measure: __?__ in.

For outside the classroom

5. How far can you jump?
Estimate: __?__ ft __?__ in.
Measure: __?__ ft __?__ in.

6. How far can you throw a ball?
Estimate: __?__ yd __?__ ft.
Measure: __?__ yd __?__ ft.

Skillkeeper

Solve the equations.

1. $\frac{3}{4} = \frac{n}{16}$ **2.** $\frac{1}{8} = \frac{n}{24}$

3. $\frac{3}{5} = \frac{n}{25}$ **4.** $\frac{3}{1} = \frac{n}{9}$

5. $\frac{1}{10} = \frac{n}{100}$ **6.** $\frac{1}{2} = \frac{n}{50}$

7. $\frac{3}{2} = \frac{n}{16}$ **8.** $\frac{2}{3} = \frac{n}{9}$

Problem Solving: Area

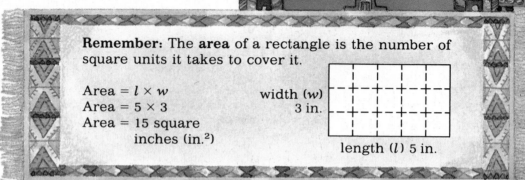

Remember: The **area** of a rectangle is the number of square units it takes to cover it.

Area = $l \times w$
Area = 5×3
Area = 15 square inches (in.²)

width (w) 3 in.

length (l) 5 in.

Solve.

1. A rug is 9 ft long and 12 ft wide. What is the area of the rug in square feet (ft²)?

2. A bag of grass seed is enough to plant 1,000 ft² of lawn. How many bags are needed to plant a lawn 85 ft wide and 112 ft long?

3. A gallon of paint will cover an area of 500 ft². If the paint costs $12.95 a gallon, how much will it cost to paint an area of 1,500 ft²?

4. The area of a garden is 1,334 ft². The width is 23 ft. How long is the garden?

5. An airport covers an area 15 mi long and 12 mi wide. What is the area of the airport?

6. Carpet costs $9.95 a square yard (yd²). How much will it cost to carpet a 12 ft by 15 ft room?

7. **DATA HUNT** How much would it cost to carpet a room in your home? Measure the length and width of the room. Find the cost of carpet at a store in your area.

8. **Try This** The area of a rectangular room is 384 ft². The length of the room is 8 ft greater than the width. What is the width of the room?

Problem Solving: Volume

Remember: The **volume** of a box is the number of cubic units it takes to fill it.

Volume = $l \times w \times h$
Volume = $4 \times 2 \times 2$
Volume = 16 cubic inches (in.^{3})

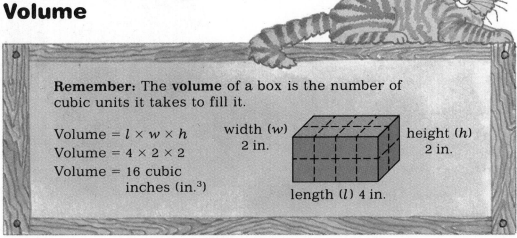

width (w) 2 in.

height (h) 2 in.

length (l) 4 in.

Solve.

1. A storage box is 6 ft long, 4 ft wide, and 3 ft high. What is the volume of the box in cubic feet (ft^3)?

2. A small air conditioner will cool about 1,000 cubic feet of air. Will it be enough to cool a room 17 ft by 11 ft by 7 ft?

1 cord of wood

4 ft

4 ft

8 ft

3. A cord of wood is a stack 4 ft wide, 8 ft long, and 4 ft deep. How many cubic feet is this?

4. The aquarium has 1,575 in.^{3} of water in it. How many more cubic inches of water will it take to fill it completely?

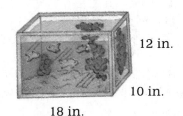

12 in.

10 in.

18 in.

5. A large trailer is 48 ft long, 10 ft wide, and 12 ft high. How many cubic feet of cargo will it hold?

6. Which cereal box has the greater volume? How much greater?

3 in.

12 in.

11 in.

7 in.

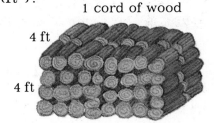

B

A

4 in.

8 in.

7. **DATA HUNT** About how many cubic feet of air are there in your classroom? If air weighs 0.08 pounds per cubic foot, what is the weight of this air?

8. **Try This** Jeff's father wants to build a fence around a swimming pool. The fence will be in the shape of a rectangle 60 ft long and 48 ft wide. The posts will be 12 ft apart. How many posts are needed?

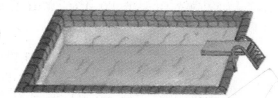

Capacity

Jeannie helps her father and mother collect sap from maple trees and make maple syrup.

As the syrup is made, it is put in gallon cans, like the one shown here.

How many quart containers can be filled from this can?

1 gallon

1 gallon   1 quart   1 quart   1 quart   1 quart

1 **gallon (gal)** will fill 4 **quarts (qt).**

1 quart   1 pint   1 pint   1 pint   1 cup   1 cup

1 quart will fill 2 **pints (pt).**   1 pint will fill 2 **cups (c).**

Use the pictures above to give the missing numbers.

1. 8 qt = ▥ gal   **2.** 4 c = ▥ qt   **3.** $\frac{1}{2}$ qt = ▥ pt

4. 4 pt = ▥ qt   **5.** 16 c = ▥ gal   **6.** $\frac{1}{2}$ pt = ▥ c

7. 3 gal = ▥ qt   **8.** 1 qt = ▥ c   **9.** $\frac{1}{2}$ gal = ▥ qt

10. 8 pt = ▥ gal   **11.** 1 gal = ▥ pt   **12.** 3 qt = ▥ pt

Problem Solving: Capacity

Solve.

1. A gallon of maple syrup costs $27.00. What does 1 qt cost?

2. It takes 43 gal of sap to make 1 gal of syrup. Jeannie's family collected 2,236 gal of sap. How many gallons of syrup will this make?

3. A collection bucket holds 3 gal of sap. How many gallons of sap can be collected from full buckets on 128 trees?

4. Which is cheaper, syrup costing $6.85 a quart or syrup costing $3.53 a pint? How much cheaper?

5. Jeannie's mother prints the number of ounces on each can of syrup. How many ounces are in a pint can? A quart can? A gallon can?

1 cup = 8 fluid ounces (fl oz)

1 tablespoon (tbsp) = $\frac{1}{2}$ fluid ounce

6. How many tablespoons are in 1 qt of syrup?

7. The volume of a gallon container is 231 in.^{3} What is the volume of a quart container, rounded to the nearest whole number?

8. **Try This** Suppose you have a barrel of syrup and a 3-qt and an 8-qt collection pail. There are no markings on either pail. How can you use these pails to get 4 quarts of syrup in the larger pail?

Weight

Don works at a supermarket. When he receives grocery shipments or answers customers' questions, it is important for Don to understand these customary units of measure.

1 **ounce (oz)**

1 **pound (lb)**

1 **ton (T)**

Delivery Record
1 truckload of watermelons
100 Melons
2,000 pounds or 1 ton

16 oz = 1 lb

2,000 lb = 1 T

Choose the best weight estimate.

1.

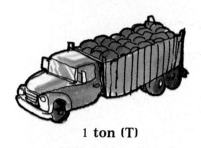

Canned ham

A 10 oz

B 10 lb

C 10 T

2.

Dried apples

A 7 oz

B 7 lb

C 7 T

3.

Delivery van

A 2 oz

B 2 lb

C 2 T

Give the missing numbers.

4. 3 lb = ▦ oz

5. 48 oz = ▦ lb

6. 6,000 lb = ▦ T

7. 4 T = ▦ lb

8. 8 lb = ▦ oz

9. 72 oz = ▦ lb

Problem Solving: Weight

Solve.

1. A customer asked Don for a pound and a half of ground beef. How many ounces is this?

2. A 1-lb bag of peaches contains 8 peaches. What is the average weight of each peach in ounces?

3. A truck delivered 600 watermelons to the supermarket. If the average weight of each melon was 20 lb, how many tons of melons were delivered?

4. A stick of butter is $\frac{1}{4}$ of a pound. How many ounces is this?

5. A 10-lb bag of potatoes costs $2.39. What is the cost of 1 lb of potatoes?

6. A 1-lb slice of watermelon sells for 17¢. How much greater is this cost per pound than the cost of a 20-lb melon that sells for $3.20?

7. Which is the better buy per ounce, a 7-oz package of dried fruit for 91¢ or a 1-lb package for $1.76? How much better?

8. **Try This**   A pound of butter and a loaf of bread cost $2.40. A pound of butter costs the same as 2 loaves of bread. What is the cost of a loaf of bread?

Temperature: Degrees Fahrenheit

Temperature is often measured using the **degree Fahrenheit (°F)** unit.

Use the information shown on this thermometer to give the best temperature estimate for each item below.

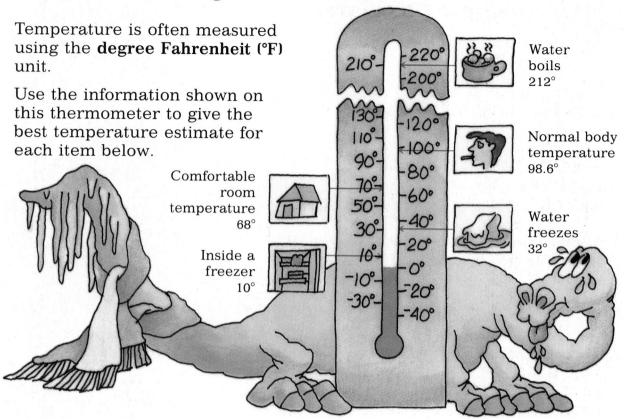

Water boils 212°

Normal body temperature 98.6°

Water freezes 32°

Comfortable room temperature 68°

Inside a freezer 10°

1. Hot soup

   A 50°F   **B** 170°F

   C 220°F

2. Frozen yogurt

   A 10°F   **B** 40°F

   C 60°F

3. Very hot summer day

   A 35°F   **B** 65°F

   C 95°F

4. Hot faucet water

   A 60°F   **B** 95°F

   C 150°F

5. Heated swimming pool

   A 20°F   **B** 80°F

   C 190°F

6. Cool fall day

   A 10°F   **B** 50°F

   C 100°F

Give each temperature in degrees Fahrenheit (°F).

7.

Hot chocolate

8.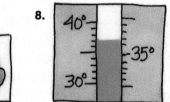

Drink with ice cubes

9.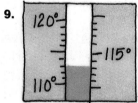

Warm bath

Problem Solving: Using a Calculator

Use a calculator to solve these special measurement problems.

1. How much greater is the number of minutes in a week than the number of hours in a year? (Use 365 days in a year.)

2. The total weight of a class of fifth-grade students is 1 T. If the students' average weight is 80 lb, how many students are in the class?

3. The weight of 5 nickels is about 1 oz. If an 80-lb fifth grader is given a bag of nickels that weighs as much as she does, how much money would she have?

4. A dollar bill is about 6 in. long. How much money would you have if you had a string of dollar bills laid end to end that was 1 mile long?

5. A rectangular house 21 yd long and 16 yd wide is built on a lot 32 yd long and 25 yd wide. How many square feet of yard space is left on the lot?

6. **DATA HUNT** How many gallons of water would be wasted if the drinking fountain got stuck and stayed on for 12 hours? Hint: Find out how many seconds it takes to fill a quart jar.

7. **Try This** Erica took a train from Chesterton to Morganville. The train made six 15-minute stops during the 232-mile trip. Its average speed between stops was 58 mph. The train arrived in Morganville at 3:10 p.m. If both cities are in the same time zone, what time was it when the train left Chesterton? (Hint: Traveling time + stopped time = Total trip time.)

Applied Problem Solving

You want a new bicycle. Should you sell your old bicycle through a newspaper advertisement, or should you trade it in on a new one?

Some Things to Consider

- You can get $70 for your old bicycle if you sell it through an advertisement in the newspaper.

- A newspaper advertisement costs $3 a day.

- A new bicycle costs $149.

- You can get $35 for your old bicycle if you use it as a trade-in on a new one.

- You would like to have a new bicycle within 8 days.

Some Questions to Answer

1. If you trade in your old bicycle, how much will you have to spend for the new one?

2. If you sell your old bicycle after running the ad for only 1 day, what will your total expenses for the new bicycle be?

3. What will your total expenses for the new bicycle be if you sell the old one after running the ad for 7 days?

4. If you run the ad for 8 days and do not sell the old bicycle, what will be the cost of the new one and the advertising minus the trade-in?

What Is Your Decision?

Will you trade in the old bicycle right away or buy the ad and see what happens?

Chapter Review-Test

Which unit would you use? Write **inches**, **feet**, **yards**, or **miles**.

1. A baseball bat is about 38 ? long.

2. An airport runway might be 2 ? long.

3. A football field is 100 ? long.

4. A car might be 13 ? long.

Complete the following.

5. 6 ft = ▦ in.

6. 3 mi = ▦ ft

7. 56 yd = ▦ ft

8. 48 in. = ▦ ft

9. 39 ft = ▦ yd

10. 16 ft = ▦ in.

11. Estimate the length of $\overline{AB}$ to the nearest inch.

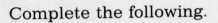

A •————————————————————• B

12. Measure the length of $\overline{AB}$ to the nearest half inch.

Complete the following.

13. 12 qt = ▦ gal

14. 8 c = ▦ pt

15. 2 gal = ▦ qt

16. 4 pt = ▦ c

17. 4 qt = ▦ pt

18. 12 pt = ▦ qt

Complete the following.

19. 4 lb = ▦ oz

20. 32 oz = ▦ lb

21. 3 T = ▦ lb

Choose the best estimate.

22. Weight of a bowling ball

   A 16 oz   **B** 16 lb   **C** 16 T

23. Temperature of a cool drink

   A 5°F   **B** 45°F   **C** 80°F

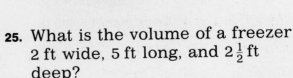

24. What is the perimeter of a lot 95 ft long and 63 ft wide? What is the area of the lot?

25. What is the volume of a freezer 2 ft wide, 5 ft long, and $2\frac{1}{2}$ ft deep?

Another Look

5 ft → 5 × 12 = 60 → 60 in.

12 inches in 1 foot

48 in. → 48 ÷ 12 = 4 → 4 ft

6 yd → 6 × 3 = 18 → 18 ft

3 feet in 1 yard

27 ft → 27 ÷ 3 = 9 → 9 yd

3 mi → 3 × 1,760 = 5,280 → 5,280 yd

1,760 yards in 1 mile

4 mi → 4 × 5,280 = 21,120 → 21,120 ft

5,280 feet in 1 mile

12 qt → 12 ÷ 4 = 3 → 3 gal

4 quarts in 1 gallon

8 gal → 8 × 4 = 32 → 32 qt

7 qt → 7 × 2 = 14 → 14 pt

2 pints in 1 quart

18 pt → 18 ÷ 2 = 9 → 9 qt

4 lb → 4 × 16 = 64 → 64 oz

16 ounces in 1 pound

3 T → 3 × 2,000 = 6,000 → 6,000 lb

2,000 pounds in 1 ton

Complete.

1. 6 ft = ▦ in.

2. 12 ft = ▦ in.

3. 84 in. = ▦ ft

4. 36 in. = ▦ ft

5. 12 yd = ▦ ft

6. 24 yd = ▦ ft

7. 36 ft = ▦ yd

8. 15 ft = ▦ yd

9. 2 mi = ▦ yd

10. 10 mi = ▦ yd

11. 3 mi = ▦ ft

12. 7 mi = ▦ ft

13. 16 qt = ▦ gal

14. 24 qt = ▦ gal

15. 9 gal = ▦ qt

16. 20 gal = ▦ qt

17. 4 qt = ▦ pt

18. 16 qt = ▦ pt

19. 16 pt = ▦ qt

20. 54 pt = ▦ qt

21. 8 lb = ▦ oz

22. 64 oz = ▦ lb

23. 5 T = ▦ lb

24. 8,000 lb = ▦ T

25. 30,000 lb = ▦ T

26. 160 oz = ▦ lb

Enrichment

Making Predictions from Samples

Each of the 25 students in Estela's class emptied a package of mixed nuts onto a paper plate. The students counted the number of each kind of nut and the total number in the package. Then they combined their data and made a table like this.

Kind of nut	Number	Percent of total
Peanuts	539	44%
Cashews	184	?
Almonds	191	?
Pecans	201	?
Brazil Nuts	110	?
	Total: 1,225	

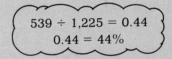

$539 \div 1,225 = 0.44$
$0.44 = 44\%$

1. Find the percent for each kind of nut in the table. (Use a calculator and round to the nearest whole percent.)

2. If you opened a package of mixed nuts like the ones Estela's class had, about how many nuts do you predict it would contain?

3. Which kind of nut would you expect to occur most often in the package?

4. Which kind of nut would you expect to occur least often?

5. Predict the number of each kind you would find in the bag.

6. Suppose that the numbers of each kind of nut found in each student's package were very different. Would you change your predictions in problems 3, 4, and 5?

Computer Drawings

Logo is a special computer language. It can be used to give a computer instructions for drawing pictures. A small triangle ▲ , called a **turtle**, moves over the computer screen and draws the pictures.

You can use the Logo commands FORWARD and BACK to make the turtle draw lines. The commands RIGHT and LEFT make the turtle turn.

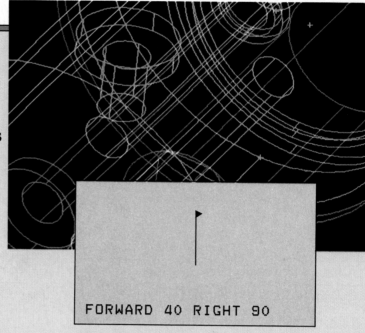

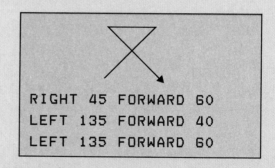

FORWARD 40 RIGHT 90

Move forward 40 units, then turn right 90 degrees.

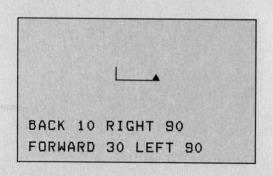

BACK 10 RIGHT 90
FORWARD 30 LEFT 90

RIGHT 45 FORWARD 60
LEFT 135 FORWARD 40
LEFT 135 FORWARD 60

When the same movement is to be made more than once, you can use the command REPEAT.

REPEAT 4 [FORWARD 20 RIGHT 90]

← This command repeats the move inside the brackets 4 times. The turtle draws a square.

REPEAT 3 [FORWARD 25 RIGHT 120]

← Following this command the turtle draws an equilateral triangle that is 25 units long on each side.

Give the missing Logo command
for each picture.

1.

FORWARD 20 _?_ 90

2.

FORWARD 30 _?_ 45
FORWARD 30

3.

_?_ 90 FORWARD 40

Give the missing number in each Logo command.

4.

BACK 20 LEFT _?_
FORWARD 20

5.

FORWARD 40 RIGHT _?_
FORWARD 30

6.

REPEAT _?_ [FORWARD
30 RIGHT 90]

Draw a picture for the commands in exercises 7–9.

7. FORWARD 30 LEFT 90
FORWARD 30 LEFT 90
FORWARD 30

8. FORWARD 20 RIGHT 90
FORWARD 20 RIGHT 90
FORWARD 20 RIGHT 90
FORWARD 20

9. REPEAT 6 [FORWARD
20 RIGHT 60]

10. Write some Logo commands of your own. Draw
the pictures for your commands.

Cumulative Review

Use this graph for items 1–2.

Books Read Last Summer

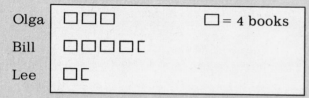

Olga	☐☐☐
Bill	☐☐☐☐☐
Lee	☐☐

☐ = 4 books

1. Who read the most books during summer vacation?
- **A** Olga
- **B** Lee
- **C** Bill
- **D** not given

2. How many books did Lee read during summer vacation?
- **A** 14
- **B** 10
- **C** 8
- **D** not given

Use this graph for items 3–4.

Growth of Mary's Plant

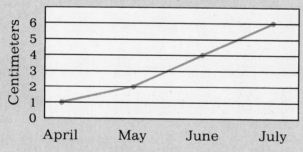

3. How many centimeters did the plant grow from May to June?
- **A** 2 cm
- **B** 1 cm
- **C** 3 cm
- **D** not given

4. During which period did the plant grow the least?
- **A** June to July
- **B** May to June
- **C** April to May
- **D** not given

5.

Tomatoes	1	2	?
Tacos	3	6	12

How many tomatoes are needed for 12 tacos?
- **A** 3
- **B** 5
- **C** 4
- **D** not given

Solve the equations.

6. $\frac{7}{2} = \frac{n}{18}$
- **A** $n = 63$
- **B** $n = 56$
- **C** $n = 72$
- **D** not given

7. $\frac{9}{10} = \frac{n}{90}$
- **A** 10
- **B** 81
- **C** 9
- **D** not given

Complete.

8. 144 in. = ▥ ft
- **A** 10
- **B** 11
- **C** 12
- **D** not given

9. 16 qt = ▥ gal
- **A** 32
- **B** 4
- **C** 14
- **D** not given

10. 10 lb = ▥ oz
- **A** 16
- **B** 1,600
- **C** 1.6
- **D** not given

11. For her art project, Lola used 7 green beads for every 9 blue beads. If she used 35 green beads, how many blue beads did she use?
- **A** 49
- **B** 45
- **C** 44
- **D** not given

Appendix

SLOAN SETS A NEW POLE VAULT RECORD

Senior track standout Greg Sloan set a new record in the pole vault yesterday during a meet at Valley Tech Stadium. Sloan cleared the bar at $15' 9\frac{3}{4}''$. This was $1\frac{1}{2}''$ higher than the old record. The final results are shown in the table.

Average Lengths of Snakes

Snake	Length (cm)	Snake	Length (cm)
Anaconda	672	Indian cobra	179
Boa constrictor	313	Indigo	238
Bull	156	King cobra	349
Copperhead	75	Rainbow	119

Name	School	Height
G. Sloan	West Side	$15' 9\frac{3}{4}''$
G. Coe	Lincoln	$15' 7\frac{1}{2}''$
B. Chin	Valley Tech	$15' 7''$
A. Ould	West Side	$15' 3\frac{1}{2}''$
M. Harrison	Sinclair	$14' 7''$
P. Carey	Valley Tech	$14' 2\frac{1}{2}''$

VALLEY TECH NEWS

GREAT LAKES STATES

State	Population	Area (Km^2)	Population Density*	Yearly Income Per Person	Highest Point
Illinois	11,418,000	146,075	78	$10,658	376 m
Indiana	5,490,000	93,993	58	8,978	383 m
Michigan	9,258,000	150,779	61	9,847	604 m
Minnesota	4,077,000	217,735	19	9,519	701 m
New York	17,557,000	128,401	137	10,143	1,629 m
Ohio	10,797,000	106,764	101	9,398	472 m
Pennsylvania	11,867,000	117,412	101	9,294	979 m
Wisconsin	4,705,000	145,438	32	9,254	595 m

*Average number of people for each square kilometer of area.

Average Heights (m)

Age	Boys	Girls
10	1.36	1.35
11	1.40	1.41
12	1.45	1.47

Daily Protein Costs

Cost in a recent year to supply a young adult with one third of daily protein needs from selected foods

Food	Cost
Peanut butter	$0.17
Turkey	0.29
Frankfurters	0.54
Beef roast	0.75
Bacon	0.99

Round-Trip Space Flight Times

From Earth to	Number of Days
• Mercury	206
• Venus	288
• Mars	514
• Jupiter	2,008
• Saturn	4,453
• Uranus	11,753
• Neptune	22,265
• Pluto	33,215

VITAMIN C CONTENT OF SELECTED BREAKFAST FOODS

FOODS	VITAMIN C (mg)
ORANGE JUICE (1 GLASS)	59.47
STRAWBERRIES (1 CUP)	88.08
GRAPEFRUIT ($\frac{1}{2}$)	52.50
MILK (1 CUP)	1.84
EGG	0
CORN FLAKES (1 CUP)	8.8
RAISIN BRAN (1 CUP)	19.75
HOT COCOA (1 CUP)	2.52
TOAST (WHOLE WHEAT)	0

RECORD AUTO SPEEDS		
Name of Auto	**Type**	**Speed (km/h)**
The Blue Flame	Rocket engine	1,016
Spirit of America—Sonic I	Jet engine	988
Bluebird	Wheel driven	691
Golden Rod	Piston engine	674
Mercedes	Diesel engine	327

TAX TABLE

Amount of Sale	Tax	Amount of Sale	Tax
7.51—7.67	0.46	8.68—8.84	0.53
7.68—7.84	0.47	8.85—9.10	0.54
7.85—8.10	0.48	9.11—9.17	0.55
8.11—8.17	0.49	9.18—9.34	0.56
8.18—8.34	0.50	9.35—9.50	0.57
8.35—8.50	0.51	9.51—9.67	0.58
8.51—8.67	0.52	9.68—9.84	0.59

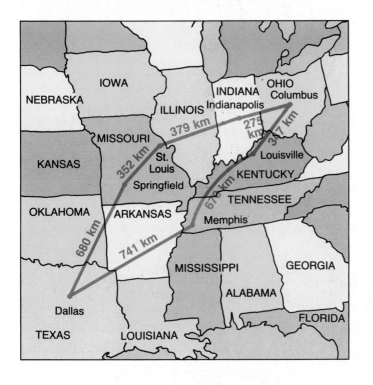

NUMBER OF DAILY GENERAL INTEREST NEWSPAPERS

Country	Number of Newspapers
United States	1,815
India	835
Soviet Union	697
Turkey	437
Brazil	280
Mexico	256
Japan	180
Indonesia	172

Average Monthly Rainfall in Charleston, S.C., and Peoria, Ill.

—— Charleston, S.C.
—— Peoria, Ill.

Amount of Rainfall (cm) vs Months

Charleston, S.C.:
- May: 8.38
- June: 12.95
- July: 15.75
- Aug.: 16.51
- Sept.: 13.21

Peoria, Ill.:
- May: 9.91
- June: 9.65
- July: 9.65
- Aug.: 8.12
- Sept.: 9.65

7 Highest Dams in the United States

Name and Location of Dam	Height (m)
Oroville (Calif.)	235
Hoover (Nev.)	221
Salisaw Creek Site (Okla.)	220
Dworshak (Ida.)	219
Glen Canyon (Ariz.)	217
New Bullards Bar (Calif.)	194
New Melones (Calif.)	192

AVERAGE DAILY* EARNINGS OF PERSONS IN SELECTED OCCUPATIONS (IN A RECENT YEAR)

Occupation	Salary
Airplane Mechanic	$ 85.40
Baker	46.80
Bulldozer Operator	65.40
Librarian	64.00
Nurse	66.40
Secretary	46.00
Sheriff	64.80

*8-hour day

WORLD RECORD ONE-MILE RUNS

Year	Name, Country	Time
1954	Roger Bannister Britain	3:59.4
1954	John Landy Australia	3:58
1957	Derek Ibbotson Britain	3:57.2
1958	Herb Elliott Australia	3:54.5
1962	Peter Snell New Zealand	3:54.4
1964	Peter Snell New Zealand	3:54.1
1965	Michel Jazy France	3:53.6
1966	Jim Ryun United States	3:51.3
1967	Jim Ryun United States	3:51.1
1975	Filbert Bayi Tanzania	3:51
1975	John Walker New Zealand	3:49.4
1979	Sebastian Coe Britain	3:49
1980	Steve Overt Britain	3:48.8

MORE PRACTICE

Set A For use after page 3

Add.

1.	7 + 4	**2.**	5 + 4	**3.**	3 + 6	**4.**	5 + 9	**5.**	4 + 1	**6.**	2 + 7	**7.**	9 + 8
8.	5 + 6	**9.**	3 + 3	**10.**	0 + 0	**11.**	1 + 3	**12.**	2 + 6	**13.**	8 + 1	**14.**	3 + 2
15.	5 + 2	**16.**	8 + 8	**17.**	6 + 9	**18.**	1 + 0	**19.**	0 + 4	**20.**	4 + 7	**21.**	4 + 2

Set B For use after page 5

Subtract.

1.	12 − 7	**2.**	6 − 5	**3.**	16 − 8	**4.**	9 − 3	**5.**	18 − 9	**6.**	12 − 6	**7.**	11 − 4
8.	7 − 2	**9.**	17 − 8	**10.**	10 − 5	**11.**	4 − 4	**12.**	15 − 7	**13.**	7 − 6	**14.**	14 − 5
15.	6 − 4	**16.**	5 − 2	**17.**	14 − 7	**18.**	3 − 2	**19.**	13 − 9	**20.**	11 − 8	**21.**	8 − 1

Set C For use after page 7

Find the sums or differences.

1.	7 + 3	**2.**	3 + 7	**3.**	4 − 0	**4.**	4 + 2	**5.**	2 + 4	**6.**	6 − 6	**7.**	0 + 6
8.	8 + 4	**9.**	4 + 8	**10.**	12 − 4	**11.**	7 − 7	**12.**	5 + 0	**13.**	9 − 6	**14.**	6 − 3
15.	4 3 + 7	**16.**	9 1 + 6	**17.**	3 8 + 1	**18.**	5 2 + 8	**19.**	3 1 + 3	**20.**	5 6 + 5	**21.**	2 0 + 9

Set A   For use after page 11

Multiply.

1. $\begin{array}{r} 1 \\ \times\ 3 \\ \hline \end{array}$	**2.** $\begin{array}{r} 7 \\ \times\ 6 \\ \hline \end{array}$	**3.** $\begin{array}{r} 5 \\ \times\ 4 \\ \hline \end{array}$	**4.** $\begin{array}{r} 9 \\ \times\ 1 \\ \hline \end{array}$	**5.** $\begin{array}{r} 3 \\ \times\ 7 \\ \hline \end{array}$	**6.** $\begin{array}{r} 2 \\ \times\ 3 \\ \hline \end{array}$	**7.** $\begin{array}{r} 4 \\ \times\ 2 \\ \hline \end{array}$
8. $\begin{array}{r} 5 \\ \times\ 5 \\ \hline \end{array}$	**9.** $\begin{array}{r} 4 \\ \times\ 1 \\ \hline \end{array}$	**10.** $\begin{array}{r} 2 \\ \times\ 4 \\ \hline \end{array}$	**11.** $\begin{array}{r} 3 \\ \times\ 7 \\ \hline \end{array}$	**12.** $\begin{array}{r} 8 \\ \times\ 5 \\ \hline \end{array}$	**13.** $\begin{array}{r} 0 \\ \times\ 7 \\ \hline \end{array}$	**14.** $\begin{array}{r} 6 \\ \times\ 4 \\ \hline \end{array}$
15. $\begin{array}{r} 3 \\ \times\ 2 \\ \hline \end{array}$	**16.** $\begin{array}{r} 8 \\ \times\ 3 \\ \hline \end{array}$	**17.** $\begin{array}{r} 9 \\ \times\ 7 \\ \hline \end{array}$	**18.** $\begin{array}{r} 0 \\ \times\ 6 \\ \hline \end{array}$	**19.** $\begin{array}{r} 1 \\ \times\ 8 \\ \hline \end{array}$	**20.** $\begin{array}{r} 3 \\ \times\ 9 \\ \hline \end{array}$	**21.** $\begin{array}{r} 5 \\ \times\ 6 \\ \hline \end{array}$

Set B   For use after page 17

Divide.

1. $10 \div 2$ **2.** $63 \div 7$ **3.** $9 \div 3$ **4.** $8 \div 4$ **5.** $30 \div 6$ **6.** $18 \div 3$

7. $12 \div 4$ **8.** $63 \div 9$ **9.** $35 \div 7$ **10.** $10 \div 5$ **11.** $48 \div 6$ **12.** $20 \div 4$

13. $3\overline{)21}$ **14.** $4\overline{)24}$ **15.** $5\overline{)20}$ **16.** $7\overline{)56}$ **17.** $6\overline{)12}$ **18.** $2\overline{)18}$

19. $4\overline{)28}$ **20.** $6\overline{)42}$ **21.** $3\overline{)27}$ **22.** $2\overline{)14}$ **23.** $8\overline{)48}$ **24.** $7\overline{)21}$

Set C   For use after page 39

Write $>$, $<$, or $=$ for each ▥.

1. 1,043 ▥ 1,403   **2.** 36,455 ▥ 36,455   **3.** 9,003 ▥ 8,973

4. 737,421 ▥ 777,981   **5.** 10,000 ▥ 9,000   **6.** 768 ▥ 876

Order from greatest to least.

7. 717; 770; 707; 170   **8.** 408,577; 488,700; 48,980

Order from least to greatest.

9. 37,090; 137,400; 37,079   **10.** 98,501; 10,999; 103,275

Set A For use after page 41

Round to the nearest ten.   Round to the nearest hundred.

1. 179 **2.** 394 **3.** 771 **4.** 17,049 **5.** 1,672

Round to the nearest thousand.

6. 4,028 **7.** 12,454 **8.** 1,987 **9.** 27,630 **10.** 5,500

Set B For use after page 51

Estimate by rounding to the nearest ten.

1.	**2.**	**3.**	**4.**	**5.**
37	21	48	91	67
+ 16	+ 46	+ 45	+ 14	+ 45

Estimate by rounding to the nearest thousand.

6.	**7.**	**8.**	**9.**	**10.**
1,050	2,500	1,329	6,117	7,277
+ 3,760	+ 1,431	+ 6,727	+ 5,089	+ 3,941

Estimate by rounding to the nearest dollar.

11.	**12.**	**13.**	**14.**	**15.**
$1.48	$7.75	$3.80	$1.85	$4.27
+ 6.72	+ 3.25	+ 4.50	+ 9.17	+ 1.88

Set C For use after page 53

Find the sums.

1.	**2.**	**3.**	**4.**	**5.**
208	475	608	117	636
+ 191	+ 162	+ 327	+ 435	+ 412

6.	**7.**	**8.**	**9.**	**10.**
154	916	414	754	77
+ 554	+ 73	+ 440	+ 823	+ 17

11.	**12.**	**13.**	**14.**	**15.**
4,516	7,120	4,006	4,128	7,046
+ 3,802	+ 1,597	+ 1,925	+ 7,361	+ 5,341

Set A   For use after page 55

Add.

1. 368 + 427	2. 424 + 978	3. 4,177 + 3,840	4. 11,088 + 5,427	5. 27,451 + 16,826
6. 7,264 + 1,966	7. 18,426 + 54,219	8. 33,427 + 18,916	9. 1,626 + 7,088	10. 27,677 + 19,281
11. $1.86 + 4.42	12. $14.60 + 9.97	13. $17.04 + 29.77	14. $11.08 + 9.77	15. $34.07 + 19.29

Set B   For use after page 57

Add.

1. 77 16 + 81	2. 744 86 + 208	3. 444 38 + 877	4. 1,327 4,418 + 805	5. 26,125 10,877 + 34,501
6. 716 84 375 + 170	7. 4,166 2,401 3,397 + 1,804	8. $7,241 1,388 214 + 4,425	9. $12.67 41.31 8.15 + 16.99	10. $14.32 27.57 18.49 + 25.00

Set C   For use after page 61

Estimate by rounding to the nearest hundred.

1. 417 − 186	2. 354 − 147	3. 1,208 − 435	4. 985 − 450	5. 1,368 − 875

Estimate by rounding to the nearest thousand or nearest dollar.

6. 7,563 − 2,088	7. 4,920 − 1,377	8. 12,187 − 4,842	9. 15,500 − 8,500	10. 13,667 − 8,095
11. $4.75 − 3.50	12. $8.95 − 2.25	13. $6.66 − 3.89	14. $15.27 − 9.61	15. $9.95 − 4.50

Set A   For use after page 63

Find the differences.

1. $\begin{array}{r} 36 \\ -\ 19 \end{array}$	**2.** $\begin{array}{r} 47 \\ -\ 28 \end{array}$	**3.** $\begin{array}{r} 618 \\ -\ 454 \end{array}$	**4.** $\begin{array}{r} 795 \\ -\ 467 \end{array}$	**5.** $\begin{array}{r} 811 \\ -\ 540 \end{array}$
6. $\begin{array}{r} 715 \\ -\ 123 \end{array}$	**7.** $\begin{array}{r} 658 \\ -\ 197 \end{array}$	**8.** $\begin{array}{r} 444 \\ -\ 183 \end{array}$	**9.** $\begin{array}{r} 764 \\ -\ 580 \end{array}$	**10.** $\begin{array}{r} 456 \\ -\ 302 \end{array}$
11. $\begin{array}{r} 9{,}663 \\ -\ 4{,}208 \end{array}$	**12.** $\begin{array}{r} 7{,}351 \\ -\ 2{,}620 \end{array}$	**13.** $\begin{array}{r} 14{,}317 \\ -\ 8{,}014 \end{array}$	**14.** $\begin{array}{r} \$27.53 \\ -\ 18.22 \end{array}$	**15.** $\begin{array}{r} \$49.37 \\ -\ 29.08 \end{array}$

Set B   For use after page 65

Subtract.

1. $\begin{array}{r} 622 \\ -\ 157 \end{array}$	**2.** $\begin{array}{r} 345 \\ -\ 196 \end{array}$	**3.** $\begin{array}{r} 814 \\ -\ 326 \end{array}$	**4.** $\begin{array}{r} 953 \\ -\ 166 \end{array}$	**5.** $\begin{array}{r} 417 \\ -\ 54 \end{array}$
6. $\begin{array}{r} 3{,}444 \\ -\ 1{,}555 \end{array}$	**7.** $\begin{array}{r} 4{,}942 \\ -\ 1{,}988 \end{array}$	**8.** $\begin{array}{r} 8{,}255 \\ -\ 4{,}880 \end{array}$	**9.** $\begin{array}{r} 395 \\ -\ 198 \end{array}$	**10.** $\begin{array}{r} 4{,}327 \\ -\ 1{,}548 \end{array}$
11. $\begin{array}{r} 27{,}365 \\ -\ 19{,}508 \end{array}$	**12.** $\begin{array}{r} 91{,}362 \\ -\ 46{,}175 \end{array}$	**13.** $\begin{array}{r} 22{,}921 \\ -\ 5{,}463 \end{array}$	**14.** $\begin{array}{r} \$82.62 \\ -\ 9.95 \end{array}$	**15.** $\begin{array}{r} \$63.59 \\ -\ 27.07 \end{array}$

Set C   For use after page 67

Subtract.

1. $\begin{array}{r} 700 \\ -\ 186 \end{array}$	**2.** $\begin{array}{r} 320 \\ -\ 113 \end{array}$	**3.** $\begin{array}{r} 405 \\ -\ 86 \end{array}$	**4.** $\begin{array}{r} 300 \\ -\ 103 \end{array}$	**5.** $\begin{array}{r} 740 \\ -\ 166 \end{array}$
6. $\begin{array}{r} 1{,}700 \\ -\ 861 \end{array}$	**7.** $\begin{array}{r} 4{,}040 \\ -\ 1{,}625 \end{array}$	**8.** $\begin{array}{r} 3{,}770 \\ -\ 1{,}308 \end{array}$	**9.** $\begin{array}{r} 4{,}000 \\ -\ 2{,}614 \end{array}$	**10.** $\begin{array}{r} 1{,}033 \\ -\ 67 \end{array}$
11. $\begin{array}{r} 27{,}500 \\ -\ 18{,}611 \end{array}$	**12.** $\begin{array}{r} 30{,}100 \\ -\ 11{,}433 \end{array}$	**13.** $\begin{array}{r} \$26.50 \\ -\ 19.66 \end{array}$	**14.** $\begin{array}{r} \$14.00 \\ -\ 6.99 \end{array}$	**15.** $\begin{array}{r} \$20.00 \\ -\ 16.77 \end{array}$

Set A   For use after page 83

Write >, <, or = for each ▦ .

1. 0.44 ▦ 0.43   2. 3.98 ▦ 3.89   3. 1.99 ▦ 1.0   4. 7 ▦ 8.7

5. 1.9 ▦ 1.90   6. 3.25 ▦ 32.5   7. 1.799 ▦ 1.4   8. 26.02 ▦ 26.2

Order from greatest to least.

9. 3.206; 3.026; 2.930; 1.500; 4.086   10. 0.677; 0.855; 0.760; 0.078; 0.541

Set B   For use after page 85

Round to the nearest whole number.

1. 6.7   2. 10.84   3. 1.3   4. 19.08   5. 5.5

6. 14.38   7. 9.9   8. 4.399   9. 7.11   10. 43.806

Round to the nearest tenth.

11. 6.25   12. 0.19   13. 5.917   14. 0.08   15. 0.459

16. 8.445   17. 7.65   18. 0.509   19. 0.621   20. 0.054

Set C   For use after page 89

Add.

1.	17.2 + 11.5	2.	4.44 + 7.81	3.	0.88 + 1.96	4.	14.5 + 9.84	5.	9.53 + 0.8
6.	7.999 + 0.010	7.	4.308 + 12.95	8.	$76.51 + 0.48	9.	$1.75 + 4.99	10.	$68.70 + 9.28
11.	17.2 11.8 + 9.5	12.	42.1 118.06 + 1.97	13.	7.335 0.862 9.577 + 1.086	14.	$42.08 16.99 16.99 + 14.36	15.	$1.99 3.67 4.42 + 1.50

Set A   For use after page 91

Subtract.

1.	2.	3.	4.	5.
4.3 − 1.9	75.08 − 16.97	65.17 − 5.9	5.367 − 2.956	459.3 − 18.65

6.	7.	8.	9.	10.
17.946 − 12.987	408.75 − 69.80	1,546.12 − 996.85	432.777 − 154.699	48.532 − 1.97

11.	12.	13.	14.	15.
0.757 − 0.219	7,764.1 − 2,362.9	44.50 − 1.75	$798.05 − 36.54	$433.67 − 248.70

Set B   For use after page 108

Estimate the products by rounding 2-digit numbers
to the nearest ten and 3-digit numbers to the
nearest hundred.

1.	2.	3.	4.	5.
27 × 3	69 × 5	55 × 4	267 × 3	195 × 4

6.	7.	8.	9.	10.
55 × 54	366 × 42	92 × 45	188 × 12	48 × 61

11.	12.	13.	14.	15.
604 × 48	912 × 377	459 × 632	850 × 275	926 × 144

Set C   For use after page 111

Multiply.

1.	2.	3.	4.	5.	6.
73 × 2	19 × 6	66 × 7	45 × 6	77 × 3	63 × 4

7.	8.	9.	10.	11.	12.
81 × 5	37 × 6	91 × 8	79 × 7	366 × 7	908 × 2

13.	14.	15.	16.	17.	18.
734 × 5	566 × 4	840 × 3	$4.14 × 7	$3.26 × 4	$5.99 × 7

Set A   For use after page 113

Multiply.

1. 6,421 × 4	**2.** 877 × 6	**3.** 4,226 × 5	**4.** 7,122 × 4	**5.** 818 × 3
6. 7,912 × 3	**7.** 4,506 × 4	**8.** 64,446 × 8	**9.** 25,284 × 3	**10.** 1,633 × 7
11. 35,446 × 4	**12.** $62.14 × 5	**13.** $48.08 × 6	**14.** $91.20 × 2	**15.** $45.65 × 3

Set B   For use after page 115

Multiply.

1. 43 × 30	**2.** 97 × 50	**3.** 29 × 70	**4.** 48 × 60	**5.** 73 × 40
6. 375 × 50	**7.** 406 × 40	**8.** 912 × 20	**9.** 775 × 40	**10.** 814 × 70
11. 694 × 600	**12.** 163 × 800	**13.** 667 × 900	**14.** 433 × 20	**15.** 546 × 500

Set C   For use after page 117

Multiply.

1. 48 × 48	**2.** 37 × 45	**3.** 62 × 49	**4.** 17 × 62	**5.** 28 × 41
6. 616 × 26	**7.** 921 × 53	**8.** 447 × 22	**9.** 146 × 72	**10.** 805 × 83
11. 736 × 41	**12.** 296 × 38	**13.** 354 × 77	**14.** 546 × 63	**15.** 660 × 48

Set A   For use after page 121

Multiply.

1. 791 $\times$ 675	**2.** 409 $\times$ 227	**3.** 343 $\times$ 511	**4.** 192 $\times$ 346	**5.** 818 $\times$ 625
6. 746 $\times$ 520	**7.** 942 $\times$ 108	**8.** 634 $\times$ 727	**9.** 811 $\times$ 546	**10.** 342 $\times$ 790
11. 818 $\times$ 264	**12.** 532 $\times$ 167	**13.** 917 $\times$ 444	**14.** 459 $\times$ 260	**15.** 114 $\times$ 362

Set B   For use after page 134

Estimate the quotients by rounding 3-digit numbers
to the nearest ten and 4-digit numbers to the
nearest hundred.

1. $2\overline{)164}$ **2.** $7\overline{)208}$ **3.** $5\overline{)446}$ **4.** $9\overline{)721}$ **5.** $7\overline{)4,899}$

6. $5\overline{)3,040}$ **7.** $2\overline{)1,798}$ **8.** $6\overline{)4,150}$ **9.** $6\overline{)3,550}$ **10.** $5\overline{)247}$

11. $8\overline{)4,780}$ **12.** $7\overline{)138}$ **13.** $3\overline{)2,090}$ **14.** $5\overline{)4,037}$ **15.** $6\overline{)2,415}$

16. $5\overline{)248}$ **17.** $6\overline{)1,825}$ **18.** $3\overline{)2,379}$ **19.** $9\overline{)3,620}$ **20.** $7\overline{)415}$

Set C   For use after page 136

Find the quotients and remainders.

1. $7\overline{)20}$ **2.** $4\overline{)18}$ **3.** $9\overline{)29}$ **4.** $7\overline{)54}$ **5.** $6\overline{)25}$

6. $4\overline{)30}$ **7.** $9\overline{)7}$ **8.** $7\overline{)27}$ **9.** $4\overline{)36}$ **10.** $2\overline{)19}$

11. $3\overline{)14}$ **12.** $8\overline{)30}$ **13.** $6\overline{)53}$ **14.** $5\overline{)37}$ **15.** $8\overline{)3}$

16. $8\overline{)32}$ **17.** $7\overline{)40}$ **18.** $9\overline{)15}$ **19.** $4\overline{)33}$ **20.** $7\overline{)29}$

Set A   For use after page 139

Divide and check.

1. $2\overline{)82}$ 2. $3\overline{)51}$ 3. $4\overline{)56}$ 4. $2\overline{)78}$ 5. $4\overline{)44}$

6. $5\overline{)75}$ 7. $3\overline{)55}$ 8. $6\overline{)64}$ 9. $3\overline{)62}$ 10. $3\overline{)95}$

11. $4\overline{)68}$ 12. $5\overline{)55}$ 13. $5\overline{)82}$ 14. $2\overline{)59}$ 15. $6\overline{)94}$

Set B   For use after page 141

Divide and check.

1. $4\overline{)884}$ 2. $5\overline{)865}$ 3. $3\overline{)737}$ 4. $4\overline{)545}$ 5. $5\overline{)573}$

6. $8\overline{)892}$ 7. $5\overline{)635}$ 8. $8\overline{)939}$ 9. $3\overline{)408}$ 10. $5\overline{)748}$

11. $2\overline{)827}$ 12. $5\overline{)585}$ 13. $3\overline{)964}$ 14. $3\overline{)635}$ 15. $5\overline{)986}$

Set C   For use after page 143

Divide and check.

1. $4\overline{)184}$ 2. $7\overline{)457}$ 3. $2\overline{)130}$ 4. $3\overline{)232}$ 5. $5\overline{)194}$

6. $3\overline{)228}$ 7. $7\overline{)131}$ 8. $6\overline{)264}$ 9. $5\overline{)193}$ 10. $3\overline{)289}$

11. $7\overline{)151}$ 12. $6\overline{)531}$ 13. $3\overline{)168}$ 14. $5\overline{)369}$ 15. $7\overline{)340}$

Set D   For use after page 144

Divide.

1. $3\overline{)625}$ 2. $6\overline{)424}$ 3. $3\overline{)913}$ 4. $6\overline{)843}$ 5. $2\overline{)416}$

6. $9\overline{)727}$ 7. $5\overline{)523}$ 8. $2\overline{)405}$ 9. $8\overline{)483}$ 10. $4\overline{)818}$

11. $9\overline{)915}$ 12. $3\overline{)918}$ 13. $5\overline{)203}$ 14. $7\overline{)760}$ 15. $2\overline{)813}$

Set A For use after page 147

Divide.

1. $6\overline{)2{,}074}$ 2. $9\overline{)5{,}570}$ 3. $8\overline{)3{,}500}$ 4. $6\overline{)2{,}432}$ 5. $5\overline{)2{,}182}$

6. $7\overline{)2{,}226}$ 7. $5\overline{)4{,}073}$ 8. $2\overline{)1{,}906}$ 9. $3\overline{)2{,}209}$ 10. $4\overline{)1{,}218}$

11. $3\overline{)3{,}813}$ 12. $6\overline{)4{,}248}$ 13. $9\overline{)1{,}186}$ 14. $6\overline{)3{,}348}$ 15. $3\overline{)8{,}163}$

Set B For use after page 149

Divide.

1. $3\overline{)\$5.01}$ 2. $5\overline{)\$4.90}$ 3. $6\overline{)\$23.22}$ 4. $5\overline{)\$9.75}$ 5. $9\overline{)\$40.50}$

6. $7\overline{)\$9.80}$ 7. $5\overline{)\$45.20}$ 8. $7\overline{)\$17.29}$ 9. $6\overline{)\$48.78}$ 10. $2\overline{)\$22.52}$

11. $6\overline{)\$25.02}$ 12. $8\overline{)\$97.60}$ 13. $5\overline{)\$88.75}$ 14. $3\overline{)\$29.97}$ 15. $6\overline{)\$27.00}$

Set C For use after page 151

Divide.

1. $4\overline{)675}$ 2. $3\overline{)807}$ 3. $7\overline{)411}$ 4. $3\overline{)255}$ 5. $7\overline{)1{,}617}$

6. $4\overline{)2{,}491}$ 7. $5\overline{)1{,}522}$ 8. $6\overline{)2{,}743}$ 9. $3\overline{)2{,}209}$ 10. $9\overline{)4{,}700}$

11. $6\overline{)4{,}380}$ 12. $4\overline{)1{,}225}$ 13. $6\overline{)7{,}002}$ 14. $7\overline{)974}$ 15. $2\overline{)8{,}483}$

Set D For use after page 152

Find the averages to the nearest whole number.

1. 34, 22, 29   2. 17, 11, 25, 26   3. 43, 26, 25, 33

4. 17, 32, 21   5. 43, 21, 32, 37   6. 14, 21, 22, 17, 20

7. 18, 31, 30, 24   8. 16, 22, 37   9. 22, 28, 24, 25, 19

Set A   For use after page 167

Divide and check.

1. $29\overline{)87}$ 2. $27\overline{)81}$ 3. $41\overline{)83}$ 4. $26\overline{)86}$ 5. $33\overline{)75}$

6. $41\overline{)181}$ 7. $17\overline{)85}$ 8. $68\overline{)214}$ 9. $61\overline{)144}$ 10. $36\overline{)191}$

11. $78\overline{)269}$ 12. $19\overline{)114}$ 13. $81\overline{)287}$ 14. $47\overline{)235}$ 15. $94\overline{)206}$

Set B   For use after page 169

Divide and check.

1. $62\overline{)191}$ 2. $16\overline{)140}$ 3. $27\overline{)190}$ 4. $43\overline{)380}$ 5. $32\overline{)275}$

6. $28\overline{)208}$ 7. $61\overline{)441}$ 8. $48\overline{)415}$ 9. $84\overline{)416}$ 10. $63\overline{)455}$

11. $27\overline{)251}$ 12. $37\overline{)232}$ 13. $22\overline{)129}$ 14. $43\overline{)373}$ 15. $72\overline{)666}$

Set C   For use after page 173

Divide and check.

1. $37\overline{)530}$ 2. $46\overline{)620}$ 3. $33\overline{)705}$ 4. $22\overline{)382}$ 5. $31\overline{)696}$

6. $35\overline{)639}$ 7. $21\overline{)491}$ 8. $41\overline{)586}$ 9. $31\overline{)594}$ 10. $11\overline{)270}$

11. $62\overline{)2,184}$ 12. $36\overline{)5,076}$ 13. $15\overline{)1,221}$ 14. $27\overline{)6,090}$ 15. $54\overline{)2,342}$

Set D   For use after page 175

Divide and check.

1. $13\overline{)661}$ 2. $46\overline{)949}$ 3. $25\overline{)514}$ 4. $22\overline{)676}$ 5. $46\overline{)953}$

6. $27\overline{)5,564}$ 7. $59\overline{)8,892}$ 8. $12\overline{)7,459}$ 9. $88\overline{)9,350}$ 10. $58\overline{)4,682}$

11. $39\overline{)14,045}$ 12. $68\overline{)55,086}$ 13. $82\overline{)25,077}$ 14. $44\overline{)4,773}$ 15. $76\overline{)65,048}$

Set A   For use after page 176

Divide and check.

1. $65\overline{)\$7.80}$ 2. $89\overline{)\$3.56}$ 3. $90\overline{)\$22.50}$ 4. $30\overline{)\$55.80}$ 5. $21\overline{)\$41.16}$

6. $74\overline{)\$604.58}$ 7. $38\overline{)\$326.04}$ 8. $65\overline{)\$66.30}$ 9. $81\overline{)\$55.89}$ 10. $58\overline{)\$124.70}$

11. $37\overline{)\$62.53}$ 12. $51\overline{)\$12.24}$ 13. $48\overline{)\$212.16}$ 14. $60\overline{)\$336.60}$ 15. $71\overline{)\$416.77}$

16. $57\overline{)\$11.40}$ 17. $26\overline{)\$25.48}$ 18. $53\overline{)\$392.73}$ 19. $12\overline{)\$13.92}$ 20. $60\overline{)\$195.60}$

Set B   For use after page 223

Give the next three equivalent fractions.

1. $\frac{3}{5}$ 2. $\frac{1}{6}$ 3. $\frac{2}{7}$ 4. $\frac{1}{5}$

Give the missing numerator.

5. $\frac{1}{3} = \frac{\text{▥}}{18}$ 6. $\frac{3}{8} = \frac{\text{▥}}{16}$ 7. $\frac{1}{4} = \frac{\text{▥}}{20}$ 8. $\frac{3}{5} = \frac{\text{▥}}{15}$

9. $\frac{1}{5} = \frac{\text{▥}}{20}$ 10. $\frac{2}{3} = \frac{\text{▥}}{15}$ 11. $\frac{1}{2} = \frac{\text{▥}}{12}$ 12. $\frac{5}{6} = \frac{\text{▥}}{12}$

Set C   For use after page 225

List the factors of each number. Then give the greatest common factor.

1. 9   2. 12   3. 5   4. 9
   18   21   30   16

5. 15   6. 25   7. 12   8. 36
   20   30   14   40

Give the greatest common factor.

9. 12   10. 32   11. 20   12. 7   13. 36   14. 15
   18   36   30   21   48   27

425

Reduce to lowest terms.

1. $\frac{9}{12}$　　**2.** $\frac{10}{12}$　　**3.** $\frac{3}{24}$　　**4.** $\frac{10}{15}$　　**5.** $\frac{14}{21}$　　**6.** $\frac{4}{16}$

7. $\frac{24}{30}$　　**8.** $\frac{6}{36}$　　**9.** $\frac{12}{16}$　　**10.** $\frac{30}{42}$　　**11.** $\frac{15}{18}$　　**12.** $\frac{16}{40}$

13. $\frac{27}{30}$　　**14.** $\frac{12}{28}$　　**15.** $\frac{15}{24}$　　**16.** $\frac{3}{18}$　　**17.** $\frac{7}{28}$　　**18.** $\frac{15}{25}$

19. $\frac{25}{35}$　　**20.** $\frac{6}{8}$　　**21.** $\frac{10}{30}$　　**22.** $\frac{7}{35}$　　**23.** $\frac{8}{48}$　　**24.** $\frac{6}{21}$

Give the correct sign, >, <, or =, for each ▥ .

1. $\frac{1}{3}$ ▥ $\frac{1}{4}$　　**2.** $\frac{2}{5}$ ▥ $\frac{1}{3}$　　**3.** $\frac{2}{7}$ ▥ $\frac{1}{3}$　　**4.** $\frac{5}{6}$ ▥ $\frac{10}{12}$

5. $\frac{3}{9}$ ▥ $\frac{3}{4}$　　**6.** $\frac{3}{4}$ ▥ $\frac{1}{16}$　　**7.** $\frac{2}{6}$ ▥ $\frac{3}{9}$　　**8.** $\frac{2}{5}$ ▥ $\frac{3}{4}$

Order from least to greatest.

9. $\frac{2}{3}, \frac{3}{4}, \frac{2}{5}$　　　　**10.** $\frac{2}{5}, \frac{1}{3}, \frac{5}{9}$　　　　**11.** $\frac{6}{7}, \frac{3}{5}, \frac{2}{3}$

Add or subtract. Reduce answers to lowest terms.

1. $\frac{1}{3}$ $+\frac{1}{3}$　　**2.** $\frac{2}{10}$ $+\frac{1}{10}$　　**3.** $\frac{2}{8}$ $+\frac{4}{8}$　　**4.** $\frac{1}{6}$ $+\frac{3}{6}$　　**5.** $\frac{2}{5}$ $+\frac{2}{5}$

6. $\frac{5}{12}$ $-\frac{1}{12}$　　**7.** $\frac{4}{5}$ $-\frac{2}{5}$　　**8.** $\frac{8}{15}$ $-\frac{3}{15}$　　**9.** $\frac{5}{6}$ $-\frac{3}{6}$　　**10.** $\frac{6}{7}$ $-\frac{2}{7}$

Set A   For use after page 235

Write as a whole number or mixed number.
Reduce the fraction to lowest terms.

1. $\frac{9}{4}$ 2. $\frac{15}{2}$ 3. $\frac{12}{10}$ 4. $\frac{11}{4}$ 5. $\frac{10}{3}$ 6. $\frac{6}{2}$

7. $\frac{15}{6}$ 8. $\frac{11}{8}$ 9. $\frac{15}{12}$ 10. $\frac{9}{4}$ 11. $\frac{7}{2}$ 12. $\frac{29}{6}$

Write each mixed number as an improper fraction.

13. $5\frac{1}{6}$ 14. $1\frac{3}{10}$ 15. $8\frac{3}{5}$ 16. $9\frac{1}{3}$ 17. $6\frac{2}{7}$ 18. $3\frac{4}{9}$

19. $12\frac{1}{2}$ 20. $8\frac{5}{6}$ 21. $11\frac{1}{8}$ 22. $15\frac{3}{4}$ 23. $7\frac{1}{7}$ 24. $25\frac{1}{2}$

Set B   For use after page 237

Find the least common denominator of each pair
of fractions.

1. $\frac{1}{6}$ 2. $\frac{1}{4}$ 3. $\frac{1}{10}$ 4. $\frac{3}{8}$ 5. $\frac{3}{5}$
   $\frac{2}{3}$ $\frac{1}{12}$ $\frac{4}{15}$ $\frac{1}{4}$ $\frac{9}{10}$

6. $\frac{2}{3}$ 7. $\frac{1}{3}$ 8. $\frac{2}{3}$ 9. $\frac{7}{8}$ 10. $\frac{7}{10}$
   $\frac{4}{8}$ $\frac{3}{5}$ $\frac{1}{4}$ $\frac{1}{10}$ $\frac{49}{100}$

Set C   For use after page 239

Add.

1. $\frac{1}{6}$ 2. $\frac{3}{4}$ 3. $\frac{1}{4}$ 4. $\frac{1}{5}$ 5. $\frac{1}{3}$
   $+\frac{1}{3}$ $+\frac{1}{2}$ $+\frac{3}{8}$ $+\frac{1}{2}$ $+\frac{3}{4}$
   _____   _____   _____   _____   _____

6. $\frac{1}{6}$ 7. $\frac{4}{5}$ 8. $\frac{5}{6}$ 9. $\frac{1}{4}$ 10. $\frac{1}{8}$
   $+\frac{1}{8}$ $+\frac{1}{10}$ $+\frac{1}{2}$ $+\frac{2}{3}$ $+\frac{2}{3}$
   _____   _____   _____   _____   _____

Set A   For use after page 241

Subtract.

1. $\frac{4}{5} - \frac{1}{2}$

2. $\frac{5}{6} - \frac{2}{3}$

3. $\frac{2}{3} - \frac{1}{12}$

4. $\frac{7}{8} - \frac{3}{4}$

5. $\frac{1}{2} - \frac{3}{8}$

6. $\frac{5}{16} - \frac{1}{8}$

7. $\frac{7}{12} - \frac{1}{6}$

8. $\frac{9}{10} - \frac{3}{5}$

9. $\frac{7}{8} - \frac{5}{6}$

10. $\frac{7}{10} - \frac{33}{100}$

11. $\frac{2}{3} - \frac{3}{5}$

12. $\frac{11}{12} - \frac{1}{4}$

13. $\frac{1}{4} - \frac{3}{20}$

14. $\frac{47}{100} - \frac{3}{10}$

15. $\frac{7}{12} - \frac{3}{8}$

Set B   For use after page 251

Add or subtract. Reduce to lowest terms.

1. $3\frac{3}{4} - 1\frac{1}{4}$

2. $2\frac{1}{3} + 3\frac{1}{3}$

3. $1\frac{4}{5} + 3\frac{1}{10}$

4. $4\frac{5}{8} + 12\frac{1}{16}$

5. $17\frac{9}{10} - 3\frac{1}{2}$

6. $14\frac{1}{2} + 10\frac{3}{8}$

7. $10\frac{2}{3} + 5\frac{1}{6}$

8. $26\frac{5}{16} - 19\frac{1}{8}$

9. $23\frac{5}{8} - 9\frac{5}{12}$

10. $43\frac{2}{3} + 3\frac{1}{8}$

Set C   For use after page 255

Add. Reduce to lowest terms.

1. $8\frac{5}{6} + 10\frac{7}{12}$

2. $8\frac{1}{2} + 3\frac{5}{8}$

3. $44\frac{3}{10} + 17\frac{7}{8}$

4. $14\frac{2}{3} + 71\frac{8}{9}$

5. $17\frac{5}{8} + 37\frac{11}{16}$

6. $29\frac{1}{2}$
   $13\frac{1}{2}$
   $+ 44\frac{3}{4}$

7. $19\frac{3}{4}$
   $26\frac{1}{2}$
   $+ 7\frac{1}{4}$

8. $30\frac{2}{3}$
   $18\frac{1}{6}$
   $+ 15\frac{3}{4}$

9. $49\frac{7}{10}$
   $42\frac{2}{5}$
   $+ 45\frac{1}{2}$

10. $8\frac{2}{3}$
    $37\frac{1}{4}$
    $+ 76\frac{1}{2}$

Set A   For use after page 257

Rename each mixed numeral.

1. $5\frac{1}{3} = 4\frac{\text{▦}}{3}$

2. $7\frac{3}{4} = 6\frac{\text{▦}}{4}$

3. $5\frac{1}{2} = 4\frac{\text{▦}}{2}$

4. $15\frac{5}{6} = 14\frac{\text{▦}}{6}$

5. $12\frac{3}{5} = 11\frac{\text{▦}}{5}$

6. $14 = 13\frac{\text{▦}}{6}$

7. $16\frac{3}{4} = \text{▦}\frac{7}{4}$

8. $9\frac{1}{5} = 8\frac{\text{▦}}{5}$

9. $10\frac{1}{2} = \text{▦}\frac{3}{2}$

10. $8\frac{1}{4} = \text{▦}\frac{5}{4}$

11. $74\frac{2}{3} = \text{▦}\frac{5}{3}$

12. $63\frac{9}{10} = 62\frac{\text{▦}}{10}$

Set B   For use after page 259

Subtract. Reduce to lowest terms.

1. $9\frac{1}{4}$ $- 3\frac{3}{4}$

2. $6\frac{1}{5}$ $- 3\frac{4}{5}$

3. $14\frac{5}{6}$ $- 1\frac{1}{6}$

4. $13\frac{7}{8}$ $- 6\frac{3}{8}$

5. 34 $- 22\frac{3}{4}$

6. $71\frac{3}{8}$ $- 42\frac{5}{8}$

7. $94\frac{1}{6}$ $- 44\frac{5}{6}$

8. $48\frac{3}{5}$ $- 23\frac{2}{5}$

9. $93\frac{6}{7}$ $- 75$

10. $62\frac{1}{3}$ $- 14\frac{2}{3}$

Set C   For use after page 261

Subtract. Reduce to lowest terms.

1. $5\frac{1}{2}$ $- 3\frac{3}{4}$

2. $16\frac{1}{8}$ $- 12\frac{1}{2}$

3. $6\frac{2}{3}$ $- 1\frac{2}{5}$

4. 41 $- 21\frac{3}{10}$

5. $95\frac{3}{4}$ $- 94\frac{9}{10}$

6. $60\frac{3}{4}$ $- 26$

7. $67\frac{2}{3}$ $- 17\frac{5}{8}$

8. 64 $- 2\frac{1}{3}$

9. $87\frac{1}{5}$ $- 16\frac{9}{10}$

10. $11\frac{1}{6}$ $- 4\frac{1}{3}$

11. 21 $- 9\frac{4}{5}$

12. $32\frac{1}{3}$ $- 30\frac{5}{6}$

13. $50\frac{7}{8}$ $- 22$

14. $43\frac{1}{4}$ $- 29\frac{5}{8}$

15. $19\frac{1}{3}$ $- 8\frac{3}{4}$

Set A For use after page 263

Add or subtract. Reduce to lowest terms.

1. $17\frac{1}{2}$
$+ \ \ 9\frac{1}{6}$

2. $\frac{6}{12}$
$+ \ \frac{3}{4}$

3. $28\frac{1}{4}$
$- \ \ 5\frac{5}{6}$

4. 35
$- \ 34\frac{6}{8}$

5. $\frac{17}{6}$
$- \ \frac{4}{3}$

6. $\frac{27}{6}$
$- \ \frac{12}{4}$

7. $45\frac{7}{10}$
$- \ 37$

8. 26
$+ \ \ \frac{3}{12}$

9. $77\frac{1}{3}$
$- \ \ \frac{3}{4}$

10. $14\frac{1}{8}$
$+ \ 11\frac{9}{10}$

Set B For use after page 305

Multiply. Write the product in lowest terms.

1. $\frac{1}{3} \times \frac{2}{4}$ **2.** $\frac{1}{6} \times \frac{1}{2}$ **3.** $\frac{3}{4} \times \frac{2}{3}$ **4.** $\frac{2}{5} \times \frac{2}{3}$

5. $\frac{2}{3} \times \frac{1}{4}$ **6.** $4 \times \frac{1}{2}$ **7.** $\frac{2}{5} \times \frac{5}{8}$ **8.** $\frac{2}{3} \times 6$

9. $\frac{3}{5} \times \frac{5}{3}$ **10.** $\frac{7}{6} \times 4$ **11.** $\frac{11}{5} \times 3$ **12.** $\frac{1}{3} \times \frac{5}{6}$

13. $\frac{9}{3} \times \frac{1}{2}$ **14.** $\frac{4}{3} \times \frac{5}{4}$ **15.** $\frac{1}{6} \times 12$ **16.** $\frac{6}{4} \times 10$

17. $\frac{2}{3} \times 18$ **18.** $\frac{3}{8} \times \frac{4}{5}$ **19.** $24 \times \frac{5}{6}$ **20.** $\frac{7}{8} \times \frac{2}{5}$

Set C For use after page 309

Multiply.

1. $1\frac{1}{2} \times 3\frac{1}{2}$ **2.** $2\frac{1}{3} \times 2\frac{1}{2}$ **3.** $\frac{2}{3} \times 1\frac{1}{4}$ **4.** $1\frac{1}{2} \times 3\frac{2}{3}$

5. $4 \times 1\frac{2}{5}$ **6.** $1\frac{1}{3} \times 2\frac{1}{4}$ **7.** $4\frac{1}{2} \times 2\frac{1}{2}$ **8.** $2\frac{3}{4} \times 1\frac{1}{5}$

9. $3\frac{1}{4} \times 1\frac{1}{3}$ **10.** $5 \times 3\frac{1}{2}$ **11.** $\frac{3}{4} \times 6$ **12.** $1\frac{2}{3} \times 3\frac{1}{5}$

13. $2\frac{1}{3} \times 2\frac{3}{4}$ **14.** $2\frac{1}{5} \times 1\frac{2}{5}$ **15.** $6\frac{1}{2} \times 3$ **16.** $\frac{3}{4} \times 5\frac{1}{5}$

17. $2\frac{1}{2} \times 1\frac{1}{5}$ **18.** $\frac{3}{10} \times 3\frac{1}{3}$ **19.** $2\frac{3}{4} \times 8$ **20.** $3\frac{1}{6} \times 3\frac{3}{5}$

Set A   For use after page 325

Multiply.

1. $\begin{array}{r} 1.6 \\ \times\ 1.9 \\ \hline \end{array}$
2. $\begin{array}{r} 7.21 \\ \times\ \ \ \ 6 \\ \hline \end{array}$
3. $\begin{array}{r} 0.3 \\ \times\ 1.4 \\ \hline \end{array}$
4. $\begin{array}{r} 4.36 \\ \times\ \ \ \ 5 \\ \hline \end{array}$
5. $\begin{array}{r} 0.6 \\ \times\ 0.7 \\ \hline \end{array}$

6. $\begin{array}{r} 0.79 \\ \times\ \ \ \ 3 \\ \hline \end{array}$
7. $\begin{array}{r} 1.8 \\ \times\ 3.6 \\ \hline \end{array}$
8. $\begin{array}{r} 12 \\ \times\ 5.9 \\ \hline \end{array}$
9. $\begin{array}{r} 1.64 \\ \times\ \ 0.4 \\ \hline \end{array}$
10. $\begin{array}{r} 7.3 \\ \times\ 0.6 \\ \hline \end{array}$

Set B   For use after page 327

Multiply.

1. $\begin{array}{r} 0.03 \\ \times\ \ 0.2 \\ \hline \end{array}$
2. $\begin{array}{r} 0.004 \\ \times\ \ \ \ \ \ 8 \\ \hline \end{array}$
3. $\begin{array}{r} 0.05 \\ \times\ \ 0.6 \\ \hline \end{array}$
4. $\begin{array}{r} 15 \\ \times\ 0.003 \\ \hline \end{array}$
5. $\begin{array}{r} 0.6 \\ \times\ 0.02 \\ \hline \end{array}$

6. $\begin{array}{r} 3.4 \\ \times\ 0.6 \\ \hline \end{array}$
7. $\begin{array}{r} 0.005 \\ \times\ \ \ \ \ \ 6 \\ \hline \end{array}$
8. $\begin{array}{r} 0.04 \\ \times\ 0.03 \\ \hline \end{array}$
9. $\begin{array}{r} 1.5 \\ \times\ 0.6 \\ \hline \end{array}$
10. $\begin{array}{r} 0.4 \\ \times\ 0.04 \\ \hline \end{array}$

Set C   For use after page 331

Divide.

1. $3\overline{)7.98}$
2. $2\overline{)52.62}$
3. $5\overline{)1.75}$
4. $2\overline{)0.86}$

5. $6\overline{)81.66}$
6. $5\overline{)0.775}$
7. $3\overline{)41.1}$
8. $2\overline{)3.78}$

9. $6\overline{)2.052}$
10. $3\overline{)4.23}$
11. $5\overline{)95.65}$
12. $8\overline{)3.496}$

Set D   For use after page 333

Divide.

1. $3\overline{)0.021}$
2. $2\overline{)3.75}$
3. $8\overline{)9.64}$
4. $4\overline{)0.052}$

5. $7\overline{)15.05}$
6. $3\overline{)1.518}$
7. $5\overline{)8.02}$
8. $2\overline{)10.1}$

9. $6\overline{)0.48}$
10. $6\overline{)6.3}$
11. $8\overline{)0.6}$
12. $2\overline{)10.08}$

Set A   For use after page 373

Solve the equations.

1. $\frac{1}{6} = \frac{n}{24}$　　　**2.** $\frac{3}{4} = \frac{n}{20}$　　　**3.** $\frac{4}{1} = \frac{n}{6}$　　　**4.** $\frac{10}{3} = \frac{n}{6}$

5. $\frac{5}{8} = \frac{n}{40}$　　　**6.** $\frac{3}{7} = \frac{n}{28}$　　　**7.** $\frac{7}{10} = \frac{n}{50}$　　　**8.** $\frac{3}{5} = \frac{n}{30}$

Set B   For use after page 375

Write each ratio as a percent.

1. 6 to 100　　　**2.** 43 to 100　　　**3.** $\frac{4}{100}$　　　**4.** $\frac{64}{100}$　　　**5.** $\frac{38}{100}$

Write each percent as a ratio in fraction form.

6. 23%　　　**7.** 19%　　　**8.** 88%　　　**9.** 20%　　　**10.** 45%

Set C   For use after page 376

Write a percent for each decimal and a decimal for each percent.

1. 0.4　　　**2.** 0.32　　　**3.** 0.02　　　**4.** 0.99

5. 36%　　　**6.** 8%　　　**7.** 20%　　　**8.** 15%

Set D   For use after page 378

Write each percent as a fraction in lowest terms.

1. 45%　　　**2.** 39%　　　**3.** 70%　　　**4.** 16%　　　**5.** 2%

Write a percent for each fraction.

6. $\frac{1}{10}$　　　**7.** $\frac{19}{20}$　　　**8.** $\frac{2}{5}$　　　**9.** $\frac{20}{25}$　　　**10.** $\frac{16}{50}$

Set E   For use after page 380

Find the percent of each number.

1. 10% of 90　　　**2.** 50% of 60　　　**3.** 18% of 300　　　**4.** 25% of 84

5. 35% of 120　　　**6.** 40% of 175　　　**7.** 90% of 350　　　**8.** 5% of 140

TABLE OF MEASURES

Metric System

Length
1 centimeter (cm)	10 millimeters (mm)
1 decimeter (dm)	100 millimeters (mm) 10 centimeters (cm)
1 meter (m)	1,000 millimeters (mm) 100 centimeters (cm) 10 decimeters (dm)
1 kilometer (km)	1,000 meters (m)

Area
1 square meter (m^2)	100 square decimeters (dm^2) 10,000 square centimeters (cm^2)

Volume
1 cubic decimeter (dm^3)	1,000 cubic centimeters (cm^3) 1 liter (L)

Capacity
1 teaspoon	5 milliliters (mL)
1 tablespoon	12.5 milliliters (mL)
1 liter (L)	1,000 milliliters (mL) 1,000 cubic centimeters (cm^3) 1 cubic decimeter (dm^3) 4 metric cups

Weight
1 gram (g)	1,000 milligrams (mg)
1 kilogram (kg)	1,000 grams (g)

Time
1 minute (min)	60 seconds (s)
1 hour (h)	60 minutes (min)
1 day (d)	24 hours (h)
1 week (w)	7 days (d)
1 month (mo)	about 4 weeks

Customary System

Length
1 foot (ft)	12 inches (in.)
1 yard (yd)	36 inches (in.) 3 feet (ft)
1 mile (m)	5,280 feet (ft) 1,760 yards (yd)

Area
1 square foot (ft^2)	144 square inches ($in.^2$)

Volume
1 cubic foot (ft^3)	1,728 cubic inches ($in.^3$)

Capacity
1 cup (c)	8 fluid ounces (fl oz)
1 pint (pt)	16 fluid ounces (fl oz) 2 cups (c)
1 quart (qt)	32 fluid ounces (fl oz) 4 cups (c) 2 pints (pt)
1 gallon (gal)	128 fluid ounces (fl oz) 16 cups (c) 8 pints (pt) 4 quarts (qt)

Weight
1 pound (lb)	16 ounces (oz)

Time
1 year (yr)	365 days 52 weeks 12 months
1 decade	10 years
1 century	100 years

433

GLOSSARY

a.m. A way to indicate time from 12:00 midnight to 12:00 noon. See also **p.m.**

addend One of the numbers to be added.

Example: $\begin{array}{r} 3 \\ + 5 \\ \hline 8 \end{array}$ addends

addition An operation that gives the total number when you put together two or more numbers.

angle Two rays from a single point.

area The measure of a region, in square units.

average The quotient when the sum of a set of numbers is divided by the number of addends.

circle A plane figure in which all the points are the same distance from a point called the center.

center —→•   ←circle

circumference The distance around a circle.

common factor A number that is a factor of two different numbers is a common factor of those two numbers.

common multiple A number that is a multiple of two different numbers is a common multiple of those two numbers.

compass An instrument used to make circles.

cone A space figure with one circular face and one vertex.

←vertex
face

congruent figures Figures that have the same size and shape.

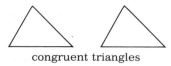

congruent triangles

coordinates Number pair used in graphing.

cross products Products obtained by multiplying the numerator of one fraction by the denominator of a second fraction, and the denominator of the first fraction by the numerator of the second fraction.

cube A space figure whose faces are all squares.

customary units of measure See Table of Measures, page 433.

cylinder A space figure with two congruent circular faces.

data bank A place where information is stored.

decimal Any base-ten numeral written using a decimal point.

3.2 ←— decimal
↳ decimal point

degree Celsius (°C) A unit for measuring temperature in the metric system.

degree Fahrenheit (°F) A unit for measuring temperature in the customary system.

denominator The number below the line in a fraction.

$\frac{3}{4}$ ←— denominator

diagonal A segment, other than a side, connecting two vertices of a polygon.

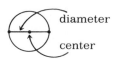
diagonal   vertex
vertex

diameter A segment containing two points of a circle and the center.

diameter
center

difference The number obtained by subtracting one number from another.

Example: $\begin{array}{r} 9 \\ - 4 \\ \hline 5 \end{array}$ ←—difference

digits The symbols used to write numerals: 0, 1, 2, 3, 4, 5, 6, 7, 8, and 9.

dividend A number to be divided.

$7\overline{)28}$ ←—dividend

division An operation that tells how many sets or how many in each set.

divisor The number by which a dividend is divided.

divisor —→ $7\overline{)28}$

edge One of the segments making up any of the faces of a space figure.

←—edge

END An instruction in a computer program that tells the computer to stop.

equilateral triangle A triangle with all 3 sides the same length and all angles the same measure.

equality (equals, or =) A mathematical relation of being exactly the same.

equation A number sentence involving the use of the equality symbol.

Example: 9 + 2 = 11

equivalent fractions Fractions that name the same amount.

Example: $\frac{1}{2}$ and $\frac{2}{4}$

estimate To find an answer that is close to the exact answer.

even number A whole number that has 0, 2, 4, 6, or 8 in the ones place.

expanded form A way to write numbers that shows the place value of each digit.

Example: 9,000 + 300 + 20 + 5

face One of the plane figures (regions) making up a space figure.

factors Numbers that are combined in the multiplication operation to give a number called the product.

factors ⟶ 6 × 7 = 42

flowchart A chart that shows a step-by-step way of doing something.

fraction A number that expresses parts of a whole or a set.

Example: $\frac{3}{4}$

gallon A unit of liquid measure. 1 gallon equals 4 quarts.

GOTO An instruction in a computer program that causes the computer to skip to a specified line in the program.

gram The basic unit for measuring weight in the metric system. A paper clip weighs about 1 gram.

graph A picture that shows information in an organized way.

greater than (>) The relationship of one number being larger than another number.

Example: 6 > 5, read "6 is greater than 5."

greatest common factor The greatest number that is a factor of each of two numbers.

grouping (associative) property When adding (or multiplying) three or more numbers, you can change the grouping and the sum (or product) is the same.

hexagon A polygon with six sides.

improper fraction A fraction whose numerator is greater than or equal to the denominator.

INPUT An instruction in a computer program that causes the computer to stop and request data while running a program.

integers The whole numbers together with their negatives.

Examples: ⁻5, 0, 23

isosceles triangle A triangle with at least 2 sides the same length and at least 2 angles the same measure.

least common denominator (LCD) The least common multiple of two denominators.

least common multiple (LCM) The smallest nonzero number that is a multiple of each of two given numbers.

less than (<) The relationship of one number being smaller than another number.

Example: 5 < 6, read "5 is less than 6."

line A straight path that is endless in both directions.

line of symmetry A line on which a figure can be folded so that the two parts fit exactly.

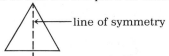

LIST A copy of a set of instructions that tells a computer what to do.

Logo A computer language that can be used for computer graphics.

lowest terms A fraction is in the lowest terms if the numerator and denominator have no common factor greater than 1.

metric units of measure See Table of Measures, page 433.

mixed number A number that has a whole number part and a fraction part, such as $2\frac{3}{4}$.

multiple A number that is the product of a given number and a whole number.

multiplication An operation that combines two numbers, called factors, to give one number, called the product.

negative number A number that is less than zero.

number line A line that shows numbers in order.

number pair Two numbers that are used to give the location of a point on a graph.

     Example: (3,2)

numeral A symbol for a number.

numerator The number above the line in a fraction.

$$\frac{3}{4} \leftarrow \text{numerator}$$

odd number A whole number that has 1, 3, 5, 7, or 9 in the ones place.

one property In multiplication, when either factor is 1, the product is the other factor.

order (commutative) property When the order of addends or factors is changed, the sum or product is the same.

ordinal number A number that is used to tell order.

     Examples: first, fifth

p.m. A way to indicate time from 12:00 noon to 12:00 midnight. See also **a.m.**

parallel lines Two lines that lie in the same plane and do not intersect.

parallelogram A quadrilateral with two pairs of parallel sides.

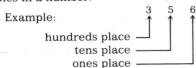
parallelogram

pentagon A polygon with five sides.

percent Per 100; a way to compare a number with 100.

perimeter The distance around a figure.

perpendicular lines Two lines that intersect at right angles.

place value The value given to the place a digit occupies in a number.

     Example:

                  3 5 6

     hundreds place ⏤
        tens place ⏤
        ones place ⏤

plane figure A figure that lies on a flat surface.

     Examples:

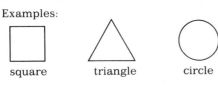

  square   triangle   circle

point A single, exact location, often represented by a dot.

polygon A closed figure formed by line segments.

prime number A number that has exactly 2 factors (the number itself and 1).

PRINT An instruction in a computer program that tells a computer to type something.

prism A space figure whose bases are congruent polygons in parallel planes and whose faces are parallelograms.

probability The probability that an event will occur in a set of equally likely outcomes is the number of ways the event can occur divided by the total number of possible outcomes.

product The result of the multiplication operation.

     Example: 6 × 7 = 42
                       ↑
                 product

program A set of instructions that tells a computer what to do.

protractor An instrument used for measuring angles.

pyramid A space figure whose base is a polygon and whose faces are triangles with a common vertex.

quadrilateral A polygon with four sides.

quotient The number (other than the remainder) that is the result of the division operation.

                              6 ← quotient

Examples: 45 ÷ 9 = 5   7)45
                 ↑   42
         quotient   3

radius A segment from the center of a circle to a point on the circle.

ratio A pair of numbers used in making certain comparisons. The ratio of 3 to 4 can be written $\frac{3}{4}$.

ray A part of a line, having only one end point.

     ray

rectangle A quadrilateral that has four right angles.

     rectangle

remainder The number less than the divisor that remains after the division process is completed.

Example:
$$7 \overline{)47} \begin{array}{r} 6 \\ \hline 42 \\ \hline 5 \end{array} \leftarrow \text{remainder}$$

rhombus A quadrilateral with all sides the same length.

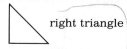
rhombus

right angle An angle that has a measure of 90 degrees.

right angle

right triangle A triangle that has one right angle.

right triangle

Roman numerals Numerals used by the Romans.

Examples:
$$I = 1$$
$$V = 5$$
$$VI = 6$$

rounding Replacing specific numbers with numbers expressed in even units, such as tens, hundreds, or thousands.

Example:

23 rounded to the nearest 10 is 20.

RUN A command that tells the computer to execute a program.

scalene triangle A triangle with no sides the same length and no angles the same measure.

segment A straight path from one point to another.

similar figures Two figures that have the same shape.

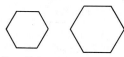
similar figures

skip counting Counting by a number other than 1.

Example: 0, 5, 10, 15
skip counting by fives

space figure A figure that has volume.

Examples:

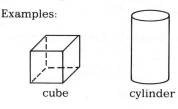
cube   cylinder

sphere A space figure in which all the points are the same distance from a center point.

sphere

square A quadrilateral with four right angles and all sides the same length.

square

subtraction An operation that tells the difference between two numbers, or how many are left when some are taken away.

sum The number obtained by adding numbers.

Example:
$$\begin{array}{r} 3 \\ + 2 \\ \hline 5 \end{array} \leftarrow \text{sum}$$

symmetric figure A plane figure that can be folded in half so that the two halves match.

trading To make a group of ten from one of the next highest place value, or one from ten of the next lowest place value. Examples: one hundred can be traded for ten tens; ten ones can be traded for one ten.

trapezoid A quadrilateral with one pair of parallel sides.

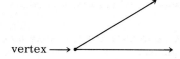
trapezoid

triangle A polygon with three sides.

unit An amount or quality used as a standard of measurement. Set Table of Measures, page 433.

vertex The point that the two rays of an angle have in common.

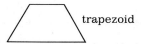
vertex →

volume The number of units of space that a space figure holds.

zero property In addition, when one addend is 0, the sum is the other addend.

INDEX